American Social Thought:
Sources and Interpretations
Volume I: Colonial Beginnings to the Civil War

Michael McGiffert
University of Denver

Robert Allen Skotheim
University of Colorado

Addison-Wesley Publishing Company
Reading, Massachusetts
Menlo Park, California · London · Don Mills, Ontario

This book is in the
ADDISON-WESLEY SERIES IN HISTORY

Consulting Editor
ROBIN W. WINKS

The Contributing Editors

Thomas F. Gossett (Ph.D., American Studies, Minnesota)

is the author of *Race, The History of an Idea in America* (1963) and is professor of American literature and American Studies at Wake Forest University.

John C. Livingston (Ph.D., History, Wisconsin)

teaches American intellectual, social, and political history at the University of Denver.

Peter Marshall (Ph.D., History, Yale)

has written extensively on early American history and British imperial history. Born in England, he has taught at Bristol University and McGill University, Montreal, where he is professor of history.

Michael McGiffert (Ph.D., American Studies, Yale)

editor of *The Character of Americans* (rev. ed., 1970) and *Puritanism and the American Experience* (1969), and author of *The Higher Learning in Colorado: An Historical Study, 1860–1964* (1964), is professor of history at the University of Denver.

Edward Pessen (Ph.D., History, Columbia)

whose writings on the Jacksonian Period include *Most Uncommon Jacksonians* (1967), *Jacksonian America: Society, Personality and Politics* (1968), and *New Perspectives on Jacksonian Politics* (1968), is professor of history in the Bernard M. Baruch College of Liberal Arts of the City University of New York.

Robert G. Pope (Ph.D., American Studies, Yale)

is the author of *The Half-way Covenant: Church Membership in Puritan New England* (1969) and teaches American history at the State University of New York at Buffalo.

General Preface to Both Volumes

During recent decades, as the history of thought has been made an integral part of the study and teaching of history, historians have paid close attention to the relations of ideas to the dynamics and patterns of social development. Consistent with this preoccupation with social thought, historians emphasize the points at which ideas affect, or are affected by, political, social, and economic experience. Few other fields of historical inquiry have produced such illuminating results.

Even though the history of social thought is a popular subject, there is neither a single ruling definition of it, nor one universally approved method of studying it. Some scholars and teachers accent the role of elite thinkers while others emphasize a wider range of public sentiment. Some study the "spirit of an age" or governing "climate of opinion," while others investigate particular ideas, or ideational systems, and their ramifications over periods of time. Some examine the impact of ideas upon behavior; others treat ideas as a part, however significant, of the total historical configuration.

These two volumes, comprised of documents and interpretive commentaries assembled by a dozen scholars, each of whom commands authority in his respective field, are intended to introduce the student to the work that is going forward on several fronts of American intellectual history. These readings reflect both the consensus on the importance of the history of social thought and some of the varying definitions, materials, and approaches to the field of study. With the exception that each contributor has been asked to include both primary and secondary source readings, no attempt has been made by the general editors to impose any rigid formula for the contents or structure of each section. The result, in both its common elements and its variety, expresses the state of scholarship in the 1970's on the history of American social ideas. Hopefully, these volumes will stimulate the interest of students in America's intellectual past and present.

Denver and Boulder, Colorado   M. McG.
October 1971   R. A. S.

Contents

Introduction

"In the beginning," wrote John Locke, "all the world was America . . ." For rationalists of Lockean persuasion America figured as the nearest modern equivalent to the "state of nature" from which, whether in history or in theory, all human societies were supposed to have sprung. What counted about this New World was the very fact of its newness—at once exhilarating and terrifying to Europeans. Its significance would be discovered (by extension of Locke's bold metaphor) in its recapitulation of mankind's progress from the state of nature to the social state. When Locke wrote in the late seventeenth century, the New World—"new" in the sense of its novelty to Europeans—was already almost exactly 200 years old, and its conversion from nature to society was far advanced even in the comparatively young colonies that England had planted along the North American littoral. It had already entered, in effect, into history; ceasing to be merely natural, its meaning had come to center in its social development—specifically in the ways it adhered to or departed from the general norms of European civilization.

Because the newness of the New World was not so much a natural as a social phenomenon, European interest—after the euphoria of discovery wore off—was directed less to the Indian cultures that, by Locke's logic, might have been viewed as the authentic social consequents of nature in America than to the Old World systems that were being imposed upon the newfound land. This shift of attention was facilitated by a general tendency to deny that the aborigines had actually advanced beyond the state of nature. "We chanced in a lande, even as God made it," declared Captain John Smith in 1612, shrugging off the "idle, improvident, scattered people" who inhabited that land. What God had made, it was man's duty to improve, but the resident savages, "carelesse of anything but from hand to mouth," had not done their duty; Smith therefore thought it needful to "bring them to be tractable civil and industrious," and to "teach them trades that the fruits of their labours might make us recompence . . ." Explaining the "thin population of America" and the "rudeness and ignorance of the people," another writer, the philosopher Francis Bacon, linked reports of the Indians' primitivism to a literal notion of the newness of their world: "you must accept your inhabitants of America as a young people, younger a thousand years, at the least, than the rest of the world." It thus became the responsibility of Englishmen, deserving due recompence, to help or make the Indian grow up: when they undertook to civilize or Christianize him—this being a main reason always given for planting colonies—they meant not to *change* his civilization but to *endow* him with civilization, not to transform his social ways but to socialize him. A child of nature, the red man had to be reclaimed from nature.

Finding nothing socially significant to learn from the Indians, European observers concentrated their attention on the white societies that rose along the transatlantic shore—on the character of their people, on their manners, morals, customs, and laws, on their political arrangements, economic activities, religious patterns, and the ordering of their social relationships, and on the purport of all these things for Europe itself. As these societies matured, emphasis came to be placed increasingly on those features which marked them as different, made them unique, gave them distinguishable identity as *American* societies. Though conceived as extensions of their mother countries, these overseas outposts did not duplicate the parental cultures; institutions and values alike were transformed by powerful determinants: the selective processes of migration, the imperatives of adaptation to the American environment, and the thrust of will on the part of many groups and individuals to improve their physical or spiritual condition. These factors, working in ways too complex, subtle, and deep to be fully understood either by those who were involved in the process of change or by historians since, produced a number of social ideas and attitudes which by the time of the Civil War, if not the Revolution, could be regarded as characteristically American. Several twentieth-century perspectives on the development and significance of these ideas and attitudes are offered in Section One of this book.

Strikingly characteristic of English America was the magnitude of the religious component of its culture. At least six of the colonies that revolted in 1776 had been founded for primarily religious purposes, and many individuals in every colony could cite religious motives for their or their ancestors' migration. The thrust of Europe into North America occurred during a period of vast religious upheaval in the Old World. England's colonial policy—unlike that of Spain or France or Portugal—was not religiously exclusive, and England's overseas territories were broad enough to accommodate without serious friction a great variety of persons who were seeking for themselves, if not for anyone else, freedom to worship as they wished. The outcome was a society that was religiously diverse beyond anything known or desired in Europe—a condition favorable to the gradual development of live-and-let-live ideas of religious toleration and liberty.

This pluralistic spread was confined, however, to the Protestant faiths; Jews and Roman Catholics composed only a tiny disadvantaged minority. Within the Protestant spectrum, moreover, one great tradition, comprising many variants, was dominant. It has been calculated that at least 50 percent of the American people at the time of the Revolution were Calvinists of one sort or another, while an overwhelming majority of the more than 3000 local churches was Calvinistic. So popular a persuasion was bound to have enormous influence in shaping the culture of Anglo-America. Its contributions to social thought would be the more pronounced because the Calvinist ethos was energetically activist rather than monastic, and because its proponents put as great stock in hard thinking as they did in hard work. Valuing intellect so highly and applying it in social action, Calvinists established the categories of social thought that subsequent American thinkers had either to account for or refute.

That is why Section Two of this volume is devoted to the social ethic of Calvinism in its American phase. Rather than concentrating narrowly on the New England Puritans, Professor Robert G. Pope, who teaches American history at the State University of New York at Buffalo and has written a valuable study, *The Half-Way Covenant: Church Membership in Puritan New England*, brings together a remarkably broad group of documents, ranging over the entire colonial period and embracing Pennsylvania Quakers and eighteenth-century evangelicals, as well as such familiar Puritan figures as John Winthrop and Roger Williams. These readings, with the commentaries that explicate them, show how the American Calvinists, whatever their denominational brand, struggled to reconcile their commitment to personal integrity and purity with their equally strong commitment to active social engagement. This struggle was reflected in their endeavor to build the holy community or Christian commonwealth whose citizens would do their best to be both godly and good. They conceived their social ideal in forms that ranged from Winthrop's magnificent "city on a hill" and William Penn's "holy experiment" in religious liberty to the humbler life of transplanted country folk who came together peacefully and comfortably in hundreds of little villages and forest settlements. Whatever its variations, the Calvinist vision of collective holiness prescribed a public order of righteousness that was all the more compelling because never wholly realized. Consequently, as Professor Pope shows and Professor Kenneth A. Lockridge confirms in the first reading of Section One, at the deepest sources of American social thought there can be found a dynamic ideal of social perfection, originally defined in religious, specifically Calvinist, terms.

As Western civilization emerged from the Age of Faith into the Age of Reason, the Calvinist foundations of American social thought were overlaid among a class of enlightened and sophisticated thinkers by concepts and commitments that derived largely from nonreligious sources. Though these intellectuals did not forego the quest for the good society—rather, they spent the better part of their lives improving the political and cultural opportunities that national independence presented to them—they no longer dreamed of founding the new City of God. Their American world was quite good enough for them; all that was needed, they believed, was to perfect its virtues, enlarge its liberties, and establish its institutions on the solid basis of reason. For some, like Thomas Jefferson, these goals entailed a firm repudiation of the Calvinist tradition, while the ideas of others, John Adams for one, represented a secularization of Calvinist beliefs about the nature of man and the right ordering of society. One and all, however, they grounded their thought in the liberal ideas of the eighteenth-century Enlightenment, adapting those ideas to the needs of revolutionary and post-revolutionary America. In Section Three John C. Livingston, associate professor of history at the University of Denver, describes the pattern of Enlightened thought, centering in the concepts of nature, reason, and science, and shows how these concepts functioned as powerful instruments of social reform, revolution, and reconstruction.

Leading American thinkers drew deeply on the writings of such English and Continental political theorists—or propagandists—as John Locke, the "Commonwealthmen," and Montesquieu, on their own experience as Americans, and on their observations of Europe at a time when the struggle for independence inspired Americans to condemn much of European culture as degenerate and meretricious. Their reading and experience alike led them to take seriously the stirring words of Thomas Paine: "We have it in our power to begin the world over again." First they placed reason at the service of revolution; then they set it to work to consolidate their revolution in durable republican institutions. Just how these institutions should be designed, and precisely what kind of social order was right for the United States, were matters of some disagreement, yet all concurred on the cardinal principles of popular sovereignty, republican polity, and government that was created and limited by constitutional contract—these being the results, as they believed, of the rule of reason rationally applied to politics. Through a rich selection of passages from the writings of John Adams, Thomas Jefferson, and James Madison, together with interpretive essays by contemporary scholars and a valuable introductory comment, Professor Livingston sets out both the basic consensus and the inner tensions in the social and political ideas of the founders of the nation.

Jefferson, Adams, and their colleagues were members of the first generation in America to become fully conscious of themselves as a new people under the Western sun. Of their predecessors Stephen Vincent Benêt writes in his epic *Western Star* that

> Those who came were resolved to be Englishmen,
> Gone to world's end, but English every one,
> And they ate the white corn kernels, parched in the sun,
> And they knew it not, but they'd not be English again.

They knew it not: that recognition was reserved for the men of the Revolution, and with its dawning they knew themselves for what they had unwittingly become—*Americans*, possessed of a way of life and a future that could be celebrated as distinct from and better than the ways of the Old World now forsworn. During the 1760's and 1770's, under the stress of conflict with the mother country, this consciousness of American identity grew clearer and stronger until it flowered in a spirit of nationalism that powerfully reinforced and directed the drive toward independence.

For social thought the emergence of nationalism was momentous. On the one hand, it dictated a narrowing of the scope of social ideas to fit within the political boundaries of the nation; on the other, it meant that those same ideas would tend to spread, more or less uniformly, over the intellectual landscape of the entire country. Thus while nationalism made social thought less cosmopolitan—one might hunt long for an ideologue of the Jacksonian period who cared to acknowledge a debt, as Franklin, Adams, and Jefferson had gladly done, to the social philosophies of Europe—it also tended to wear down the barriers of social class, geographic section, and religious sectarianism that divided Americans among themselves. Though the transformation was neither swift nor uniform in all parts of the country, from this point forward, for better or worse, the moral idea of the nation would provide the context of social thought, and all forms of social thought would become increasingly nationalistic. In Section Four Professor Peter Marshall, who teaches history at McGill University, Montreal, and has written on the American Revolution and related subjects, traces the beginnings of this development from the War of Independence to the death of Andrew Jackson. His selections offer a variety of perspectives on the character of American nationalism during the critical time when Americans had the chance, however limited, to "begin the world over again" by shaping their new nation as they wished.

Probably none of the Founding Fathers expected to build so well as to leave to posterity only the job of making occasional repairs in the fabric of society and state. Realists all, and modest in the face of history, they knew that all human works were impermanent, that the good society, like happiness, was always to be pursued and never quite caught. The test of their accomplishment and the confirmation of their skepticism came during the first half of the nineteenth century when the United States experienced an immense enlargement of population, economic production, and inhabited territory. These changes inspired patriotic boosters to hail the greatness and progress of the country where to get bigger was naturally to get better. They also evoked, however, the worried criticism of moralists who feared lest in gaining the world, Americans should lose their souls, along with their virtue. When Americans made the most of their material abundance, they were charged with the vices of materialism; pursuing happiness across the continent or up the ladder of success, they were accused of opportunism or worse; racing in hot competition on the way to wealth, they were indicted for individualism—originally a term of reproach. Whatever the truth of these criticisms, they bespoke a deep division in American thought over the character of the American people and their social ideal.

Undoubtedly many Americans—*white* Americans, at least—were tolerably content with their measure of this world's assets or had likely prospects of getting enough and more. But there were some—a not insignificant few—who defined utopia in terms of spiritual values rather than material goods or social status, and still others who sought a more equalitarian distribution of goods and power through the reconstruction of capitalist institutions. These were the perfectionists, whether spiritual or secular, whom Edward Pessen, professor of history at the City University of New York and author of *Jacksonian America* and *The Uncommon Jacksonians*, discusses in Section Five. Rather than review the course of democratic thought, the rise of "Manifest Destiny," or the record of social reform in the Jacksonian period—all well-worn topics—Professor Pessen focuses on two major expressions of the utopian ethos—the religious perfectionism of the Oneida Community and comparable undertakings, and the secular perfectionism of the labor socialists who organized the working men's movement. Though their goals and values differed—the spiritualists aiming at the moral regeneration of individuals, the secularists at an equitable economic order—they were at one in attributing the ills of American society to basic faults in its institutions, not in the character of its citizens. In addition, they agreed that the good society could be achieved only by a drastic reorganization of the whole social system, patchwork reform being worse than useless because if it worked it gave longer life to the status quo. These perfectionistic attitudes of the early nineteenth century marked a moving stage in the current of thought that flowed from the "utopian communes" of early New England to the egalitarian, libertarian, and communitarian impulses of many young Americans in the mid-twentieth century.

When Americans defined their social principles, they commonly set them off against the repudiated systems of the Old World, and they often fell into the logical error of comparing the American ideal with the European reality (as they thought it), much to their own gratification. In so doing, they tended to ignore the sorry fact that not all Americans had an equal chance to share in the blessings of liberty and that some—rarely acknowledged as genuine Americans or even as genuine human beings because of their dark skin and slave status—were entirely excluded from the good things of the American dream. Utopian visions and perfectionist programs, with few exceptions, did not cross the color line; Thomas Paine's "we" who had it in "our" power to remake the world simply did not include the blacks who, when Paine wrote in 1776, made up one-fifth of the population of the new nation. The "newness of the New World" was impartially permissive: it offered opportunity as generously to new systems of bondage for blacks as to freshening hopes of liberty for whites. And over the years, as the white pursuit of happiness came to depend increasingly on the degradation of blacks, this contrast—institutionalized in slavery and reinforced by racist attitudes and ideas—was magnified into America's most persistent, intractable, and agonizing dilemma. This is the challenging subject of Section Six, "Racism and Slavery Before the Civil War," compiled by Thomas F. Gossett, professor of English at Wake Forest University and author of an important study entitled *Race, the History of an Idea in America.*

"Racism," a word that lends itself easily to loose usage and sloganistic thinking, involves the passing of judgment on people according to their race. This judgment is collective rather than individual, and because it is made more or less in ignorance it is correctly termed a pre-judgment or prejudice. Central to this prejudice is the belief that persons of another race are inferior *as a race* to persons of one's own race. Also central is the belief that racial distinctions are founded in nature, given by birth—that they are both hereditary and indelible. Because whites in the United States have had both the power and the incentives to enact their prejudices into law and establish them in custom, their definitions of racial superiority and inferiority have been socially dominant.

Thus white ideologues, especially in the ante-bellum South, asserted not only that slavery was the appropriate status for blacks but that black slavery had to be perpetual, for the ideology of racism declared that no degree or kind of environmental change, no measure of social reform, could improve the character of the blacks so as to fit them for freedom in a racially mixed society. In this respect, for the slaveholders and their spokesmen, public law merely confirmed the fixed decree of nature: blacks were born to be slaves. Racist views were also generally, though perhaps more superficially, held in the North, even after slavery had been extinguished there in the period of the Revolution. Discrimination against blacks in the job market; segregated housing, churches, and schools; exclusion of blacks from the vote were all evidences of white racism in the Northern "free" states, and even the appeals of Northern abolitionists were more or less deeply tinctured by race prejudice. The readings chosen by Professor Gossett amply document the extent, intensity, and varieties of racism in the social thinking of white Americans on both sides of the Mason-Dixon line during the years when the country was stumbling toward a Civil War that would put an end to slavery but would not set blacks and whites in a new relation of equality.

Some observers today, citing the grim history, sociology, and psychology of race relations in the United States, hold that racism is so deeply ingrained in the American character as to be virtually irreducible: to be an American, they claim, is to be a racist, and nothing much can be done to remedy that. Others maintain, however, that race prejudice is more a fact of culture than a fact of nature, that it is therefore open to the counter-influences of culture, and that in America these ethical counter-influences can be strong. American culture, it is contended, supplies principles of equity, individuality, and humanity which might be extended to embrace impartially persons of races other than one's own. These potentially anti-racist principles may be reinforced by an abiding faith in the newness of the experience of human beings in this land. Americans have long been accustomed to believe that the future need not be inexorably ruled by the past—and this hostility to history, whatever the drawbacks of its naivete, may hold the makings of redemptive change. Thus individuals, whether black or white, yellow or red, who try to think free of their own racism may be sustained in the effort by values that are drawn from the lively traditions of American perfectionism. And if their recollection of the original newness of this New World has grown dim, they may nevertheless maintain a commitment to the possibility of social renewal in time to come.

M.McG.

Section One
Perspectives on Early American Social Thought

MICHAEL McGIFFERT

Contents

Social thought in America began with the religious folk who in the 1620's and 1630's undertook to found the kingdom of God in what turned out to be, disappointingly, merely a new (though different) England. Their puritanic ideas were essentially traditional and, of course, theological. They believed in ranking men by birth, in the heritability of social status, in a doctrine of calling that was socially static, in a fixed pattern of authority and submission. To this conservative social ethic they attached such biblical notions as the idea of the chosen people under covenant with God to build His holy city and usher in the imminent millennium. Though this covenant, as some historians have claimed, may have contained germs of a democratic, constitutionalistic polity, the Puritan leadership valued it chiefly as an instrument of direction. cohesion, and control for the New Jerusalem that was theirs to create. Executing their "errand into the wilderness," they did not contemplate a free-for-all society in which each person would do his or her own thing. Hence when Thomas Morton put up his maypole at Merrymount, the religious establishment of Plymouth Colony went right out and chopped it down. *That* sort of "merrie olde Englande" was not wanted in the "new world" of America.

What *was* wanted were committed people whose aims and ideas conformed to those of the John Winthrops, William Bradfords, Thomas Hookers, and John Davenports who directed the early enterprises of religious colonization. These leaders were distinguished, far beyond the fact of the theological warp of their thought—a point they held in common with every social thinker of that age of faith—by their assumption that truth, to be true, had to be *public*. Being public, it could be kept under official surveillance; each individual's thought could be made subject to a common standard of rightness; no one would have a right to be wrong. That was why dissidents like Anne Hutchinson, the notorious "antinomian" of the 1630's, and the Quakers, several of whom were hanged in Massachusetts in the 1650's, were obnoxious: they asserted private "truth," grounded in subjective revelation, protected by the claim of the sanctity of the individual conscience. Later ages have seen these seventeenth-century nonconformists as great individualists. In fact, they were conforming to the will of God just as closely as were their persecutors—but they read God's will differently and their comprehension of it, being essentially private, projected a principle of social order which those who were running the system could not distinguish from anarchy. The norms of thought, in their American beginnings, were theological, conservative, and significantly social: the same attitudes and convictions that marked the Puritan elite as authoritarian also made their thought invariably communal, and its significance rested in their insistence on the public character of truth.

The Puritans' undertaking, as Kenneth A. Lockridge points out in the reading that heads this section, had roots in both the puritanical and the peasant backgrounds of those who dreamed and worked New England into existence. Their intent, according to Professor Lockridge, was utopian, and their utopian vision, articulated by such leaders as John Winthrop, was both English and biblical. What they desired was what they, or perhaps their forebears, had known at home, purged of its defects—a piece of tillable soil, owned free and clear; a fair trade; religious freedom for themselves and those who agreed with them; a chance, in short, of body and spirit that was denied them before. To these goals they added the puritanic ideal of the new city of God to be erected, God helping, in the American forest. Such were the hopes and purposes that gave ideological integrity to the "holy communities" of New England in the generation of their founding. In them was laid the original pattern of American social thought.

Professor Lockridge, who teaches American history at the University of Michigan, holds high rank among a number of scholars who are re-examining the history of early America—specifically colonial New England—in the light of documents that had been insufficiently exploited by their predecessors. These newly developed sources include land and tax records, wills, property inventories, and the vital statistics of births, marriages, and deaths, as well as such more familiar materials as church rolls and town-meeting minutes. From such evidence come fresh views of the living experience of New Englanders in the seventeenth century. Maintaining an emphasis on social thought, while undergirding his account with solid documentary data, Lockridge focuses on the "utopian" faith of the Puritan settlers to show how their vision of a truly Christian community was realized, by and large, at Dedham, Massachusetts, a New World "commune." He stresses the formative influence of the traditions of medieval English peasant culture: the Puritans' "communal ideal," he writes, "repeated so many features of the peasant ideal that their Puritanism seemed a mere continuation of the peasant ethos." But while both Puritanism and the peasant ethos were sociologically conservative, they contained elements of instability and change, summed up by Lockridge in the term "voluntarism," that pointed toward more democratic social forms than those prescribed by the founders of New England. From the historical standpoint Dedham thus has interest for what it was intended to be, what it was, and what it would become—illustrating in its evolution, as Lockridge aptly observes, a major phase of the "American experience."

In the eighteenth century, as politics replaced religion as the frame and center of social thought in both Europe and America, the dreams of reason acquired talismanic power. Among these were ideals of individual liberty, social equality, and political democracy, resting on the recognition of natural rights and pointing toward a radical reordering of existing structures of intellectual and institutional authority. Historians have examined the widening divergence between old forms and new attitudes everywhere in the Western World during the Age of Reason. They have described the American experience as part of, yet distinct within, the larger patterns of transatlantic culture. They have explored the relations of changes in thought to changes in behavior, some emphasizing the motive force of ideals behind the social upheavals of the late eighteenth century, others holding the social ideologies of the Enlightenment to have been little more than rationalizations of warring political or economic interests.

These issues of interpretation are treated in the second and third selections by Bernard Bailyn, professor of history at Harvard University. Bailyn stresses the seriousness with which American thinkers took the social ideas of Locke, Voltaire, Montesquieu, and *a fortiori* the antiestablishmentarian, libertarian views of English radical pamphleteers such as Gordon and Trenchard, authors of "Cato's Letters." From these sources the promoters of the American Revolution drew, as Bailyn observes, "a common vocabulary and a common pattern of thought, and, when the time came, common principles of political reform." Enacting the ideals of eighteenth-century liberty, they would acclaim with Thomas Paine the power of reason to "make the world over again." In reality, however, many of their most celebrated reforms had already been accomplished, almost without notice, before the Revolution occurred. Enlightened ideas, crystalizing in the 1760's and 1770's, were thus much less the inspiration for social change than an after-the-fact articulation, intensification, or explanation of changes previously set in motion. This gave to these ideas, according to Bailyn, peculiar significance: "precisely because so many social and institutional reforms had already taken place in America, the revolutionary movement there, more than elsewhere, was a matter of doctrine, ideas, and comprehension."

Consequently, although the Revolution was not consciously launched to bring about considerable social change, it did transform society through its influence on thought. Under the stress of the struggle for home rule Americans challenged the assumptions that had formed the basis of their social relations. So great was the "contagion of liberty" that the attack on the authority of Parliament and of the king's administrators in the colonies quickly developed into defiance of established authority in general. The hierarchical premises of social thought, dating back in America to the time of John Winthrop, were giving way to republican inspirations; already undermined by experience, institutions of prescriptive order, theretofore deemed sacrosanct, now were put increasingly on the defensive by an equalitarian thrust of enormous force. Forms of authority that had once seemed reasonable were now seen to be arbitrary, and when they became thus intellectually vulnerable their defenders tended to resort to tactics which made their reasonableness still more doubtful. The upshot was a democratic transformation of the social ethos of America, the implications of which would be worked out in still more democratic dimensions by the post-Revolutionary generations.

It has often been asserted that the great exception to the triumph of the democratic dogma in the epochs of Jefferson and Jackson was the institution of black slavery. There, if anywhere, survived the old commitment to a social ideal that ranked men by their birth, posited the heritability of social status, approved a conservative doctrine of calling in which there was a predetermined place for everyone and everyone was expected to stay locked in his place, and prescribed a rigid pattern of power and obedience. As a system of bond labor, slavery denied black men and women the right to decide for themselves how to make their way in life. As the foundation of the rule of the planter aristocracy, slavery sustained the politics of elitism. As a way of regulating the relations of races, slavery violated the individualistic "self-help" ethic by putting a permanent brand of inferiority upon the members of one race. Thus democracy stopped at the color line, despite the sincere attempts of conscientious reformers to apply to slaves the same principles of liberty whose blessings they claimed for themselves.

In another perspective, however, slavery may be seen not so much as an exception to the democratic rule as a social and psychological prop for it. As Winthrop D. Jordan, professor of history at the University of California, Berkeley, observes in the book from which the next reading is taken,

> In committing themselves to a slavery whose logic rested . . . on racial differences, the colonists may in fact have enhanced the fluidity of the American social structure above the racial line. For the firmness of Negro exclusion may have served as a bedrock of assured but inexpressible confidence that the structure of the community was indeed as firmly ordered as it should be, thus permitting the revolutionary new social mobility among white persons to develop without the crippling apprehensiveness that proper social ordering was going entirely by the board.[1]

Not only did the white man's social rights, liberties, and opportunities rest,

[1] Winthrop D. Jordan, *White Over Black: American Attitudes Toward the Negro, 1550–1812* (Chapel Hill: Published for the Institute of Early American History and Culture by The University of North Carolina Press, 1968), p. 134.

to no small degree, on the black man's slavery, but slavery with its corollaries of white supremacy and black inferiority furnished the psychological ground for the white man's identity as American and as human being. It is thus a major theme of Jordan's study, as one of its reviewers noted, that "American society became *functionally* based on a rationale of racial superiority."[2]

Probably no white American before the Civil War was more acutely sensitive to the strains of racism in the white American way of life than Thomas Jefferson, revolutionist, libertarian, and slaveowner. Certainly none spread his troubled feelings on the public record more influentially or with so revealing a mixture of ingenuousness and casuistry. Jefferson hated slavery: it stood in pointblank contradiction to his dearest political and humanitarian convictions. But he believed blacks to be innately inferior to whites and thought them unfit for freedom in white society. He claimed to base this judgment on scientific observation, yet he never really comprehended how observation might be biased by prejudice nor did he fully recognize the degree to which the conditions of slavery itself might be responsible for traits of character that he asserted were inborn. Not only was Jefferson unable to reconcile his practice with his principles; more subtly destructive was the intellectual confusion that resulted from the tapping of deep unconscious springs of racial feeling, intensified, as Professor Jordan points out, by sexual stress. As Jefferson's agonies go to show, social thought in America would not proceed serenely on a lofty plane of ideality when the problem of race intruded. At the bottom of the problem lay the inability or refusal of a high-minded man like Thomas Jefferson to face, and by facing perhaps to transcend, the knowledge that he *was* Thomas Jefferson, America's leading spokesman for the rights of man, precisely because he owned slaves and his slaves were black.

Through the period of grace while, in Jefferson's doom-filled phrase, God's justice slept on the slavery question, Americans elaborated a governmental system that would embody and enact, as faithfully as might be, the essential affirmations of New World social thought. Simultaneously they perfected a political style in which organized political parties, earlier distrusted as divisive factions or selfish interest groups, engaged in contests that by the necessities of the case drove them toward even larger commitments to popularism, both in rhetoric and in practice. Anti-party animus diminished, as Michael Wallace, who teaches American history at Franconia College, shows in the last reading in this section, as parties became more democratic and politicos learned to pin their party pennants to the great principles of republican liberty. Included in the pro-party case were the arguments, quite characteristic of a time that saw the proliferation of all sorts of voluntary associations, that liberty was grounded in competition, that partisan vitality was both a sign

[2] David Brion Davis in *William and Mary Qtly*, 3rd ser., XXVI (Jan., 1969), p. 112.

and a guarantee of public freedoms, and that parties were in many ways essential to the welfare and progress of the nation: what was good for parties, in short, was good for the country. This reasoning made an adroit interlocking of ideas and institutions: party organization advanced the highest ideals of the republic, while those ideals, energetically invoked by party leaders, made party organization legitimate. This dynamic relation of parties and principles is described by Mr. Wallace through an analysis of the rhetoric of a group of rising politicians, the so-called Albany Regency, who flourished in New York State on the eve of the Age of Jackson.

Over the nearly 200 years that separated the ascendency of the Albany Regency from the founding of Puritan Dedham, the norms of social thought shifted in America from hierarchy toward equality, from prescription toward voluntarism, from elitism toward popularism, from communalism toward individualism. As old assumptions about status and deference were eroded by broadening socio-economic opportunities and by the pressure of an expanding population on the supply of land, Americans changed their concepts of the good society to conform to their experience. The communalistic, authoritarian precepts of the Dedham utopians came to seem utterly nonsensical to the brash republicans of the Age of Jackson who redefined social order as the automatic result of the full, free assertion of individual and associational liberties. The readings in this section illustrate aspects of this general movement of social thought from its theological and conservative beginnings to its secular and liberal outcomes. Each selection opens fresh perspectives on the history of American social ideas; each points ahead to the successive parts of this book wherein the issues introduced here, and many others, are more fully developed.

In the first decades of its existence Dedham was a remarkably stable agricultural community. It was also a utopian experiment, hardly less so than the famous Amana, Oneida, and Brook Farm experiments of the nineteenth century. The founders of this community set out to construct a unified social organism in which the whole would be more than the sum of the parts. To a considerable degree, they succeeded.

Scattered among the first waves of the Puritan exodus, they had arrived in the Massachusetts Bay colony in the years between 1630 and 1635. Many of them still strangers to one another, they had taken up temporary residence in several of the earliest settlements along the shores of the Bay. Sheer circumstance helped draw them together: it happened that most of them had found refuge in Watertown, where scores of immigrants were crowding in upon one another and where much of the best land had already been parceled out to the first arrivals. Yet behind the pressure of circumstance lay motives common to most of the Puritan immigrants. Within the limits set by the emerging policies of the colony, groups of settlers everywhere were coalescing and searching for the opportunity to create a communal life, seeking to shape in their own agricultural villages their own versions of the good society. So it was with the men who were to found the town of Dedham.

In 1635 they petitioned the General Court of the colony for a grant of land for a "plantation" south of Watertown. In polite phrases the petitioners asked for full control of the distribution of such lands as might be granted them, for exemption from taxes during the next four years, and for immunity from military obligations except in dire emergencies. Though the advice of the Court was solicited, the petition carried the implication that "the well ordering of . . . our society according to the best rule" would be left largely to the petitioners themselves. Significantly, the name which the founders would have given their plantation was "Contentment." Prosaic minds in the General Court changed "Contentment" to "Dedham," but the substance of the petition was granted.

Kenneth A. Lockridge, *A New England Town: The First Hundred Years.* Reprinted by permission of W. W. Norton & Company, Inc. Copyright © 1970 by W. W. Norton & Company, Inc. Footnotes omitted by permission.

Late in the summer of 1636 about thirty families excised from the broad ranks of the English middle classes, coming from the towns and villages of several regions, found themselves in possession of nearly 200 square miles of American wilderness. The hilly, rocky tract stretched from the south-western boundary of Boston down to what was to become the Rhode Island border. Except for several score Indians, who were quickly persuaded to re-linquish their claims for a small sum, the area was free of human habitation. Since Adam awoke in Paradise there had been no moments in which mankind had been given a clean slate, but the founders of Dedham came as close as men had ever come. They brought to their task the inevitable cultural baggage of Englishmen: language, rank, religion. They were subject to the broad guidance of the General Court. The rest, how they chose to organize what was in the most immediate sense *their* town, was up to them.

The way in which they began demonstrates the coherent social vision which had prompted this collection of men to seek their own community:

"*One*—We whose names are here unto subscribed do, in the fear and rever-ence of our Almighty God, mutually and severally promise amongst ourselves and each other to profess and practice one truth according to that most perfect rule, the foundation whereof is everlasting love." This was the first clause of the Dedham Covenant, a document in which the founders of the town simul-taneously set forth their social ideal, outlined the policies by which they would attempt to bring that ideal to reality, and pledged themselves to obey those policies. Every future townsman would be expected to signify his acceptance of its terms by signing his name beneath those of the founders. The Covenant began by binding every man to each of his fellows before God in a pledge to practice Christian love in their daily lives. The unity of men living according to this "one truth and most perfect rule" was to be the bedrock of the intended community. In four more clauses the Covenant further articulated the foun-ders' vision of social perfection.

"*Two*—That we shall by all means labor to keep off from us all such as are contrary minded, and receive only such unto us as may be probably of one heart with us, [and such] as that we either know or may well and truly be in-formed to walk in a peaceable conversation with all meekness of spirit, [this] for the edification of each other in the knowledge and faith of the Lord Jesus, and the mutual encouragement unto all temporal comforts in all things, seek-ing the good of each other, out of which may be derived true peace." They expected that all townsmen would begin as humble seekers after that true faith in the Lord Jesus out of which came the capacity for genuine Christian love. All would go together in their search for faith and would be united by the mutual love that would arise in the course of the search and would reach its culmination in their achieved faith. A deep and abiding peace within each man and pervading the whole community would be the fruit of their com-panionship in this course. But in such a community there could be no place for the contrary minded or the proud of spirit. These would be warned off or, if need be, expelled. The founders saw no contradiction in the idea that the ideal society was to be built upon a policy of rigid exclusiveness.

"*Three*—That if at any time differences shall rise between parties of our said town, that then such party or parties shall presently refer all such differences unto some one, two, or three others of our said society to be fully accorded and determined without any further delay, if it possibly may be." The founders were striving for social perfection, but they were realistic about the means leading to its achievement. Even among the most carefully selected human material there would be some men who would now and then in the course of the common search for faith forget their pledges and quarrel. Indeed, there would be men who for all their trying would never achieve a valid Christian faith. Damned by eternally flawed natures unredeemed by God's grace, time and time again they would disrupt the harmony of the community. So the founders wrote into the Covenant a secular policy designed to achieve from without what Christian love would in most cases guarantee from within. This was that all men should promise to submit their "differences," as they so delicately put it, to a gentle mediation by several of their fellows. A little sincere persuasion would remind the disputing parties of their obligations and restore the community, if not their souls, to unity and to peace.

"*Four*—That every man that . . . shall have lots [land] in our said town shall pay his share in all such . . . charges as shall be imposed on him . . ., as also become freely subject unto all such orders and constitutions as shall be . . . made now or at any time hereafter from this day forward, as well for loving and comfortable society in our said town as also for the prosperous and thriving condition of our said fellowship, especially respecting the fear of God, in which we desire to begin and continue whatsoever we shall by his loving favor take into hand." Implied in this clause was the assumption that the ideal community was to be characterized by more than a vague atmosphere of peace and unity generated by Christian love and further preserved by local mediation. "Orders and constitutions" would be made to arrange the practical details of life so as to ensure a comfortable and thriving society. Pleasing to the men who lived therein, such a society would also be pleasing to a God who reserved his special wrath for disorderly communities. Accordingly, a free but strict obedience to the policies which would provide this good order was the final promise exacted of each townsman. Continuing dissent and debate were not to be permitted; once a policy was established, all men were to accept it without reservation.

"*Five*—And for the better manifestation of our true resolution herein, every man so received [into the town is] to subscribe hereunto his name, thereby obliging both himself and his successors after him for ever, as we have done." It was more than a lifetime contract which the founders intended; it was a contract in perpetuity, binding posterity in a continuing testimony to the hunger for social perfection which had seized a handful of Englishmen in the midst of a wilderness.

They meant what they said. The story of Dedham through the first decades of its existence is above all the story of the implementation of the policies of perfection written into the Covenant. Because true Christian love could only grow within each man's soul, perhaps with the help of the church, the leaders of secular society could do little to nourish this element of the covenential ideal. But they could and did follow the guidance of the Covenant in excluding those who would disrupt Christian unity, mediating the disputes of those who broke the peace, and instituting and obeying countless ordinances which brought every area of life into a stable secular order. Thus the promises of the Covenant were kept and there emerged a community that realized the vision of the founders . . .

The mutuality preached in the Covenant . . . notwithstanding, a clearly defined social hierarchy was also a part of the ideal of the founders, and the town's land policies were set accordingly. For Christian love toward all men does not have to imply absolute human equality, and in fact this particular Christian commune was not about to practice Christian Communism. To the contrary, the men of Dedham held fast to the belief of their Puritan culture in the natural inequality of men. It was foreordained by God that some men should have both greater capabilities and virtues than others and should rise and prosper. It was equally fated that some men should be incompetents and sinners who would lag behind the rest. Nor was this without its social purpose, since obedience to men of high rank was the cement of an orderly society, while the needs of less fortunate souls kept men attentive to their duties of Christian charity. Thus, the settlers did not see any necessary contradiction between their emphasis on mutuality to the point of a form of collectivism, and a frank recognition that a certain hierarchy of wealth and status was as desirable as it was inevitable, for in the view of their culture each tended in its own way to ensure social harmony. As long as within the levels of society the gap between the high and the low was not too extreme, as long as men of rank acquitted themselves responsibly and with a proper modesty, and as long as the lower ranks freely respected the upper, hierarchy was expected to add to collectivism yet another source of harmony, not to detract from it.

Hence, ever attentive to the will of God and to the advantages of social harmony, the founders of Dedham made "men's rank and quality" major criteria for the assignment of land. Though few if any of the settlers affected much "rank and quality" as an English courtier would have defined these, there were among them men who had been relatively wealthy or somewhat prominent in the localities from whence they came. These men received larger portions of each division of land, while men without such distinctions had to show large families or accept the smaller allotments appropriate to their lesser stations. Those who had, got, because in the Puritan lexicon those who had, deserved; and by this light Dedham acted in yet another way to perfect itself as it saw perfection.

The juxtaposition of a small band of Englishmen and a huge tract of wilderness was one of the most striking characteristics of early Dedham, but even more striking was the reaction of these Englishmen to the prospect of hundreds of thousands of acres of virgin land. Far from indulging appetites long held in check by the scarcity of land in England, the Dedham settlers' initial reaction was to turn their backs on the wilderness. During the first twenty years they divided among themselves less than 3,000 acres. They deliberately refused to indulge in the rapid assignment of large individual farms which had taken place in Watertown. Instead they parceled out to each man tiny houselots, with additional strips of arable, meadow and woodland scattered around the village. Each strip ranged from two to twelve acres, depending on the size of a man's family, his usefulness and rank; each was located in a large field in which every man had a similar strip of land and in which the common decisions of the group were to determine what crop would be sown in the field, its care and harvesting. The slow process of allotment enabled the town to enforce its social priorities with precision, while the common fields brought men into continual contact with one another and kept the village from disintegrating into isolated farms out in the countryside. Slowly, as ever larger areas of the common land were divided, as individual holdings were bought and sold and thereby consolidated into farms, the rigid pattern was to dissolve. Until it did, the village remained a cohesive social organism . . .

Out of their vision of society and out of the wilderness tract with which they had begun the founders of Dedham created what might best be described as a Christian Utopian Closed Corporate Community. Christian because they saw Christian love as the force which would most completely unite their community. Utopian because theirs was a highly conscious attempt to build the most perfect possible community, as perfectly united, perfectly at peace, and perfectly ordered as man could arrange. Closed because its membership was selected while outsiders were treated with suspicion or rejected altogether. And Corporate because the commune demanded the loyalty of its members, offering in exchange privileges which could be obtained only through membership, not the least of which were peace and good order. The corporative nature of the town was confirmed by the practices of the colony: the typical inhabitant of Massachusetts could obtain land only by belonging to a particular town, since the allotment of most of the land in settled areas had been delegated to the towns by the General Court; and a man was represented in the House of Deputies (the lower house of the General Court) only if he was a member of a town, since representatives were elected from the town corporations rather than from electoral districts containing a certain number of inhabitants.

The obvious origin of the Christian Utopian Closed Corporate Community lay in the Puritan ideology. The very term "Puritan" was coined to describe the desire for perfection which drove many of these otherwise typical Englishmen into martyrdom or exile. Purity in the church itself was the chief goal. The Puritans sought an end to bishops, vestments, ritual—to "papistry" in whatever form it might take. Their consciences required a return to the simple forms of primitive Christianity and a ministry which would preach the unadorned Word of God as it appeared in the Bible. What has often been passed over, however, is the intensity of the drive for social purity which likewise characterized Puritanism. If the Puritan sometimes dreamed of a church whose membership was confined to "visible saints," he also dreamed on occasion of a society dominated by secular saints, men able to live in harmony with their fellowmen as God had commanded.

Most immediately, the policies of perfection in Dedham were the products of a vivid utopian spirit which came to possess most of the leaders and many of the rank and file of the Puritan emigration as they approached America. They were aware that a great opportunity awaited them in the confrontation of the Puritan social ideal with the New World. Here was a chance to begin again, leaving behind the compromises of an established culture. Governor John Winthrop's famous "Modell of Christian Charity," a sermon delivered aboard the *Arbella* on the way to America, is proof of the excitement and trepidation with which he approached the unique opportunity opened to his people. With God's help they would build in their colony a "city upon a hill" which would stand as a shining example to all men. The plan of the society Winthrop hoped to construct in Massachusetts was the plan of early Dedham writ large, a holy covenanted corporation mixing mutuality with hierarchy and Christian love with exclusiveness.

But the origins of the Dedham commune ran deeper than the Puritan ideology, deeper even than Christianity. At first glance they seem to run back to the English rural culture which had done so much to shape the social ideals of Puritanism. Any number of institutions and customs found in Dedham were direct transplantations from the English villages of the time. Genuine as this line of descent is, it is also deceptive. For the deepest secular origins of this Utopian Closed Corporate Community lay not merely in English villages but in a major strain of peasant culture also found in medieval and modern villages of France and Spain, and in modern Indian and Javanese villages.

An anthropologist entirely unaware of the internal structure of the New England Town has described the "Closed Corporate Peasant Community" common to all these places and times [Eric Wolf, *Peasants* (Englewood Cliffs, N.J., 1966)]. His description fits Dedham nicely. Social relationships in these rural communities are "many-stranded and polyadic"; the villagers tend to form a single social coalition which deals with all the issues of village life— land, taxation, regulation, morality. A "Closed Corporate Peasant Community" restricts its membership, retains ultimate authority over the alienation of land, seeks to guarantee its members equal access to resources, and maintains its internal order by enforcing common standards of behavior (by accusations of witchcraft, if all else fails). "The community thus acquires the form of a corporation, an enduring organization of rights and duties held by a stable membership; and it will tend to fight off changes and innovations as potential threats to the internal order that it strives to maintain." Indeed, the constant possibility of disruptions imposed by outside forces generates a powerful hostility toward everything strange, a hostility which further protects the internal order by uniting the villages in a shared emotional experience. Conscious utopianism may be found in these as in all peasant communities, for from them arise movements centering on a "myth of a social order," looking forward to "the establishment of a new order on earth."

So the utopia of the Puritan émigrés who founded Dedham was in many respects a peasant utopia. The communal ideal of these men repeated so many features of the peasant ideal that their Puritanism seemed a mere continuation of the peasant ethos. The dichotomy of mutual devotion within and hostility without, which had been practiced by a multitude of villages all over the world for thousands of years, was in turn both preached and practiced in Puritan Dedham, and all the characteristic implications of this corporative form were worked out in full detail. Further, the tendency of medieval peasants to look on the villages of an imaginary golden past as their model for the future regeneration of society was repeated in the Puritan idealization of the communes as a model for some features of Dedham's organization. Precedents for the peculiar mixture of hierarchy with collectivism manifested in Puritan Dedham could even be found in the history of peasant utopianism. The Puritan source did not simply echo the peasant; they were directly linked. The social ethic of Englishmen of the day still owed much to the peasant experience which had once dominated the English scene, and among the Puritans as among all Englishmen were many men whose families were only a few generations removed from villeinage and still lived in hamlets that were essentially peasant.

Did this really mean that for the men of Dedham Puritanism was nothing more than the continuation of traditional impulses? Not entirely. Puritanism was above all a new religious impulse, part of the Reformation which swept over Europe in the sixteenth and seventeenth centuries and which in its origins and effects was far more than a mere offshoot of the peasant ethos. This new impulse would color the history of Dedham, and indeed it had brought the townsmen there in the first place. Yet somehow when these creatures of the Reformation came to articulate their ideal of social organization, they not only continued but actually perfected and sanctified the ideal of the peasant past. The two sources, Puritan and peasant, were not identical, but by some inscrutable chemistry they came together in a mixture which was as powerful as it was inseparable.

It may be that the catalyst was the American wilderness, whose frightening presence turned the settlers back upon the old ways engrained in them and their forbears. If this was the case, then Puritanism was somewhat incidental to that intensification of the peasant tradition found in Dedham; Puritanism had brought the townsmen face to face with the wilderness and had provided the rhetoric by which their social reaction to this alarming prospect could be sanctified, but it had not directly urged them to their conservative social ideal. Yet it may be also that within Puritanism itself was a fear of the future which tended to send its advocates to the past for their definition of the holy society.

Whatever the exact nature of the mixture, Dedham was at once a Puritan and a peasant utopia. It partook of the desire for a reformed religion which had seized Europeans in all walks of life and at the same time it embraced half-conscious patterns which had arisen in peasant villages long before the discovery of America. It blended these sources into an ideology strong enough to unite men from diverse parts of England into a coherent social organism. Ironically, what was most uniquely "American" about the policies of earliest Dedham was the intensity of their utopianism. For here in the New World the settlers could heed almost without restriction whatever mysterious fears urged them to reconstruct in new perfection the ancient patterns of social organization . . .

Though a new age of revolutionary political theories was even then beginning, order was still the highest political value in the seventeenth century, as it had been for some centuries before. Thomas Hobbes was no innovator when he observed that human society is naturally inclined to chaos. Hobbes' argument in favor of strong rulers merely secularized the old Christian justification of government. God had given man the capacity to sin, Adam and Eve had sinned, thenceforth men were forever imperfect, forever condemned to fall into immorality and discord. As sin was divinely ordained, so was government. The state existed to restrain the sinful impulse and punish the sinner, not simply because sin was wrong, but because the visible church needed an orderly world in which to fulfill its part of God's plan. A society in which violence interrupted the work of the clergy and unbridled license smothered all examples of virtue was not a proper arena for man's struggle for salvation. The much-maligned James I was only invoking the commonplace when he spoke of the divine right of kings, for traditional theory gave divine sanction to the rulers of the state. Likewise Shakespeare's frequent sallies in praise of order were no more than resounding summations of the deep-rooted spirit of his age. And similarly, much of the "reform" thought of the radical English Protestants of the seventeenth century envisioned not a new and mobile society stressing individual opportunity but rather a social commonwealth whose prime features were security and Christian love.

The Puritans of New England had ample reason to hold to and indeed to extend the seventeenth century's faith in order. Their conception of a whole society bound to God by a covenant made the existence of sin an immediate danger, for to allow sin was to breach the contract with God, thereby inviting his wrath down upon them all. Further, their desire to build a perfect visible church accented the need for a state which would give the church an orderly social setting for its work. Circumstance lent practical force to these arguments; England might use any sign of discord in Massachusetts as an excuse to revoke their charter and take over the government in the name of good order. Such a move would shatter the emigrants' covenant and with it their "city on a hill."

But it does not require Hobbesean skepticism, original sin, or Puritan perfectionism to explain the love of order. All were present, but beneath all, as ever, lay the peasant's inbred fear of chaos. Robbery, extortion, war with its legalized murder—few peasant villages had not lived precariously close to these disasters. Only late in the fifteenth century had the Tudor state ended the bloody baronial feuds which had kept England in turmoil for generations, and it would be at least another century before the age of inchoate popular uprisings would come to an end. The confidence generated by uniform legal order imposed by a central monarchy was new to Englishmen's experience. A little below the surface were folk memories of violence and a longing for peace and certainty.

Such was the background of Dedham's peculiar political behavior. A product of its time, the town Covenant had obliged men to pledge obedience and had gone to some lengths to provide mechanisms for the preservation of order. Men of their time, and also men aware of the dangers involved in founding a perfect society in the wilderness, the townsmen of Dedham took the Covenant to heart. They settled their disputes peacefully and used their electoral powers to elevate a handful of substantial men, leaving in their hands the direction of the community. Sanctified by their election, the leaders of Dedham were further sanctified by their success in keeping order, and thereby they gained re-election repeatedly. Today's praise for democracy as the key to opportunity and for dissent as the harbinger of change would have been grotesquely out of place in such a society, where order outranked opportunity and the changes brought by dissent were not expected to be fruitful.

But a narrow-minded passion for order was not the only source of the town's political behavior. Had it been, there would have been no need for a town meeting. The founders or the colony's Governor could have imposed a set of lifetime rulers who would name their own successors, a complete oligarchy in short. The Puritans' desire for order was more sophisticated than this. Their intense Christianity led them to see in unity rather than in repression the essence of true order. They "demanded that in society all men, at least all regenerate men, be marshalled in one united array . . . The theorists of New England thought of society as a unity, bound together by inviolable ties; they thought of it not as an aggregation of individuals, but as an organism, functioning for a definite purpose, with . . . all members contributing a definite share.". . . Therefore, a degree of popular participation was valued, for it would both symbolize and strengthen the unity of all men in the common Christian society. Consent would strengthen unity and that unity would lead to a higher form of order.

So there was in the Puritan political philosophy a door through which the generality could enter to participate in the workings of government. But, at least on the level of the colony's theoreticians and leaders, it was seen as a very narrow door. It was only the saints who could hope to achieve genuine Christian unity, and therefore it was their participation that was the center of concern. Even in their case, "the commanders were not to trim their policies by the desires of the people . . . the officers were above the common men. . . ." The emphasis was on obedience: "When the Lord sets himself over a people, he frames them unto a willing and voluntary submission unto him . . . they follow Him not forcedly, but as far as they are sanctified by his grace, they submit willingly to his regiment." The chief participatory acts envisioned were the consent to covenants and the election of a few leaders, acts which would enhance the unity of the participating saints and at the same time give extra cachet to the leaders and to the political framework which they had established. Beyond this, participation was likely to be viewed as interference, conducive to disorder.

John Winthrop expressed it in this way: "It is yourselves who have called us to . . . office, and being called by you, we have authority from God." As for liberty, "[the] liberty you are to stand for is a liberty to [do] that only which is good, just, and honest . . . This liberty is maintained and exercised in a way of subjection to authority." A good subject was to resemble a good wife, for, "the woman's own choice makes such a man her husband; yet being so chosen, he is her lord, and she is to be subject to him, yet in a way of liberty, not of bondage; and a true wife accounts her subjection her honor and freedom. . . ." Though Winthrop's statement exaggerated its authoritarian aspects, the fundamentals of the theory prevailed as the usual ideological justification for popular participation. The colony law continued to insist that church members alone were qualified to vote for colony officers because they alone could be trusted to perceive "that which is good, just, and honest" and to submit themselves to leaders with a like perception.

Perhaps because it was grafted onto a tradition of local consensus and cooperation which had long characterized English peasant communities, the theory had more positive overtones on the local level. The vote was not confined to church members (after 1647) and voters had the right to join in substantive decisions as well as to elect leaders. Still, the town's behavior reveals that the popular voice in Dedham acted in a manner consonant with the Puritan theory of popular participation. Men had signed the Covenant voluntarily and they voluntarily lived according to its commands. Their votes were customarily "by general agreement"—a voluntary consensus. In electing a man, they were asking him to lead a society united in love under the rule of the gospel; in obeying his decisions they were marching together freely in the practice of the "one truth" desired by all. The matching restraint of the selectmen derived more from their own stake in the common unity than from any fear of retaliation. And out of the unity thereby voluntarily achieved, the townsmen also enjoyed an enduring order such as no amount of force could have imposed.

Sixty-nine men of Dedham explicitly approved the prevailing theory in a petition of support sent to the General Court in 1665 to aid the government in its battle against English interference in the affairs of the colony. None of them was qualified to vote in colony elections and some could not participate in the town meeting, yet every last one expressed appreciation of "the great blessing we enjoy ... in a Godly, righteous, and peaceable government." These men said quite frankly that they valued a government "Godly, righteous, and peaceable" over the limited blessing of the suffrage. In an age in which the suffrage was viewed as one more way of maintaining unity and preserving order, the democrat's worship of the vote was far in the future.

To put it another way, conditions were not ripe for a philosophy of individualism. "The basic sociological findings ... show that modern individualism depends appreciably upon extensive division of labor, institutional differentiation and cultural diversity." The democracy of differing religions, immigration, urbanization, and contending economic interests was out of the question in the simple society of seventeenth-century Dedham. Diversity had not yet been forced upon men. Until it was, a man's concern would be more with harmonizing himself with the one true way than with protecting his right to vote in a pluralistic world where individual rights had become the only refuge.

The political phenomenon at hand, which might be labeled "Conservative Corporate Voluntarism," actually lies not one but two layers deep in American history. A long distance from the popular democracy of the nineteenth century, it was only beginning to merge into the mechanistic political philosophy which was to characterize eighteenth-century Americans—particularly those eighteenth-century Americans familiar with Enlightenment thought and with contemporary English political theorists. Dedham's political system was intricate, yet ultimately what had made political harmony in Dedham was not a clockwork balance of one power against another but voluntary restraint on the part of all concerned. Eighteenth-century thinkers would de-emphasize the notion of an organic society held together by voluntary restraint. In its place would come an emphasis on the balance of political elements, monarchy, aristocracy, and democracy, each with its own virtues and vices. Ideally, each would contribute its virtues while holding in check the vices of the others. Democracy would contribute the representation of a certain class of interests and the innate good sense of the commonry. The instability of democracy would be cancelled partially by restricting the suffrage to propertied men, partially by the stability of the monarchical and aristocratic elements. The theory of the eighteenth century allowed popular participation at once a greater and a lesser role than its predecessor. By justifying the participation of the commonry in a legislative role and by freeing the suffrage of religious restrictions, it opened a door to the later deification of democracy. Yet by destroying the Puritan notion of popular participation as a holy recognition of the organic unity of men (or at least of all believers) in their society, the eighteenth-century outlook stripped the popular voice of a mystical level of human significance which it has since regained, alas, largely in the perverted world of plebescitary totalitarianism.

"Conservative Corporate Voluntarism" in politics, like the closed corporate community in which it operated, was "American" chiefly in that it was a uniquely intense expression of Old World ideals. Only in the most tenuous sense can the roots of modern American democracy be traced back to the political experience of seventeenth-century Dedham. Its limitations and conservative theoretical context notwithstanding, the suffrage *was* significantly wider in Dedham than in England. Both in Dedham and in Massachusetts at large the many officers subject to election by this wider electorate exercised powers which were in the aggregate greater than the powers exercised by elected officers in England. In such innovations lay the deepest foundation of an American participatory mentality, a mentality born of a widened public role in government, which eventually would lead increasing numbers of men to demand a still wider role in their own governance . . . And perhaps it is possible to see in the divine sanction with which all New England Puritans endowed a limited popular voice the beginnings of the later secular sanctification of Everyman's right to participate which paved the way for the triumph of democracy as a supreme virtue. But it must not be forgotten that modern democracy whether in practice or in theory was a long way in the future. It took far more than moderately wide participation, occasional popular protests, or veiled scriptural justifications to create that democracy . . .

Dedham's age of utopian communalism contained within itself the seeds of change, just as later the age in which change would become the dominant theme of the town's history would contain in turn the continuing impulse of the past.

As any Puritan would have been the first to admit, the impulse toward perfection is doomed to failure. Crippled by original sin, man's reason cannot discern the nature of God's plan for the universe. Still less can human reason put into practice and maintain whatever chimera of social perfection it happens to light upon. This theory was never better illustrated than in the case of earliest Dedham. Though no violent changes disturbed the even tenor of village life, the overriding utopian concern gradually evaporated. All the covenants, catechisms, and bylaws in the world could not have stopped the process, for at its heart lay the everlasting inability of human nature to satisfy its own recurring hunger for the absolute. By the end of the first half-century, the policies of perfection no longer held sway.

The process of decline began with the beginning of the community. Even as town and church wrote their covenants and set about putting their principles into practice, imperfections arose. What Plato called "the recalcitrance of the medium" made itself felt in seemingly trival ways: "Contentment" was renamed "Dedham" by an unimaginative General Court; Thomas Cakebread, a skilled miller, decided not to add his skills to the new community; the respected and learned John Phillips was unable to join the church as its first minister. But as the years passed, trival disappointments were replaced by imperfections of ever larger consequence until at last the failings had so eroded the successes that the integral utopian spirit could no longer be said to exist.

A little of the intended unity was sacrificed as early as 1639, when the meeting of all townsmen delegated its powers to the selectmen. Perhaps "the general meeting of so many men" *had* "wasted much time," but it had also enabled every townsman to participate directly in every decision. Now the pure consensual unity of the founders would disappear and most decisions would pass into the hands of a few leaders—all in the name of efficiency.

It had been the town's practice to set aside six days out of each year for work on the highways and to require each man to work any four of the six days. On the appointed day, the townsmen would work shoulder-to-shoulder until the roads were once again in good repair. But here, too, the communal ideal fell short when an early bylaw allowed a man to hire a substitute. Instead of displaying in their soiled hands the evidence of a common obligation, thenceforth the more successful townsmen could use their wealth to lift themselves above the herd. Eventually, a similar procedure would allow the well-off to buy themselves out of their turn at the burdensome office of constable. By the terms of the Covenant all townsmen were equally privileged and equally bound, but money soon made some more equal than others.

By the 1650's circumstances had begun to create a series of privileged subcorporations within the community, further undermining the total unity envisioned in the Covenant. The tapering off of new memberships in the church which began in these years had led by 1670 to a congregation which excluded a majority of the townsmen. The formal proprietorship of the town lands was shared by nearly all townsmen at the inception of that institution in 1656, but thereafter new arrivals unable to purchase shares from an existing proprietor were shut out of this privilege. The town corporation itself ceased to be identical with the community since, after about 1660, new arrivals were not always invited to sign the Covenant. Thus, a group of six or eight Scotsmen settled in Dedham in the 1660's without subscribing to the pact. They were not warned out; they paid taxes, worked and even married in the community just as did any townsman; but they were by implication second-class citizens. The irony in all of this is that the founders' drive for perfection carried the seeds of its own failure. Their perfect church had the imperfection of excluding some townsmen from its sacraments, while their perfect town excluded some of its inhabitants from the proprietorship and from its Covenant. It could not be helped.

If the corporate unity of the village was slowly eroding, so was its physical coherence. The common field system began disintegrating almost from the day of its inception. Already in the 1640's the town permitted men to "fence their lots in particular" and presumably to grow in these lots whatever crops they wished. By the 1670's it had become usual for men to take up both special "convenience grants" and their usual shares of each new dividend in locations as close as possible to their existing lots, practices which aided the consolidation of individual holdings. The process encouraged by public policy was completed by private transactions, for an active market in small parcels of land soon emerged, a market in which most farmers sought to sell distant lands and buy lands closer to their main holdings. The net result was the coalescence of private farms. From here, it would be but two short steps for farmers whose holdings were centered in outlying areas to move their barns and then their houses from the village out to their lands. As of 1686 few seem to have taken these steps, but the way had been prepared and the days of a society totally enclosed by the village were numbered. In any event the common-field system was gone, taking with it the common decisions and the frequent encounters of every farmer with his fellows which it entailed ...

The waning of the explicit social synthesis of the Dedham Covenant was a subtle thing, as subtle yet as pervasive as the synthesis itself. There had been no dramatic social upheaval brought on by irresistible material forces, nor had a cathartic moral crisis replaced the old synthesis with a new. The village remained a small, slowly growing community with traditional views and unchanging institutions. It was just that the utopian aura was gone. Something almost intangible had happened, then, and for almost inscrutable reasons. The townsmen might as well have attributed the change to a dozen small shifts of circumstance as to the gradually waning spiritual energies which, at times, they seemed to think were at fault. Most likely, they simply subsumed all causes under the wrath of a truly inscrutable God who could punish men both by altering their circumstances and by sapping their faith. That was cause enough. But, whether the forces of nature, the fallibility of the human spirit, or the wrath of God was most responsible, the fact is that something most certainly had happened. By 1686, the Covenant was no longer enforced and would never again be the guide for every policy and every action. The harmonious society so painstakingly built under its influence no longer existed in all its original integrity.

The only satisfaction the townsmen could have salvaged was that it all appeared to have happened according to strict Puritan theory. In "A Modell of Christian Charity," John Winthrop had predicated the successful application of Christian love upon the existence of a large majority of saints, who were able to sustain that love because they had received God's restoring grace. In Dedham, when the saints dwindled and died away, the rule of love dwindled and died with them. In this sense, too, the New England preachers of the 1670's and 80's could take some satisfaction in being right. Their famous laments over the decline of the spirit of the founders were justified by events in Dedham. Small wonder the wrath of God was now descending.

Perhaps, in retrospect, there is another satisfaction to be gained. Though all too short from the point of view of a Puritan divine, the life of the utopian commune had been longer than anyone had a right to expect. Created in the midst of a howling wilderness, it had remained essentially intact well into the lifetime of the second generation. It has been said that America is the place where utopias are put into practice ... and found impracticable. This is true, but among all the social blueprints brought to reality on these shores, among the Pennsylvanias and Georgias and Brook Farms, the Dedham experiment stands out by virtue of its relative endurance. In the long history of American utopias, any which lasted the better part of fifty years must be accounted a success ...

Insofar as the history of one New England town cannot be repeated in the history of any other, the story of Dedham must stand alone as one atom of our national experience. But clearly Dedham was not entirely unique. The forces which most shaped the history of this town—the residual peasant outlook and Puritan social ideal of the founders, for example, or the later growth and dispersal of the population—were general forces which must have affected other towns. Hence, in its main features the story of Dedham could well have been the story of many New England towns and so of much of early America. In this sense the history of one town can and should be used to illuminate the larger history of its times and nation.

To what extent was the history of Dedham actually duplicated in other towns? To a great extent. And what does the illumination which Dedham's history, thus enlarged, provides, reveal about the American experience? It reveals that this part of colonial America was moving away from a powerful corporate impulse deeply indebted to the European past, toward an age of pluralism, individualism, and liberty. Yet in the end the history of this and of its companion towns also suggests that the evolution of a libertarian society in America was neither as rapid nor as direct as might be thought ...

... the power of the American environment to transform human society has been exaggerated. Thousands upon thousands of the earliest Americans turned their backs on the wilderness. Aided by the fact that the material and social opportunities of the New World were not so great as to overpower all social coherence, they refused to let its undeniable abundance spin them outward into the incoherence of individual opportunism. In searching for a social ideal with which to shape the first layer of a new history, they looked back to the ideals of the past. These ideals encouraged men to strive for perfection, but defined perfection as peace, unity, and order. Because they were successfully implemented, for decades life in this part of America was intimately linked in all its phases to the intellectual and social traditions of medieval Europe and to a worldwide peasant tradition dating from the origin of recorded history. So persistent was the desire to define social perfection in terms of stability, so satisfying was the achievement of that desire, that elements of the communal ideal derived from the past remained alive in the towns of New England and of the northwestern territories of the United States even after the passing of Jefferson and the coming of Andrew Jackson.

This deepest layer of the American experience was in every way conservative. It was conservative in that it looked to the past for wisdom. It was conservative in that the substance of the wisdom it found in the past was skepticism: that in a world inclined to chaos the most men could hope for was a stable life within a small community. It was conservative in that the outlook it created resisted change long after it had become obvious that the skeptical lessons of the past did not entirely apply to America, after it was clear that opportunity and individual freedom within a fluid national society could be achieved without fatal disorder. On this conservative foundation a large part of the history of our nation has been constructed. In the depths of the American experience lies a craving for peace, unity, and order within the confines of a simple society. Though it is not à la mode to say so, next to it lies a willingness to exclude whatever men and to ignore whatever events threaten the fulfillment of that hunger.

But there were in this earliest age the seeds of a more optimistic America, which after the further evolution of the national experience would burst into flower. At first the remarkably pervasive utopian impulse, an impulse that on one occasion could weld a hundred strangers from diverse parts of England into the social organism known as Dedham, was inseparable from the conservatism of the age. But time would leach away some of the conservatism, leaving a widespread desire for perfection and the belief that it was to be found in America. Then it would matter that at least some part of America had possessed from the beginning an ingrained utopianism, a utopianism not just of leaders or visionaries but of the common man. The optimistic visionary Thomas Jefferson would find awaiting him a number of believers in an American utopia, whose confidence would help make of him the leader of a national political machine dedicated to the realization of a utopia of opportunity and freedom. Similarly the initial abundance of land and the economic equality which it fostered, together with the relatively wide base of political participation characteristic of this part of early America, would take on new significance after the time of Jefferson; they would cease to be the accidental or subordinate parts of a synthesis which looked to the past, and would become instead the dominant elements of a new synthesis which welcomed the future.

2 / Bernard Bailyn
Political Experience and Enlightenment Ideas in
Eighteenth-Century America

Considering the material at hand, old and new, that bears on the question [of the relation of American political experience to Enlightenment ideas], one discovers an apparent paradox. There appear to be two primary and contradictory sets of facts. The first and more obvious is the undeniable evidence of the seriousness with which colonial and revolutionary leaders took ideas, and the deliberateness of their efforts during the Revolution to reshape institutions in their pattern. The more we know about these American provincials the clearer it is that among them were remarkably well-informed students of contemporary social and political theory. There never was a dark age that destroyed the cultural contacts between Europe and America. The sources of transmission had been numerous in the seventeenth century; they increased in the eighteenth. There were not only the impersonal agencies of newspapers, books, and pamphlets, but also continuous personal contact through travel and correspondence. Above all, there were Pan-Atlantic, mainly Anglo-American, interest groups that occasioned a continuous flow of fresh information and ideas between Europe and the mainland colonies in America. Of these, the most important were the English dissenters and their numerous codenominationalists in America. Located perforce on the left of the English political spectrum, acutely alive to ideas of reform that might increase their security in England, they were, for the almost endemically nonconformist colonists, a rich source of political and social theory. It was largely through nonconformist connections, as Caroline Robbins' recent book, *The Eighteenth-Century Commonwealthman* (1959), suggests, that the commonwealth radicalism of seventeenth-century England continued to flow to the colonists, blending, ultimately, with other strains of thought to form a common body of advanced theory.

In every colony and in every legislature there were people who knew

Bernard Bailyn, *American Historical Review*, LXVII (January, 1962), pp. 343–351. Reprinted without footnotes by permission of the author.

Locke and Beccaria, Montesquieu and Voltaire; but perhaps more important, there was in every village of every colony someone who knew such transmitters of English nonconformist thought as Watts, Neal, and Burgh; later Priestley and Price—lesser writers, no doubt, but staunch opponents of traditional authority, and they spoke in a familiar idiom. In the bitterly contentious pamphlet literature of mid-eighteenth-century American politics, the most frequently cited authority on matters of principle and theory was not Locke or Montesquieu but *Cato's Letters*, a series of radically libertarian essays written in London in 1720–1723 by two supporters of the dissenting interest, John Trenchard and Thomas Gordon. Through such writers, as well as through the major authors, leading colonists kept contact with a powerful tradition of enlightened thought.

This body of doctrine fell naturally into play in the controversy over the power of the imperial government. For the revolutionary leaders it supplied a common vocabulary and a common pattern of thought, and, when the time came, common principles of political reform. That reform was sought and seriously if unevenly undertaken, there can be no doubt. Institutions were remodeled, laws altered, practices questioned all in accordance with advanced doctrine on the nature of liberty and of the institutions needed to achieve it. The Americans were acutely aware of being innovators, of bringing mankind a long step forward. They believed that they had so far succeeded in their effort to reshape circumstances to conform to enlightened ideas and ideals that they had introduced a new era in human affairs. And they were supported in this by the opinion of informed thinkers in Europe. The contemporary image of the American Revolution at home and abroad was complex; but no one doubted that a revolution that threatened the existing order and portended new social and political arrangements had been made, and made in the name of reason.

Thus, throughout the eighteenth century there were prominent, politically active Americans who were well aware of the development of European thinking, took ideas seriously, and during the Revolution deliberately used them in an effort to reform the institutional basis of society. This much seems obvious. But, paradoxically, and less obviously, it is equally true that many, indeed most, of what these leaders considered to be their greatest achievements during the Revolution—reforms that made America seem to half the world like the veritable heavenly city of the eighteenth-century philosophers—had been matters of fact before they were matters of theory and revolutionary doctrine.

No reform in the entire Revolution appeared of greater importance to Jefferson than the Virginia acts abolishing primogeniture and entail. This action, he later wrote, was part of "a system by which every fibre would be eradicated of antient or future aristocracy; and a foundation laid for a government truly republican." But primogeniture and entail had never taken deep roots in America, not even in tidewater Virginia. Where land was cheap and easily available such legal restrictions proved to be encumbrances profiting few. Often they tended to threaten rather than secure the survival of the family, as Jefferson himself realized when in 1774 he petitioned the Assembly to break an entail on his wife's estate on the very practical, untheoretical, and common ground that to do so would be "greatly to their [the petitioners'] Interest and that of their Families." The legal abolition of primogeniture and entail during and after the Revolution was of little material consequence. Their demise had been effectively decreed years before by the circumstances of life in a wilderness environment.

Similarly, the disestablishment of religion—a major goal of revolutionary reform—was carried out, to the extent that it was, in circumstances so favorable to it that one wonders not how it was done but why it was not done more thoroughly. There is no more eloquent, moving testimony to revolutionary idealism than the Virginia Act for Establishing Religious Freedom: it is the essence of Enlightenment faith. But what did it, and the disestablishment legislation that had preceded it, reform? What had the establishment of religion meant in prerevolutionary Virginia? The Church of England was the state church, but dissent was tolerated well beyond the limits of the English Acts of Toleration. The law required nonconformist organizations to be licensed by the government, but dissenters were not barred from their own worship nor penalized for failure to attend the Anglican communion, and they were commonly exempted from parish taxes. Nonconformity excluded no one from voting and only the very few Catholics from enjoying public office. And when the itineracy of revivalist preachers led the establishment to contemplate more restrictive measures, the Baptists and Presbyterians advanced to the point of arguing publicly, and pragmatically, that the toleration they had so far enjoyed was an encumbrance, and that the only proper solution was total liberty: in effect, disestablishment.

Virginia was if anything more conservative than most colonies. The legal establishment of the Church of England was in fact no more rigorous in South Carolina and Georgia: it was considerably weaker in North Carolina. It hardly existed at all in the middle colonies (there was of course no vestige of it in Pennsylvania), and where it did, as in four counties of New York, it was either ignored or had become embattled by violent opposition well before the Revolution. And in Massachusetts and Connecticut, where the establishment, being nonconformist according to English law, was legally tenuous to begin with, tolerance in worship and relief from church taxation had been extended to the major dissenting groups early in the century, resulting well before the Revolution in what was, in effect if not in law, a multiple establishment. And this had been further weakened by the splintering effect of the Great Awakening. Almost everywhere the Church of England, the established church of the highest state authority, was embattled and defensive—driven to rely more and more on its missionary arm, the Society for the Propagation of the Gospel, to sustain it against the cohorts of dissent.

None of this had resulted from Enlightenment theory. It had been created by the mundane exigencies of the situation: by the distance that separated Americans from ecclesiastical centers in England and the Continent; by the never-ending need to encourage immigration to the colonies; by the variety, the mere numbers, of religious groups, each by itself a minority, forced to live together; and by the weakness of the coercive powers of the state, its inability to control the social forces within it.

Even more gradual and less contested had been the process by which government in the colonies had become government by the consent of the governed. What had been proved about the franchise in early Massachusetts—that it was open for practically the entire free adult male population—can be proved to a lesser or greater extent for all the colonies. But the extraordinary breadth of the franchise in the American colonies had not resulted from popular demands: there had been no cries for universal manhood suffrage, nor were there popular theories claiming, or even justifying, general participation in politics. Nowhere in eighteenth-century America was there "democracy"—middle-class or otherwise—as we use the term. The main reason for the wide franchise was that the traditional English laws limiting suffrage to freeholders of certain competences proved in the colonies, where freehold property was almost universal, to be not restrictive but widely permissive.

Representation would seem to be different, since before the Revolution complaints had been voiced against the inequity of its apportioning, especially in the Pennsylvania and North Carolina assemblies. But these complaints were based on an assumption that would have seemed natural and reasonable almost nowhere else in the Western world: the assumption that representation in governing assemblages was a proper and rightful attribute of people as such—of regular units of population, or of populated land—rather than the privilege of particular groups, institutions, or regions. Complaints there were, bitter ones. But they were complaints claiming injury and deprivation, not abstract ideals or unfamiliar desires. They assumed from common experience the normalcy of regular and systematic representation. And how should it have been otherwise? The Colonial assemblies had not, like ancient parliaments, grown to satisfy a monarch's need for the support of particular groups or individuals or to protect the interests of a social order, and they had not developed insensibly from precedent to precedent. They had been created at a stroke, and they were in their composition necessarily regular and systematic. Nor did the process, the character, of representation as it was known in the colonies derive from theory. For colonial Americans, representation had none of the symbolic and little of the purely deliberative qualities which, as a result of the revolutionary debates and of Burke's speeches, would become celebrated as "virtual." To the colonists it was direct and actual: it was, most often, a kind of agency, a delegation of powers, to individuals commonly required to be residents of their constituencies and, often, bound by instructions from them—with the result that eighteenth-century American legislatures frequently resembled, in spirit if not otherwise, those "ancient assemblies" of New York, composed, the contemporary historian William Smith wrote, "of plain, illiterate husbandmen, whose views seldom extended farther than to the regulation of highways, the destruction of wolves, wild cats, and foxes, and the advancement of the other little interests of the particular counties which they were chosen to represent." There was no theoretical basis for such direct and actual representation. It had been created and was continuously reinforced by the pressure of local politics in the colonies and by the political circumstances in England, to which the colonists had found it necessary to send closely instructed, paid representatives—agents, so called—from the very beginning.

But franchise and representation are mere mechanisms of government by consent. At its heart lie freedom from executive power, from the independent action of state authority, and the concentration of power in representative bodies and elected officials. The greatest achievement of the Revolution was of course the repudiation of just such state authority and the transfer of power to popular legislatures. No one will deny that this action was taken in accordance with the highest principles of Enlightenment theory. But the way had been paved by fifty years of grinding factionalism in colonial politics. In the details of prerevolutionary American politics, in the complicated maneuverings of provincial politicians seeking the benefits of government, in the patterns of local patronage and the forms of factional groupings, there lies a history of progressive alienation from the state which resulted, at least by the 1750's, in what Professor Robert Palmer has lucidly described as a revolutionary situation: a condition

> . . . in which confidence in the justice or reasonableness of existing authority is undermined; where old loyalties fade, obligations are felt as impositions, law seems arbitrary, and respect for superiors is felt as a form of humiliation; where existing sources of prestige seem undeserved . . . and government is sensed as distant, apart from the governed and not really "representing" them.

Such a situation had developed in mid-eighteenth-century America, not from theories of government or Enlightenment ideas but from the factional opposition that had grown up against a succession of legally powerful, but often cynically self-seeking, inept, and above all politically weak officers of state.

Surrounding all of these circumstances and in various ways controlling them is the fact that that great goal of the European revolutions of the late eighteenth century, equality of status before the law—the abolition of legal privilege—had been reached almost everywhere in the American colonies at least by the early years of the eighteenth century. Analogies between the upper strata of colonial society and the European aristocracies are misleading. Social stratification existed, of course; but the differences between aristocracies in eighteenth-century Europe and in America are more important than the similarities. So far was legal privilege, or even distinction, absent in the colonies that where it existed it was an open sore of festering discontent, leading not merely, as in the case of the Penn family's hereditary claims to tax exemption, to formal protests, but, as in the case of the powers enjoyed by the Hudson River land magnates, to violent opposition as well. More important, the colonial aristocracy, such as it was, had no formal, institutional role in government. No public office or function was legally a prerogative of birth. As there were no social orders in the eyes of the law, so there were no governmental bodies to represent them. The only claim that has been made to the contrary is that, in effect, the governors' Councils constituted political institutions in the service of the aristocracy. But this claim—of dubious value in any case because of the steadily declining political importance of the Councils in the eighteenth century—cannot be substantiated. It is true that certain families tended to dominate the Councils, but they had less legal claim to places in those bodies than certain royal officials who, though hardly members of an American aristocracy, sat on the Councils by virtue of their office. Councilors could be and were removed by simple political maneuver. Council seats were filled either by appointment or election: when appointive, they were vulnerable to political pressure in England; when elective, to the vagaries of public opinion at home. Thus on the one hand it took William Byrd II three years of maneuvering in London to get himself appointed to the seat on the Virginia Council vacated by his father's death in 1704, and on the other, when in 1766 the Hutchinson faction's control of the Massachusetts Council proved unpopular, it was simply removed wholesale by being voted out of office at the next election. As there were no special privileges, no peculiar group possessions, manners, or attitudes to distinguish councilors from other affluent Americans, so there were no separate political interests expressed in the Councils as such. Councilors joined as directly as others in the factional disputes of the time, associating with groups of all sorts, from minute and transient American opposition parties to massive English-centered political syndicates. A century before the Revolution and not as the result of antiaristocratic ideas, the colonial aristocracy had become a vaguely defined, fluid group whose power—in no way guaranteed, buttressed, or even recognized in law—was competitively maintained and dependent on continuous, popular support.

Other examples could be given. Were written constitutions felt to be particular guarantees of liberty in enlightened states? Americans had known them in the form of colonial charters and governors' instructions for a century before the Revolution; and after 1763, seeking a basis for their claims against the constitutionality of specific acts of Parliament, they had been driven, out of sheer logical necessity and not out of principle, to generalize that experience. But the point is perhaps clear enough. Major attributes of enlightened polities had developed naturally, spontaneously, early in the history of the American colonies, and they existed as simple matters of social and political fact on the eve of the Revolution.

But if all this is true, what did the Revolution accomplish? Of what real significance were the ideals and ideas? What was the bearing of Enlightenment thought on the political experience of eighteenth-century Americans?

Perhaps this much may be said. What had evolved spontaneously from the demands of place and time was not self-justifying, nor was it universally welcomed. New developments, however gradual, were suspect by some, resisted in part, and confined in their effects. If it was true that the establishment of religion was everywhere weak in the colonies and that in some places it was even difficult to know what was orthodoxy and what was not, it was nevertheless also true that faith in the idea of orthodoxy persisted and with it belief in the propriety of a privileged state religion. If, as a matter of fact, the spread of freehold tenure qualified large populations for voting, it did not create new reasons for using that power nor make the victims of its use content with what, in terms of the dominant ideal of balance in the state, seemed a disproportionate influence of "the democracy." If many colonists came naturally to assume that representation should be direct and actual, growing with the population and bearing some relation to its distribution, crown officials did not, and they had the weight of precedent and theory as well as of authority with them and hence justification for resistance. If state authority was seen increasingly as alien and hostile and was forced to fight for survival within an abrasive, kaleidoscopic factionalism, the traditional idea nevertheless persisted that the common good was somehow defined by the state and that political parties or factions—organized opposition to established government—were seditious. A traditional aristocracy did not in fact exist; but the assumption that superiority was indivisible, that social eminence and political influence had a natural affinity to each other, did. The colonists instinctively conceded to the claims of the well-born and rich to exercise public office, and in this sense politics remained aristocratic. Behavior had changed—had had to change—with the circumstances of everyday life; but habits of mind and the sense of rightness lagged behind. Many felt the changes to be *away from*, not *toward*, something: that they represented deviance; that they lacked, in a word, legitimacy.

This divergence between habits of mind and belief on the one hand and experience and behavior on the other was ended at the Revolution. A rebellion that destroyed the traditional sources of public authority called forth the full range of advanced ideas. Long-settled attitudes were jolted and loosened. The grounds of legitimacy suddenly shifted. What had happened was seen to have been good and proper, steps in the right direction. The glass was half full, not half empty; and to complete the work of fate and nature, further thought must be taken, theories tested, ideas applied. Precisely because so many social and institutional reforms had already taken place in America, the revolutionary movement there, more than elsewhere, was a matter of doctrine, ideas, and comprehension.

And so it remained. Social change and social conflict of course took place during the revolutionary years; but the essential developments of the period lay elsewhere, in the effort to think through and to apply under the most favorable, permissive circumstances enlightened ideas of government and society. The problems were many, often unexpected and difficult; some were only gradually perceived. Social and personal privilege, for example, could easily be eliminated—it hardly existed; but what of the impersonal privileges of corporate bodies? Legal orders and ranks within society could be outlawed without creating the slightest tremor, and executive power with equal ease subordinated to the legislative: but how was balance within a polity to be achieved? What were the elements to be balanced and how were they to be separated? It was not even necessary formally to abolish the interest of state as a symbol and determinant of the common good; it was simply dissolved: but what was left to keep clashing factions from tearing a government apart? The problems were pressing, and the efforts to solve them mark the stages of revolutionary history.

In behalf of Enlightenment liberalism the revolutionary leaders undertook to complete, formalize, systematize, and symbolize what previously had been only partially realized, confused, and disputed matters of fact. Enlightenment ideas were not instruments of a particular social group, nor did they destroy a social order. They did not create new social and political forces in America. They released those that had long existed, and vastly increased their power. This completion, this rationalization, this symbolization, this lifting into consciousness and endowing with high moral purpose inchoate, confused elements of social and political change—this was the American Revolution.

3 / Bernard Bailyn
The Ideological Origins of the American Revolution:
The Contagion of Liberty

In no obvious sense was the American Revolution undertaken as a social revolution. No one, that is, deliberately worked for the destruction or even the substantial alteration of the order of society as it had been known. Yet

Bernard Bailyn, *The Ideological Origins of the American Revolution*. Cambridge, Mass.: The Belknap Press of Harvard University Press, Copyright, 1967 by the President and Fellows of Harvard College, pp. 302–305, 306, 307–311. Excerpted by permission of the publishers. Footnotes omitted by permission.

it was transformed as a result of the Revolution, and not merely because Loyalist property was confiscated and redistributed, or because the resulting war destroyed the economic bases of some people's lives and created opportunities for others that would not otherwise have existed. Seizure of Loyalist property and displacements in the economy did in fact take place, and the latter if not the former does account for a spurt in social mobility that led earlier arrivés to remark, "When the pot boils, the scum will rise." Yet these were superficial changes; they affected a small part of the population only, and they did not alter the organization of society.

What did now affect the essentials of social organization—what in time would help permanently to transform them—were changes in the realm of belief and attitude. The views men held toward the relationships that bound them to each other—the discipline and pattern of society—moved in a new direction in the decade before Independence.

Americans of 1760 continued to assume, as had their predecessors for generations before, that a healthy society was a hierarchical society, in which it was natural for some to be rich and some poor, some honored and some obscure, some powerful and some weak. And it was believed that superiority was unitary, that the attributes of the favored—wealth, wisdom, power—had a natural affinity to each other, and hence that political leadership would naturally rest in the hands of the social leaders. Movement, of course, there would be: some would fall and some would rise; but manifest, external differences among men, reflecting the principle of hierarchical order, were necessary and proper, and would remain; they were intrinsic to the nature of things.

Circumstances had pressed harshly against such assumptions. The wilderness environment from the beginning had threatened the maintenance of elaborate social distinctions; many of them in the passage of time had in fact been worn away. Puritanism, in addition, and the epidemic evangelicalism of the mid-eighteenth century, had created challenges to the traditional notions of social stratification by generating the conviction that the ultimate quality of men was to be found elsewhere than in their external condition, and that a cosmic achievement lay within each man's grasp. And the peculiar configuration of colonial politics—a constant broil of petty factions struggling almost formlessly, with little discipline or control, for the benefits of public authority—had tended to erode the respect traditionally accorded the institutions and officers of the state.

Yet nowhere, at any time in the colonial years, were the implications of these circumstances articulated or justified. The assumption remained that society, in its maturity if not in its confused infancy, would conform to the pattern of the past; that authority would continue to exist without challenge, and that those in superior positions would be responsible and wise, and those beneath them respectful and content. These premises and expectations were deeply lodged; they were not easily or quickly displaced. But the Revolution brought with it arguments and attitudes bred of arguments endlessly repeated, that undermined these premises of the *ancien régime*.

For a decade or more defiance to the highest constituted powers poured from the colonial presses and was hurled from half the pulpits of the land. The right, the need, the absolute obligation to disobey legally constituted authority had become the universal cry. Cautions and qualifications became ritualistic: formal exercises in ancient pieties. One might preface one's charge to disobedience with homilies on the inevitable imperfections of all governments and the necessity to bear "some injuries" patiently and peaceably. But what needed and received demonstration and defense was not the caution, but the injunction: the argument that when injuries touched on "fundamental rights" (and who could say when they did not?) then nothing less than "duty to God and religion, to themselves, to the community, and to unborn posterity require such to assert and defend their rights by all lawful, most prudent, and effectual means in their power." Obedience as a principle was only too well known; disobedience as a doctrine was not. It was therefore asserted again and again that resistance to constituted authority was "a doctrine according to godliness—the doctrine of the English nation . . . by which our rights and constitution have often been defended and repeatedly rescued out of the hands of encroaching tyranny . . . This is the doctrine and grand pillar of the ever memorable and glorious Revolution, and upon which our gracious sovereign George III holds the crown of the British empire." What better credentials could there be? How lame to add that obedience too "is an eminent part of Christian duty without which government must disband and dreadful anarchy and confusion (with all its horrors) take place and reign without control"—how lame, especially in view of the fact that one could easily mistake this "Christian obedience" for that "blind, enslaving obedience which is no part of the Christian institution but is highly injurious to religion, to every free government, and to the good of mankind, and is the stirrup of tyranny, and grand engine of slavery.". . .

In such declarations a political argument became a moral imperative. The principle of justifiable disobedience and the instinct to question public authority before accepting it acquired a new sanction and a new vigor. Originally, of course, the doctrine of resistance was applied to Parliament, a nonrepresentative assembly 3,000 miles away. But the composition and location of the institution had not been as crucial in creating opposition as had the character of the actions Parliament had taken. Were provincial assemblies, simply because they were local and representative, exempt from scrutiny and resistance? Were they any less susceptible than Parliament to the rule that when their authority is extended beyond "the bounds of the law of God and the free constitution . . . 'their acts are, *ipso facto*, void, and cannot oblige any to obedience'"? There could be no doubt of the answer. Any legislature, wherever located or however composed, deserved only the obedience it could command by the justice and wisdom of its proceedings. Representative or not, local or not, any agency of the state could be defied . . .

"Rights" obviously lay at the heart of the Anglo-American controversy: the rights of Englishmen, the rights of mankind, chartered rights. But *"rights,"* wrote Richard Bland—that least egalitarian of Revolutionary leaders— "imply *equality* in the instances to which they belong and must be treated without respect to the dignity of the persons concerned in them." This was by no means simply a worn cliché, for while "equality before the law" was a commonplace of the time, "equality without respect to the dignity of the persons concerned" was not; its emphasis on social equivalence was significant, and though in its immediate context the remark was directed to the invidious distinctions believed to have been drawn between Englishmen and Americans its broader applicability was apparent. Others seized upon it, and developed it, especially in the fluid years of transition when new forms of government were being sought to replace those believed to have proved fatal to liberty. "An affectation of rank" and "the assumed distinction of 'men of consequence'" had been the blight of the Proprietary party, a Pennsylvania pamphleteer wrote in 1776. Riches in a new country like America signified nothing more than the accident of prior settlement. The accumulation of wealth had been "unavoidable to the descendants of the early settlers" since the land, originally cheap, had appreciated naturally with the growth of settlement.

> Perhaps it is owing to this accidental manner of becoming rich that wealth does not obtain the same degree of influence here which it does in old countries. Rank, at present, in America is derived more from qualification than property; a sound moral character, amiable manners, and firmness in principle constitute the first class, and will continue to do so till the origin of families be forgotten, and the proud follies of the old world overrun the simplicity of the new.

Therefore, under the new dispensation, "no reflection ought to be made on any man on account of birth, provided that his manners rises decently with his circumstances, and that he affects not to forget the level he came from."

The idea was, in its very nature, corrosive to the traditional authority of magistrates and of established institutions. And it activated other, similar thoughts whose potential threat to stability lay till then inert. There was no more familiar notion in eighteenth-century political thought—it was propounded in every tract on government and every ministerial exhortation to the civil magistracy—than that those who wield power were "servants of society" as well as "ministers of God," and as such had to be specially qualified: they must be acquainted with the affairs of men; they must have wisdom, knowledge, prudence; and they must be men of virtue and true religion. But how far should one go with this idea? The doctrine that the qualifications for magistracy were moral, spiritual, and intellectual could lead to conflict with the expectation that public leaders would be people of external dignity and social superiority; it could be dangerous to the establishment in any settled society. For the ancient notion that leadership must devolve on men whose

"personal authority and greatness," whose "eminence or nobility," were such
that "every man subordinate is ready to yield a willing submission without
contempt or repining"—ordinary people not easily conceding to an authority
"conferred upon a mean man ... no better than selected out of their own
rank"—this traditional notion had never been repudiated, was still honored
and repeated. But now, in the heated atmosphere of incipent rebellion, the
idea of leaders as servants of the people was pushed to its logical extreme,
and its subversive potentialities revealed. By 1774 it followed from the belief
that "lawful rulers are the servants of the people" that they were "exalted
above their brethren not for their own sakes, but for the benefit of the people;
and submission is yielded, not on account of their persons considered exclusively on the authority they are clothed with, but of those laws which in the
exercise of this authority are made by them conformably to the laws of nature
and equity." In the distribution of offices, it was said in 1770, "merit only in
the candidate" should count—not birth, or wealth, or loyalty to the great;
but merit only. Even a deliberately judicious statement of this theme rang with
defiance to traditional forms of authority: "It is not wealth—it is not family—
it is not either of these alone, nor both of them together, though I readily allow
neither is to be disregarded, that will qualify men for important seats in
government, unless they are rich and honorable in other and more important
respects." Indeed, one could make a complete inversion and claim that,
properly, the external affluence of magistrates should be the consequence of,
not the prior qualification for, the judicious exercise of public authority over
others.

Where would it end? Two generations earlier, in the fertile seedtime of
what would become the Revolutionary ideology, the ultimate subversiveness
of the arguments advanced by "the men of the rights" had already been
glimpsed. "The sum of the matter betwixt Mr. Hoadly and me," the Jacobite,
High Church polemicist Charles Leslie had written in 1711, is this:

I think it most natural that *authority* should *descend*, that is, be *derived*
from a *superior* to an *inferior*, from God to *fathers* and *kings*, and from
kings and *fathers* to *sons* and *servants*. But Mr. Hoadly would have it *ascend*
from *sons* to *fathers* and from *subjects* to *sovereigns*, nay to God himself,
whose *kingship* the men of the *rights* say is *derived* to *Him* from the *people!*
And the *argument* does naturally carry it all that *way*. For if *authority* does
ascend, it must *ascend* to the *height*.

By 1774 it seemed undeniable to many, uninvolved in or hostile to the
Revolutionary effort, that declarations "before God ... that it is no rebellion
to oppose any king, ministry, or governor [who] destroys by any violence or
authority whatever the rights of the people" threatened the most elemental
principles of order and discipline in society. A group of writers, opposed not
merely to the politics of resistance but to the effect it would have on the primary linkages of society—on that patterning of human relations that dis-

tinguishes a civilized community from a primitive mob—attempted to recall to the colonists the lessons of the past, the wisdom, as they thought of it, of the ages. Citing adages and principles that once had guided men's thoughts on the structure of society; equating all communities, and England's empire in particular, with families; quoting generously from Filmer if not from Leslie; and explaining that anarchy results when social inferiors claim political authority, they argued, with increasing anxiety, that the essence of social stability was being threatened by the political agitation of the time. Their warnings, full of nostalgia for ancient certainties, were largely ignored. But in the very extremism of their reaction to the events of the time there lies a measure of the distance Revolutionary thought had moved from an old to a very new world.

4 / Winthrop D. Jordan
Thomas Jefferson and the Agony of Race

Against the backdrop of changing attitudes and actions concerning Negroes and Negro slavery, the writings of one man become a fixed and central point of reference and influence. In the years after the Revolution the speculations of Thomas Jefferson were of great importance because so many people read and reacted to them. His remarks about Negroes in the only book he ever wrote were more widely read, in all probability, than any others until the mid-nineteenth century. In addition to his demonstrable impact upon other men, Jefferson is important—or perhaps more accurately, valuable to historical analysis—because he permits (without intending to) a depth and range of insight into the workings of ideas about Negroes within one man as he stood in relationship to his culture. Jefferson's energetic facility with the pen makes it possible, uniquely so in this period of history, to glimpse some of the inward springs of feeling which supported certain attitudes towards Negroes. It then becomes possible to see the intricate interlacing of one man's personality with his social surroundings, the values of his culture, and the ideas with which he had contact. Thomas Jefferson was not a typical nor an ordinary man, but his enormous breadth of interest and his lack of originality make him an effective sounding board for his culture. On some important matters, therefore, he may be taken as accurately reflecting common presuppositions and sensitivities even though many Americans disagreed with some of his conclusions.

Winthrop D. Jordan, *White Over Black: American Attitudes Toward the Negro, 1550–1812.* Published by The University of North Carolina Press for The Institute of Early American History and Culture. Copyright © by The University of North Carolina Press. Reprinted by permission of the publisher. Footnotes omitted by permission.

To contemplate any man-in-culture is to savor complexity. It will be easiest to start with Jefferson's central dilemma; he hated slavery but thought Negroes inferior to white men ...

Jefferson was personally involved in Negro slavery. On his own plantations he stood confronted by the practical necessity of making slave labor pay and by the usual frustrating combination of slave recalcitrance and inefficiency. Keeping the Negro men and especially the women and children clad, bedded, and fed was expensive, and keeping them busy was a task in itself. Nor was his load lightened by daily supervision of a system which he genuinely hated, nor by realization that his livelihood depended on its continuation. This dependence almost inevitably meant that, for Jefferson the planter, Negroes sometimes became mere objects of financial calculation. "I have observed," he once wrote, "that our families of negroes double in about 25 years, which is an increase of the capital, invested in them, of 4 percent over and above keeping up the original number." Successful maintenance of several plantations made for a measure of moral callousness: "The first step towards the recovery of our lands," he advised John Taylor, "is to find substitutes for corn and bacon. I count on potatoes, clover, and sheep. The two former to feed every animal on the farm except my negroes, and the latter to feed them, diversified with rations of salted fish and molasses, both of them wholesome, agreeable, and cheap articles of food." For a man of Jefferson's convictions, entanglement in Negro slavery was genuinely tragic. Guiltily he referred to his Negroes as "servants," thus presaging the euphemism of the nineteenth century. His hopes for transforming his slaves into tenants evidenced a desire to seek a way out, but financial considerations perpetually precluded action. In the end he freed a few of them, but more than a hundred remained in slavery. He never doubted that his monetary debts constituted a more immediate obligation than manumission. Most Americans would have agreed.

Jefferson's heartfelt hatred of slavery did not derive so much from this harassing personal entanglement in the practicalities of slavery as from the system of politics in which he was enmeshed mentally. "Enmeshed" seems the appropriate term because the natural rights philosophy was the governing aspect of his theology and his science; it formed a part of his being, and his most original contribution was the graceful lucidity with which he continually restated the doctrine. Yet in Jefferson's hands natural rights took on a peculiar cast, for he thought of rights as being natural in a very literal sense. Rights belonged to men as biological beings, inhering in them, as he said in his draft of the Declaration of Independence, because "all men are created equal and independent" and because "from that equal creation they derive rights inherent and inalienable." The central fact was creation: the Creator, whose primary attribute was tidiness, would scarcely have been so careless as to create a single species equipped with more than one set of rights. If Jefferson's own passion for order was reflected in these phrases, so was his agrarian penchant for solitude. What was reflected most clearly of all, though, was the extent to which the natural world dominated Jefferson's thinking. Creation was the central "fact" because it explained nature. And Jefferson was awed by nature, if "awe" may be used in connection with a man so immensely capable of placid receptivity. While apparently working from a "Supreme Being" to an orderly nature, in fact Jefferson derived his Creator from what He had created—a nature which was by axiom orderly. In the same way, he derived God-given rights from the existence of the class of natural beings known as men. To know whether certain men possessed natural rights one had only to inquire whether they were human beings.

Without question Negroes were members of that class. Hence Jefferson never for a moment considered the possibility that they might rightfully be enslaved. He felt the personal guilt of slaveholding deeply, for he was daily depriving other men of their rightful liberty. With "my debts once cleared off," he wrote with a highly revealing slip of the pen, "I shall try some plan of making their situation happier, determined to content myself with a small portion of their ~~liberty~~ labour." His vigorous antislavery pronouncements, however, were always redolent more of the library than the field. Slavery was an injustice not so much for the specific Negroes held in bondage as for any member of the human species. It was not simply that Jefferson was a benevolent master and had little contact with the cruelty of slavery, but that his approach to human society was always phylogenic. His most heartfelt denunciation of the notorious horrors of the slave trade, for example, consisted of a reference to "the unhappy human beings ... forcibly brought away from their native country." Wherever he encountered human cruelty, as he assuredly did in France, he saw not cruelty but injustice; as in so many other matters he was inclined to universalize particulars. Yet he was always the observer of particulars and too much interested in the welfare of Virginia to let his vision of slavery remain entirely academic. Slavery was an evil as well as an injustice, and from this standpoint Jefferson wrote one of the classic denunciations of the institution. In his *Notes on the State of Virginia*, written in 1781–1782 in reply to queries from the secretary of the French legation in Philadelphia, François Barbé-Marbois, Jefferson answered a question on the "particular customs and manners that may happen to be received in that state" by discussing one matter only—the deleterious effects of slavery.

There must doubtless be an unhappy influence on the manners of our people produced by the existence of slavery among us. The whole commerce between master and slave is a perpetual exercise of the most boisterous passions, the most unremitting despotism on the one part, and degrading submissions on the other. Our children see this, and learn to imitate it; for man is an imitative animal ... The parent storms, the child looks on, catches the lineaments of wrath, puts on the same airs in the circle of smaller slaves, gives a loose to his worst of passions, and thus nursed, educated, and daily exercised in tyranny, cannot but be stamped by it with odious peculiarities. The man must be a prodigy who can retain his manners and morals undepraved by such circumstances. And with what execration should the statesman be loaded, who permitting one half the citizens thus to trample on the rights of the other, transforms those into despots, and these into enemies, destroys the morals of the one part, and the amor patriæ of the other. For if a slave can have a country in this world, it must be any other in preference to that in which he is born to live and labour for another: in which he must lock up the faculties of his nature, contribute as far as depends on his individual endeavours to the evanishment of the human race, or entail his own miserable condition on the endless generations proceeding from him. With the morals of the people, their industry also is destroyed. For in a warm climate, no man will labour for himself who can make another labour for him. This is so true, that of the proprietors of slaves a very small proportion indeed are ever seen to labour. And can the liberties of a nation be thought secure when we have removed their only firm basis, a conviction in the minds of the people that these liberties are of the gift of God? That they are not to be violated but with his wrath?

While he recognized the condition of slaves as "miserable," the weight of Jefferson's concern was reserved for the malevolent effects of slavery upon masters. These effects had always concerned antislavery men of every stripe, but with most of them one is not left wondering what would have remained of their antislavery views had they found slavery beneficial to white society. Fortunately Jefferson went to his grave convinced that slavery was a blight on the white community. With slavery's effect on black men he simply was not overly concerned.

Indicative of Jefferson's approach toward the institution was his horror of slave rebellion. His apprehension was of course shared by most Americans, but he gave it expression at an unusually early date, some years before the disaster in St. Domingo. When denouncing slavery in the *Notes on Virginia* he gave vent to forebodings of a possible upheaval in America in a passage clouded with dark indirection. "Indeed I tremble for my country," he wrote passionately, "when I reflect that God is just: that his justice cannot sleep for ever: that considering numbers, nature and natural means only, a revolution of the wheel of fortune, an exchange of situation, is among possible events: that it may become probable by supernatural interference! The Almighty has no attribute which can take side with us in such a contest." The depth of his feeling was apparent, for he rarely resorted to exclamation marks and still less often to miracles without skepticism. Later, Negro rebellion in St. Domingo confirmed his fears, the more so because he was utterly unable to condemn it. Always blandly receptive to revolution as a mechanism of change, he foresaw a strange future for the Caribbean islands. "I become daily more and more convinced," he wrote in 1793, "that all the West India

Islands will remain in the hands of the people of colour, and a total expulsion of the whites sooner or later take place." From the islands he gloomily turned to his own country. "It is high time we should forsee the bloody scenes which our children certainly, and possibly ourselves (south of the Potommac,) have to wade through, and try to avert them." St. Domingo, he became convinced, was merely "the first chapter"; and his mind dwelt on the possible second chapter almost morbidly: "if something is not done," he wrote melodramatically in 1797, "and done soon, we shall be the murderers of our own children." Then in the summer of 1800 the second chapter appeared to open, and Jefferson wrote self-consolingly from Monticello: "We are truly to be pitied." Twenty years later at the time of the Missouri Compromise he was still murmuring of his fears. Still adamant that Negroes must be free, he characteristically fused obligation with future fact: "Nothing is more certainly written in the book of fate than that these people are to be free." Only the means were at question: white men must liberate Negroes in justice, or Negroes would liberate themselves in blood.

While Jefferson thus hitched fear of rebellion to the antislavery cause, he refused to allow strong feelings on both matters to override his judgment as to the appropriate course of practical action. As a youth, in the first blush of Revolutionary enthusiasm, he had urged upon his native Virginia a program of gradual emancipation. "But it was found," he wrote years later in 1821, "that the public mind would not yet bear the proposition, nor will it bear it even at this day." As early as the 1780's Jefferson fully recognized the difficulties involved in any practical program for freedom and shrank from publishing his *Notes on Virginia* because it contained strong antislavery expressions. His friend Charles Thomson agreed that there were just grounds for fearing southern reaction while agreeing too that if the "cancer" was not wiped out "by religion, reason and philosophy" it would be someday "by blood." James Monroe, on the other hand, thought the antislavery sentiments could well be published. They finally did appear, of course, but Jefferson remained pessimistic. He wrote in 1786 concerning possible legislative action in Virginia that "an unsuccessful effort, as too often happens, would only rivet still closer the chains of bondage, and retard the moment of delivery to this oppressed description of men." Later he steadfastly refused to condemn slavery publicly, refused to join antislavery organizations, refused to endorse the publications of abolitionists, in each case because he thought that premature endorsement by a figure of his prominence might easily damage the antislavery cause. It was neither timidity nor concern for reputation which restrained him; in fact he had good reason to think that antislavery pronouncements might solidify the institution. Francis Kinloch wrote him from South Carolina of "the general alarm" which a certain "passage in your Notes occasioned amongst us. It is not easy to get rid of old prejudices, and the word 'emancipation' operates like an apparition upon a South Carolina planter." From wide experience Jefferson had acquired a strong sense of "how difficult it is to move or inflect the great machine of society, how impossible to advance the notions of a whole people suddenly to ideal right." He was acutely conscious of "the passions, the prejudices, and the real difficulties" compounded in American Negro slavery.

His sensitive reaction to social "passions" and "prejudices" was heightened by dim recognition that they operated powerfully within himself, though of course he never realized how deepseated his anti-Negro feelings were. On the surface of these thoughts lay genuine doubts concerning the Negro's inherent fitness for freedom and recognition of the tensions inherent in racial slavery. He was firmly convinced, as he demonstrated in the *Notes on Virginia*, that Negroes could never be incorporated into white society on equal terms.

Deep rooted prejudices entertained by the whites; ten thousand recollections, by the blacks, of the injuries they have sustained; new provocations; the real distinction which nature has made; and many other circumstances, will divide us into parties, and produce convulsions which will probably never end but in the extermination of the one or the other race.—To these objections, which are political, may be added others, which are physical and moral.

The "real distinction which nature has made" was for Jefferson not only physical but temperamental and mental. Negroes seemed to "require less sleep," for "after hard labour through the day," they were "induced by the slightest amusements to sit up till midnight, or later" though aware that they must rise at "first dawn." They were "at least as brave" as whites, and "more adventuresome." "But," he wrote, withdrawing even this mild encomium, "this may perhaps proceed from a want of forethought, which prevents their seeing a danger till it be present. When present, they do not go through it with more coolness or steadiness than the whites." Negroes were "more ardent," their griefs "transient." "In general," he concluded, "their existence appears to participate more of sensation than reflection. To this must be ascribed their disposition to sleep when abstracted from their diversions, and unemployed in labour. An animal whose body is at rest, and who does not reflect, must be disposed to sleep of course." Within the confines of this logic there was no room for even a hint that daily toil for another's benefit might have disposed slaves to frolic and to sleep.

Of far more serious import for the Negro's future were Jefferson's remarks on mental capacity. More than any other single person he framed the terms of the debate still carried on today.

Comparing them by their faculties of memory, reason, and imagination, it appears to me, that in memory they are equal to the whites; in reason much inferior, as I think one could scarcely be found capable of tracing and comprehending the investigations of Euclid; and that in imagination

they are dull, tasteless, and anomalous. It would be unfair to follow them
to Africa for this investigation. We will consider them here, on the same
stage with the whites, and where the facts are not apocryphal on which a
judgment is to be formed. It will be right to make great allowances for the
difference of condition, of education, of conversation, of the sphere in
which they move. Many millions of them have been brought to, and born
in America. Most of them indeed have been confined to tillage, to their
own homes, and their own society: yet many have been so situated, they
might have availed themselves of the conversation of their masters; many
have been brought up to the handicraft arts, and from that circumstance
have always been associated with the whites. Some have been liberally
educated, and all have lived in countries where the arts and sciences are
cultivated to a considerable degree, and have had before their eyes samples
of the best works from abroad . . . But never yet could I find that a black
had uttered a thought above the level of plain narration; never see even an
elementary trait of painting or sculpture.

Despite his stress on the necessity for "great allowance," Jefferson seemed
unable to push the logic of environmentalism very far; in fact he stopped at
just the point where that logic made a case for Negro inferiority. He seemed
incapable of complimenting Negroes without immediately adding qualifications. "In music," he continued, picking up a widespread popular belief,
"they are more generally gifted than the whites with accurate ears for tune
and time, and they have been found capable of imagining a small catch."
Further ability was "yet to be proved."

Not content with a general assessment, Jefferson went on to disparage the
widely known Negroes who had been puffed by the antislavery people as
examples of the Negro's equal capacities. Those known to him were poets,
and by speculating on the theoretical effects of slavery upon poetry he twisted
the environmentalist logic into anti-Negro shape. "Misery is often the parent
of the most affecting touches in poetry.—Among the blacks is misery enough,
God knows, but no poetry. Love is the peculiar oestrum of the poet. Their
love is ardent, but it kindles the sense only, not the imagination." He dismissed
Phyllis Wheatley with the airy remark that she was "not . . . a poet. The compositions published under her name are below the dignity of criticism."
Ignatius Sancho he treated with more respect but decided that Sancho's works
did "more honour to the heart than the head" and substituted "sentiment
for demonstration." Sancho was the best of his race, but among literary figures
in England "we are compelled to enroll him at the bottom of the column," if,
Jefferson added pointedly, he was in fact the real author of the material
"published under his name." This higher criticism was surprising in a man
who wrote twenty years later that "of all men living I am the last who should
undertake to decide as to the merits of poetry. In earlier life I was fond of it,
and easily pleased."

Jefferson was thoroughly aware that the environmentalist argument could serve (and actually had) to make a case for Negro equality, and hence he went to great lengths to prove that the Negroes' lack of talent did not stem from their condition. He turned to the slavery of classical times and wandered happily and discursively among the Romans and the Greeks, arguing that ancient slavery was more harsh than America's yet produced slaves of talent and demonstrable achievement. Unaware that he might be inverting cause and effect he noted that some ancient slaves excelled "in science, insomuch as to be usually employed as tutors to their master's children." There had been slaves, then, who had demonstrated significant attainments; and those who had "were of the race of whites." As for Negroes, he concluded, "It is not their condition then, but nature, which has produced the distinction."

Having baldly stated his belief in innate inferiority, Jefferson immediately introduced his next subject by reopening the question he had just closed: "Whether further observation will or will not verify the conjecture, that nature has been less bountiful to them in the endowments of the head. . . ." What he now asked was suspension of decision, for he became increasingly aware of how far he had allowed himself to go. Genuine alarm underlay his admonition, toward the *end* of his passage on Negroes, that caution must be exercised "where our conclusion would degrade a whole race of men from the rank in the scale of beings which their Creator may perhaps have given them." But he extricated himself in highly satisfying fashion by dumping the whole problem in the broad lap of American science, thus permitting qualification of his previously stated position to the point of inconsistency. "The opinion, that they are inferior in the faculties of reason and imagination, must be hazarded with great diffidence. To justify a general conclusion, requires many observations, even where the subject may be submitted to the Anatomical knife, to Optical glasses, to analysis by fire, or by solvents. How much more then where it is a faculty, not a substance, we are examining; where it eludes the research of all the senses; where the conditions of its existence are various and variously combined; where the effects of those which are present or absent bid defiance to calculation."

Growing happier with his solution he thus labored the obvious fact that assessing mental ability was an immensely difficult task. With nearly audible relief he remodeled an anti-Negro diatribe into a scientific hypothesis, thus effectively depersonalizing a matter which was for him obviously of some personal importance. "To our reproach it must be said, that though for a century and a half we have had under our eyes the races of black and of red men, they have never yet been viewed by us as subjects of natural history. I advance it therefore as a suspicion only, that the blacks, whether originally a distinct race, or made distinct by time and circumstances, are inferior to the whites in the endowments both of body and mind. It is not against experience to suppose, that . . . [they] may possess different qualifications." A "suspicion only" of "different qualifications" represented a rather different proposition from "It is not their condition then, but nature, which has produced the distinction."

In assessing one important quality in Negroes, however, Jefferson always remained firmly consistent. The "moral sense" was as fully developed in Negroes as in whites. On this subject Jefferson suddenly pressed environmentalist logic as far as it would go. "That disposition to theft with which they have been branded," he declared categorically, "must be ascribed to their situation." With dry detachment he explained the justice of Negro thievery: "The man, in whose favour no laws of property exist, probably feels himself less bound to respect those made in favour of others." Might not the slave "justifiably take a little from one, who has taken all from him?"

Jefferson's strikingly divergent conclusions on the Negro's moral sense and on his intellect were reached without a particle of inconsistency, for the two qualities were, as far as he and many of his post-Revolutionary contemporaries were concerned, thoroughly discrete. The "moral sense, or conscience," as Jefferson explained, was "as much a part of man as his leg or arm" and was "made a part of his physical constitution, as necessary for a social being." To say that the Negro possessed it was the Jeffersonian analogue of the Christian axiom that the Negro possessed a soul. Just as the traditional Christian God had provided the soul, the Jeffersonian Creator had endowed men with the properties necessary for their existence, and no kinds of men could be assumed to lack what they could not live together without. Had the Creator not provided men with a moral sense He would have been "a pitiful bungler." The moral sense might be temporarily impaired by slavery, but Negroes must be said to possess it, else Negroes could never be free. Indeed they could not even be men without it. No such requirement, on the other hand, pertained to the Negro's intellectual endowment . . .

Jefferson's confusion at times became monumental. On the one hand he had intellectually derived his belief in human equality from the existence of an orderly creation which had shaped every natural species each to its own mold; and on the other he possessed a larger unquestioning faith, strengthened by his political experience, which predisposed him toward equality. The problem of the Negro's intellect stripped these approaches of their apparent congruity. For he could not rid himself of the suspicion that the Negro was naturally inferior. If this were in fact the case, then it was axiomatic that the Creator had so created the Negro and no amount of education or freedom or any other tinkering could undo the facts of nature. Thus Jefferson suspected that the Creator might have in fact created men unequal; and he could not say this without giving his assertion exactly the same logical force as his famous statement to the contrary. His science-theology rammed squarely into his larger faith, and the result was intellectual wreckage. In the *Notes*, for example, he explained the Indian's apparent deficiencies as resulting wholly from environmental influences. Yet in 1785 he wrote to the Marquis de

Chastellux, "I believe the Indian then to be in body and mind equal to the whiteman. I have supposed the blackman, in his present state, might not be so. But it would be hazardous to affirm that, equally cultivated for a few generations, he would not become so." This was all very well as a declaration of faith, but intellectually it made no sense at all. Logically the Indian could retrieve an original equality. But if the Negro was not originally equal he could never "become" so, not if equality really stemmed from "that equal creation" from which Jefferson had derived it in the Declaration.

As he grew older Jefferson grew increasingly irritated on the subject, dimly aware of the trap in which he was placed. When in 1809 the Abbé Henri Gregoire sent him a book puffing the extraordinary achievements of various Negroes, he replied to Gregoire with his usual protestations of inconclusiveness. "Be assured that no person living wishes more sincerely than I do, to see a complete refutation of the doubts I have myself entertained and expressed on the grade of understanding allotted to them by nature, and to find that in this respect they are on a par with ourselves. My doubts were the result of personal observation on the limited sphere of my own State, where the opportunities for the development of their genius were not favorable, and those of exercising it still less so. I expressed them therefore with great hesitation." But then his nervousness came spilling forth, revealing the gap between his science and his equalitarian faith: "but whatever be their degree of talent it is no measure of their rights. Because Sir Isaac Newton was superior to others in understanding, he was not therefore lord of the person or property of others." The reference to Newton was a dangerous red herring and the separation of the rights of a group from their talent, while vindicating freedom for the Negro, came perilously close to impugning the tidiness of the Author of Nature from whom freedom was derived. Jefferson exploded to his friend Joel Barlow that the book in question was a fantastic collection of unauthenticated tales, though he had given Gregoire "a very soft answer." "The whole do not amount in point of evidence, to what we know ourselves of Banneker." As for that case, Jefferson declared, "We know he had spherical trigonometry enough to make almanacs, but not without the suspicion of aid from Ellicot, who was his neighbor and friend, and never missed an opportunity of puffing him. I have a long letter from Banneker, which shows him to have had a mind of very common stature indeed." Jefferson had become irritated, one might well conclude, by contact with an issue he could not successfully handle ...

Until well into the nineteenth century Jefferson's judgment on [the intellectual capacity of the Negro], with all its confused tentativeness, stood as the strongest suggestion of inferiority expressed by any native American. To some extent sectional differences help account for his opinion, for Jefferson was the only person in Virginia or southward to tackle the problem, and his opponents were chiefly northerners. He wrote at length on a matter upon which Virginians generally were silent, but he may well have been speaking for many of them. His acquaintance St. George Tucker, a Virginia lawyer, referred casually in 1795 (after, it should be noted, he had read the *Notes on Virginia*) to "the general opinion [in Virginia] of their mental inferiority," but this statement appears to be the only contemporary testimony concerning what Virginian opinion actually was. It is striking that even when defending slavery Virginians seem to have felt no need to advance suggestions of Negro inferiority. No such suggestions were made, for example, in several emphatic petitions to the legislature which defended slavery in advocating repeal of the 1782 act facilitating manumission. Similarly, Governor John Drayton of South Carolina, one of a handful of men in that state to aspire successfully to authorship (in conscious imitation of Jefferson's *Notes*), defended slavery at some length in 1802 chiefly on grounds of necessity and without once mentioning the possibility of Negro inferiority. The only southerner to object directly to Jefferson about the remarks in the *Notes* was David Ramsay. Both a physician and a historian, Ramsay had been born in Pennsylvania and had migrated to Charleston at age twenty-three, where he became a moderately successful politician; though he owned slaves he was regarded by many persons in the state as distinctly unsound on the subject of slavery. It is therefore perhaps not surprising that after reading Jefferson's *Notes* in manuscript he wrote to congratulate the author and commented unfavorably on only one passage: "I admire your generous indignation at slavery; but think you have depressed the negroes too low."

Opinion in the North, on the other hand, was distinctly different though far from unanimous. When St. George Tucker addressed queries concerning Negroes in Massachusetts to Jeremy Belknap in 1795, he asked specifically for information concerning mental capacity, and Belknap in turn made enquiries among his prominent friends in Boston. Judge James Winthrop replied magisterially, "There are a few instances of their appearing as authors, and some of their productions are not contemptible. I have not heard of their dipping into the more abstruse parts of science, and in general they are not estimated for speculative abilities." James Sullivan, less pompous but more verbose, explained that Negroes were not now the equal of whites but that if they were given the same "prospects," "motives," and "advantages" for three or four generations "they may exceed the white people." Belknap summarized his little survey by reporting that gentlemen in Massachusetts who had studied the matter "do not scruple to say, that there is no more difference between them and those whites who have had the same education, and have lived in the same habits, than there is among different persons of that class of whites. In this opinion I am inclined to acquiesce. It is neither birth nor colour, but education and habit, which form the human character."

Though it is difficult to judge exactly what most Virginians or other southerners would have thought of this statement, it is clear that only one man in the South felt compelled to take the opposite position publicly. Jefferson alone spoke forth, and this fact in itself suggests, at very least, strong feeling on his part, an uncommon need to discourse upon the subject. It was not that he alone felt need for scientific experiment. George Wythe, Jefferson's much-admired mentor, undertook to give both his own nephew and his mulatto servant boy classical educations as a comparative test of the Negro's ability. On the other hand, Jefferson, who delighted in compiling the facts of the natural world, never attempted any such experiment despite ample opportunity. And the structure of his relevant passage in the *Notes*, where his appeal to science followed lengthy and very definite pronouncements on Negro inferiority, indicated clearly that his appeal to that highest court was not the starting point for his thoughts about Negroes but a safe refuge from them.

Jefferson started, in fact, with a brief assertion of the necessity for colonizing Negroes elsewhere once they had been freed. "Why not retain and incorporate the blacks into the state?" Only later did his answer find wide acceptance in Virginia, especially after September 1800. "Deep rooted prejudices entertained by the whites; ten thousand recollections, by the blacks, of the injuries they have sustained; new provocations; the real distinctions which nature has made; and many other circumstances, will . . . produce convulsions which will probably never end but in the extermination of the one or the other race." His ensuing remarks made evident which factor carried greatest weight with him, for he immediately entered into a long discussion of other "objections" which were "physical and moral." "The first difference which strikes us" he wrote in accurate summary of his countrymen's perceptions, "is that of colour." Accepting the chromatically inaccurate but universally accepted metaphor of the Negro's "black" color, he continued, "Whether the black of the negro resides in the reticular membrane between the skin and scarf-skin, or in the scarf-skin itself; whether it proceeds from the colour of the blood, the colour of the bile, or from that of some other secretion, the difference is fixed in nature, and is as real as if its seat and cause were better known to us." For Jefferson, the overwhelming aspect of the Negro's color was its *reality*; he simply shelved the important scientific question of its cause. Even when he considered the question in a more neutral context, in his discussion of albino Negroes in the section on "Productions Mineral, Vegetable and Animal," he refused (or perhaps was unable) to offer a word of speculation about a matter on which other scientists speculated freely. Instead he rushed on, spilling forth words which revealed what the "reality" of the "difference" was for Thomas Jefferson. The passionate underpinnings of his feelings were laid bare.

And is this difference of no importance? Is it not the foundation of a greater or less share of beauty in the two races? Are not the fine mixtures of red and white, the expressions of every passion by greater or less suffusions of colour in the one, preferable to that eternal monotony, which reigns in the countenances, that immoveable veil of black which covers all the emotions of the other race? Add to these, flowing hair, a more elegant symmetry of form, and their own judgment in favour of the whites, declared by their preference of them, as uniformly as is the preference of the Oran-ootan for the black women over those of his own species. The circumstance of superior beauty, is thought worthy attention in the propagation of our horses, dogs, and other domestic animals; why not in that of man?

With this geyser of libidinal energy Jefferson recapitulated major tenets of the American racial complex. Merely on a factual level he passed along several notions which had long been floating about, some since the first years of confrontation in Africa. Red and white were the ingredients of beauty, and Negroes were pronouncedly less beautiful than whites; Negroes desired sexual relations especially with whites; black women had relations with orang-outangs. On a deeper level the pattern of his remarks was more revealing of Jefferson himself. Embedded in his thoughts on beauty was the feeling that whites were subtler and more delicate in their passions and that Negroes, conversely, were more crude. He felt Negroes to be sexually more animal—hence the gratuitous intrusion of the man-like ape. His libidinal desires, unacceptable and inadmissible to his society and to his higher self, were effectively transferred to others and thereby drained of their intolerable immediacy. Having allowed these dynamic emotions perilously close to the surface in the form of the orang-outang, he had immediately shifted to the safe neutral ground of horse-breeding, thus denying his exposure by caricaturing it. Without fully recognizing the adversary within, he continued to flee, taking refuge on higher and higher ground. "They have less hair on the face and body." Not quite safe enough, but he was reaching the safe temple of science. "They secrete less by the kidnies, and more by the glands of the skin," he wrote, carefully placing the rationale before the important fact, "which gives them a very strong and disagreeable odour." Having taken as given the facts of Negro secretion, about which many contemporaries were uncertain, he applied them as proof to a less emotion-laden folk belief. "This greater degree of transpiration renders them more tolerant of heat, and less so of cold, than the whites." He came to rest finally in convoluted speculation. "Perhaps too a difference of structure in the pulmonary apparatus, which a late ingenious experimentalist [Adair Crawford, *Experiments . . . on Animal Heat*] has discovered to be the principal regulator of animal heat, may have disabled them from extricating, in the act of inspiration, so much of that fluid from the outer air, or obliged them in expiration, to part with more of it."

Yet Jefferson was never completely at rest. His picture of Negroes as crudely sensual beings, which was at once an offprint of popular belief and a functional displacement of his own emotional drives, kept popping up whenever Negroes came to mind. That it did not appear on other, irrelevant occasions indicated that there were limits to its personal importance, yet most of Jefferson's widely-read remarks on the Negro were tinged by it. When discussing the Negro's over-all temperament he wrote, "They are more ardent after their female: but love seems with them to be more an eager desire, than a tender delicate mixture of sentiment and sensation." In the original manuscript he had stated this even more baldly. Elsewhere in the *Notes* he commented in defense of the masculinity of Indian men despite the sparsity of their hair: "Negroes have notoriously less hair than the whites; yet they are more ardent."

Jefferson had framed old beliefs about the Negro's sexuality in newly deprecatory terms, and defenders of the Negro rose in his behalf. Gilbert Imlay laid his finger on the core of Jefferson's argument with acute intuition but faltering analysis:

Were a man, who, with all the ardour of a youthful passion, had just been gazing upon the fair bosom of a loved and beautiful mistress, and afterwards marked the contrast of that paradise of sublunary bliss, to the African or Indian hue, to exclaim in the terms which Mr. Jefferson has used, he might be judged excusable on account of the intoxication of his heated senses—But when a grave philosopher, who has passed the meridian of life, sits down to meliorate, by his writings and opinions, the condition of the slaves of his country, whose fetters have fixed an obliquity upon the virtue and humanity of the southern Americans, I confess it appears to me not a little jejune and inconsistent.

The Reverend Samuel Stanhope Smith of Princeton, however, was affronted by Jefferson's assertions of ardency which kindled "the senses only, not the imagination," and seized the opportunity of reading an environmentalist lecture in morals to slaveowners. "With what fine tints can imagination invest the rags, the dirt, or the nakedness so often seen in a quarter of negro labourers? Besides, to awaken the exquisite sentiments of a delicate love, and to surround it with all the enchantment of the imagination, this passion requires to be placed under certain moral restraints which are seldom formed in the coarse familiarity, and promiscuous intercourse permitted, and too often encouraged among the American slaves." Smith was careful to discharge the other barrel by declaring that he had seen many instances of the highest sentiments of love among Negroes. Jefferson never replied to these attacks . . .

American tenderness on mixture of the races had been unrelieved by the Revolutionary upheaval of thought concerning the Negro. Indeed certain shifts in thought in the latter part of the eighteenth century may have served to deepen objection to intermixture. While conceiving of man's social and political activities as taking place within the ordered realm of nature (most obviously in the natural rights philosophy), Americans also brought biological preconceptions to the consideration of human beings. In nature, likes begat likes in ordered succession. Could Americans be entirely happy, then, with even the superficial confusion of appearances brought about by miscegenation? The "mulatto breed" was an affront to anyone with a sense of tidiness. In the 1790's, too, the Negro rebellions added urgency to all consideration of interracial relationships, and the growing sense of the separateness of Negroes meant more frequent expressions of alarm concerning mongrelization. Given a new nation, with slavery now recognized as a national concern, the omnipresent fact of miscegenation was perforce seen in a somewhat different light than in earlier years. Cases of intermixture once of only local pertinence had now become ingredients in the larger problem of the integrity of the blood of the national community. Hence national councils became forums for denunciation of intermixture. Pennsylvania's James Wilson announced during discussion of the three-fifths clause in the Constitutional Convention that he "had some apprehensions also from the tendency of the blending of the blacks with the whites, to give disgust to the people of Pena." William Loughton Smith, defending slavery in the congressional debate of 1790, declared that any "mixture of the races would degenerate the whites" and that as far as the future of America was concerned if Negroes intermarried "with the whites, then the white race would be extinct, and the American people would be all of the mulatto breed." And a nationalistic President Jefferson remarked concerning the Negro's future that "it is impossible not to look forward to distant times, when our rapid multiplication will expand itself beyond those [present] limits, and cover the whole northern, if not the southern continent, with a people speaking the same language, governed in similar forms, and by similar laws; nor can we contemplate with satisfaction either blot or mixture on that surface.". . .

Beneath all pronouncements on the undesirability of racial mixture lay a substructure of feeling about interracial sex. Jefferson's feelings were of course partially molded by specific beliefs about Negroes which constituted readily visible manifestations of feelings prevailing in his culture not merely about Negroes but about life in general. It seems legitimate and profitable to speak of an entire culture as having feelings, partly because every society demands—and gets—a large measure of the behavior it "wants" (i.e., needs) from individuals and partly because in a literate culture expressions of individual feeling accrete through time, thus forming a common pool of expressed feelings. Usually, but by no means always, these expressions are highly intellectualized, that is, detached from direct functional connection with powerful emotional drives. Sometimes they are not, as they sometimes were not when Thomas Jefferson wrote about Negroes. It seems evident that his feelings, his affective life, his emotions—whatever term one prefers— were being expressed in some of his beliefs or opinions about the Negro. His opinions were thus sometimes quite directly the product of his repressions. And it seems axiomatic, given the assumptions about the nature of culture prevailing in the twentieth century, that variants of his repressions operated in so many individuals that one can speak of deep-seated feelings about the Negro as being social in character, that is, as characterizing an entire society. It seems important to remember that the explicit *content* of social attitudes stemmed not directly from the emotions being repressed but from the mechanisms of repression. The resultant attitudes, moreover, through constant communication within society, acquired autonomous energy and a viability independent of emotional underpinnings. Hence many individuals subscribed to beliefs about Negroes which performed no very vital function in their personality, and these beliefs may be considered as being part of the cultural environment.

It is with this final consideration in mind that such manifestations of attitudes as laws on interracial sexual relations must be considered; it saves us from despair at being unable to obtain much personal information on individual legislators. Again, it constitutes a useful way of looking at sectional differences in attitudes. Differences between North and South concerning interracial sex were not in kind but in vehemence, if vehemence is defined as the product of the degree of individual involvement and proportion of people involved. In New York in 1785, for example, the assembly passed a gradual emancipation bill which would have barred Negroes from the polls and from marrying whites. The senate objected to the intermarriage clause because "in so important a connection they thought the free subjects of this State ought to be left to their free choice." The assembly again voted narrowly to retain the clause and then, after conference with the senate, finally receded on it by a narrow margin, though later for other reasons the entire bill was lost. In Massachusetts, however, an act of 1786 on the "Solemnization of Marriage" voided marriages between whites and Negroes. Rhode Island passed a similar law in 1798. The Pennsylvania emancipation bill also contained a similar provision which was dropped before final passage. On the whole, this random pattern in the North suggests both the existence of sentiment against intermixture and a lack of great vehemence underlying it.

In the South, on the other hand, where there were more Negroes (wearing fewer clothes) there is evidence suggesting greater tension. For the most part laws prohibiting racial mixture were already on the books and nobody wanted them off. The Virginia legislature's refusal to accept Jefferson's provision in the revisal for banishment of white women bearing mulattoes stemmed more from objection to the harsh penalty than from willingness to countenance interracial matches. One foreign traveler observed that the unusually large number of mulattoes in the state was occasioned only by greater length of settlement and that public opinion was firmly set against interracial unions. Liaisons were carried on in secrecy, he explained, for "no white man is known to live regularly with a black woman." The converse relationship was of course another matter; though white women still occasionally slept with Negro men, southern society was as determined as ever to punish rigorously any Negro sexual attacks on white women. In 1769, Virginia had excluded castration from the penal code except as punishment for that offense. The brutality of castration had become offensive to humanitarian sentiment, however, and the legislature refused to enact Jefferson's revisal bill based on the *lex talionis*. Yet as late as 1792 emasculation was specifically declared by the legislature to be permissible punishment for any slave "convicted of an attempt to ravish a white woman." In practice the courts seem usually to have hanged such offenders but there was at least one case of sentence to castration, in 1797. The penalty was finally abolished in a general amendment to the penal code in 1805. Despite tension on the matter, some Virginians refused to be blinded by their feelings. In the 1800's several petitions to the governor asked clemency for Negroes condemned for rape on grounds that the white woman involved was of low character. Elsewhere in the South, however, there was evidence of smoldering emotion. In North Carolina a tradition was inaugurated at the turn of the century when lynching parties burned a Negro for rape and castrated a slave for remarking that he was going to have some white women. Georgia in 1806 enacted a mandatory death penalty for any Negro raping or attempting to rape a white woman. As late as 1827 a Georgia court sentenced a Negro to castration and deportation for attempted rape, and the *Macon Telegraph* castigated the court for its leniency.

The dynamics of the interracial sexual situation did not, of course, invariably tend toward emotional abandon. For one thing, in regions where slavery was firmly rooted in a high proportion of Negroes, the traditional European double standard for the sexes was subject to caricatural polarization. More sexual freedom for white men meant less for white women. Throughout the eighteenth century South Carolina had shown the effects of this tendency, though far less than the British West Indian societies. Despite difficulties created by the biases of travelers, it seems clear that the same tendency still operated in the deep South in the early years of the nineteenth century. One American traveler, the prominent ornithologist of Philadelphia, Alexander Wilson, described his unfavorable impressions by first lamenting that the "superabundance of Negroes" had "destroyed the activity of the whites," who "stand with their hands in their pockets, overlooking their negroes." In his letter to William Bartram in 1809 (here given as published much later in the century), Wilson went on to say,

These, however, are not one-tenth of the curses slavery has brought on the Southern States. Nothing has surprised me more than the cold, melancholy reserve of the females, of the best families, in South Carolina and Georgia. Old and young, single and married, all have that dull frigid insipidity, and reserve, which is attributed to solitary old maids. Even in their own houses they scarce utter anything to a stranger but yes or no, and one is perpetually puzzled to know whether it proceeds from awkwardness or dislike. Those who have been at some of their Balls [in Charleston] say that the ladies hardly even speak or smile, but dance with as much gravity, as if they were performing some ceremony of devotion. On the contrary, the negro wenches are all sprightliness and gayety; and if report be not a defamer—(*here there is a hiatus in the manuscript*) which render the men callous to all the finer sensations of love, and female excellence.

While one suspects that the "hiatus" may not have been the author's, the description clearly points to deep alienation on the part of white women. Their rightful consorts were often otherwise engaged, and their resulting shell of "dull frigid insipidity" was hardened by the utter necessity of avoiding any resemblance to women of the other race. Perhaps they sensed, too, that the protection they received against Negro men constituted a very perverse variety of affection. Their proper function, moreover, was to preserve the forms and symbols of civilization—they were, after all, bearers of white civilization in a literal sense—and to serve as priestesses in the temples, performing, in Wilson's perceptive phrase, a "ceremony of devotion."

The relationship between miscegenation and society was intricately reciprocal. While miscegenation altered the tone of society, the social institution of slavery helped reshape the definition of miscegenation from fusion of that which was different to fusion of higher and lower; hence slavery was of course responsible for much of the normative judgment implied in the concept of miscegenation. Yet both slavery and miscegenation rested, in the final analysis, upon a *perception of difference* between the races, a perception founded on physiognomic fact. When Jefferson, for example, set out to prove that emancipated Negroes must be removed from white society he predicated "the real distinctions nature has made," moved immediately into a discussion of appearance, and only then went on to less tangible differences in temperament and intellect. Underlying his discussion of the Negro, and everyone else's, was an axiomatic separation of Negroes from white men based on appearance.

5 / Michael Wallace
An American Dynamic—Parties and Principles:
New York, 1815–1828

During the first thirty years of its existence the United States developed, quite unintentionally, a party system. Organized popular parties regularly contested for power; Federalists and Republicans fought passionately and acrimoniously in Congress and cabinet, in town squares and county courthouses throughout the nation. The evidences of party spirit alarmed many Americans, for the existence of parties and their constant contention violated powerful and ancient traditions of proper political behavior. According to canons inherited from British and colonial thought and practice, parties were evil: they were associations of factious men bent on self-aggrandizement. Political competition was evil: the ideal society was one where unity and consensus prevailed, where the national interest was peacefully determined by national leaders. Because partisan behavior violated normal ethical standards, many men, politicians among them, saw in the rise of parties a sign of moral decline. Not until a new generation of politicians emerged—men who had been raised in parties and had grown to maturity in a world that included party competition as a fixture of political life—were Americans able to re-evaluate the ancient traditions and establish new ones that justified their political activities.

Much of this re-evaluation and development of new ideals took place in New York State in the 1820's. There a group of professional politicians, leaders of the Republican party known as the Albany Regency, developed the modern concept of a political party and declared party associations to be eminently desirable. They adhered to a set of values that insisted on preserving, not destroying, political parties. They denounced and derided the consensus ideal and praised permanent political competition as being beneficial to society . . .

The regency politicians justified their political party by distinguishing it from the parties characteristic of English and colonial American politics. They asserted that while the old type of party had been a personal clique satisfying nothing but the greed and whims of its aristocratic leaders—thus meriting the odium it had received—the new type of party was a popular, democratically run organization that enabled the people to participate in government; it was, therefore, praiseworthy. By distinguishing between old

Michael Wallace, "Changing Concepts of Party in the United States: New York, 1815–1828," *American Historical Review*, LXXIV (December, 1968), pp. 453–491. Reprinted by permission of the author. Footnotes omitted by permission.

and new parties, and by applying the epithets of the antiparty tradition only to the former, they freed their own association from condemnation. They were able to make this distinction because in fact the parties they were familiar with were quite different from their eighteenth-century forebears: the regency ratified a change that had already occurred.

In eighteenth-century England, "parties," "factions," or "connections" were cliques of parliamentary notables, organized about one or more prominent leaders. They were held together primarily by hopes of obtaining office. As Sir Lewis Namier tells us, "whoever in the eighteenth century had the 'attractive power' of office, received an accession of followers, and whoever retained it for some time was able to form a party." In addition to patronage, kinship and friendship were the basic ligaments of these primary political units. Lacking an organizational basis, however, these connections were quite unstable: "Such parties ... were bound to melt, ... for the basis of the various groups was eminently personal." Several such groups would merge to form the coalitions that made up ministries, but these coalitions were themselves highly unstable and in a crisis tended to dissolve into their constituent elements. Denominations such as Whig and Tory were often meaningful designations, but they denoted broad stylistic and ideological characteristics, not cohesive structures. "There were no proper party organizations ... though party names and cant were current."

Colonial politics in New York adhered to the English pattern: an intricate interplay of family cliques that occurred largely within the confines of the Assembly. This is not to say that contests were simply affairs of personal pique; significant economic and social interests were often at stake. Yet the processes of adjustment and reconciliation of interests were not carried on through the medium of such stable groupings as political parties. The units of political organization were shifting alliances of patrician families or elite individuals: New York's political history was a dense tangle of Livingstonians and DeLanceyites, of Lewisites, Burrites, and Clintonians.

From the Revolution to the 1820's, the English model of party was altered, and a distinctively American form emerged. The Revolution forced the elite factions, whose power had been rooted in connections with England, social prestige, or economic power, to turn to the public, to attempt to bolster their positions by soliciting mass support; this increased dependency on the legitimizing power of numbers produced what one historian has called a shift from a politics of status to a politics of opinion. The mobilization of popular support behind specific political positions or leaders became increasingly crucial in American politics, and the political party emerged as the mechanism for organizing that support. In the 1780's and 1790's, debate over such national issues as the adoption of the Constitution, the Hamiltonian program, the Jay Treaty, and the Genêt mission drew great numbers of previously uninvolved people into the expanding political parties. The parties changed from cliques in Congress to popular associations, as men sought to influence the composition and character of political leadership by concerted action at the polls.

Parties began to develop identities, personas, that were separable from the personalities and positions of their leaders; structures, too, were becoming less communal, more impersonal, as parties stretched to absorb ever-larger numbers of adherents. Changing terminology marked the process: in New York, where DeLanceyites had fought Livingstonians, Federalists now fought Republicans. Yet by the War of 1812 the process was far from complete; the New York Republican party, for instance, remained primarily a coalition of family factions, which tended to fracture repeatedly along the lines of its component parts. The first generation of party members, generally unaware of the larger processes at work, maintained a greater allegiance to their personal factions than to the larger entity, the party. The structure, function, size, and scope of the party had changed, but not men's attitudes toward it. Because the transformation was unplanned, a series of *ad hoc* reactions to events, the conception of party remained unchanged. What looked like a modern party had evolved, but because change had preceded intellectual awareness, old attitudes toward parties prevailed.

In New York, after the War of 1812, a new conception of party emerged, modeled more closely on reality; in turn, the new definition of what a party ought to be legitimated existing structures. This re-evaluation developed out of what at first seemed just one more intraparty feud among New York Republicans, but that rapidly took a new and significant turn. The focus of the struggle was De Witt Clinton, in 1817 the leader of the party. Clinton held to the old view of party: he was a patrician politician who considered the party his personal property. This attitude is not surprising, given the nature of his career. Clinton assumed his position of leadership effortlessly, inheriting control of the faction that had been led by his uncle, George Clinton, New York's Revolutionary War governor. Despite the fact that the organization he headed in 1817 was quite different from what it had been when he entered politics in the 1790's, his style of leadership remained characteristic of the earlier period. Snobbish, spiteful, and supercilious, he was forbiddingly aristocratic. He craved flattery, he rejected advice from subordinates that conflicted with his own political judgments, and he directed the party largely as he saw fit. Above all, he dispensed the rewards of the party—political patronage and party nominations—as he pleased, often to personal friends, often to Federalists at the expense of deserving Republicans.

This type of leadership became increasingly unacceptable to a group of younger politicians in the party. As the party had become richer, more powerful, more obviously a vital route to a-successful career in public life, many men whose allegiance lay not to any person or family but to the party itself had joined the organization. Inevitably such men would resent the idiosyncratic and unpredictable quality of party life, particularly the capricious dispensation of party rewards. Beginning about 1817, a group of these younger politicians known as the Bucktails began a quiet campaign to oust Clinton from the leadership. They were not interested merely in substituting one set of leaders for another. Rather their position may be likened to that of a group of young executives in a family firm who think that the business is being misrun because familial, not managerial, standards govern its operation.

By 1819 the Bucktails, who included such able men as Martin Van Buren, Benjamin Franklin Butler, Silas Wright, William Learned Marcy, and Azariah Cutting Flagg, felt ready to challenge Clinton openly. At first they attacked him personally, charging that he put his own interests above those of the organization. "De Witt Clinton, has acted incompatibly with his situation as the head of the republican party of this state, and in direct hostility to its best interest and prosperity . . ." "Personal aggrandizement," they declared, "has been his personal maxim, even at the sacrifice of the republican party." As one Bucktail wrote in the Albany *Argus*, the organ of the insurgents, "notwithstanding his capacity, his manners are too repulsive, his temper too capricious and imperious, his deportment too dictatorial and tyrannical to acquire the affections or retain the confidence of any party."

The Bucktails wanted to go beyond indicting Clinton's personal style and to get at the anachronistic system of personal politics that he represented. Yet it was difficult to criticize Clinton's kind of leadership within the traditional framework of ideas about parties, for he was acting in accord with centuries-old standards of behavior. They were thus forced to proclaim a new definition of party and new standards of proper behavior for party politicians that would discredit both Clinton and his style of politics. They accomplished this task by adopting the rhetoric of democracy and egalitarianism and applying it to intraparty organization. Parties, they declared, should be democratic associations, run by the majority of the membership. It was a simple assertion, but it immediately put them in a position of strength. The ideal was virtually unassailable; to undermine the Bucktail position, critics would have to denounce republicanism itself—in the 1820's a political impossibility. Republican ideals became the Bucktails' weapons, and they were weapons that Clinton could not counter.

The Bucktails asserted that a party organized about an individual or patrician family was unacceptable as it was not republican. Personal parties were not parties at all, but factions, aristocratic remnants from the deferential days of colonial politics. Clinton was denounced as "raising up not only an aristocracy, but what has more hideous features, a species of monarchy." He was "the chieftain and head of an aristocracy"; his followers, "governed by no principle or party discipline," were "servile dependents . . . solely devoted to his views"; they were a "dangerous faction, bearing the badge of his family name," and solely concerned with "ministering to personal ambition." His patronage policy was denounced, not simply as unfair, but as producing undemocratic concentrations of power: "Devotion to the person of a chief becomes a passport to public distinction, and servility to men in power is rewarded . . . by honors and emoluments." In sum, Clinton's whole vision of politics, "characterized by personal attachments on the one hand and by personal antipathies on the other," was "highly prejudicial to the interests of the people, and if successful [would] have a tendency to subvert our republican form of government."

The proper form of political organization in a democratic state, the Bucktails argued, was not a personal faction but a political party. A true party was not the property of a man or a family, but transcended any of its members. Like a corporation it outlived its officers and did not, as had been the rule, expire when its leaders died or were removed from office. The proper party was "bound to the fortunes of no aspiring chief." A political party, moreover, was responsible to the mass of its members: it was a democratic organization. The "cardinal maxim with the great republican party [should be] . . . always to seek for, and when ascertained, always to follow the will of the majority." Politicians like Clinton, who felt themselves to be above the majority, could no longer be tolerated. "Those who refuse to 'abide by the fairly expressed will of the majority' . . . forfeit all claims to the character of republicans, and become recreant to the principles of that party." This did not mean an end to leadership: "Republicans know full well that . . . some must bear the brunt of the battle, and that to some hands must be consigned the interest and honor of the party; the system, the management, the labor and the anxiety." But leaders were expected to consider themselves the instruments or agents of an organization, not its owners. He "whose talents and zeal have benefitted the republican party will be supported as long as he consults the interests and ascendancy of that party, and no longer." The proper criteria for advancement were faithful dedication to the party and long service in its support, not pedigree or property.

By these standards, Van Buren was a model party leader. He proclaimed his obligation to the organization: "There are few men in the state," he told a gathering of the faithful, "more indebted to the favor of the Republican Party than myself and none more willing to acknowledge it." He rose to power in the prescribed fashion: "We speak of him with pride," declared a mass meeting of Albany Republicans in 1820, "because without the influence of fortune, or the factitious aid of a family name, he has, by his entire devotion to the republican cause, raised himself to the first grade as a statesman and a patriot."

By 1820 the Bucktail revolt had succeeded. Largely because they were able to convince many of the party that they were more faithful to the organization and the will of its majority than was Clinton, they managed to oust Clinton and his adherents; they then appropriated the apparatus and symbols of the Republican party entirely for themselves. Despite vigorous protests at being read out of the party because they failed to measure up to the new criteria, the Clintonians were relegated to the status of a distinct personal party. Van Buren and his fellow Republicans entrenched themselves in the legislature and all of the executive branch but the governorship and came to be characterized, by Clintonian and Federalist opponents, as the Albany Regency.

The Bucktails thus succeeded in distinguishing between party and faction in both the theory and actuality of New York politics. A party (such as their own) was a democratically structured, permanent organization; a faction (such as the Clintonians) was a transient, aristocratic, personal clique. "On one side is arrayed the old republican party, and on the other the followers of a man." Personal factions were bad: they were aristocratic and concerned only with enriching their leader. But parties were good: they allowed all members an equal voice; gave all members an equal chance to rise to positions of leadership and to receive party nominations for important elective positions; and provided all members an equal chance at receiving patronage, now no longer dispensed at the whim of an arbitrary leader. The degree to which the newer politicians rejected the antiparty tradition and the personal basis of politics can be seen in their extraordinary degree of attachment to their organization. They went far beyond merely justifying the existence of their party in ideological and practical terms and developed a system of political discipline that enjoined every politician, at whatever cost to himself, to preserve and perpetuate the party . . .

The length to which legislators would occasionally go in subordinating their interests to those of the organization is illustrated by the political suicide committed by seventeen state senators in 1824. Party strategy required the defeat of the extremely popular electoral bill (which would have given the choice of presidential electors to the people and blocked the regency's delivering the state's united electoral vote to William Crawford, the caucus choice that year). Van Buren urged "the Republican members of both houses [to] act in concert and magnanimously sacrifice individual preferences for the general good." With perfect foreknowledge of the consequences, these seventeen voted, as the party required, to defeat the democratic measure. As Senator John Suydam phrased it, "I have discharged my duty fearlessly but conscientiously." Most of these political Spartans ended their legislative careers with that vote; the hatred generated among the people was extraordinarily intense. Their only recompense, aside from those few who were rewarded substantially with executive appointments, judgeships and the like, was the overwhelming gratitude of their party brethren . . .

[In 1797 few had] disagreed with Washington's classic restatement of the consensus ideal in his Farewell Address. Warning his countrymen against "the baneful effects of the spirit of party," he insisted that partisan conflict "serves always to distract the public councils and enfeeble the public administration"; that it "agitates the community with ill-founded jealousies and false alarms"; that it "kindles the animosity of one part against another"; and that it was therefore definitely "a spirit not to be encouraged." Despite Washington's words, reality remained refractory. At bottom the consensus ideal rested on the view that a "national interest" existed, a common good that rational men could agree upon. But in the young republic men agreed upon very little. To Washington's dismay, parties formed, advancing conceptions of the proper organization of society and the structure of government, representing conflicting economic and social interests, pressing differing views on foreign policy, contesting particular actions of the administration. And these parties were even more obnoxious to upholders of the old tradition than were English parties, to their detractors, for they represented not merely parliamentary cliques but popular movements, reaching deep down into society. Unheralded, unplanned for, and, for most Americans, unwanted, the first party system had come into being.

The growth of political competition had little impact on the consensus ideal. Departure from ideals seldom changes them, for the deviations are attributed rather to a lack of virtue in the transgressors than to lack of validity in the ideals themselves. Usually denunciations of violators grow shriller, and the virtue of the tradition is insisted on the more ferociously. That is what happened in the United States in the early nineteenth century. Although there were glimmerings of a re-evaluation of the consensus mentality during the Federalist and Jeffersonian eras—stray remarks about the value of party competition in the writings of Thomas Jefferson, Robert Goodloe Harper, Fisher Ames, and John Adams coexist with more conventional denunciations of party, and James Madison achieved a major break-through on the subject of interest groups, though not political parties—the voices seem lost and isolated, exceptions that prove the rule. The intellectual lag behind institutional practice increased.

After 1815 an attempt was made to align theory and practice, but in a reactionary fashion: men tried to reshape reality to conform to the older ideals. The bitter animosities of the War of 1812 had convinced many that parties had to be eliminated. The most popular political book of the day was Mathew Carey's *The Olive Branch: or Faults on Both Sides, Federal and Democratic—A Serious Appeal on the Necessity of Mutual Forgiveness and Harmony, Dedicated to a Beloved but Bleeding Country, Torn in Pieces by Factious and Ruinous Contests for Power*. Peace in 1815, marking the passing of older issues, oriented to foreign policy, seemed a perfect opportunity to eliminate conflict. The nation's political leaders, noting the decline of the Federalist party, declared that political divisions were a thing of the past, that a time of harmony, unity, and consensus had arrived. It was to be an Era of Good Feelings in which the remnants of parties would come together in a celebration of national unity.

The idea of Good Feelings was professed nationally by men of the stature of James Monroe, John Quincy Adams, and Andrew Jackson. In his inaugural address, Monroe declared that parties were not needed. Echoing Bolingbroke, he announced that "the American people constitute one great family with a common interest." That national interest was so obvious that there could be no deviation from it. "Discord," he declared, "does not belong to our system." Privately Monroe noted that a "great undertaking" would be to "exterminate all party divisions in our country." Adams declared too that he would "break up the remnant of old party distinctions, and bring the whole people together in sentiment as much as possible." In his inaugural address, he asserted that party competition had ended; "the baneful weed of party strife" had been uprooted. It remained for those who had "heretofore followed the standards of political party" to make "one effort of magnanimity, one sacrifice of prejudice and passion," that of "discarding every remnant of rancor against each other" and "embracing as countrymen and friends." And in 1817 Jackson wrote President Monroe that "party and party feelings ought to be laid out of view." "Now," he argued, "is the time to exterminate that monster called party spirit."

This was the standard approach to parties and political competition in the 1820's. Against this background, the innovations of the regency politicians in New York once again take on special interest. The attitudes they had evolved toward their opponents in the normal course of political life determined to a large extent how they would react when the Good Feelings persuasion was advanced and used against them on their home grounds in 1824.

The primary goal of regency politicians was to preserve their party. This is of utmost importance for understanding their attitudes toward their opponents in New York politics. Their goal was not to destroy, overwhelm, or eliminate their opponents; they were not ideologues bent on the destruction of evildoers. They were able, therefore, to realize that the continued existence of an opposition was necessary, from the perspective of perpetuating their own party; opposition was highly useful, a constant spur to their own party's discipline. While the party might, it was argued, "suffer temporary defeats" in the interparty struggle, "it is certain to acquire additional strength . . . by the attacks of adverse parties." Indeed, the party was "most in jeopardy when an opposition is not sufficiently defined." As another writer noted, "there is such a thing as a party being too strong; a small and firm majority is more to be relied upon than an overwhelming and loose one." The politicians were aware that during "the contest between the great rival parties . . . each found in the strength of the other a powerful motive of union and vigor."

This need for opposition led to a fertile paradox. The Federalists and their latter-day avatars, the Clintonians, were, of course, guilty of heinous political sins: they were aristocrats, personalists, factionalists, no-party heretics. Yet they were also the opposition. As a consequence, the Federalist party (a label Republicans attached to their major opponents of the moment), while condemned, was simultaneously praised; it was the strong, flourishing, and virtuous organization to which Republicans would accede should it obtain the support of the state's majority . . .

The regency . . . had no desire to eliminate its opponents. Rather it hoped for a "tranquil though determined opposition." . . . This acceptance of the continued existence of [its] opponents engendered a sportsmanlike attitude toward the competition . . . Republican politicians even envisioned occasionally ceding power to their enemies. They had, after all, done it often enough. Alternating in power with political opponents was a recurring experience. Yet they had a theoretical justification for this alternation that allowed them to deal with ejection from power quite calmly: they applied the doctrine of majoritarianism to interparty relations, a process less elegantly known as the spoils system. Just as they thought that the minority of the party must submit to the greater number, so they thought that the party that obtained a majority of the votes of the state should rule completely, until such time as the minority party managed to convert itself into the majority party . . .

These were the attitudes regency politicans developed toward their opponents amid daily political struggles. Their lack of ideological fervor and their emphasis on preserving their institution contributed to a lowering of the political temperature. In the cooler atmosphere of the 1820's the politicians perceived that an opposition was necessary, and they came to think in terms of the continued existence of two parties, each sincere, legitimate, and capable of administering the government. Within this framework of attitudes a re-evaluation of the consensus ideal could easily emerge. But ideas seldom spring forth without some encouragement, no matter how conducive the times. A stimulus was needed, some reason to force the regency men to think about their political universe and to make them articulate their attitudes toward political parties. The stimulus came in the mid-twenties with a barrage of antiparty criticism from their New York opponents. Only when confronted with a severe challenge to their habits and practices would they formulate a rebuttal. A brief look at the position of the New York antiparty spokesmen may help us understand what provoked the regency response.

The New York opponents of the Albany Regency, drawing on the antiparty spirit of the national leaders, reasserted the old consensus ideal. Clinton, for example, declared that the clash of parties has "rent us asunder, degraded our character, and impared our ability for doing good." He too felt there was no need for division:

I hardly understand the nomenclature of parties. They are all republicans, and yet a portion of the people assume the title of republican, as an

exclusive right . . . It is easy to see that the difference is nominal—
that the whole controversy is about office, and that the country is constantly assailed by ambitious demagogues for the purpose of gratifying
their cupidity . . .

The solution was obvious: eliminate parties. If one could "knock aside
all artificial arrangements and the whole machinery of party," it would
prevent the "citizens of the state having their sentiments perverted by intrigue
and corruption." If parties could not be exorcised, they could at least be
merged and amalgamated, particularly as there existed no difference between
them . . .

When it became apparent that the Republicans had no intention of merging with their opponents, much less of dissolving, the antiparty men moved
beyond rhetoric. They organized. They formed, of all things, a party, an
antiparty party, a party to end parties. The People's party, formed in 1823
by Clintonians, Federalists, and dissident Republicans, appealed to the electorate "not in the spirit of *party* warfare, for this is emphatically the cause
of the People." "We contend," the People's men declared, "not for the
aggrandizement of a party of men, leagued together for selfish purposes, but
for a great COMMON CAUSE, interesting to the people of this state." Their
candidates were picked "without reference to PARTY POLITICS," as it had
been deemed "best to sacrifice party considerations on the altar of public
good." They offered their party as a means whereby members of all groups
could unite, but it was highly unlikely that many regency Republicans would
be lured into support of the fledgling party in light of the candidate it chose
to support in 1824—De Witt Clinton. Yet here a theoretical assault on party
was linked to a potentially powerful organization and a popular candidate.
If the antiparty message appealed to many in the electorate, the regency was
in trouble. The emergence of the People's party threatened regency hegemony
and forced its members to defend the party system that had evolved in New
York. This they consciously set about to do. As the Albany *Argus* states, "the
doctrines of dissolution and amalgamation . . . must be met and resisted."

The regency defense against the amalgamation attack took five forms.
Their first, most parochial, and probably most effective position was that
the philosophy of amalgamation, for all its seeming disinterestedness, was
actually an opposition trick, the purpose of which was not to unite the country
but to destroy the Republican party. Secondly, on a more theoretical level,
regency Republicans denied that parties had dissolved, but rather that they
continued in undiminished strength, a result traceable to powerful ideological
and historical forces perpetuating them, which the Good Feelings men had
ignored. Thirdly, they rejected the entire vision of a society based on consensus; the proper political universe was characterized by constant contention; the truly moral man was not one who put himself above party, but
was a committed partisan. Fourthly, . . . they declared that parties had to

exist in a free state, that the elimination of parties occurred only under despotism. Fifthly, and most broadly, they declared that, for several reasons, competition between parties benefited the state . . .

Republicans declared that advocacy of Good Feelings was a Federalist plot. By persuading Republicans that parties no longer existed, or by convincing them that they no longer should exist, the Federalists would loosen the bands of party discipline so vital to the party, and it would dissolve; then the Federalists would step in and recapture the government. "The great design and hope now is to abolish the old political distinctions," warned the Albany *Argus*, "and as a revolutionary consequence TO DESTROY THE DEMOCRATIC PARTY." The glorification of unity was a ruse: "the affections of union, and of the dissolution of all parties, is [*sic*] only a snare for [Republican] feet." . . .

The regency's second, more muted response to the amalgamationists was also more radical. Parties, they declared, were not simply ideologically coherent organizations, at odds over fundamental issues. They were social institutions in their own right, largely independent of their earlier ideological stances . . .

New issues did not require new parties; rather the two traditional organizations remained to act as vehicles for opposing positions. The parties maintained themselves not so much by love of "principle" as by the attachment of the members to the organization itself. The men composing parties "are bound together by a thousand affinities and alliances; the alliance is cemented by time and strengthened by the strongest affections and antipathies; real or fancied persecutions rivet the bonds of union." These loyalties were then transmitted to the next generation. "The succession of generations renders them the more enduring, and the transmission of the sentiments and feelings of the father to the son is generally regular and unbroken . . . The parties remain unaltered; they are embodied in the constitutions and inherent in the minds of men."

Association with a political party, therefore, was not simply the result of a conscious decision; parties were not to be dissolved after certain issues were resolved. Rather, party affiliation and thus party divisions were handed down, like heirlooms, from generation to generation. Once again, amalgamation was precluded.

The Republicans' third rejection of amalgamation was perhaps their most radical, for it condemned the consensus ideal itself, declaring that it led to politically immoral behavior. The regency conception of what comprised political honesty and morality was not an avoidance of party, but a consistent adherence to party. Amalgamationists insisted that party men of opposite faiths should come together; with Republicans it was an article of political morality for them to remain apart. The Republicans did not respect the man who, following the consensus tradition, put himself above party. They were partisans and respected only other partisans . . . A man who disengaged from politics and affected aloofness from parties was not praiseworthy. He might be a trimmer: "in all times, men of incorruptible integrity and virtue have been found in the ranks of parties; and the affected denial of their existence, or an assumed independence of them springs rather from a propensity to trim, and a hankering after official rewards, than from any elevated and patriotic feeling." Or he might be a despot: "it is easy for those whose ambition is as insatiable as the sea, and who to gratify their inordinate lust for power, would overleap all bounds, to affect to be independent of all things, except for the good of the whole, to act for the nation and not for a party, to be patriots and not politicians."

Men who abandoned one party for another were thoroughly denounced. They were condemned, with almost ecclesiastical fervor, as "apostates." But even worse than apostasy was vacillation. The politician who drifted from party to party was condemned as "inconsistent"; Butler lucidly outlined the immorality of this attitude. Writing to Van Buren, Butler declared that "*political consistency* [is] as indispensable as any other *moral qualification*. For say what you will it is a *moral* qualification." This was so because the "man who is dishonest and unstable in his politics" is "equally dishonest and unstable in the relations of his private life.".... This partisan spirit proved the deadliest foe of the consensus mentality. It governed relations between party organizations, not just party members, and thus barred amalgamation. Partisans did not switch, and parties did not mix: organizations as well as individuals were consistent ...

The fourth argument advanced by the Republicans concerned the inevitability of parties in a free state; their absence or amalgamation was evidence of repression. Republicans assumed that in any society there would be more than one conception of the national interest. In order to express these differences, men form parties: those whose "general interests are the same" will always combine to promulgate their ideas, for "all experience has shown, that efforts to be powerful, must be concentrated." It followed that society normally contained parties contending with one another. "Diversity of opinion results from the infirmity of human judgment; and party spirit is but the passion with which opposing opinions are urged in the strife for the possession of power." The development of parties was considered to be a natural and irresistible phenomenon: "It is the vainest thing in the world to deny the existence of parties. They will exist."

Yet they might not exist, if repressed: parties developed only in societies that tolerated organized dissent. The very existence of parties was, therefore, an indication that freedom of expression existed. Parties "will prevail where there is the least degree of liberty of action on the part of the public agents, or their constituents; ... they are ... inseparable from a free government." The association of parties and freedom was a basic theme of the regency defense. "Parties," they declared, "will ever exist, in a free state." The maintenance of parties, they asserted, was "necessary to the just exercise of the powers of free governments." Because this was such an obvious equation, they hinted darkly that their Good Feelings opponents, in calling for an end to parties, were contemplating an end of freedom. It was much commented on that military men like Jackson were fervent advocates of eliminating parties, and they contrasted such behavior with their own: "Fortunately for our country, and its institutions, there is another class of politicians, whom we delight to honor, who believe, that when party distinctions are no longer known and recognized, our freedom will be in jeopardy, as the 'calm of despotism' will then be visible." Party competition was the hallmark of a free society.

The fifth ground for rejecting the consensus ideal derived from the belief that permanent competition between political parties was a positive benefit to the state. This was their broadest argument, most likely to appeal to nonpoliticians. "We are party men, attached to party systems," they declared, but added, "we think them necessary to the general safety . . ." And again, "for the safety of the republic & the good of the people" it was imperative to "keep up and adhere to old party distinctions." How did they justify this position? For one thing, party competition provided a check upon the government; it was an extraconstitutional aid to the people. "The spirit of party," they declared, was "the vigilant watchman over the conduct of those in power." The parties were "among the firmest bulwarks of civil liberty," and politicians insisted that they were "necessary to keep alive the vigilance of the people, and to compel their servants to act up to principle." But exactly how did they do this? One of their major functions was to inform the people.

> [Parties] on either side of the question, become the counsel who argue the cause before the people . . . The solicitude and interest of political rival-ship, will sufficiently expose the crimes, and even the failings, of competitors for the people's confidence. Competitors of this description *force* into notice facts, . . . which the people at large could never have derived from the ordinary commerce of thought.

The people are thus presented with expert watchdogs: "leading men, on both sides of the question check one another," and the people, presented with informed alternatives, "know when to support and when to oppose." Governor Enos Throop asserted that the party system allowed the people to participate intelligently in government.

> Those party divisions which are based upon conflicting opinions in regard to the constitution of the government, or the measures of the administration of it, interest every citizen, and tend, inevitably, in the spirit of emulation and proselytism, to reduce the many shades of opinion into two opposing parties . . . [The] organized parties watch and scan each other's doings, the public mind is instructed by ample discussions of public measures, and acts of violence are restrained by the convictions of the people, that the prevailing measures are the results of enlightened reason.

Party competition had another value: it agitated the public and kept the mass of people interested in the operation of the government. It produced discord, and discord, despite the attitudes of the men who advocated Good Feelings, was of utmost value to republics. For, in the eyes of the Bucktails, the real danger to republics was not division, as in consensus cosmology, but apathy. And the surest cure for apathy was party competition . . .

Then, paradoxically, party competition bound the country together. Here was one of the shrewdest observations that the politicians made. While only in its formative stages in the 1820's, this idea would quickly enter the main current of ante bellum thought. Van Buren and his colleagues realized that contrary to antiparty mythology, the really divisive threat to the nation was not party, but section. Party associations that cut across sectional lines were, in fact, an antidote to interregional stress. The Good Feelings men, by calling for the elimination of parties, were exacerbating sectionalism. Republicans accused them of wanting "to ABROGATE THE OLD PARTY DISTINCTIONS" in order to "organize new ones founded in the territorial prejudices of the people." The consequence of abolishing the old political distinctions would be "to array republicans against each other under such new artificial distinctions . . . as geographical locations, such as North and South, East and West." Van Buren rested much of his case for the maintenance of the old parties on this ground: "We must always have party distinctions, and the old ones are the best . . . If the old ones are suppressed, geographical differences founded on local instincts or what is worse, prejudices between free & slave holding states will inevitably take their place."

Finally, contests between political parties benefited society by eliminating the fierce contentions of personal parties. Decrying the "cant and self-interests" that "utter lamentations over the prevalence of party division and the exhibition of party feelings," Butler wrote that

we are not of that fastidious sect which can desire the extinction of the old parties—which would sweep away the associations . . . and give us in their stead the bitter contentions of personal feuds, and the degrading personalities of an individual vassalage . . . The old divisions are virtues which we . . . cherish. The contests which grow out of them are salutary and needful for the preservation of the community.

It was now obvious, as Throop noted, that it was "one of the peculiar benefits of a well-regulated party spirit in a commonwealth, that it employs the passions actively in a milder mood, and thus shuts the door against faction . . ."

By the end of the 1820's, the amalgamation attack had been met, the consensus tradition rejected. "Let us be greeted no more," demanded the Albany *Argus*, "by the cant and whining about the extinction of party feelings and the impropriety of endeavoring to keep them alive." "Parties of some sort must exist. 'Tis in the nature and genius of our government."

Section Two
American Calvinism, 1607–1765

ROBERT G. POPE

Contents

Selected Additional Readings

Introduction

Prior to independence the influence of the Calvinist tradition pervaded the American experience. The relationship of God, man, and nature elaborated by the Reformed theology, adapted to the wilderness and constantly changing within it, became an instrument for shaping and reshaping the political and social institutions of America. Throughout colonial America, from New England to the back country of the south, men carried with them shared religious values which unified them far more than denominational rivalry and local isolation would suggest. Congregationalists, Presbyterians, Baptists, Quakers, Dutch and German Reformed, even Anglicans and Methodists, could claim roots in Calvin's Geneva. As these denominations dominated American Protestantism they tended to force even those churches outside this religious tradition into their mold. On the eve of the American Revolution at least three-fourths of the congregations in the rebellious colonies still professed, if they did not strictly adhere to, the tenets of Reformed theology. The interaction of Calvinism, the wilderness, and the transported English culture provided the dynamic for an emerging America. Together they challenged Americans and the world with a new vision of the "city upon a hill."

Calvinism defies simple definition because nothing in the original creed proved immutable. As men asked new questions of their reformed faith and received new answers, they altered the stern decrees and the blinding sovereignty of Calvin's God. In turn, the doctrines of grace, predestination, depravity, and divine authority were challenged, defended, and adapted for successive generations of Calvinists. Calvinism acquired over two and a half centuries a diversity that all but hid the common origin. The mutations never ceased, but the essential Christian questions remained: What must I do to be saved? What is the Christian life? As they answered these questions, Calvinists reflected their common heritage.

The Reformed theologians—Calvin in Geneva, Zwingli and Bullinger in Zurich, Bucer in Strasbourg—shared Luther's negations and many of his affirmations. With him they rejected papal authority, celibacy, and the efficacy of good works; with him they accepted the emphasis on scriptures and faith, on reduction of the number of the sacraments, and on worldly vocation. The most radical break which separated the Lutheran and Reformed traditions was the significance that Calvinists attributed to scriptural law. For Lutherans the world was governed by the laws of creation, and the gospel was "good news," not a source of law that directed Christian life.

The underlying spirit of Lutheranism was *agape* (spiritual love); the essence of Calvinism was the *nomos*, the law, and it was in this respect Christian Judaism. Calvin's *Institutes* (1536) began with the assertion of God's sovereignty and depraved man's dependence, but law became the fundamental and absolute derivative of God's will. Law entered into every aspect of life—in worship, in daily morals, in vocation, in the life of the world; it was the great teacher. From the law Calvinists derived their attack on existing liturgy and polity, and it guided them in building anew from the "word of God," rather than from expediency. It served as the standard for what man should do and what he should not do, and its enforcement by the state restrained the lawless impulses of men. Moral law regulated men's lives, and obedience to the law became a measure of men. All men, whether "elect" or damned, were bound to external obedience. Thus Calvinists, despite their assertion of depravity and predestination, became moral activists with a conversionist attitude toward society. The law could be imposed on the world and transform it. The Reformed tradition put the Christian on the cutting edge between the reality of sin and the divine moral injunctions.

Disciples carried this legalistic theology out of the Swiss cantons into the Lowlands and across the channel into Scotland and England. To the dismay of later Stuart kings, John Knox built the Scottish Presbyterian kirks on Genevan models; continental reformers crowded the England of Edward VI. When Elizabeth firmly established her *via media* upon Anglicanism, Calvinism permeated the doctrine but it was mixed with other traditions to create an unstable, if comprehensive, half-way house. Two Calvinist currents challenged the new establishment. The incompleteness of reform led many to advocate further purification of the churches; in particular, they demanded the abolition of the episcopal hierarchy and "Romish remnants" (candles, clerical vestments, crosses, etc.) which lacked scriptural warrant. Secondly, out of a reawakening of personal piety there developed increasing condemnation of the moral laxity and excesses of Elizabethan England. Together they created the Puritan movement.

However, in the century between publication of the *Institutes* and the great Puritan migration of the 1630's the sovereignty of Calvin's God became less comforting to Calvin's heirs, and they sought new assurances of His grace and order. In the rational framework of the Federal or covenant theology, usually associated with English Puritans but also part of the continental Reformed tradition, they imposed new restraints on divine will. They taught that God, in

His mercy, had voluntarily bound Himself in a series of "contracts" that made the workings of divine grace comprehensible to man. In the fall, Adam broke the "covenant of works" and graceless man thereby lost forever the possibility of achieving salvation through meritorious good works. But in a second covenant, the "covenant of grace" made originally with Abraham and renewed with Christ, God promised eternal life to those who believed in Him. However, faith sprang not from the will of corrupt men but from the will of God; through the gift of God's grace men received saving faith. Since the most a man could do was be ready when God made the offer, a new question assumed primary importance for Puritans—How can I know if I am among the elect? Calvin had warned men against attempting to penetrate the labyrinth of God's mind wherein such secrets were stored, but covenant theology and practical experience made Puritans more optimistic.

As Puritan ministers wrote, preached and counseled they recognized a regularity in the process of conversion that changed men from reprobates to saints. Their "morphology of conversion" not only offered comfort and guidance to the individual's spiritual pilgrimage, it also served as a yardstick. The final stage of conversion was the reflection in daily life, through good works, of "sanctification." Saints, unlike carnal men, were morally capable, if not perfect, and their lives would exemplify their faith. The two central elements of conversion, the divine gift of grace and the external morality that flowed from it, created a precarious tightrope requiring a fine sense of balance. Too much emphasis on the indwelling of the Holy Spirit could denigrate moral behavior and risk antinomianism; too much emphasis on good works denied God's free grace and risked Arminianism. For every Calvinist sect that came to America this tension between piety and moralism ultimately precipitated a denominational crisis.

Although the New World in the seventeenth century lured tens of thousands of Englishmen in search of fame, fortune, and escape, embattled English sectaries attached a special meaning to America. There, in the security of isolation, Puritans in the 1630's and Quakers in the 1680's consciously strove to create a Zion in the wilderness. Neither sect entertained utopian illusions; in their Calvinist heritage both Puritan and Quaker shared too clear a sense of man's potential for evil and the imperfection of the world. But they sought to create a society where—within the limits of human ability endowed by grace—godliness, order, and authority could be established; they would recreate in the wilderness the organic, almost medieval community which had disappeared from Stuart England. Although they fled from persecution, more important than their personal discomfort under the Stuarts was their abhorrence of the prevailing moral disorder and their sense of impending disaster. One cannot dismiss this sense of disaster; it pervaded the Calvinist tradition. The reality of apocalyptic thought, the possibility that every moment might be the last, in large measure sustained and explains the initial zeal. The reflections of John Winthrop and William Penn just prior to their emigrations, although separated by half a century, reveal remarkably similar apprehensions, and inherent in each of the communities they guided was the notion of "a saving remnant."

Although Congregationalist and Quaker social structures differed radically, the failure of each sect to achieve its vision of a Zion lay in the same roots. H. Richard Niebuhr has suggested that no sect can last longer than a single generation, since it must compromise its own separateness to inculcate the religious values and discipline in its own children. The second generation of Congregationalists and Quakers reached maturity without ever experiencing Laud's pursuivants, or the Tower, or distraint of their property—for which blessings their parents most certainly thanked God. But with the creation of moral order in their wilderness Zions, these sects also removed the opportunity for those experiences which had led to their own experiential piety. The regenerative experience of the Puritan and the Inner Light of the Quaker—the heart of piety to the first generations—became increasingly stylized and routinized in the children. Formalism succeeded the prophetic. As the following generations acquired membership by birthright rather than personal piety, the sects lost their voluntaristic character and were transformed into churches. Neither Puritan nor Quaker was blind to the alterations; when their children failed to experience the "soul shattering" conversion, they consciously changed the requirements rather than leave them outside. The prerequisites for membership became increasingly tribal and moral. Within another generation morality itself would be equated with personal religion.

The "this-worldly asceticism" ascribed to both sects by Max Weber also contributed to the destruction of their sense of community. A Zion in the wilderness required that the welfare of the whole take precedence over the welfare of the individual, but ultimately the temptations of mammon proved too strong. Dedicated to work as a godly vocation and an act of worship, and rejecting conspicuous consumption, Puritans and Quakers rapidly achieved material prosperity. With the waning of piety the restrictions on acquisitiveness lost their force. Though the Quakers continuously tempered it with benevolence, the merchant princes of Philadelphia and Boston were a far cry from the ideals espoused by George Fox and John Cotton. Success in the marketplace had begun that transformation of Calvinist values that would culminate in Andrew Carnegie and the gospel of wealth.

Finally, the increasing emotional aridity of the Age of Reason and the Enlightenment settled over all the churches of colonial America. Religion became as "corpse-cold" and as formal as the Unitarianism Emerson rejected a century later. It offered little emotional satisfaction; it asked for little more than common civility and when found, labelled it faith; it often accepted much less. Dully read sermons, infrequent conversions, and church membership increasingly dependent on external conformity to doctrine and morality—

these were just the obvious manifestations of religious torpor. The ripples of revival that occasionally broke the calm damned by contrast the religious quiet that normally lay over the land.

The Great Awakening shattered that tranquility. No one, from the Maine lands to Georgia escaped its impact as thousands of colonials opened their hearts to the emotional appeals of Whitefield, Edwards, the Tennents, and a score of itinerant preachers. Even those who scorned the emotionalism watched the revival profoundly alter the world in which they lived. The bitterness and schism aroused by the Awakening divided American Calvinism into two distinct streams. Both had been present for more than a generation but were obscured. As men searched for new answers to the perpetual Christian questions or justified old answers in new terms, they redefined piety and morality. Neither evangelical nor rationalist rejected the traditional Calvinist concepts of divine grace and morality, but they bitterly disagreed over the essential qualities of the religious experience.

The rationalist, anti-revivalist faction emphasized the mind as the core of the conversion process. Emotionalism, essentially irrational because it stemmed from the heart and not the head, inhibited conversion and on those grounds deserved condemnation. Religious orthodoxy to the rationalists most often meant stable, settled, comfortable lives in conformity with the ethical demands of the community and acceptance of traditional doctrinal statements. Although it tended to favor a static social order, it was potentially revisionary toward political and theological traditions.

Revivalists saw the only meaningful conversion as a spiritual rebirth, a "heart circumcision," that could come only after men recognized their sinfulness and depravity. Moral capability came only when God had given grace. The evangelicals' attack on sin, social as well as individual, gave it a potential for moral reform that by the nineteenth century dominated the tradition. The individualism of the conversion experience also pulled the revivalists in new directions. It provided a basis for challenging the existing sources of religious and social authority; the regenerate man had less need for intermediaries and they appeared to him to have less divine authority within them. Because the evangelical tradition de-emphasized the mind in conversion, the potential for anti-intellectualism was great. Divine grace alone, it could be argued, not education or social graces, qualified men to preach the word; indeed, education might be a real handicap to conversion. Finally, the evangelical, as he preached conversion, steadily encroached on God's freedom and developed more and more individual, human responsibility for salvation or damnation. Ironically, both rationalists and evangelicals made man a free agent.

The dilemma of the Calvinist tradition in America is, with only minor theological variations, the Christian dilemma. H. Richard Niebuhr describes it: "the very essence of Christianity lies in the tension which it presupposes or creates between the worlds of nature and of spirit, and in its resolution of that conflict by means of justifying faith. It demands the impossible in conduct and belief; it runs counter to the instinctive life of man and exalts the rationality of the irrational; in a world of relativity it calls for unyielding loyalty to unchangeable absolutes." [1] The dilemma of churches no less than individuals is how to live in the world and not be of the world.

[1] H. Richard Niebuhr, *The Social Sources of Denominationalism* (New York, 1963), p. 4.

Part One

Zion in the Wilderness

John Winthrop and William Penn, in the first three selections of this section, clearly express some of the ideals which underlay the attempt by Puritans and Quakers to create their new Canaans in America. Both men stress the relationship of law, authority, and the individual in realizing and sustaining the ideal community, and although they share the same sense of the necessity for government, each assigns priorities to different factors that he feels essential to achieving community. Note, for example, the contrast between Winthrop's conception of magisterial authority and Penn's relative indifference to the forms of government; yet each emphasizes "liberty" as a prerequisite of society. Winthrop's vision of the holy commonwealth is further clarified by Perry Miller's essay, and Miller suggests two central components of Puritan political-social thought which provided a basis for repression in the first decades and a legacy for democracy in succeeding generations. This same theme is developed by Sydney Ahlstrom's emphasis on Puritan "responsibility" without which the community could not have existed and which was also susceptible to secularization.

Frederick B. Tolles' discussion of the Quakers emphasizes the balance of internal or mystic elements with the pressure of the external community in the creation of the "Holy Experiment" of William Penn. He also indicates many of the difficulties Quakers would encounter in Pennsylvania. The remaining selections—by Darrett B. Rutman, Gary B. Nash, Perry Miller, and Timothy L. Smith—attempt to outline, through various historical approaches, the difficulties that each community faced as it matured in a new and American environment. The focus is still on community, but now it is on the dissolution, or at least the altering, of the community and the development and articulation of conflict. Most notable in all these selections is the contest between individual interest and the community welfare.

1 / John Winthrop
A Model of Christian Charity

(1630)

It rests now to make some application of this discourse by the present design which gave the occasion of writing of it. Herein are four things to be propounded: first the persons, secondly, the work, thirdly, the end, fourthly, the means.

1. For the persons, we are a company professing ourselves fellow members of Christ, in which respect only, though we were absent from each other many miles and had our employments as far distant, yet we ought to account ourselves knit together by this bond of love, and live in the exercise of it, if we would have comfort of our being in Christ. This was notorious in the practice of the Christians in former times, as is testified of the Waldenses from the mouth of one of their adversaries, Aeneas Sylvius, *mutuo [solent amare] pene antequam norint*, they used to love any of their own religion even before they were acquainted with them.

2. For the work we have in hand, it is by a mutual consent through a special overruling providence and a more than an ordinary approbation of the churches of Christ to seek out a place of cohabitation and consortship under a due form of government both civil and ecclesiastical. In such cases as this the care of the public must oversway all private respects, by which not only conscience but mere civil policy doth bind us; for it is a true rule that particular estates cannot subsist in the ruin of the public.

3. The end is to improve our lives to do more service to the Lord the comfort and increase of the body of Christ whereof we are members that ourselves and posterity may be the better preserved from the common corruptions of this evil world to serve the Lord and work out our salvation under the power and purity of His holy ordinances.

4. For the means whereby this must be effected, they are twofold. A conformity with the work and end we aim at: these we see are extraordinary; therefore we must not content ourselves with usual ordinary means. Whatsoever we did or ought to have done when we lived in England, the same must we do and more also where we go. That which the most in their churches maintain as a truth in profession only, we must bring into familiar and

John Winthrop, "A Model of Christian Charity," *The Winthrop Papers*, vol. II (Boston, 1931), pp. 292–95. Spelling and punctuation revised. Reprinted with permission of the Massachusetts Historical Society.

constant practice, as in this duty of love we must love brotherly without dissimulation, we must love one another with a pure heart fervently, we must bear one another's burdens, we must not look only on our own things, but also on the things of our brethren. Neither must we think that the Lord will bear with such failings at our hands as He doth from those among whom we have lived, and that for three reasons.

1. In regard of the more near bond of marriage between Him and us, wherein He hath taken us to be His after a most strict and peculiar manner which will make Him the more jealous of our love and obedience. So He tells the people of Israel, "You only have I known of all the families of the earth, therefore will I punish you for your transgressions."

2. Because the Lord will be sanctified in them that come near Him . . .

3. When God gives a special commission He looks to have it strictly observed in every article . . . Thus stands the cause between God and us: we are entered into covenant with Him for this work, we have taken out a commission, the Lord hath given us leave to draw our own articles. We have professed to enterprise these actions upon these and these ends; we have hereupon besought Him of favor and blessing. Now if the Lord shall please to hear us, and bring us in peace to the place we desire, then hath He ratified this Covenant and sealed our commission, [and] will expect a strict performance of the articles contained in it. But if we shall neglect the observation of these articles which are the ends we have propounded, and, dissembling with our God, shall fall to embrace this present world and prosecute our carnal intentions, seeking great things for ourselves and our posterity, the Lord will surely break out in wrath against us, be revenged of such a perjured people, and make us know the price of the breach of such a Covenant.

Now the only way to avoid this shipwreck and to provide for our posterity is to follow the counsel of Micah, to do justly, to love mercy, to walk humbly with our God. For this end we must be knit together in this work as one man, we must entertain each other in brotherly affection, we must be willing to abridge ourselves of our superfluities, for the supply of others' necessities. We must uphold a familiar commerce together in all meekness, gentleness, patience and liberality. We must delight in each other, make others' conditions our own, rejoice together, mourn together, labor and suffer together, always having before our eyes our commission and community in the work, our community as members of the same body. So shall we keep the unity of the spirit in the bond of peace. The Lord will be our God and delight to dwell among us, as his own people and will command a blessing upon us in all our ways, so that we shall see much more of His wisdom, power, goodness, and truth than formerly we have been acquainted with. We shall find that the God of Israel is among us, when He shall make us a praise and glory, that man shall say of succeeding plantations, "The Lord make it like that of

New England." For we must consider that we shall be as a city upon a hill, and the eyes of all people are upon us. So that if we shall deal falsely with our God in this work we have undertaken and so cause Him to withdraw His present help from us, we shall be made a story and a byword through the world. We shall open the mouths of enemies to speak evil of the ways of God and all professors for God's sake. We shall shame the faces of many of God's worthy servants, and cause their prayers to be turned into curses upon us till we be consumed out of the good land whither we are going. And to shut up this discourse with that exhortation of Moses, that faithful servant of the Lord, in his last farewell to Israel, Deuteronomy 30: Beloved there is now set before us life and good, death and evil in that we are commanded this day to love the Lord our God, and to love one another, to walk in his ways, and to keep his Commandments and His ordinance and His laws and the articles of our Covenant with Him that we may live and be multiplied, and that the Lord our God may bless us in the land whither we go to possess it. But if our hearts shall turn away so that we will not obey, but shall be seduced and worship other gods, our pleasures and profits, and serve them, it is propounded unto us this day, we shall surely perish out of the good land whither we pass over this vast sea to possess it.

> Therefore, let us choose life,
> that we, and our seed,
> may live; by obeying His
> voice, and cleaving to Him,
> for He is our life, and
> our posterity.

2 / John Winthrop
Little Speech on Liberty

(1645)

I also acknowledge the justice of the court, and, for mine own part, I am well satisfied. I was publicly charged, and I am publicly and legally acquitted, which is all I did expect or desire. And though this be sufficient for my justification before men, yet not so before the God ... It may be of some good

---

John Winthrop, "Little Speech on Liberty," James Savage, ed., *The History of New England from 1630 to 1649. By John Winthrop, esq., "Winthrop's Journal"* (Boston, 1826), vol. II, pp. 228–30.

use, to inform and rectify the judgments of some of the people, and may prevent such distempers as have arisen amongst us. The great questions that have troubled the country, are about the authority of the magistrates and the liberty of the people. It is yourselves who have called us to this office, and being called by you, we have our authority from God, in way of an ordinance, such as hath the image of God eminently stamped upon it, the contempt and violation whereof hath been vindicated with examples of divine vengeance. I entreat you to consider, that when you choose magistrates, you take them from among yourselves, men subject to like passions as you are. Therefore when you see infirmities in us, you should reflect upon your own, and that would make you bear the more with us, and not be severe censurers of the failings of your magistrates, when you have continual experience of the like infirmities in yourselves and others ... The covenant between you and us is the oath you have taken of us, which is to this purpose, that we shall govern you and judge your causes by the rules of God's laws and our own, according to our best skill. When you agree with a workman to build you a ship or house, etc., he undertakes as well for his skill as for his faithfulness, for it is his profession, and you pay him for both. But when you call one to be a magistrate, he doth not profess nor undertake to have sufficient skill for that office, nor can you furnish him with gifts, etc., therefore you must run the hazard of his skill and ability. But if he fail in faithfulness, which by his oath he is bound unto, that he must answer for. If it fall out that the case be clear to common apprehension, and the rule clear also, if he transgress here, the error is not in the skill, but in the evil of the will: it must be required of him. But if the case be doubtful, or the rule doubtful, to men of such understanding and parts as your magistrates are, if your magistrates should err here, yourselves must bear it.

For the other point concerning liberty, I observe a great mistake in the country about that. There is a twofold liberty, natural (I mean as our nature is now corrupt) and civil or federal. The first is common to man with beasts and other creatures. By this, man ... hath liberty to do what he lists; it is a liberty to evil as well as to good. This liberty is incompatible and inconsistent with authority, and cannot endure the least restraint of the most just authority ... The other kind of liberty I call civil or federal; this liberty is the proper end and object of authority, and cannot subsist without it; and it is a liberty to that only which is good, just, and honest. On the other side, ye know who they are that complain of this yoke and say, let us break their bands, etc., we will not have this man to rule over us. Even so, brethren, it will be between you and your magistrates. If you stand for your natural corrupt liberties, and will do what is good in your own eyes, you will not endure the least weight of authority, but will murmur, and oppose, and be always striving to shake off that yoke; but if you will be satisfied to enjoy such civil and lawful liberties, such as Christ allows you, then will you quietly and cheerfully submit unto that authority which is set over you, in all the administrations of it, for your good. Wherein, if we fail at any time, we hope we shall be willing (by God's assistance) to hearken to good advice from any of you, or in any other way of God; so shall your liberties be preserved, in upholding the honor and power of authority amongst you.

3 / William Penn
Pennsylvania Frame of Government

(1682)

When the great and wise God had made the world, of all his creatures it pleased him to choose man his deputy to rule it, and to fit him for so great a charge and trust he did not only qualify him with skill and power, but with integrity to use them justly. This native goodness was equally his honour and his happiness, and whilst he stood here, all went well; there was no need of coercive or compulsive means; the precept of divine love and truth in his bosom was the guide and keeper of his innocency. But lust prevailing against duty, made a lamentable breach upon it, and the law that before had no power over him, took place upon him and his disobedient posterity, that such as would not live conformable to the holy law within, should fall under the reproof and correction of the just law without, in a judicial administration.

This the apostle teaches us in divers of his epistles. The law (says he) was added because of transgression; in another place, knowing that the law was not made for the righteous man but for the disobedient and ungodly, for sinners, for unholy and profane, for murderers, for whoremongers, for them that defile themselves with mankind, and for menstealers, for liars, for perjured persons, etc. But this is not all. He opens and carries the matter of government a little further: let every soul be subject to the higher powers for there is no power but of God. The powers that be are ordained of God: whosoever therefore resisteth the power, resisteth the ordinance of God. For rulers are not a terror to good works, but to evil; wilt thou then not be afraid of the power? Do that which is good, and thou shalt have praise of the same. He is the minister of God to thee for good. Wherefore ye must needs be subject, not only for wrath, but for conscience' sake.

This settles the divine right of government beyond exception, and that for two ends: first, to terrify evil-doers; secondly, to cherish those that do well, which gives government a life beyond corruption and makes it as durable in the world as good men shall be. So that government seems to me a part of

From *Minutes of the Provincial Council of Pennsylvania*, 10 vols. (Philadelphia and Harrisburg, 1852–1853), vol. I, pp. 29–32.

religion itself, a thing sacred in its institution and end. For if it does not directly remove the cause, it crushes the effects of evil, and is as such (though a lower yet) an emanation of the same Divine Power that is both author and object of pure religion; the difference lying here, that the one is more free and mental, the other more corporal and compulsive in its operations, but that is only to evil-doers; government itself being otherwise as capable of kindness, goodness and charity as a more private society. They weakly err that think there is no other use of government than correction, which is the coarsest part of it; daily experience tells us that the care and regulation of many other affairs more soft and daily necessary make up much the greatest part of government and which must have followed the peopling of the world had Adam never fell, and will continue among men on earth under the highest attainments they may arrive at, by the coming of the blessed second Adam, the Lord from heaven. Thus much of government in general, as to its rise and end.

For particular frames and models it will become me to say little, and comparatively I will say nothing. My reasons are: first, that the age is too nice and difficult for it, there being nothing the wits of men are more busy and divided upon. 'Tis true, they seem to agree in the end, to wit, happiness, but in the means they differ as to divine, so to this human felicity, and the cause is much the same, not always want of light and knowledge, but want of using them rightly. Men side with their passions against their reason, and their sinister interests have so strong a bias upon their minds that they lean to them against the good of the things they know.

Secondly, I do not find a model in the world that time, place, and some singular emergences have not necessarily altered; nor is it easy to frame a civil government that shall serve all places alike.

Thirdly, I know what is said by the several admirers of monarchy, aristocracy and democracy, which are the rule of one, a few, and many, and are the three common ideas of government, when men discourse on that subject. But I choose to solve the controversy with this small distinction, and it belongs to all three: any government is free to the people under it (whatever be the frame) where the laws rule, and the people are a party to those laws, and more than this is tyranny, oligarchy, and confusion.

But lastly, when all is said, there is hardly one frame of government in the world so ill designed by its first founders that in good hands would not do well enough, and history tells us the best in ill ones can do nothing that is great or good; witness the Jewish and Roman states. Governments, like clocks, go from the motion men give them, and as governments are made and moved by men, so by them they are ruined too. Wherefore governments rather depend upon men than men upon governments. Let men be good, and the government cannot be bad; if it be ill, they will cure it. But if men be bad, let the government be never so good, they will endeavour to warp and spoil to their turn.

I know some say, let us have good laws and no matter for the men that execute them. But let them consider that though good laws do well, good men do better; for good laws may want good men, and be abolished or invaded by ill men; but good men will never want good laws, nor suffer ill ones ...

... we have (with reverence to God and good conscience to men) to the best of our skill, contrived and composed the FRAME and LAWS of this government to the great end of all government, viz., to support power in reverence with the people and to secure the people from the abuse of power, that they may be free by their just obedience, and the magistrates honourable for their just administration; for liberty without obedience is confusion, and obedience without liberty is slavery.

4 / Perry Miller
The Puritan State and Puritan Society

(1956)

The Puritan theory of the state began with the hypothesis of original sin. Had Adam transmitted undiminished to his descendants the image of God in which he had been created, no government would ever have been necessary among men; they would all then have done justice to each other without the supervision of a judge, they would have respected each other's rights without the intervention of a policeman. But the Bible said—and experience proved—that since the Fall, without the policeman, the judge, the jail, the law, and the magistrate, men will rob, murder, and fight among themselves; without a coercive state to restrain evil impulses and administer punishments, no life will be safe, no property secure, no honor observed. Therefore, upon Adam's apostasy, God Himself instituted governments among men. He left the particular form to be determined by circumstance—this was one important human art on which the Puritans said the Bible was not an absolute and imperious lawgiver—but He enacted that all men should be under some sort of corporate rule, that they should all submit to the sway of their superiors, that no man should live apart from his fellows, that the government should have full power to enforce obedience and to inflict every punishment that the crimes of men deserved.

There was, it is true, a strong element of individualism in the Puritan creed; every man had to work out his own salvation, each soul had to face his maker alone. But at the same time, the Puritan philosophy demanded that in

Perry Miller, *Errand Into the Wilderness*, Cambridge, Mass.: The Belknap Press of Harvard University Press, Copyright 1956 by the President and Fellows of Harvard College, pp. 142–147. Reprinted by permission of the publishers.

society all men, at least all regenerate men, be marshaled into one united array. The lone horseman, the single trapper, the solitary hunter was not a figure of the Puritan frontier; Puritans moved in groups and towns, settled in whole communities, and maintained firm government over all units. Neither were the individualistic business man, the shopkeeper who seized every opportunity to enlarge his profits, the speculator who contrived to gain wealth at the expense of his fellows, neither were these typical figures of the original Puritan society. Puritan opinion was at the opposite pole from Jefferson's feeling that the best government governs as little as possible. The theorists of New England thought of society as a unit, bound together by inviolable ties; they thought of it not as an aggregation of individuals but as an organism, functioning for a definite purpose, with all parts subordinate to the whole, all members contributing a definite share, every person occupying a particular status. "Society in all sorts of humane affaires is better than Solitariness," said John Cotton. The society of early New England was decidedly "regimented." Puritans did not think that the state was merely an umpire, standing on the side lines of a contest, limited to checking egregious fouls but otherwise allowing men free play according to their abilities and the breaks of the game. They would have expected laissez faire to result in a reign of rapine and horror. The state to them was an active instrument of leadership, discipline, and, wherever necessary, of coercion; it legislated over any or all aspects of human behavior, it not merely regulated misconduct but undertook to inspire and direct all conduct. The commanders were not to trim their policies by the desires of the people, but to drive ahead upon the predetermined course; the people were all to turn out as they were ordered, and together they were to crowd sail to the full capacity of the vessel. The officers were above the common men, as the quarter-deck is above the forecastle. There was no idea of the equality of all men. There was no questioning that men who would not serve the purposes of the society should be whipped into line. The objectives were clear and unmistakable; any one's disinclination to dedicate himself to them was obviously so much recalcitrancy and depravity. The government of Massachusetts, and of Connecticut as well, was a dictatorship, and never pretended to be anything else; it was a dictatorship, not of a single tyrant, or of an economic class, or of a political faction, but of the holy and regenerate. Those who did not hold with the ideals entertained by the righteous, or who believed God had preached other principles, or who desired that in religious belief, morality, and ecclesiastical preferences all men should be left at liberty to do as they wished—such persons had every liberty, as Nathaniel Ward said, to stay away from New England. If they did come, they were expected to keep their opinions to themselves; if they discussed them in public or attempted to act upon them, they were exiled; if they persisted in returning, they were cast out again, if they still came back, as did four Quakers, they were hanged on Boston Common. And from the Puritan point of view, it was good riddance.

These views of the nature and function of the state were not peculiar to the Puritans of New England; they were the heritage of the past, the ideals, if not always the actuality, of the previous centuries. That government was established by God in order to save depraved men from their own depravity had been orthodox Christian teaching for centuries; that men should be arranged in serried ranks, inferiors obeying superiors, was the essence of feudalism; that men should live a social life, that profit-making should be restrained within the limits of the "just price," that the welfare of the whole took precedence over any individual advantage, was the doctrine of the medieval church, and of the Church of England in the early seventeenth century. Furthermore, in addition to these general principles, there were two or three more doctrines in the New England philosophy which also were common to the age and the background: all the world at that moment believed with them that the church was to be maintained and protected by the civil authority, and a certain part of the world was contending that government must be limited by fundamental law and that it takes its origin from the consent of the people.

Every respectable state in the Western world assumed that it could allow only one church to exist within its borders, that every citizen should be compelled to attend it and conform to its requirements, and that all inhabitants should pay taxes for its support. When the Puritans came to New England the idea had not yet dawned that a government could safely permit several creeds to exist side by side within the confines of a single nation. They had not been fighting in England for any milk-and-water toleration, and had they been offered such religious freedom as dissenters now enjoy in Great Britain they would have scorned to accept the terms. Only a hypocrite, a person who did not really believe what he professed, would be content to practice his religion under those conditions. The Puritans were assured that they alone knew the exact truth, as it was contained in the written word of God, and they were fighting to enthrone it in England and to extirpate utterly and mercilessly all other pretended versions of Christianity. When they could not succeed at home, they came to America, where they could establish a society in which the one and only truth should reign forever. There is nothing so idle as to praise the Puritans for being in any sense conscious or deliberate pioneers of religious liberty—unless, indeed, it is still more idle to berate them because in America they persecuted dissenters for their beliefs after themselves had undergone persecution for differing with the bishops. To allow no dissent from the truth was exactly the reason they had come to America. They maintained here precisely what they had maintained in England, and if they exiled, fined, jailed, whipped, or hanged those who disagreed with them in New England, they would have done the same thing in England could they have secured the power. It is almost pathetic to trace the puzzlement of New England leaders at the end of the seventeenth century, when the idea of toleration was becoming more and more respectable in European thought.

They could hardly understand what was happening in the world, and they could not for a long time be persuaded that they had any reason to be ashamed of their record of so many Quakers whipped, blasphemers punished by the amputation of ears, Antinomians exiled, Anabaptists fined, or witches executed. By all the lights which had prevailed in Europe at the time the Puritans had left, these were achievements to which any government could point with pride. In 1681 a congregation of Anabaptists, who led a stormy and precarious existence for several years in Charlestown, published an attack upon the government of Massachusetts Bay; they justified themselves by appealing to the example of the first settlers, claiming that like themselves the founders had been nonconformists and had fled to New England to establish a refuge for persecuted consciences. When Samuel Willard, minister of the Third Church in Boston, read this, he could hardly believe his eyes; he hastened to assure the authors that they did not know what they were talking about:

> I perceive they are mistaken in the design of our first Planters, whose business was not Toleration; but were professed Enemies of it, and could leave the World professing they died no Libertines. Their business was to settle, and (as much as in them lay) secure Religion to Posterity, according to that way which they believed was of God.

For the pamphlet in which Willard penned these lines Increase Mather wrote an approving preface. Forty years later, he and his son Cotton participated in the ordination of a Baptist minister in Boston, and he then preached on the need for harmony between differing sects. But by that time much water had gone under the bridge, the old charter had been revoked, there was danger that the Church of England might be made the established church of the colonies, theology had come to be of less importance in men's minds than morality, the tone of the eighteenth century was beginning to influence opinion—even in Boston. Increase was old and weary. Puritanism, in the true sense of the word, was dead.

Of course, the whole Puritan philosophy of church and state rested upon the assumption that the Word of God was clear and explicit, that the divines had interpreted it correctly, and that no one who was not either a knave or a fool could deny their demonstrations. Ergo, it seemed plain, those who did deny them should be punished for being obstinate. John Cotton said that offenders should not be disciplined for their wrong opinions, but for persisting in them; he said that Roger Williams was turned out of Massachusetts not for his conscience but for sinning against his own conscience. Roger Williams and John Cotton debated the question of "persecution" through several hundred pages; after they had finished, I think it is very doubtful whether Cotton had even begun to see his adversary's point. And still today it is hard to make clear the exact grounds upon which Roger Williams became the great apostle of religious liberty. Williams was not, like Thomas Jefferson, a man to whom theology and divine grace had become stuff and nonsense; on the contrary he was pious with a fervor and passion that went beyond most of his contemporaries. So exalted was his conception of the spiritual life that he could not bear to have it polluted with earthly considerations. He did not believe that any man could determine the precise intention of Scripture with such dreadful certainty as the New England clergy claimed to possess. Furthermore, it seemed to him that even if their version were true, submission to truth itself was worth nothing at all when forced upon men by the sword. Williams evolved from an orthodox Puritan into the champion of religious liberty because he came to see spiritual truth as so rare, so elevated, so supernal a loveliness that it could not be chained to a worldly establishment and a vested interest. He was a libertarian because he contemned the world, and he wanted to separate church and state so that the church would not be contaminated by the state; Thomas Jefferson loved the world and was dubious about the spirit, and he sought to separate church and state so that the state would not be contaminated by the church. But John Cotton believed that the state and church were partners in furthering the cause of truth; he knew that the truth was clear, definite, reasonable, and undeniable; he expected all good men to live by it voluntarily, and he was sure that all men who did not do so were obviously bad man. Bad men were criminals, whether their offense was theft or a belief in the "inner light," and they should be punished. Moses and Aaron, the priest and the statesman, were equally the vice-regents of God, and the notion that one could contaminate the other was utter insanity.

The two other ideas derived from the background of the age, rule by fundamental law and the social compact, were also special tenets of English Puritanism. For three decades before the settlement of Massachusetts the Puritan party in England had been working hand in glove with the Parliament against the King. The absolutist Stuarts were allied with the bishops, and the Puritan agitator and the Parliamentary leader made common cause against them both. As a result of this combination, the Puritan theorists had taken over the essentials of the Parliamentary conception of society, the contention that the power of the ruler should be exercised in accordance with established fundamental law, and that the government should owe its existence to a compact of the governed. Because these ideas were strategically invaluable in England, they became ingrained in the Puritan consciousness; they were carried to the New England wilderness and were preached from every pulpit in the land.

The Puritans did not see any conflict between them and their religious intentions. In New England the fundamental law was the Bible. The magistrates were to have full power to rule men for the specific purposes to which the society was dedicated; but they as well as their subordinates were tied to the specific purposes, and could not go beyond the prescribed limits. The Bible was clear and definite on the form of the church, on the code of punishments for crimes, on the general purposes of social existence; its specifications were binding on all, magistrates, ministers, and citizens. Consequently, the Puritans did not find it difficult to conclude that in those matters upon which the Bible left men free to follow their own discretion, the society itself should establish basic rules. The New England leaders and the people frequently disagreed about what these rules were, or how detailed they should be made, but neither side ever doubted that the community must abide by whatever laws had been enacted, either by God or by the state. The government of New England was, as I have said, a dictatorship, but the dictators were not absolute and irresponsible. John Cotton was the clerical spokesman for the Massachusetts rulers, but he stoutly demanded "that all power that is on earth be limited."

The belief that government originated in the consent of the governed was equally congenial to the Puritan creed. The theology is often enough described as deterministic, because it held that men were predestined to Heaven or Hell; but we are always in danger of forgetting that the life of the Puritan was completely voluntaristic. The natural man was indeed bound in slavery to sin and unable to make exertions toward his own salvation; but the man into whose soul grace had been infused was liberated from that bondage and made free to undertake the responsibilities and obligations of virtue and decency. The holy society was erected upon the belief that the right sort of men could of their own free will and choice carry through the creation and administration of the right sort of community. The churches of New England were made up of "saints," who came into the church because they wanted membership, not because they were born in it, or were forced into it, or joined because of policy and convention. Though every resident was obliged to attend and to pay taxes for the support of the churches, no one became an actual member who did not signify his strong desire to be one. The saints were expected to act positively because they had in them a spirit of God that made them capable of every exertion. No doubt the Puritans maintained that government originated in the consent of the people because that theory was an implement for chastening the absolutism of the Stuarts; but they maintained it also because they did not believe that any society, civil or ecclesiastical, into which men did not enter of themselves was worthy of the name.

5 / Sydney E. Ahlstrom
Puritanism and Democratic Citizenship

(1963)

Despite their views of man's Fall, [Puritans] faced the World with a "conversionist" (or transformationist) attitude. The Puritan sought to control and subdue the lawlessness of men; and he was emboldened by his faith in God's power and providence to feel that such a feat was possible wherever God's call to action was clearly heard and decisively answered. He thus faced culture and the state with a realistic kind of optimism; the world was the theater of God's redemptive activity. It could be humbled and disciplined. That each true Christian was a predestined instrument in this cause, and that his "city on a hill" figured concretely in God's plan for redeeming the world, only strengthened him in his zeal.

Possibly most operative in the formation of latter-day civic or social attitudes was the Puritan's awe-filled concern for God's almighty will, His Law. Thomas Hooker formulated this concern in the second of the three heads of his famous sermon to the Connecticut Court: "The privilege of election, which belongs to the people, therefore, must not be exercised according to their humours, but according to the blessed will and law of God." Even this assertion would be little more than a pious platitude had the Puritans not made it an operative factor in society. But this they did. The Puritan was a legalist . . . On the Law of Moses they meditated long and often; ancient Israel, indeed, was a kind of legal model for them. As for the gospel, the message of the New Testament, here was the Law of Christ. Covenant obligations at the heart of the Puritan's scheme of salvation were stated in terms of law. The Puritan was steeped in a concern for law. Nowhere more than in the Bible Commonwealth would "antinominianism" (i.e. opposition to the law) be viewed with holy horror!

It followed that the Puritan viewed other-worldliness and forthright statements of "Christian freedom" with alarm. God's law was both judge and teacher. It was God's way of ordering his world and controlling man's sinfulness. It was also His dread means of exposing man's sinful shortcomings, of bringing man to "legal terrors," repentance, and humiliation. It was finally a guide for the true Christian in his search for holiness. A "God-fearing man" was thus a law-abiding man in the deepest, most thorough

Sydney E. Ahlstrom, "Thomas Hooker—Puritanism and Democratic Citizenship," *Church History*, XXXII (December, 1963), pp. 425–429. Reprinted with permission of author and publisher. Footnotes omitted by permission. For a more extended discussion see Sydney E. Ahlstrom, "The Puritan Ethic and the Spirit of American Democracy," in George L. Hunt, ed., *Calvinism and the Political Order* (Philadelphia: The Westminster Press, 1965), Ch. 5.

sense of the term ... Thus all men were to be brought and kept under the law by the state, by the church, by the ministry, and by the visible saints ...

One of the distinctive features of Reformed legalism was the powerful way in which man's Christian duty was expressed through the doctrine of vocation. Christian obedience was defined not in terms of otherworldly counsels of perfection but of a person's calling within the instituted structure of the Creation—the family, the state, the church, the market place, etc.—each with its disciplines, demands, and laws. The Christian's place was in the world. In time this doctrine of vocation became almost the way, the truth, and the life, working with immense power on the individual's sense of duty and on his performance in the calling.

Ineluctably, however, the doctrine would be secularized. By a steady, half-noticed process it would be drained of its corollaries in piety ... Lamented Cotton Mather: "Religion brought forth prosperity, and the daughter destroyed the mother." "Legal terrors" were no longer felt by law-abiding, dutiful men. Those whom Schneider calls the "Ungodly Puritans," men such as Benjamin Franklin, had left their piety behind; they could forget about being "a new man in Christ" and live by the code. ... One may observe, therefore, a steady line of progression from the Puritan doctrine of vocation to the Yankee gospel of work and from that, in due course, to the Gilded Age's gospel of wealth ... The incipiency of this secularizing, yet immensely powerful, practical tendency is one of the most notable features of Puritanism. As Max Weber contended, moreover, Puritan vocational doctrines bore an affinity to capitalism that helps account for their joint penetration of American life and ideals.

The matter cannot be left here, however. To conclude that Puritan ethics was merely a matter of imbuing men with a compulsion to work, turn profits, and increase productivity would be the worst kind of caricature. Puritanism could never countenance individualism in its full and anarchistic sense. It regularly exhibited a profound public concern; it retained the idea of a "community of righteousness." It did not shrug problems of the state. Its piety led to Bible Commonwealths and Holy Experiments ...

The calling of the Christian man, moreover, was as much to responsible citizenship in a well-ordered commonwealth as to steadfast performance in the market place, though it is the latter duty that has received so much scholarly attention. A man was led to serve God and neighbor in and through his vocation as citizen or magistrate no less than as cobbler or tradesman ... And in this context the importance of one's *civic* vocation was vastly increased. The Puritan doctrine, in other words, contributes to the very essence of American citizenship ...

It is not at all mysterious that men should move in this direction. Neither is it strange, considering the moral intensity and traditionary force of the whole Puritan ethos, that men should continue to propagate and live by the secularized principles with the same vigor and austerity. Puritanism thus can almost be said to have offered itself as a sacrifice to responsible citizenship. It was enormously influential almost *because* it was secularized . . .

In conclusion let me recur to my major theme: the cruciality of the *nomos motif* in Puritan life and thought and the direct relation of this legalism to the movement's impact on the sense of civic responsibility of latter-day Americans. In this perspective more than any other we see Connecticut's "founder" in a vital relationship to a fundamental feature of American democracy. Legalism, broadly speaking, was the Achilles' Heel of Puritanism. In several ways it guaranteed the movement's declension and transformation. Yet, the Puritan's concern for law, duty, and civil obligation—the calling to citizenship and the citizen's concern for the commonwealth—was negotiable. It could be secularized but not easily or quickly extinguished.

Americans are not paragons of civisme, yet, comparatively speaking, they have grounds for a modest measure of pride. To that extent they are justly indebted to Thomas Hooker and his Puritan brethren.

6 / Frederick B. Tolles
The Two Plantations

(1948)

As the first Quaker colonists set sail for Pennsylvania in 1682, they carried with them sober words of advice and caution from George Fox, founder of the Society of Friends: "My friends, that are gone, and are going over to plant, and make outward plantations in America, keep your own plantations in your hearts, with the spirit and power of God, that your own vines and lilies will be not hurt.". . .

The typical experience of the early Quaker was, however, no Nirvanic contemplation, no *via negativa* leading to ecstatic absorption in the Godhead. The religious temper of primitive Quakerism was not mysticism in the classical sense, but rather what contemporaries in fear and scorn called "enthusiasm." It was activism, not quietism. In their religious experience George Fox and his compeers had more in common with the Hebrew prophets than with the great mystics of the Church. There was a strong prophetic strain in the preaching of the early Quakers. They traveled about England in the power of the Spirit, calling men off from the sins and vanities of the world, exhorting them

Frederick B. Tolles, *Meeting House and Counting House: The Quaker Merchants of Colonial Philadelphia* (Chapel Hill: The University of North Carolina Press for The Institute of Early American History and Culture, 1948) pp. 3, 5–7, 9–10. Reprinted without footnotes by permission of the publisher.

to be faithful to the Inward Light of Christ. In their insistent dwelling upon the moral demands of the Christian religion, they yielded nothing to Puritan prophets of righteousness.

Indeed the early Friends went beyond their Puritan contemporaries in this respect. They were frankly perfectionist in their ethical teachings. They insisted that the Holy Spirit enabled men to overcome the disabilities of the body of sin and death and to live in accordance with the injunctions of the Sermon on the Mount, not in a future Kingdom of Heaven but here and now in this world of flesh and blood . . .

The possibility of turning to the Light and thereby entering upon a state of sinless perfection was not limited to a small body of the elect. There was "that of God" in every man, Jew or Gentile, bond or free; and the Friends often quoted the words of John: "That there was the true light which lighteth every man that cometh into the world." The Friends of the first generation took literally the universalistic implications of their faith and set out to bring the whole world to the inward teacher, not overlooking the Pope and the Grand Turk. It was only later, when the pristine evangelical ardor had cooled, that the Society of Friends abandoned its global outreach and concentrated upon perfecting the spiritual life of a "peculiar people."

The religious faith of the Quaker immigrants to Pennsylvania thus represented an equilibrium of four elements: mysticism, prophetism, perfectionism, and universalism. These four strains, each with its peculiar spiritual dynamic, mingled to produce a religious compound of extraordinary potency. By virtue of this equilibrium and of the organizing genius of its founder, Quakerism achieved a stability and survival power not given to most of the other sects of Commonwealth England.

The Quakerism of the immigrants is misconstrued, however, if it is regarded as rampant individualism or anarchism in religion. Since the God from whom each private revelation came was forever *one*, there could be no final disharmony between the light vouchsafed to one individual and that of any other truly enlightened person, including the prophets and apostles who recorded their revelations in the Bible. Moreover, the Spirit of God as experienced in corporate worship was felt as a unifying power, binding the worshippers together in love and unity . . . So far did Friends carry their conviction that God revealed himself to groups that in their monthly, quarterly, and yearly meetings for discipline they acted always in accordance with the "sense of the meeting" as gathered by a clerk; the corporate judgment thus reached was regarded as having greater validity than the often imperfect and clouded light of an individual. This strong sense of community, arising in the first instance out of the common experience of the divine presence, and fostered by persecution, which drove Friends in upon themselves, offset the centrifugal tendencies inherent in the doctrine of the Inner Light, and substituted an organic social theory for one that might otherwise have been wholly atomistic. For the Quakers who settled Pennsylvania, the solidarity generated by the intangible but deeply felt presence of the Spirit was as real and as effectual as that represented by the outward covenants of the Puritans. As with the Mennonites and other groups in the Anabaptist tradition, however, there was an exclusive aspect to the "holy community" which presently came to overshadow the sense of world mission.

. . . Identifying divine law primarily with the Sermon on the Mount, they regarded its ethics of love and non-resistance as literally binding upon them as followers of Christ and dwellers in the Light. With this Anabaptist position, however, they combined the essentially Calvinistic conviction that religion must be integrated with life on the natural plane; in other words, they recognized no cleavage between the spheres of divine and natural law. Unwilling at this stage to withdraw, Mennonite-fashion, behind protecting walls thrown up around the *Gemeinschaft*, Quakers participated actively in politics wherever they were not disqualified by law or excluded by popular prejudice. In 1682 William Penn expressed the conviction that government was "a part of religion itself, a thing sacred in its institution and end." For the early Quakers there was but one morality for the individual and for the state, and that was dictated by the uncompromising demands of the Gospel. During the seventy-five years of Quaker rule in Pennsylvania this faith in the practical applicability of the Sermon on the Mount to the governing of men was to be subject to severe tensions . . .

7 / Darrett B. Rutman
Winthrop's Boston

(1965)

Much has been written of Puritanism in America, as though somehow it had injected a constant factor into the moving stream of history. But in the beginning, if one is to judge from the vantage point of Boston, there was no Puritan way, no constant to be injected, merely actions, reactions, interactions . . . If what eventually emerged was uniquely American—and Americans regularly seek to explain their peculiarities—it was only because one found here a continuing juxtaposition of varied elements which could not be duplicated elsewhere . . .

Darrett B. Rutman, *Winthrop's Boston: Portrait of a Puritan Town* (Chapel Hill: The University of North Carolina Press for the Institute of Early American History and Culture, 1965) pp. 274–277. Reprinted by permission of the publisher.

What emerged from the succession of actions and counteractions in early Massachusetts? A peculiar Puritan state? A Bible commonwealth? An oligarchy to be disposed of in the latter half of the century? Historians have written in such terms, but they are meaningless. They neither fit the facts that one finds in Winthrop's Boston nor establish a basis upon which to proceed through American history. One can find, however, certain institutions, practices, and attitudes emerging in the town and exemplifying general tendencies observable in subsequent periods. Some have long been recognized: the town form of government, congregationalism, a concern for the young, and the beginnings of public education. Others are less obvious.

There is individualism and the pursuit by the individual of his own material well-being. Indeed, it confronts even the casual observer of the Boston scene. And while one is inclined to bemoan the materialism and the individualism which so regularly thwarted the Governor's concern for the community and marked the decline of his ideal, the definition of social good in terms of the well-being of the free individual was to be the way of the future, a new ideal. Of course, the assumptions of the Massachusetts Bay society, as voiced from the pulpit and magistrate's bench, still reflected the idealized community; not for over a hundred years would the individual be so ardently idealized. But the reality of New England was changing faster than its assumptions.

One finds an abiding, pervasive morality in the town. Although the Bostonian was solicitous for his own advancement in the world, and he tended to ignore the arbitrary morality demanded by the ministers, the proper cut of one's hair, for example, when the church lamented the mode of wearing it long, nevertheless the pulpit and the law—the latter through the misguided notion that moral conduct can be precisely legislated—had their effect. Also important in strengthening morality was the very nearness to God of the seventeenth-century man, for whom the divine presence was made more awful by the strenuous preaching of the New England minister. With few exceptions, the Bostonian was ever concerned with his soul. He was, however, defining salvation in terms of the moral and good life and thus establishing at that early date the climate from which emerged Benjamin Franklin's dictates about frugality, industry, and prudence. The easiest way to heaven for the Bostonian of the seventeenth century was essentially the way of Franklin in the eighteenth . . .

One finds a separation of church and state, too, for though the two were linked throughout the period—the elders of the churches constituting a pressure group, soliciting protection, advising, cajoling, the civil authorities ever responsive to their pressure—the church and the state were irrevocably drifting apart. In the early 1650's the separation was symbolized by the removal of town and commonwealth government from Boston's meeting-house, where the General Court and town meetings had previously gathered, to a newly completed Town House. The medieval unity of church and state, their existence as but two facets of the same society, was disappearing. The church in Boston in the 1640's consciously embraced only a part of the population; and with the multiplying of churches after 1650, with their diversity in matters of doctrine (the First and Third Churches divided on the issue of the half-way covenant), any single church included only a fraction of the town. Moreover, church and state had varied concerns. Both played vital roles, being the separate poles around which the community revolved. But the concern of the church—both in the sense of one congregation and in the sense of the synodical union of churches—was increasingly its own denominational purity, the accenting of God's truth, even though the elders could not agree upon truth, for its own sake rather than for the sake of the community. To an extent the church busied itself about the doings and misdoings of its communicants, even attempting to extend its sway within the community by compromising purity and practicality in that movement culminating in the half-way covenant. Reflecting the way of its communicants, its sermons more and more stressed conduct and morality and less and less God's free grace. Yet from the latter 1630's it tended to ignore the broad social role of organized religion insofar as the whole community was concerned. Within the walls of the church, within its ever more formal, more institutional framework, the Bostonians periodically sought communion with God, but life itself was being lived outside.

As the church tended to withdraw from life, the secular authorities of both town and commonwealth assumed a broader and broader social function ... But in part, too, necessity required the assumption of social functions ... Within this fragmented society, where long-established relationships were nonexistent, where families were disrupted, where the church itself was a divisive element, where materialism and individualism were tending toward social chaos, only the secular authority—the political organization of society—could unite, could define the relationships of one individual to another. It was, in effect, becoming the grand arbiter that it is in theory today, the impartial, amoral arbiter regulating in order to avoid collisions as the members of society followed their individual yet concentric orbits.

8 / Gary B. Nash
Pennsylvania Quakers: Dynamics of Instability

(1968)

No more dramatic symbol of the failure of the Quaker polity in Pennsylvania could be found that the Keithian schism [1692–1693].[1] For more than a decade, since their first arrival in 1682, Quakers had wrestled with the problem of political disunity and social instability. Now the fires of contention had spread to the religious community itself.

For historians this decay of Quaker solidarity has proved a thorny problem. Why should the Quakers, released from persecution in England and given a government of their own in a fertile, strategically located river valley, fall prey to political and religious guerrilla warfare? Why should the shared values, the common outlook, the sense of community which had solidified Quakers in England, provide so little cohesive force in Pennsylvania? Most historians have skirted the issue, either taking little account of the chronic friction of the early years or passing it off as a kind of prodromal sign of eighteenth-century revolutionary democracy . . .

In the end, no fruitful attempt can be made to rank precisely the factors which contributed to Quaker instability in Pennsylvania. The anti-authoritarian strain in the Quaker makeup and the unstructured nature of the society seem of particular importance. But it is more significant that all of these factors interpenetrated so that no single thread in the cloth of Quaker experience can be entirely separated from the others. The crucial point is that almost all of the elements which distinguished the Quaker's existencc in Pennsylvania from his life in England seemed to promote rather than restrain the atomistic component in his cultural pattern. The vastness of the wilderness and the availability of cheap land tended to break down the sense of corporateness while at the same time complicating the disciplinary functions of the Monthly Meeting. The utopian hopes raised by Penn led to inevitable dissillusionment, for they elevated expectations to a level that could never be fulfilled. The unprecedented access to office which the Quakers enjoyed led to a scramble for position and place as men sought to achieve what had been beyond their remotest hopes in England. And, ironically, that absence of persecution deprived the Quakers in Pennsylvania of an important annealing force which

Gary B. Nash, *Quakers and Politics: Pennsylvania, 1681–1726.* Copyright © 1968 by Princeton University Press, pp. 161, 178–180. Reprinted by permission of the publisher. Footnotes omitted by permission.
[1] Led by George Keith (1638–1716) a Scots Quaker and Philadelphia schoolmaster who sought a comprehensive creed and more emphasis on the Bible to combat the centrifugal tendencies present in Pennsylvania. However, the support Keith received among Quakers stemmed more from economic and political tensions than from sympathy with his theological innovations. (ed. note)

had operated in England. In the Old World the Quakers' insularity was a form of self-protection and a source of unity. But in Pennsylvania, where they represented the dominant culture, Quakers had no need to cling together in mutual defense. In England a side-effect of persecution was fusion; in Pennsylvania the absence of persecution contributed to fission. In England Quakers looked inward; in Pennsylvania they looked outward. Anti-authoritarian tendencies and the psychological effects of the wilderness put insupportable burdens on institutions which were inherently frail, and fragile institutions encouraged resistance to authority.

Religious values, though of great importance in sustaining the Quaker community, could never overcome entirely the atomizing tendencies of life in Pennsylvania or stifle the immoderate quest for political and economic advantage. Just as the leading Quakers who gathered around Thomas Lloyd had initially opposed Penn's proprietary circle and later overpowered his deputy governor, the lesser men in the colony, as if forgetful of the Old World concept of an ordered society, now sought to curb the power of the ruling group. Ultimately, controversy in the secular sphere spilled over into the inner sanctum of the Society of Friends—the last preserve of unity in Pennsylvania. Keith's doctrinal crusade against the Quaker leaders was deeply intellectual in its origins; but for his followers it came to represent a means of responding to unfavorable economic and political conditions which seemed to them to stem from self-interest in the Lloydian circle. The composition of Keith's following signified better than anything else the unsettled nature of colonial society: the Quaker leaders, who had so recently gained power at the expense of the proprietor's supporters, were now themselves challenged from below.

These same problems arose in the other American colonies but not in such an acute form as they did in Pennsylvania. The Quaker as a social type was simply an exaggerated form of the Puritan as a social type. The effect of the wilderness in Pennsylvania was not much different than in New England or in the colonies on the Chesapeake. The proprietary system of land management only added a further dimension to the governmental and social problems which everywhere embroiled English colonists in the seventeenth century. Pennsylvania, however, differed from New England in its failure, in the first few decades, to develop a mechanism for ridding itself of its more strenuous malcontents. Though John Winthrop saw the splintering of the Massachusetts Bay Colony into "a hundred earnest little Utopias" as the most crucial problem he faced, he unwittingly succeeded in maintaining a semblance of stability in the colony because he failed to keep the dissident elements within his fold. Pennsylvania, on the other hand, developed no art of casting out its malcontents or encouraging them to stake out settlements of their own farther to the west. Instead antagonistic factions within Pennsylvania society were allowed to remain in the colony and to resolve their differences as best they could.

9 / Perry Miller
The Protestant Ethic

(1953)

The husbandmen and traders were doing nothing but what they had been told to do. They worked in their callings—and brought multiplicity out of unity. There were perceptibly "more divisions in times of prosperity than in times of adversity, and when Satan cant destroy them by outward violence he will endeavour to undo them by Strife and variance." Saints waited upon God for the reward—and became social climbers. The more everybody labored, the more society was transformed. The more diligently the people applied themselves—on the frontier, in the meadows, in the countinghouse or on the Banks of Newfoundland—the more they produced a decay of religion and a corruption of morals, a society they did not want, one that seemed less and less attractive. From the beginning, the city on a hill was to have social classes, but status ordained by God should not become the prize of competition; the jeremiad could not arrest the process in which names rose and fell, but by grieving over the incomprehensible it provided a method of endurance.

Hence we may see in the sermons more than ministerial nagging of worldlings, more than hypocritical show, more than rhetoric. They were releases from a grief and a sickness of soul which otherwise found no surcease. They were professions of a society that knew it was doing wrong, but could not help itself, because the wrong thing was also the right thing. From such ceremonies men arose with new strength and courage: having acknowledged what was amiss, the populace could go back to their fields and benches and ships, trusting that a covenanted Jehovah would remember His bond. When again they grew apprehensive, they could look into their own hearts, find what was festering there, and hasten once more to cleanse their bosoms of poisonous stuff by public confession. Although jeremiads and the Reforming Synod called for an alteration of social habits, the result was only more days of humiliation. Knowing their impotence, the people needed a method for paying tribute to their sense of guilt and yet for moving with the times. Realizing that they had betrayed their fathers, and were still betraying them, they paid the requisite homage in a ritual of humiliation, and by confessing iniquities regained at least a portion of self-respect.

A literary form does not come into flower unless it answers some deep necessity of the time and the place. As drama was the ideal articulation of Elizabethan London, the jeremiad was for the tiny communities of New

Perry Miller, *The New England Mind: From Colony to Province*, Cambridge, Mass.: Harvard University Press. Copyright 1953 by the President and Fellows of Harvard College, pp. 51–52. Reprinted by permission of the publisher.

England. The form suited their needs, on the one hand satisfying a passionate desire to remain faithful to the Puritan inheritance and on the other inculcating the ethic which was steadily undermining that heritage. Devotion to business, accumulation of estates, acquisition of houses and lands: these were the duties of Christians. What they gained of elegance or luxury was the just reward of blessed diligence, yet business and riches meant devotion to the world, and luxury meant pride. The sins paraded in the sermons were not so much those of the notoriously scandalous but such as were bound to increase among good men. They thus had to be all the more vigorously condemned because they were incurable: after proper obeisance to the past, the society was better prepared to march into its future.

10 / Timothy L. Smith
Congregation, State, and Denomination

(1968)

Little wonder that when respite came briefly from loneliness, danger, and toil, or when illness interrupted the busy round of life, weary minds threw a bridge of memory across the Atlantic and longed for the order and security of the villages they had left behind. In such moments was bred a deep hunger for kinship and community in the new settlements which they now must call home. But how did one create community, when the only kind he had known seemed a natural inheritance, not a human contrivance? ...

To men reared in an age of faith, this crisis of community inevitably seemed a religious one. They took it for granted that the church congregation must be the nucleus of all their new associations. Awe and reverence alone seemed to them able to generate the mystic force required to knit erstwhile strangers into units of belonging ... Herein lies the meaning of the exaggerated emotions which characterized congregational life in the New World. In Virginia, it was not simply the heritage of the reformation piety which, as Perry Miller has suggested, turned men's minds to God. The anxieties awakened by their taking leave of England and their arrival in America, strangers to one another and in a strange land, also played a part. Likewise in New England, the solemn ceremonies of church founding and church joining bespoke a search for long lost community as well as a testimony to newfound

Timothy L. Smith, "Congregation, State, and Denomination: The Forming of the American Religious Structure," *William and Mary Quarterly*, 3rd ser., XXV (April, 1968), pp. 159–160, 164, 175. Reprinted, without footnotes, by permission of the author.

grace. Later, Pennsylvania pietism, though originally imported from Europe, was nurtured by the need which both British and German immigrants felt for personal identity, for recognition and response, in a threatening wilderness . . .

The seventeenth-century settlers turned instinctively to the political authorities for aid, regardless of the theory of church-state relationships they had held in Europe. The earliest American tradition became, therefore, not religious liberty, but state control. The difficulties which beset the first attempts of congregations to establish community life on a religious basis largely explain this development. The actions of provincial governments and county courts in ecclesiastical, moral, and educational matters aimed not at displacing the family and the congregation by a "secular" authority but at supporting their efforts to stabilize behavior in a mobile and remarkably pluralistic setting. Nor was the establishment of democracy or aristocracy the primary issue, for the experience of the first settlers was limited to a hierarchical status system, and they expected nothing different here. To them, as Bernard Bailyn has pointed out, the larger problem was the threat of social disorder, of barbarization, which hung over their common enterprise. They believed the creation of a Christian community was the only reliable protection from this threat . . .

Viewing in retrospect the entire history of colonial Protestantism, I think the use of the term "Great Awakening" to describe the wide-spread effort to solve the problems of evangelism, of education, and of congregational order which took place in the eighteenth century serves more to confuse than to clarify our understanding of what was happening. What we have called the "Awakening" certainly occurred at widely separated times and places. It began, perhaps we may say, with Frelinghuysen's labors in New Jersey, and it burned out (or, possibly, simply took off across the mountains) on the Carolina frontier in the 1790's. With a little more imagination, one might say it began with John Cotton's arrival in Boston and continued, but did not stop, with Daddy Grace.

Part Two

New Wine

The revivals which disrupted the American colonies and splintered the churches for the 1730's down to and beyond the Revolution polarized men's conceptions of God and themselves, and thus, ultimately, shaped their attitudes toward the standing order—social, political, and ecclesiastical. In the first selection Alan Heimert outlines the basic theme of this section, the bifurcation of American thought. He criticizes the historians who by focusing on the bewildering variety of denominational labels and institutions have lost sight of the fundamental intellectual cleavage. He returns to the same theme in the final selection as he discusses the social ramifications of the Awakening, although his interpretations have been bitterly contested by a number of contemporary historians.

Leonard Trinterud describes the gulf—part ethnic and part theological—which separated Presbyterians in the middle colonies and made the Great Awakening so divisive. Samuel Blair, a "New Side" Presbyterian minister, in his account of a "typical" congregation, indicts the prevailing religious climate on the eve of the revival. The four succeeding selections illustrate the issues at stake in the Awakening and the response of various segments to the outpourings of emotionalism and the tactics employed to generate it. Frederick B. Tolles' analysis of the Quakers' response to the revivals demonstrates once again the changes that a half century in America had produced among the Friends. The excerpts from Paul K. Conkin, Jonathan Edwards, and Charles Chauncy try to suggest the radical distinction between the evangelical's sense of virtue, grace, and the revivals and that associated with the rationalists.

The final selections from Richard L. Bushman, William G. McLoughlin, Sidney E. Mead, and Alan Heimert assess the ways the Great Awakening generated attitudes which, despite the passing of the revivals, altered colonial society and the religious framework. Both Bushman and Heimert emphasize the challenge the Awakening created to the traditional sources of authority and they suggest the necessity for a reinterpretation of the revivals as a social movement. Similarly McLoughlin, by focusing on the radical evangelical, Isaac Backus, and Mead demonstrate the impetus for the separation of church and state and a redefinition of freedom that is most often associated with the rationalist tradition. One thing is certain, religious thought in colonial America was not an isolated stream separated from the "realities" of life. Although the initial focus and impact of religious thought may have been theological and denominational, it rarely remained confined within ecclesiastical boundaries. Not only man's relation with God, but man's relation with man—in state, in church, in society—felt the influence of the Calvinist tradition.

11 / Alan Heimert
Religion and the American Mind

(1966)

The Great Awakening was the series of religious revivals which, foreshadowed in the "refreshings" in New Jersey and New England in 1734–1735, rose to intercolonial crescendo in 1740. In the estimation of the Awakening's most outspoken critic, the revivals of the 1740's caused American Protestantism to be "divided into Parties" for the first time since the Antinomian Crisis of the 1630's. Actually, divisions existed within the American churches even before the Great Awakening. The Presbyterian Church, for instance, was torn by various issues throughout the 1730's. Likewise the Congregational ministers of New England differed on such questions as the standards of church membership and, though no open breach had as yet appeared, were aligning themselves into clearly identifiable groups. What the Awakening did was crystallize these differences, giving them objective form, and more importantly, expand them beyond the clergy, making partisans of the laity as well. The "two armies, separated, and drawn up in battle array" which Jonathan Edwards espied in 1742 were not clerical factions merely but hosts whose confrontation embodied a fundamental cleavage within the colonial populace itself.

One way of assessing the divisive consequences of the Awakening is that which has often been followed by historians of American Christianity—by considering the manner in which the Awakening altered the denominational structure of the colonies. The two churches most directly involved in the revival were fragmented. Presbyterianism was split into the Synod of Philadelphia, dominated by the "Old Side" opposers of the Awakening, and that

Alan Heimert, *Religion and the American Mind*, Cambridge, Mass.: Harvard University Press. Copyright, 1966 by the President and Fellows of Harvard College, pp. 2–3, 10–11. Excerpted by permission of the publisher. Footnotes omitted by permission.

of New York, whose members were the "New Side" partisans of the revival. In Connecticut the Congregational Church was similarly, though not so dramatically, sundered into "Old Lights" and "New Lights." There, also, "Separate" conventicles were established in defiance of the parish system and the semi-Presbyterial Saybrook Platform. Indeed, throughout New England evangelical congregations declared their independence from the associations and consociations that had developed over the course of a century. Some defined themselves as Baptists, and a few even as Presbyterians, but most simply stood as autonomous, and disaffected, seceders from the New England Way. Moreover, the revival impulse encouraged the growth of Presbyterianism in the South, where previously the Anglican Church had enjoyed a near monopoly. In Pennsylvania and New Jersey, and eventually in New England, the Baptists rose into new prominence as the beneficiaries of the revival. Throughout the North the Church of England, whose spokesmen were almost unanimously opposed to the Awakening, grew in numbers by virtue of its appeal to citizens offended by the enthusiasm of the revival.

But such a chronicle of sectarian division and proliferation obscures the fact that the "parties" thrown up by the Awakening were hardly so numerous as any listing of denominations might suggest. The fundamental post-Awakening division of the American mind was one that transcended both the inherited denominational structure and that created by the revival. There were in substance only *two* parties on the American religious scene in the period after the Great Awakening. Generally speaking, one consisted of the opponents of the revival, the other of its advocates, each of which over the succeeding years evolved a religious philosophy consistent with its involvement in and attitude toward the Awakening. These parties were of course not organizational entities, though it is true that the tendency of the century was toward more explicit and formal alignments. The parties into which American Protestantism was divided by the Awakening are best understood, and most accurately described, in intellectual terms. Both represented a casting off from the intellectual universe of Protestant scholasticism, and each marked the independent fulfillment of one of the strains that in Puritanism had been held in precarious balance: "piety" and "reason."

Such a division within Protestantism has long been acknowledged to be the intellectual characteristic of the eighteenth century. Indeed from one perspective what happened in America seems "merely one variant of a universal occurrence in Western culture." In England and on the Continent, as well as in the colonies, the "educated classes" turned to the "generalities of eighteenth-century rationalism," and the "spiritual hungers of the lower classes" found expression in the revivals, in Pietism or what is called Evangelicalism. Such a division has been characterized by a recent chronicler of the Great Awakening in New England as the divergence and confrontation of the eighteenth-century forces of "Pietism" and the "Enlightenment." However, the evangelical religion of the colonies differed markedly from the pietism of Europe, and the "rational religion" that arose to thwart the revival impulse was hardly identical to the faith of the Encyclopedists. The Great Awakening in America was a unique and profound crisis in the history of the "indigenous culture." ...

Even in 1740, ... it escaped no one's notice that those who possessed "a greater measure of this world's goods" were less disposed toward the Awakening, or that evangelical religion held a greater appeal for the "lower classes" of American society. Yet at no time was the division between Calvinist and Liberal one merely of economic or social class—any more than the Great Awakening itself was "a revolt of the backcountry producers from the stringent controls of the mercantile aristocracy." Such interpretations of the eighteenth century do as much violence to the American temper as accounts of the Great Migration that portray New England as originally a plantation of trade. The parties and debates of eighteenth-century American religion simply will not yield to the categories of Marx and Beard, for the reason that the fundamental post-Awakening division was an intellectual one—one more aesthetic, in fact, than economic or social ... What distinguished Americans, so far as the "great debate" of the eighteenth century was concerned, were differences not of income but, in substance, of taste.

Implicit in the "new light" of the revival was a forswearing of the pragmatic and rather hardheaded differences in policy that before the Awakening had distinguished colonial partisanship. But from the moment when the eyes of some citizens of the colonies were taken from their "ordinary secular business" and turned to the "great things of religion" the stage was being prepared for a new kind of party struggle, but one hardly less vehement. In the contest between rational and evangelical religion was embodied, indeed, one of those fundamental value disagreements from which, according to many historians, America has from the beginning been free. When Edwards first challenged Arminian rationalism he proclaimed that the differences between his "scheme" and the "legal one" were multiform and irreconcilable. When the "foundation" is so different, he went on to insist, "the whole scheme becomes exceeding diverse and contrary." Over the remainder of the century this contrariety was to be manifested in nearly every area of thought and behavior.

... The great debate of the eighteenth century focused on such questions as the nature and needs of the human personality, the pattern and tendency of history (and of American history in particular), the nature of the good society—phrased both as judgment on the social order of colonial America and as conviction as to what the civilization of the New World might and should be—and the role of the intellectual, and of ideas and expression, in translating ideals into practice.

12 / Leonard J. Trinterud
The New Light

(1949)

The driving force that shaped American Presbyterianism in its formative years ... was the reinterpretation of the Christian life which inspired the Great Awakening. This conception of the Christian life was introduced by the Log College men, who in turn had heard it preached and taught by William Tennent. Against it one group in the Church had united in what came to be known as the Old Side. Toward it the New England group were drawn and they, together with the Log College men, eventually became the New Side group ...

The more rationalistic group usually [declared that in] his own time and way, the Holy Spirit working immediately would infuse the principle of grace into the elect sinner. Ministers accordingly were to preach sound doctrine and the faithful observance of the moral law, leaving to God himself the matter of infusion or regeneration. Church members were to be faithful in their obligations to the Church, and to live sober, moral lives, waiting patiently and hopefully for God to give them a new principle. Even a sinner knew the moral law and could obey it in some measure. Moreover, whenever he was regenerated, if he was of the elect, he would still find the meaning of his life in that obedience. Therefore, regenerate or not, this was his great business.

To the more evangelical, or the experimental, Puritans this extreme rationalistic attitude was unacceptable. God did not work immediately and wholly unpredictably. He worked rather through the means of grace that he had himself instituted—preaching, the sacraments, Bible-reading, prayer, and Church discipline. The Holy Spirit working through these means of grace called men out of the city of destruction and sent them on a pilgrimage to the celestial city. This pilgrimage led through the "terrors of the law," under which the sinner saw his self-righteousness compared with the law of God and was driven to abandon all hope of being saved by his own goodness or efforts. When, then, he saw afar off the righteousness of Christ, which alone could save him, he was led on his journey by that sight. Passing through the gate of repentance, he found himself at the foot of the cross. There he laid down his burden of guilt and knew his sins forgiven. Looking up, he saw before him now the road that henceforth was to be his only home. Far down the years, at the end of the road, lay the Holy City ...

In the end, for the evangelical Puritan, the pilgrimage, the Christian life, was the essential. The theology was important, but it was only the rational explanation on the stages of the pilgrimage. Anyone might memorize all the theology but never become a pilgrim, whereas even a rather ignorant pilgrim could conceivably make it through to the Holy City somehow by God's good grace. Hence theology was always subservient to preaching and piety in evangelical Puritanism. Illogicalities in theology were not nearly so serious as self-righteousness, complacency, legalism, and coldness of heart. No heresy was so evil as a bad life.

For the rationalistic Puritan, theology was primary. Orthodox theology gave a true statement of God's relationship to man, and God would not take lightly any falsification of his glory, wisdom, power, or righteousness. Therefore it was utterly essential that men have and retain right ideas about God and themselves. Whenever, accordingly, the unpredictable spontaneity of the religious life clashed with the theology, the former must be laid aside. That alone could stand which was rational, logical, and according to the eternal natural law . . .

While many of the Old Side men remained upright, moral, and sober men, others of them became libertines. He who had faith (i.e., believed in orthodox doctrine) was of the elect. Hence he could not be lost. He might be a source of scandal to the name of God, but if he held sound doctrine he could not be called an unbeliever or an apostate. Therefore, the Tennents' ways were wholly illogical, and were mere "enthusiasm." If a man could believe the pure truths of right doctrine, with all their deprecation of man's sinful state, helplessness, unworthiness, vileness, etc., this was ample witness that into him God had indeed infused the principle of grace. No "natural" or "unregenerate" man would ever assent to doctrines that taught such things about himself. Unfortunate though these failures in conduct might be, the gradual ways of sanctification would care for these problems in due time, and do so far better than the Tennents' excoriations would.

Moreover, no elect people could be seriously harmed by any failures of the clergy, for the number and identity of these elect also had been fixed from eternity. They might not like what their pastor did, but it did them no real hurt. Therefore they should bear and forswear. Going to hear the Log College revival preachers, however, was a breach of faith with their pastor, and was as bad as adultery. Contempt of a presbytery was contempt of God, for God had himself ordained that presbyteries should govern his Church . . .

It was against such a background as this that the Log College men had revived the evangelical Puritan interpretation of Federalism. The old Puritan doctrines of "convictions" and "assurance," and the pilgrimage motif, were the spear points of the Tennent evangelistic preaching, although even during the revival their sermons touched on the whole range of doctrine. Under such treatment the static character of the Federal doctrine [was] broken up, but so [was] the peace of the Church. The Old Side rationalistic Federalists . . . reacted violently against the introduction of this evangelical interpretation of Federalism.

13 / Samuel Blair
An Account of Fagg's Manor

(1740)

If they performed these duties pretty punctually in their seasons, and, as they thought, with a good meaning, out of conscience, and not just to obtain a name for religion among men, then they were ready to conclude that they were truly and sincerely religious. A very lamentable ignorance of the main essentials of true practical religion, and the doctrines nearly relating thereunto, very generally prevailed. The nature and necessity of the *new birth* was but little known or thought of, the necessity of a conviction of sin and misery, by the Holy Spirit's opening and applying the law to the conscience, in order to a saving closure with Christ, was hardly known at all to the most. It was thought, that if there was any need of a heart-distressing sight of the soul's danger, and fear of divine wrath, it was only needful for the grosser sort of sinners; and for any others to be deeply exercised this way (as there might be some rare instances observable), this was generally looked upon to be a great evil and temptation that had befallen those persons. The common names for such soul-concern were, *melancholy*, *trouble of mind*, or *despair*. These terms were in common, so far as I have been acquainted, indifferently used as synonymous; and *trouble of mind* was looked upon as a great evil, which all persons that made any sober profession and practice of religion, ought carefully to avoid . . . There was scarcely any suspicion at all, in general, of any danger of depending upon self-righteousness, and not upon the righteousness of Christ alone for salvation. Baptists and Quakers would be readily acknowledged guilty of this crime, but hardly any professed Presbyterian. The necessity of being first in Christ by a vital union, and in a justified state, before our religious services can be well pleasing to God, was very little understood or thought of; but the common notion seemed to be, that if people were aiming to be in the way of duty as well as they could, as they imagined, there was no reason to be much afraid . . .

Leonard J. Trinterud, The Forming of an American Tradition. Copyright MCMXLIX by W. L. Jenkins, The Westminster Press. Used by permission.

14 / Gilbert Tennent
The Danger of an Unconverted Ministry

(1741)

And Jesus, when he came out, saw much People and was moved with Compassion towards them, because they were as Sheep not having a Shepard.

But notwithstanding of the great Crowds of these Orthodox, Letter-learned and regular Pharisees, our Lord laments the unhappy Case of that great Number of People, who, in the Days of his Flesh, had no better Guides: Because that those were as good as none (in many Respects) in our Saviour's Judgment. For all them, the People were as Sheep without a Sheperd ...

Natural Men, not having true Love to Christ and the Souls of their Fellow-Creatures, hence their Discourses are cold and sapless, and as it were freeze between their Lips ... And Pharisee-Teachers, having no Experience of a special Work of the Holy Ghost, upon their own Souls, are therefore neither inclined to, nor fitted for, Discoursing ... upon such important Subjects ... They often strengthen the Hands of the Wicked, by promising him Life. They comfort People, before they convince them; sow before they plow ... These fooling Builders do but strengthen Men's carnal Security by their soft, selfish, cowardly Discourses ...

That such who are contented under a *dead Ministry*, have not in them the Temper of that Saviour they profess. It's an awful Sign, that they are as blind as Moles, and as dead as Stones, without any spiritual Taste and Relish. And alas! Isn't this the Case of Multitudes? If they can get one, that has the Name of a Minister, with a Band, and a black Coat or Gown to carry on a *Sabbathdays* among them, although never so coldly, and *insuccessfully*; if he is free from gross Crimes in Practice, and takes good Care to keep at a due Distance from their Consciences, and is never troubled about his Insuccessfulness ...

If the Ministry of natural Men be as it has been represented; Then it is both lawful and expedient to go from them to hear Godly Persons; yea, it's so far from being sinful to do this, that one who lives under a pious Minister of lesser Gifts, after having honestly endeavour'd to get Benefit by his Ministry, and yet gets little or none, but doth find real Benefit and more Benefit elsewhere; I say, he may *lawfully* go, and that *frequently*, where he gets most Good to his precious Soul, after regular Application to the Pastor where he lives, for his Consent, and proposing the Reason thereof; when this is done in the Spirit of Love and Meekness, without Contempt of any, as also without rash

---

Gilbert Tennent, *The Danger of an Unconverted Ministry* (Philadelphia, 1741).

Anger or vain *Curiosity* . . . To bind Men to a particular Minister, against their Judgment and Inclinations, when they are more edified elsewhere, is carnal with a Witness; a cruel oppression of tender Consciences, a compelling of Men to Sin . . .

And as for Breaking of Congregations to Pieces, upon the Account of People's Going from Place to Place, to hear the Word, with a View to get greater Good; that spiritual Blindness and Death, that so generally prevails, will put this out of Danger. It is but a very few, that have got any spiritual Relish; the most will venture their Souls with any Formalist, and be well satisfied with the sapless Discourses of such dead Drones . . . And let those who live under the Ministry of dead Men, whether they have the Form of Religion or not, repair to the Living, where they may be edified.

15 / Thomas Prince
Christian History

(1745)

Conviction is quite another Sort of a Thing. It is the Work of the Spirit of God, a sovereign, free and almighty Agent; wherein he gives the sinful Soul such a clear and lively View of the Glory of the divine Sovereignty, Omnipresence, Holiness, Justice, Truth and Power; the Extensiveness, Spirituality and Strictness of his *Law*, the binding Nature, Efficacy and Dreadfulness of his *Curses*; the Multitude and Heinousness of its *Sins* both of Commission and Omission; the horrible Vileness, Wickedness, Perverseness and Hypocrisy of the *Heart*, with its utter *Impotence* either rightly to repent, or believe in Christ, or change itself: so that it sees itself in a lost, *undone* and perishing State; without the least Degree of *Worthiness* to recommend it to the holy and righteous God, and the least Degree of *Strength* to help itself out of this Condition. These Discoveries are made by Means of some *revealed Truths*, either in the *Reading*, *Hearing*, or *Remembrance*: when in the *Hearing*, sometimes by Words of Terror, and sometimes by Words of Tenderness: And the Holy Spirit with such internal Evidence and Power so applies them to the Conscience, that they become as *sharp Arrows* piercing into the *Heart*, wounding, paining and sticking in it, when all the mechanical Impressions of frightful Sounds are over, sometimes for *many Days, Weeks* and *Months*, if not *Years* together; until this DIVINE AGENT, by these and other Convictions, agreeable to his inspired *Word*, intirely subdues the Soul to Christ; or being

Thomas Prince, *The Christian History Containing Accounts of the Revival and Propagation of Religion in Great Britain and America*, 101 (Boston, 1745), pp. 389–90.

ungratefully treated, withdraws his convincing influence, and leaves the Heart and Conscience to greater and more dangerous Hardness and Stupidity than ever.

Such were the *Convictions* wrought in *many Hundreds* in this Town by Mr. *Tennent's searching* Ministry: And such was the Case of those *many Scores* of several other Congregations as well as mine, who came to me and others for Direction under them. And indeed by all their Converse I found, it was not so much the *Terror* as the *searching* Nature of his Ministry, that was the principal Means of their *Conviction*. It was not meerly nor so much his laying open the *Terrors* of the Law and Wrath of God, or Damnation of Hell; (for this they could pretty well bear, as long as they hoped these belonged not to them, or they could easily avoid them;) as his laying open their many vain and secret *Shifts* and *Refuges, counterfeit Resemblances* of Grace, *delusive* and *damning Hopes*, their utter *Impotence*, and impending Danger of Destruction: whereby they found all their Hopes and Refuges of Lies to fail them, and themselves exposed to eternal Ruin, unable to help themselves, and in a lost Condition. This *searching* Preaching was both the *suitable* and principle *Means* of their *Conviction*: Tho' 'tis most evident, the *most proper Means* are utterly *insufficient*; and wholly depend on the *sovereign Will* of God, to put forth his *Power* and apply them by this or that Instrument, on this or that Person, at this or that Season, in this or that Way or Manner; with these or those permitted Circumstances, Infirmities, Corruptions, Errors, Agencies, Oppositions; and to what Degree, Duration and Event he pleases.

16 / Testimony Against Several Errors

(1743)

We, the pastors of the churches of Christ in the province of Massachusetts Bay, in New England, at our Annual Convention, May 25, 1743, taking into consideration several errors of doctrine and disorders in practice that have of late obtained in various parts of the land, look upon ourselves bound, in duty to our great Lord and Master, Jesus Christ, and in concern for the purity and welfare of these churches, in the most public manner to bear our testimony against them.

I. As to errors in doctrine; we observe that some in our land look upon what are called secret impulses upon their minds, without due regard to the written word, the rule of their conduct; that none are converted but such as know they are converted, and the time when; that assurance is of the essence

The Testimony of the Pastors of the Churches in the Province of Massachusetts Bay . . . against several Errors in Doctrine and Disorders (Boston, 1743).

of saving faith; that sanctification is no evidence of justification; with other Antinomian and Familistical errors which flow from these; all which, as we judge, are contrary to the pure doctrines of the Gospel, and testified against and confuted in the Acts of the Synod of August, 1637 . . .

II. As to disorders in practice, we judge.

1. The itinerancy, as it is called, by which either ordained ministers or young candidates go from place to place, and without knowledge, or contrary to the leave of the stated pastors in such places, assemble their people to hear themselves preach,—arising, we fear, from too great an opinion of themselves, and an uncharitable opinion of those pastors, and a want of faith in the great Head of the churches, is a breach of order . . .

2. Private persons of no education and but low attainments in knowledge and in the great doctrines of the gospel, without any regular call, under a pretence of exhorting, taking upon themselves to be preachers of the word of God, we judge to be a heinous invasion of the ministerial office, offensive to God, and destructive to these churches . . .

3. The ordaining or separating of any persons to the work of the evangelical ministry at large, and without any relation to a particular charge, which some of late have unhappily gone into, we look upon as contrary to the Scriptures . . .

4. The spirit and practice of separation from the particular flocks to which persons belong, to join themselves with, and support lay exhorters or itinerants, is very subversive of the churches of Christ, opposite to the rule of the gospel . . . and contrary to their covenant engagements.

5. Persons assuming to themselves the prerogatives of God, to look into and judge the hearts of their neighbours, censure and condemn their brethren, especially their ministers, as Pharisees, Arminians, blind and unconverted, &c., when their doctrines are agreeable to the gospel and their lives to their Christian profession, is, we think, most contrary to the spirit and precepts of the gospel and the example of Christ . . .

6. Though we deny not that the human mind, under the operations of the Divine Spirit, may be overborne with terrors and joys; yet the many confusions that have appeared in some places, from the vanity of mind and ungoverned passions of the people, either in the excess of sorrow or joy, with the disorderly tumults and indecent behaviour of persons, we judge to be so far from an indication of the special presence of God with those preachers that have industriously excited and countenanced them or in the assemblies where they prevail, that they are a plain evidence of the weakness of human nature . . .

17 / Testimony and Advice . . . Occasioned by the Late Happy Revival

(1743)

The Testimony and Advice of an Assembly of Pastors of Churches in New England, at a meeting in Boston, July 7, 1743, occasioned by the late happy Revival of Religion in many parts of the Land. If it is the duty of everyone capable of observation and reflection, to take a constant religious notice of what occurs in the daily course of common providence; how much more is it expected that those events in the divine economy, wherein there is a signal display of the power, grace and mercy of God in behalf of the Church, should be observed with sacred wonder, pleasure, and gratitude! Nor should the people of God content themselves with a silent notice, but publish with the voice of thanksgiving, and tell of all his wondrous works . . .

For these and other reasons, we . . . think it our indispensable duty, (without judging or censuring such of our brethren as cannot at present see things in the same light with us,) in this open and conjunct manner to declare, to the glory of sovereign grace, our full persuasion, either from what we have seen ourselves, or received upon credible testimony, that there has been a happy and remarkable revival of religion in many parts of this land, through an uncommon divine influence; after a long time of great decay and deadness, and a sensible and very awful withdraw of the Holy Spirit from his sanctuary among us . . .

But who can wonder, if at such a time as this, Satan should intermingle himself, to hinder and blemish a work so directly contrary to the interests of his own kingdom? . . . We would therefore, in the bowels of Jesus, beseech such as have been partakers of this work, or are zealous to promote it, that they be not ignorant of Satan's devices; that they watch and pray against errors and misconduct of every kind, lest they blemish and hinder that which they desire to honor and advance . . . And while we would meekly exhort both ministers and Christians, so as is consistent with truth and holiness, to follow the things that make for peace; we would most earnestly warn all sorts of persons not to despise these outpourings of the Spirit, least a holy God be provoked to withhold them, and instead thereof, to pour out upon this people the vials of his wrath, in temporal judgments and spiritual plagues . . .

The Testimony and Advice of an Assembly of Pastors of Churches in New England . . . occasioned by the late happy Revival of Religion (Boston, 1743).

18 / Frederick B. Tolles
Quietism versus Enthusiasm

(1960)

By 1739, when George Whitefield first appeared in Philadelphia, the Quaker movement was nearly a century old. It had left behind it the ardors and extravagances of its primitive period. No longer as in the days of George Fox and James Nayler were Friends reviled as wild enthusiasts and hysterical fanatics; no longer were they thrown into jail as heretics, firebrands, and disturbers of the peace. With the advent of toleration, the passing of the first-generation leaders, and the adoption of birthright membership, they had settled into a period characterized by a less prophetic ministry, a more introspective mysticism, and a fear of "creaturely activity."

Not only had Friends become reserved and introverted religiously; they had also become socially respectable. The early Friends had been recruited largely from the lower strata of society, from among the artisans, shopkeepers, domestic servants, yeoman farmers, and husbandmen of Commonwealth and Restoration England. By the practice of the economic virtues of diligence, prudence, and thrift, they had risen in the course of years to the status of substantial and respected upper-middle-class citizens. A little aloof, perhaps, from "the world" and its follies, preserving their character as a "peculiar people" by certain singularities of dress and address, they had attained, both in England and in the colonies, to a secure place in the upper ranks of society . . .

The typical Quaker attitude toward the revival at its outset was compounded of an aloof but tolerant amusement at the antics of the preachers and a somewhat grudging admiration for their success in mending the morals of the Philadelphians . . .

The Quaker characteristically emphasized the inward working of the Holy Spirit, the Christ formed in man's soul, whereas the Evangelical rested his faith on the objective historic Christ and His vicarious atonement. The eighteenth-century Friends laid less stress on external factors or "outward helps" in religion than George Fox had done, and it was natural that Whitefield should be shocked by their concern with the Christ within almost to the exclusion of the historic Christ . . . Here are the heirs of one movement of uninhibited emotional religion pronouncing judgment from the vantage point of a century-long development into emotional restraint and social respectability upon a cognate movement of vital popular religion in the first flush of its exuberant youth. The relatively sophisticated Quaker of the eighteenth century looked upon the excesses of religious frenzy produced by the

Reprinted with permission of The Macmillan Company from *The Quakers and the Atlantic Culture* by Frederick B. Tolles. Copyright 1947, 1951, 1960 by Frederick B. Tolles.

revival with distaste, forgetting, even denying, that his seventeenth-century forbears had allowed their religious emotions to express themselves with equal abandon and equal scorn for the norms of civilized behavior ...

That which the two movements had in common was a central persuasion that God reveals Himself directly to individual men through the Holy Spirit. The historical function of both movements in their time was to shift the basis of religious authority from outward belief to inward experience, from intellectual assent to experiential certainty ... The mood of quietism crept over the Society of Friends in the early eighteenth century, however, and the enthusiast gave way to the mystic as the normal Quaker type. No longer was the sudden dazzling and transforming experience and thereafter the constant presence of the Godhead, prompting to action. Instead there was more likely to be a slow and gradual development with frequent extended periods of "dryness" ...

Here on the streets of Philadelphia two of the most characteristic religious movements in Anglo-Saxon Protestantism in a sense confronted each other. Theologically they were at one in many essential respects. In 1740, however, they were in different stages in their historical development. The Evangelical movement, then in its robust and dynamic infancy, was characterized by that type of powerful sensibility known as enthusiasm, and drew its strength chiefly from the lower classes. Quakerism, on the other hand, was well advanced in that historical development to which such religious movements appear to be inevitably subject: it had passed from uninhibited enthusiasm to quietistic mysticism, and what had once been a plebian movement had become in Philadelphia the religion of a substantial mercantile aristocracy.

19 / Paul K. Conkin
Jonathan Edwards: Theology

(1968)

Jonathan Edwards was a Christian and a genius. But many of his contemporaries were so blinded by his Christian orthodoxy that they failed to recognize his genius. Edwards, a solitary figure in eighteenth-century America, observed with disgust much of the formative, adolescent period in the development of American (and also modern) thought. He was vehemently critical of his age, for in it man was slowly but decisively taking the place of God. Piety was being replaced by pride; Christianity by a benevolent humanism. Edwards' protests were quite ineffective. For the next 200 years man would at least play at being God, with only occasional moments of revulsion, or even sheer horror, at the enormity of his presumption. But today,

Paul K. Conkin, *Puritans and Pragmatists*. Copyright © 1968 by Dodd, Mead & Company, Inc. Reprinted by permission of the publisher.

when the horror is widespread, when so many are embracing either cynicism or some new orthodoxy, it is easy, once again, to view Jonathan Edwards as an astute prophet rather than as a curious anachronism. In any case, no one today denies his solitary brilliance. Even if he failed to provide an adequate defense of his beliefs, he certainly left a penetrating criticism of the developments of his day and, through these, of much that is contemporary.

Edwards has often been characterized, or contemptuously dismissed, as the last great American defender of a strict form of Calvinism. But even to label him a Calvinist is to invite immense semantic confusion. Edwards was as far removed from the narrow scholasticism of some of the professed Calvinists of the seventeenth century as were his closest spiritual kinsmen, the Cambridge Platonists. Yet such rigid Calvinism, with its absolute reprobation, its unrelenting decrees, and its facile rationalism, was in spirit if not in word far removed from the burning fervor of Calvin. The often ambiguous *Institutes*, as most prophetic manifestoes, suffered from too much literalistic and legalistic exegesis.

Likewise, Edwards hardly resembled those few orthodox Puritans still on exhibit in New England pulpits. He cared little for many of the doctrines of earlier Puritans. Except in sermons, he rarely used the stilted axioms of earlier ministers or even the literal language of the Bible. As a philosopher, he moved well beyond (but not away from) conventional Christian orthodoxy. In his lofty philosophical theology, he seemed to be on an entirely different plane than even Calvin. Yet, by his philosophical ideas, he tried to save the essence and spirit of Augustinian Christianity. To do this, he usually ignored the highly stylized arguments that had so long divided traditional Calvinists and humanistic Arminians (free-will advocates). Historically, the Arminians had already won this battle, for orthodox Calvinism was becoming an oddity even in New England. Thus, Edwards raised his sights and, in an original philosophical perspective, tried to do battle with the whole spirit and tenor of an Arminian age and to show the terrible emptiness of the Arminian victory. To do this, he revived, and gave conceptual respectability to, an earlier Puritan spirituality, meanwhile clarifying the esthetic and experimental aspects of any true religion. By a Neoplatonic merging of morality and esthetics and by a new, sensationalist psychology, he attacked the cold rationalism and staid propriety not only of liberal Puritans but, by implication, even of orthodox Calvinists.

As a brilliant Christian theologian, Edwards tried to use the latest and, for the time, most convincing scientific and philosophical ideas in defense of a religious faith which, for him, was vindicated by reason and even more by immediate and inescapable experience. In this, he fulfilled the perennial role of theologians ... Neither his subjective experience nor, closely related, his basic assumptions paralleled that of a majority of his eighteenth-century contemporaries. Yet, his brilliance made him more than a match for any American. He started with the same conceptual tools as Benjamin Franklin or John Adams, but by combining them with his unique religious experience he created a world view that seemed somewhat out of place in the age of

Enlightenment. God, not man, was at its core and infused it throughout. Into a vast intellectual homage to an overwhelming God that men were ever less inclined to treat as God, Edwards poured all of himself . . .

Without quite recognizing it, the Arminians were headed toward Unitarianism and, eventually, complete humanism. To Edwards, this escape to free will had to stop, and quickly; otherwise man would soon forget his utter sinfulness and his complete dependence on God for all righteousness. The common-sense (and Calvinist) condemnation of people with bad habits and a natural inclination to evil had to be restored. If morality were tied to an Arminian definition of freedom, all moral judgment and all morality would eventually cease to exist.

The essence of Calvinist harshness was a refusal to accept excuses. Edwards was a strict Calvinist in this respect—he would permit no relaxation, allow no weakness, pardon no inability. The Calvinist condemned nothing so much as moral inability. Not the lack of choice of God, but the moral inability to choose God was what was wrong with all men unaided by special grace. This, not the action or inaction, was prior in the scale of evil, and permitted a harsh judgment even of children. This attitude toward moral inability contrasted sharply with the Anabaptist tradition in Protestantism, which was radically free will and which placed blame directly on the evil act . . . The Calvinist position also differed radically from the sacramental emphasis of Roman Catholicism, in which baptism removed the blight of original sin and thus removed any necessity for a radical conversion. This Calvinist harshness was conducive to the most explosive revivalism. For any Calvinist, conversion was a single, radical, undeserved transformation wrought by God. Ordinarily, but not necessarily, conversion occurred as a step in an ordained sequence of events which included preaching, conviction, and repentance, but it was always, nonetheless, a complete gift, totally undeserved . . .

Edwards grasped the central dilemma of the indeterminists—a tendency to find everything distasteful to be determined and thus beyond judgment. Not moral relativism but a suspension of moral judgments was the danger. Edwards believed that the Calvinist position was closest to the common-sense view and that it was really less involved in metaphysical subtleties. The average man rightly condemned any deed if it was a person's own deed, obviously evil, and done by choice. In asking for one further test—is the choice free?—the Arminians confused the issue by directing attention to some cloudy, undetectable element in back of an ordinary act of volition. By seeking this obscure freedom behind a choice, they were really leaving the will under the guidance of *nothing* . . .

Edwards lived in an age when humanitarian sentiments had virtually captured the realm of moral philosophy. Particularly popular in the Enlightenment was a concept of a special moral sense, a principle or faculty of moral judgment implanted in all men by nature or by God. By tying virtue to grace and to the holy affections of the Christian elect, Edwards was emphatically denying that virtue consists of such a moral sense.

20 / Jonathan Edwards
Some Thoughts Concerning the Present Revival
of Religion in New England

(1740)

It is not unlikely that this work of God's spirit, that is so extraordinary and wonderful, is the dawning, or at least, a prelude of that glorious work of God, so often foretold in Scripture, which in the progress and issue of it shall renew the world of mankind. If we consider how long since, the things foretold, as what should precede this great event have been accomplished; and how long this event has been expected by the church of God, and thought to be nigh by the most eminent men of God in the church ... we cannot reasonably think otherwise, than that the beginning of this great work of God must be near. And there are many things that make it probable that this work will begin in America. It is signified that it shall begin in some very remote part of the world, that the rest of the world will have no communication with but by navigation, in Isa. 1x. 9: "Surely the Isles will wait for me, and the ships of Tarshish first, to bring my sons from afar." It is exceeding manifest that this chapter is a prophecy of the prosperity of the church, in its most glorious state on earth, in the latter days; and I cannot think that any thing else can here be intended by America, by the isles that are afar off ... This prophecy therefore seems plainly to point out America, as the first fruits of that glorious day.

God has made as it were two worlds here below, the old and the new (according to the names they are now called by), two great habitable continents, far separated one from the other; the latter is but newly discovered, it was formerly wholly unknown, from age to age, and is as it were now but newly created: it has been, until of late, wholly the possession of Satan, the church of God having never been in it, as it has been in the other continent, from the beginning of the world. This new world is probably now discovered, that the new and most glorious state of God's church on earth might commence there; that God might in it begin a new world in a spiritual respect, when he creates the new heavens and new earth ...

And so it is probable that that will come to pass in spirituals, that has in temporals, with respect to America; that whereas till of late, the world was supplied with its silver and gold and earthly treasures from the old continent, now it is supplied chiefly from the new, so the course of things in spiritual respects will be in like manner turned.

And it is worthy to be noted that America was discovered about the time of the reformation, or but little before: which reformation was the first thing that God did towards the glorious renovation of the world ... So that as soon as this new world is (as it were) created, and stands forth in

London: James Black and Son, 1817.

view, God presently goes about doing some great thing to make way for the introduction of the church's latter day glory, that is to have its first seat in, and is to take its rise from that new world . . .

And if we may suppose that this glorious work of God shall begin in any part of America, I think if we consider the circumstances of the settlement of New England, it must needs appear the most likely of all American colonies, to be the place whence this work shall principally take its rise.

And if these things are so, it gives more abundant reason to hope that what is now seen in America, and especially in New England, may prove the dawn of that glorious day: and the very uncommon and wonderful circumstances and events of this work, seem to me strongly to argue that God intends it as the beginning or forerunner of something vastly great.

I have thus long insisted on this point, because if these things are so, it greatly manifests how much it behooves us to encourage and promote this work, and how dangerous it will be to forbear so to do.

21 / Charles Chauncy
Seasonable Thoughts

(1743)

'Tis true, we read of the coming on of a *glorious State* of Things in the LAST DAYS: Nor will the *Vision fail*.—We may rely upon it, the Prophesies, foretelling the Glory of the REDEEMER'S *Kingdom*, will have their Accomplishment to the making this Earth of *Paradise*, in Compare with what it now is. But for the *particular Time* when this will be, it *is not for us to know it, the Father having put it in his own Power*: And whoever pretend to such Knowledge, they are wise above what is written: and tho' they may think they know much, they really know nothing as to this Matter.

It may be suggested, that "the Work of God's SPIRIT that is so extraordinary and wonderful, is the *dawning*, or at lest, a *Prelude* of that *glorious Work of* GOD, so often foretold in Scripture, which, in the Progress and Issue of it, shall renew the whole World." But what are such Suggestions, but the Fruit of Imagination? Or at best, uncertain Conjecture? And can any good End be answered in endeavouring, upon Evidence absolutely precarious, to instill into the Minds of People a Notion of the *millenium* State, as what is Now going to be introduced; yea, and of AMERICA, as that Part of the World, which is pointed out in the *Revelations* of GOD for the Place, where this glorious Scene of Things, "will, probably, first begin?" How often, at other Times, and in other Places, has the Conceit been propagated among

Charles Chauncy, *Seasonable Thoughts on the State of Religion* (Boston, 1743).

People ...? And what has been the Effect, but their running wild? So it was in GERMANY, in the Beginnings of the Reformation.

While I was writing this Page, I received a Letter from a worthy Gentleman, in which, speaking of Mr. EDWARDS'S late *Book*, he has these Words, "I am sur-priz'd at his long Labour to prove the *Millenium* shall begin in AMERICA.— He has been so modest as to conceal the Reason of this; but it may easily be gathered from what he has *often said to private Persons, viz.* that he doubted not, the *Millenium* began when there was such an Awakening at NORTH-HAMPTON 8 Years past."—So that Salvation is gone forth from NORTH-HAMPTON, and NORTH-HAMPTON must have the Praise of being first brought into it.

To which let me add a few Words, from the late venerable Dr. INCREASE MATHER, which will shew, how widely good Men may differ from one another, in Matters of *meer Conjecture*. They are these, "I know there is a blessed Day to the visible Church not far off: But it is the Judgment of very learned Men, that, in the glorious Times promised to the Church on Earth, AMERICA will be HELL. And, although there is a Number of the Elect of GOD to be born here, I am verily afraid, that, in Process of Time, NEW-ENGLAND will be the wofullest Place in all AMERICA."

22 / Richard L. Bushman
A New Social Order

(1967)

Measured against seventeenth-century standards, Puritan social institu-tions had deteriorated sadly by 1765. The social order no longer restrained unruly human passion, and the rulers of Connecticut were unable to fulfill their commission from God to keep peace and order. The old ambiguity about economic ambition, which had formerly discomfited only a small section of the community, now troubled virtually the whole population. Men of all classes who were eagerly seeking wealth clashed with the institutions designed to keep order. The town, the churches, and the civil government felt the pres-sures of a generation bent on expanding its worldly inheritance through land or trade and increasingly impatient with the limitations the rulers imposed.

The conflict between ambition and traditional authority found a release in the Great Awakening. The guilty men surrendered to God, admitted their culpability, and called upon Him to save them by His grace. But the God to whom they surrendered was not He whose authority invested social institu-

Richard L. Bushman, *From Puritan to Yankee: Character and the Social Order in Con-necticut, 1690–1765.* Cambridge, Mass.: Harvard University Press. Copyright 1967 by the President and Fellows of Harvard College, pp. 267–279. Excerpted by permission of the publisher. Footnotes omitted by permission.

tions. Newborn men relied wholly on the God they had discovered in a personal experience. Far from instilling submission to the old authority, the revival planted the conviction that God's power was given to individuals, clearing the way for men to resist in good conscience when the occasion arose . . .

To reinforce the failing strength of the rulers, election preachers of both political factions stressed the familiar formula for civil obedience: God instituted governments among men to keep the peace; the authority of rulers was derived from God; therefore, men were conscience-bound to submit ... The Awakening controversies seriously undercut the civil authorities' claims to divine approval. Neither branch of the New Lights was very impressed by the assertion that the rulers were God's vice-regents . . . At the same time the word "liberty" assumed new political usages. At the beginning of the century the love of liberty was used as an incentive for submission to authority, since only rigid enforcement of the law adequately guaranteed each man his rights. The argument was well grounded so long as a consensus about the definitions of individual rights existed ... But the argument broke down when the boundaries between the rights of the people and the power of the state were in dispute . . .

. . . This widespread uncertainty about the precise limitations of liberty, which in various forms troubled Americans ever after, weakened the link to order. Liberty thenceforth could imply resistance to authority as well as submission, and the older formula for civil obedience lost much of its power.

The traditional conceptions of the social order were not wholly obsolete. They remained in the armory of election sermon preachers for many years, too thoroughly integrated into the colony's theology to be discarded. Yet the old ideas were ineffective. Civil authority was disparaged, faction reigned in politics, and the people called for still greater liberties. A new rationale for the social order was needed as a basis on which to appeal to the people for submission to authority and obedience to law.

The 1750's and 1760's were a period of experimentation in social theory because everyday experience confronted people with the problem. Submission or resistance, liberty versus authority, orderliness or confusion, these were crucial alternatives. Not surprisingly, the theories born in this era were projections of personal methods for dealing with life and without strict correspondence to party lines ... Important centers of feelings and thought can be identified, but few pronouncements on social theory were pure expressions of a single conception.

Among Anglicans there had always been an aversion to disorder. Samuel Johnson accounted for his conversion to Episcopacy by remembering how distasteful he had found the "great animosities" and "virulent separations" in Congregationalism at the beginning of the century. The same dislike of "divisions and separations" precipitated a flood of conversions [to Anglicanism] . . .

Samuel Johnson probably numbered the New Divinity men among the enthusiasts he despised, yet their view of society also aimed to restore order ... Sensitized by their religious experience to the odiousness of sin, New Lights were zealous to crush immorality by stringent laws ... But, for all their impatience with the manifestations of sin, many New Lights recognized that no reinforcement of authority would stop the vices of the people. ... Law could eliminate only the symptoms, not the inner heart of evil, whence all disorder sprang.

The New Lights, particularly the New Divinity men, taught that the new birth alone could heal society, just as it alone had healed individual souls. The idea was not new, for the contribution of religious morality to civil government had long been a cliché of the election sermons ... But in the Awakening the weary old belief came to life again ... The large number of conversions made it seem quite likely that God's grace might subdue people as law and authority had not ...

More worldly individuals, the rationalists of their generation, felt that it was useless and probably unnecessary to fight human nature and preferred to construct a society frankly founded on self-interest ... [and] propounded a distinctly new definition of self-interest. Instead of limiting themselves to seventeenth-century values, they recognized that economic expansion had generated vital new concerns having to do more with trade and agriculture than morality. If the state supported these interests, which had led to turmoil in the first place, people might very well sustain government ...

These appeals to self-interest offended many New Lights. The rationalists seemed to be enlarging the role of self-love in society to monstrous proportions. No objection could be made to enumerating the blessings of government as an incentive to obedience so long as government was acknowledged to rest on God's desire and authority; but the rationalists who made the satisfaction of human desires the main end of government seemed to think that self-interest, if enlightened, could be given a free rein and made the very foundation of civil society.

The New Divinity men regarded this indulgence of self-interest as a dangerous and un-Christian attempt to reconcile egotistical impulses with the good of the whole. Religious experiences committed them to a total subjection of the human will to God. The retention of prideful desires in any form was a devilish scheme to prevent the abasement that had to precede rebirth ...

23 / William G. McLoughlin
Isaac Backus

(1967)

The essence of the religious revolution which the Separatist movement began (and the Baptists finished) lay in church government and not in theology—

William G. McLoughlin, *Isaac Backus*, pp. 23–25, 31, 63–64, 120–123. Copyright © 1967 by William G. McLoughlin. Reprinted by permission of Little, Brown and Co.

though it became necessary eventually to modify Calvinism in order that it might conform more nearly to the unforeseen ramifications of the new practices in church discipline and polity. The major issues involved in church government were the autonomy and purity of the church, the nature of the ministry, and the relationship between Church and State. The revolution came because the existing structure and practice of the New England churches could not contain the new energy and outlook released by the experience of the revival. The challenge to individual parish churches grew into a challenge to the associations or presbyteries which stood above them; when these proved unable to suppress or confine the new energies, the State itself became involved in the disorder. For the Church and the State were so intricately interwoven in the corporate system of New England that a breakdown at the local level ultimately compelled a realignment of the whole social and political structure ...

When the Awakening began to get out of hand after 1742, the established ministers called upon the State to pass a law preventing itinerant evangelists from preaching in a parish without the permission of the parish minister. The legislature duly passed such a law under which many itinerants were punished, though local authorities by no means enforced it strictly. In 1743 the legislature also rescinded the Toleration Act of 1708 which allowed county courts to license dissenting churches whose members complied with the British Toleration Act of 1689; after 1743 only the legislature could do so. This effectively stifled several incipient Separate movements. In addition the legislature took disciplinary action against members of the Council and General Assembly known to sympathize with the New Lights ...

The right of lay ordination was one of the most fundamental tenets of the Separatist reformation. Majority rule in and by the church was essential. The Separates constantly harped on the theme that the established clergy were "lording it over" the brethren, the church members, by refusing to let the laity exercise their gifts and by exercising the right to veto the wishes of the majority ... The right of ordaining their own pastors without the concurrence of a ministerial association or the license of the state was part of the democratic rebellion against the prevailing ecclesiastical constitution ...

The Puritans had said that the attempt to form pure churches of the converted was sheer fanaticism and arrogance. And the Separates, by continuing to baptize infants would face the same problem the Puritans had when they adopted the Halfway Covenant in 1662: What status did a baptized infant have in a pure church after he came of age but was not converted? The Puritans had decided to abandon their earlier pietistic and perfectionist notion of a gathered church consisting only of visible saints. They had come to believe that religious education and nurture somehow prepared baptized infants for salvation. They enacted ecclesiastical laws to preserve good order in the churches and to support them by compulsion, because they believed that God would be more willing to convert those who lived in a

Christian Commonwealth. In short, the Puritans had conceived of Christianity in organic terms, as a process of growth and continuity—an evolutionary rather than a revolutionary process. And they disliked the Anabaptist view which left the continuity of the church and hence of the commonwealth up to the contingency of wholly adventitious conversions in adulthood. God's grace was miraculous but not fortuitous; no community, no corporate Christian state, could depend upon this kind of spasmodic action if it was to have stability and order. The Puritans feared the depravity of man too much to trust that God would be willing to save souls with sufficient regularity to preserve Christian civilization without considerable support and assistance from the institutions of Church and State. That was why he had ordained them . . .

The Baptists finally reached the point of exasperation in 1773, a year which Backus considered a turning point in his own life as well as in the movement itself. The Baptists then decided to adopt a policy of massive civil disobedience to assert their rights of conscience. They had exhausted all of the lawful means of redress for their grievances and had patiently borne a long train of abuses; now they had no choice but to stand up and fight by unlawful means . . . "Liberty of conscience, the great and most important article of liberty, is evidently not allowed as it ought to be in this country, not even by the very men who are now making loud complaints of encroachments upon their own liberties [by Parliament]." The "root of all these difficulties" was the assumption by civil rulers of a power to govern ecclesiastical affairs or to use "force to support ministers." No connection between Church and State was justifiable if it limited the freedom of "ecclesiastical affairs." The Baptists were no longer content to act within the prevailing system, to accept a policy of mere toleration. They wanted religious liberty as a general principle, as a natural right, and not a denominational privilege . . .

Backus, however, by no means identified liberty with government by the majority, for it was the tyranny of the majority in New England which denied the rights of the Baptists. Like a true pietist, he placed as much reliance upon Biblical texts as upon the works of Locke to prove the necessity for separation of Church and State . . .

Basic to the Baptist position was the belief that all direct connections between the state and institutionalized religion must be broken in order that America might become a truly Christian country. Backus, like Jefferson and Madison, believed that "Truth is great and will prevail"—but by "Truth" he meant the revealed doctrines of grace. His fundamental assumption was that "God has appointed two different kinds of government in the world which are different in their nature and ought never to be confounded together; one of which is called civil, the other ecclesiastical government."

(1963)

Much more important for the future than left-wing influence was the move-ment called Pietism. Originating in the European right-wing state churches during the last quarter of the seventeenth century, its leaders were seeking for more palatable spiritual food for the hungry souls of the common folk than current Protestant scholasticism and formalism afforded. Conceived and projected as a movement *within* churches aimed at the revitalization of the personal religious life of the members and a restoration of Christian unity, Pietism did tend to develop its own patterns of doctrine and polity. While assuming the validity and continuance of traditional standards and practices, Pietists tended to make personal religious experience more impor-tant than assent to correctly formulated belief and the observance of ecclesiastical forms. Here was an intimation that the essence of a church was the voluntary association of individuals who had had the experience.

Stress on the intuitive religion of the heart "strangely warmed" by "faith in Christ," as John Wesley was later to put it, became a possible seedbed for the dreaded religious "enthusiasm." However, in Europe the movement was always somewhat constrained by the sheer existence and accepted forms of the powerful state churches.

But, sprouting indigenously in America, or transplanted thereto by such leaders as Freylinghuysen, Muhlenberg, Zinzendorf, and the great White-field, where such constraining ecclesiastical forms were already weakened, Pietism, cross-fertilized by other movements, grew rankly and blossomed into the spectacular phenomena associated with the Great Awakenings. It swept the colonies from the 1720's to the Revolution, transforming the religious complexion of the land as it went.

Jonathan Edwards' experience in Northampton indicates how short was the step from preaching even the most traditional doctrines out of a heart "strangely warmed," to the outbreak of a surprising revival in the church that soon led to "strange enthusiastic delusions" which threatened to disrupt established parish customs. To a modern student the emotional upheavals created by George Whitefield's preaching seem to be out of proportion to that noted evangelist's reputed powers that so impressed Benjamin Franklin.

Back of this was the peculiar religious situation that had been developing in the colonies for a century. Concurrent with the fracturing of uniformity

Sidney E. Mead, *The Lively Experiment*, pp. 29–31, 33–37. Copyright © by Sidney E. Mead. Reprinted by permission of Harper & Row, Publishers, Inc. Footnotes omitted by permission.

had come the obvious decline of vital religion which concerned clergymen throughout the colonies during the twilight years of the seventeenth century and often turned their sermons into lamentations. The churches were not reaching the masses of the people, and they now confronted a greater proportion of unchurched adults than existed in any other Christian country. This grim statistic reflected the breakdown of the traditional pattern of church membership by birth into a commonwealth and baptism into a church that was coextensive with it, as well as the passing of support induced by coercion, at a time when no new, effective, and acceptable method for recruiting and holding members had emerged.

There was also the general cultural attrition associated with living on the frontier of western civilization where so much of the vital energy of the prosperous went into practical affairs—usually related to immediate profits—and of the poor in the even more engrossing problem of survival. The end of the seventeenth century has been called with reason the lowest ebb tide of the cultural amenities in America... Hence... at the very time when the tried old dams of civil and ecclesiastical law and custom were crumbling, there was building up behind them a religious yearning waiting to be released in floods of religious enthusiasm. And the revivals came, doing just that.

Most of the early revivalists were pietistically inclined ministers who more or less unwittingly stumbled upon this technique. It so perfectly met the immediate needs of the churches that it seemed a direct answer to their prayers and a sign of the divine approbation of their doctrines. The revivalists were obviously successful in carrying the gospel to the masses of indifferent people, in recruiting members from among the large body of the unchurched, and in filling the pews with convinced and committed Christians. The revivals demonstrated the spectacular effectiveness of persuasion alone to churches rapidly being shorn of coercive power.

In the context of our general interpretation it is important to note two things. The first is that the revivals took place largely within the entrenched and dominant churches of right-wing tradition. The second is that everywhere, whether among Dutch Reformed and Presbyterians in the middle colonies, Congregationalists in New England or Anglicans in the South, head-on clashes developed between the pietistic revivalists and the powerful defenders of the traditional authoritarian Protestant patterns of doctrine and polity. For the latter correctly sensed that the revivalists stressed religious experience and results—namely conversions—more than correctness of belief, adherence to creedal statements, and proper observance of traditional forms. They knew that in the long run this emphasis might undermine all standards...

The revivalists—harassed by traditionalists—naturally developed a kind of anticlericalism and antiecclesiasticism that helped to blur the lines between them and those of more authentic left-wing origin. Compounding this confusion between the revivalists and authentic left wingers was the fact that ever since the time of Munster, every departure from accepted order in the Protestant churches was apt to conjure up visions of an imminent upsurge of familism, antinomianism, anabaptism, and enthusiasm. These were terms that the traditionalists used freely but loosely during the heat of the controversies over revivalism.

Actually all the outstanding revivalists belonged to churches of right-wing tradition, and it might cogently be argued that what growth accrued to left-wing groups as a result of the revivals came largely through their ability to reap where others had sown. Thus, for example, the Baptists in New England apparently took little part in the Awakenings there, looking upon them as a movement within the churches of their Congregational oppressors. But when conflict led to a separatist movement, and Separate Congregationalists were treated even more harshly than Baptists by their erstwhile Congregational brethren, many separatists became Baptists.

Once this point is clear, we see that during the clash between traditionalists and revivalists, the latter were thrown willy-nilly—but somewhat incidentally—on the side of greater toleration and freedom. It was not that they developed clearly formulated theories about religious freedom. In fact the striking thing about the whole pietistic movement, as A. N. Whitehead pointed out, was that it "was singularly devoid of new ideas." Rather it appears that the revivalists were prompted by a practical desire for freedom from the immediate restraints imposed by the dominant churchmen. They fought for the right to promote their own point of view in their own way unmolested by traditional civil and ecclesiastical customs and laws.

Simultaneously the rationalist permeation of the intellectual world during the eighteenth century led to a situation where any man or group that appeared to be fighting for wider toleration of religious differences would attract the sympathetic attention of "enlightened" men in positions of social and political leadership. Furthermore, these men, unlike the pietists, were interested in giving religious freedom rational, theoretical justification. However much they might abhor "enthusiasm," they could take a sympathetic view of the practical moral application of the revivalist's gospel and the concomitant pietistic appeal to the teachings and simple religion of Jesus. As these rationalists observed the controversies in and between the religious "sects" occasioned by the revivals, along with the attempts of entrenched traditionalists to preserve order through the use of power, their sympathies were with the revivalists who appeared to be on the side of freedom.

Hence came that apparently strange coalition of rationalists with pietistic-revivalistic sectarians during the last quarter of the eighteenth century. Together, they provided much of the propelling energy behind the final thrust for the religious freedom that was written into the constitution of the new nation. This coalition seems less strange if we keep in mind that at the time, religious freedom was for both more a practical and legal problem than a theoretical one. They agreed on the practical goal.

. . . Having suggested how it had come to be, we may briefly describe the situation in 1787 that necessitated the declaration for religious freedom in the new nation.

First, the churches of right-wing background were still dominant in every area. But no one of them, and no possible combination of them, was in a position to make a successful bid for a national establishment even if those of the Calvinistic tradition were numerous and powerful enough to give Jefferson reason to fear the possibility. Meanwhile the sweep of pietistic sentiments through these right-wing churches during the revivals had undermined much of their desire for establishment. On the question of religious freedom for all, there were many shades of opinion in these churches, but all were practically unanimous on one point: each wanted freedom for itself. And by this time it had become clear that the only way to get it for themselves was to grant it to all others.

Second, the situation had actually made all previous distinctions between established churches and sects, between right- and left-wing groups, practically meaningless. In the South all but the Anglican Church were dissenting sects, as in New England were all but Congregational churches. In this respect, there was no difference between historically right-wing groups such as Presbyterians, Lutherans, and Anglicans, and historically left-wing groups such as Quakers and Baptists. The latter, of course, had traditionally held for religious freedom on principle, while the former had recently come to accept it of necessity. But since the immediate problem of such freedom was practical and legal, all worked together for it—each for his own complete freedom to publish his own point of view in his own way.

Hence the true picture is not that of the "triumph" in America of right-wing or left-wing, of churches or sects, but rather a mingling through frustration, controversy, confusion, and compromise of all the diverse ecclesiastical patterns transplanted from Europe, with other patterns improvised on the spot. The result was a complex pattern of religious thought and institutional life that was peculiarly "American," and is probably best described as "denominationalism."

Most of the effectively powerful intellectual, social, and political leaders were rationalists, and these men made sense theoretically out of the actual, practical situation which demanded religious freedom. They gave it tangible form and legal structure. This the churches, each intent on its own freedom, accepted in practice but without reconciling themselves to it intellectually by developing theoretical defenses of religious freedom that were legitimately rooted in their professed theological positions. And they never have. Anson Phelps Stokes' massive three-volume work on *Church and State in the United States*, proceeding over the historical evidence like a vacuum cleaner over a rug, is notable for the paucity of positive Protestant pronouncements on religious freedom that it sweeps up.

The religious groups that were everywhere dominant in America throughout the colonial period seem to have placed their feet unwittingly on the road to religious freedom. Rather than following the cloud and pillar of articulated aspiration in that direction they granted it (insofar as any can be said to have "granted" it) not as the kind of cheerful givers their Lord is said to love, but grudgingly and of necessity.

Meanwhile, by the time that the original intention to preserve religious uniformity was seen to be impossible of fulfillment in the new land, there had been incubated, largely within the dissenting groups (which were not necessarily left wing), ideas, theories, and practices that pointed the way toward a new kind of "church" consistent with the practice of religious freedom. During the colonial upheavals of the Great Awakenings, these dissenters' patterns of thought and practice infiltrated the dominant churches, and through the misty atmosphere of confusion and compromise, there began that historical merging of the traditional European patterns of "church" and "sect," "right" and "left" wings into a new kind of organization combining features of both plus features growing out of the immediate situation. The resulting organizational form was unlike anything that had preceded it in Christendom, and for purposes of distinctive clarity it is best known as the "denomination."

25 / Alan Heimert
Legacies of the Great Awakening

(1967)

In the Awakening, the followers of Edwards believed, God had not simply promised that the millennium would begin in America; he had called on his American people to exert their wills in order to bring that good society into being. Brainerd's endeavors [in Indian missionary work] were only one way of "promoting" God's historical design; other men were also required to aid the cause by expressing, at every opportunity, "a great and universal benevolence." Such a definition of true virtue . . . was what actually distinguished evangelical religion from the rationalism that arose in post-Awakening America. For the ultimate issue, as between those most conspicuous and persisting streams of American Protestantism, was not the place of emotion in the conversion experience, but the nature and the goals of man's moral endeavor.

At the time of the Awakening, Arminian morality assumed a static, even structured, social order, in which each man's "duties" were defined according

Alan Heimert and Perry Miller, eds., *The Great Awakening*. Copyright © by The Bobbs-Merrill Company, Inc. Reprinted by permission of the publisher.

to his place and station in society. Eventually rational religion opened the possibility of individual advancement, but it continued to argue that man's happiness and holiness derived solely from a reasonable assessment of, and conformity to, the dictates of his environment. Thus rationalism's two objections to Calvinism were not truly distinct. Critics of Calvinism complained that allowing emotion into man's life put him "out of the Power of distinguishing what is right from what is wrong. For this cannot be done but by man's Reasoning and Perceptive Power, by which he compares things to form his Judgment." The critics also argued (with increasing vehemence in the late 1740's) that Calvinism, by its denigration of "works," encouraged an all-licensed immorality. Both charges assumed that morality was the result of reason and calculation, and, for that matter, strongly implied that worldly prosperity was at least as valuable an end toward which to work as salvation. Evangelical religion, on the other hand, considered true virtue possible only after justification, and virtuous acts as flowing spontaneously (as Edwards conceived the personality) outward from the fountain that was the "vital indwelling principle" of grace. A regenerate heart made it possible for man to choose the good, and to pursue it, "without being at the trouble of a train of reasoning." In this contrast of premises and perspectives was contained no less than opposing judgments of the worth of the existing social order. For Calvinism released men from the vise of traditional obligations and relationships, but not into self-indulgence. It was the duty of the Calvinist "saint" to fulfill "the royal law of love"—to serve, that is, not himself but his fellow man and even, if necessary, to join with him in common endeavors to change society.

At the heart of the evangelical ethic was the hope of human betterment, the vision of a great community in which men, instinctively as it were, would seek the general welfare. Where evangelical virtue might lead America was disclosed in the sermons of the 1740's and 1750's denouncing the acquisitive ethic of Arminian rationalism. But Calvinism was not merely negative in its social attitudes, and most of the drama of the decade after the Awakening consisted in the effort of the Calvinist mind to find new and positive means of applying its definition of true virtue in American society—in the life of the body politic as well as in that of individuals. Rapidly and radically Calvinism's vision of the social good flowed into political protest, into challenges to the "rulers" of colonial society, and, eventually, into the discussion and the activity that preceded and accompanied the American Revolution.

Selected Additional Reading

Dunn, Richard S. *Puritans and Yankees: The Winthrop Dynasty of New England* (Princeton, 1962).

Erikson, Kai. *Wayward Puritans: A Study in the Sociology of Deviance* (New York, 1966).

Gaustad, Edwin S. *The Great Awakening in New England* (New York, 1957).

Gewehr, Wesley F. *The Great Awakening in Virginia, 1740–1790* (Durham, 1930).

Goen, C. C. *Revivalism and Separatism in New England, 1740–1800* (New Haven, 1962).

Haroutunian, Joseph. *Piety versus Moralism* (New York, 1932).

Haskins, George L. *Law and Authority in Early Massachusetts* (New York, 1960).

James, Sydney V. *A People Among Peoples: Quaker Benevolence in Eighteenth-Century America* (Cambridge, Mass., 1963).

Jones, Rufus. *Quakers in the American Colonies* (New York, 1966).

Miller, Perry. *The New England Mind: The Seventeenth Century* (Cambridge, Mass., 1939).

———. *The New England Mind: From Colony to Province* (Cambridge, Mass., 1953).

———. *Orthodoxy in Massachusetts* (Cambridge, Mass., 1933).

Morgan, Edmund S. *The Puritan Dilemma* (Boston, 1958).

———. *The Puritan Family* (New York, 1966).

———. *Roger Williams: The Church and the State* (New York, 1967).

———. *Visible Saints: The History of a Puritan Idea* (New York, 1963).

Niebuhr, H. Richard. *The Kingdom of God in America* (New York, 1937).

Perry, Ralph B. *Puritanism and Democracy* (New York, 1944).

Pettit, Norman. *The Heart Prepared: Grace and Conversion in Puritan Spiritual Life* (New Haven, 1966).

Pope, Robert G. *The Half-Way Covenant: Church Membership in Puritan New England* (Princeton, 1969).

Simpson, Alan. *Puritanism in Old and New England* (Chicago, 1955).

Tolles, Frederick B. *James Logan and the Culture of Provincial America* (Boston, 1957).

Vann, Richard T. *The Social Development of English Quakerism, 1655–1755* (Cambridge, Mass., 1969).

Walzer, Michael. *The Revolution of the Saints* (Cambridge, Mass., 1965).

Section Three
The American Enlightenment:
Reason and Revolution

JOHN C. LIVINGSTON

Contents

Introduction

The eighteenth century has long been designated the Age of Reason or the Enlightenment by intellectual historians. Certainly these are precisely the terms in which the thinkers of the eighteenth century conceived of themselves. They believed that they were enlightened men of reason, and that their generation marked a revolution in the thought patterns of western civilization. But against what tradition did the philosophers of the eighteenth century rebel? By what standard did they measure their rationality and enlightenment and condemn their adversaries for irrationality and ignorance? Universally the intellectual community of the eighteenth century responded that the enemy was orthodox Christianity and the rigid dogmas of formal theology. Above all else, then, the men of the Enlightenment directed their intellectual energies toward a secularization of thought. They did not completely dismiss God or religion, but they did emphasize the human condition rather than the heavenly state, the worldly rather than the spiritual, life rather than death.

In part, the eighteenth-century intellectual's secularism derived from an increasing faith in man, a movement that the most recent historian of the Enlightenment has called the "recovery of nerve."[1] As philosophers waxed enthusiastic over the potential of man, they tended to downgrade the omnipotence of God. The characteristic conception of God in the Age of Reason was that of God the watchmaker, the Creator who had fashioned the universe and then withdrew, permitting His creation to function according to its natural laws. But eighteenth-century secularism was also the result of a vigorous attack on Christianity as a theology founded on myth and reinforced by the lies of the clergy. As Thomas Jefferson explained to John Adams: "I can never join Calvin in addressing *his* God. He was indeed an atheist, which I can never be; or rather his religion was daemonism. If ever man worshiped a false God, he did. The being described in his five points, is not the God whom you and I acknowledge and adore, the Creator and benevolent Governor of the world; but a daemon of malignant spirit. It would be more pardonable to

[1] Peter Gay, *The Enlightenment: An Interpretation*, II (New York, 1969), pp. 3–56.

believe in no God at all, than to blaspheme Him by the atrocious attributes of Calvin."[2]

In both aspects of its anti-theological animus the resulting secularism of the Enlightenment reflected the impact of eighteenth-century science on all areas of thought. The scientific titan of the age, the model all Enlightenment intellectuals sought to emulate, was Sir Isaac Newton. Newton had performed the feat of explaining what forces held God's universe together. Even more remarkably, he had demonstrated that the universe was ruled by laws that were regular, uniform, predictable, and therefore discoverable by man through the use of his reason. Borrowing directly from the Newtonian example, eighteenth-century thinkers came to accept three fundamental concepts as defining the intellectual Zeitgeist of the age. The three concepts, belief in which united all Enlightened philosophers regardless of geographic region, nationality, or class, were nature, reason, and science. These ideas defined the boundaries within which Enlightened philosophers sought the truth.

Convinced by the obvious success of Newtonian physics and struggling to free themselves from the shackles, as they thought, of orthodox theology, the philosophers of the Age of Reason agreed that reality was grounded in the material universe. They were content with the world of the senses as the source from which all knowledge flowed; they conceived of nature, physical nature, as God's handiwork within which He had included all that man could possibly seek and desire to know.

It would be mistaken, however, to confuse the eighteenth-century conception of nature with twentieth-century scientific views of the natural world. For the Age of the Enlightenment, but not for the Age of the Atom, nature provided values as well as the bedrock upon which all reality stood. Nature was, that is, normative as well as existential. For the eighteenth-century mind, what was natural was also good. What the laws of nature decreed as right, man was morally bound to pursue. It was directly to nature and natural law that Jefferson appealed when he wrote in the Declaration of Independence that all men "are endowed by their Creator with certain unalienable Rights, that among these are Life, Liberty and the pursuit of Happiness." Jefferson did not claim these rights as a matter of theological principle but as ordained by God *in* nature and thus "self-evident" to all who bothered to look in that place.

When Jefferson wrote that certain rights were self-evident, he introduced the second element of the eighteenth-century philosophical trinity: reason. To the mind of the Enlightenment man's reason made possible the investigation of nature and the discovery of all that was true and beautiful. After all, had not Newton simply exercised his human reason to unfold the mysteries

---

[2] Thomas Jefferson to John Adams, April 11, 1823, in Adrienne Koch and William Peden, *The Life and Selected Writings of Thomas Jefferson* (N.Y., 1944), pp. 705–706.

of how the universe held together? Furthermore, reason was natural to man, part of his fundamental nature. Amidst the variety and confusion of the changing human scene, eighteenth-century thinkers identified one absolute and immutable characteristic of all men, at all times, in all places: all men were endowed by nature with reason. This held true for the primitive savage and the civilized sophisticate alike. It was on the assumption of the universal element of reason in man that Jefferson claimed certain rights as "self-evident." What he meant, of course, was that it was self-evident to the reason of all men that each man possessed a natural right to life, liberty, and happiness.

Exactly what the eighteenth century meant by reason is not always perfectly clear. The term was employed to cover a multitude of virtues, but it generally encompassed at least two elements. On one level the Age of the Enlightenment defined reason by contrasting it with its opposite—passion. Passion was subjective, individual, misleading, and corrupt. Reason was objective, universal, truthful, and beneficent. In this sense reason signified for the Enlightenment a mood or temperament of calm reflection requisite to counter man's tendency to act rashly and unwisely when impelled by the power of his passions. On another level, however, reason connoted an approach to knowledge, a way of comprehending the reality of nature, a method of discovering the truth. Voltaire caught the essence of this usage of the term reason when he urged his contemporaries never to "make hypotheses; we must never say: let us begin by making principles according to which we explain everything; We should say rather: Let us make an exact analysis of things . . . When we cannot utilize the compass of mathematics or the torch of experience and physics, it is certain that we cannot take a single step forward."[3] When employed in this fashion, as a synonym for induction as opposed to deduction, the term reason stood for the third basic principle of Enlightenment philosophy: science.

The advance of science in the eighteenth century, especially the omnipresent example of Newtonian physics, was that which gave the Enlightenment a faith in progress. The ideas of man's reason and the morality of nature were borrowings by the "modern" philosophers from their ancient predecessors in Greece and Rome, and the intellectual debt owed the past was freely confessed in the eighteenth century. But the new Age of Reason could and did take pride that it had surpassed the ancients in scientific prowess. Indeed, the scientific discoveries of the eighteenth century were awe-inspiring, ranging all the way from Newton's laws of motion to Benjamin Franklin's experiments with electricity. Without much reflection the eighteenth century took the breakthroughs in the physical sciences as objective proof for the reality of universal progress. Enlightenment thinkers easily jumped to the conclusion that the method of science could be applied with equal chances for success

[3] Voltaire quoted in Ernst Cassirer, *The Philosophy of the Enlightenment* (Boston, 1951), p. 12.

in every facet of human endeavor. Suddenly the problems of morality as well as medicine, of psychology as well as physics, of aesthetics as well as sociology were soluble by exercising human reason through the scientific method to unlock the philosophical secrets hidden in the laws of nature. Assuming that nature, reason, and science could establish all truth, the eighteenth-century philosophers set forth to discover, among other things, the laws of society.

The philosophers enthusiastically undertook the work of fashioning a body of social thought agreeable to the age, for they optimistically believed that a science of society must lead to better social organization and thus advance the chances for human happiness. In accordance with the Enlightenment's general tendency toward secularization, they subjected the theological, traditionalist, and static social philosophy of the seventeenth-century to ridicule and scorn. If the debt owed their predecessors was greater than they wished to acknowledge, it was nonetheless true that eighteenth-century social theorists chose science as the ultimate source for guidelines to the organization of society, recognized an element of dynamic activism as present in every community, and often emphasized the individualistic rather than the corporate origins of the social organism. John Winthrop would have been a lonely stranger in this intellectual atmosphere.

The reception of the European Enlightenment in the New World was enthusiastic but selective. The English colonists of North America borrowed from the Old World those ideas and assumptions which seemed best suited to their needs. The selection was partly controlled by the fact that the colonies recognized a cultural dependence upon the Mother Country as well as a political and economic subservience. Further, the social composition of the colonies was less aristocratic than that of England, which may account for the predominantly middle-class origins of the philosophers of the American Enlightenment as compared to the somewhat higher social standing of their English counterparts.

One indicator of the difference between the English and American Enlightenments was the all but total absence in America of any concern with aesthetic questions. The American Enlightenment centered almost exclusively on religious and political issues. John Adams once attempted to explain this phenomenon to his wife. "I must study politics and war," John informed Abigail, "that my sons may have liberty to study mathematics and philosophy, geography, natural history and naval architecture, navigation, commerce, and agriculture, in order to give their children a right to study painting, poetry, music, architecture, statuary, tapestry, and porcelain."[4] The arts could wait until the colonies had established their political and economic independence from the Mother Country.

The effects of the Enlightenment upon theology and the religious es-

[4] John Adams to Abigail Adams, 1780, as quoted in Adrienne Koch, *The American Enlightenment* (New York, 1965), p. 88.

tablishment in the provincial society of the New World were dramatic but perhaps less striking than in the cosmopolitan centers of Europe. As Louis Hartz has pointed out, "Despite the European flavor of a Jefferson or a Franklin, the American refused to join in the great Enlightenment enterprise of shattering the Christian concept of sin, replacing it with an unlimited humanism, and then emerging with an earthly paradise as glittering as the heavenly one that had been destroyed."[5]

The colonists uncovered deists in their midst—Jefferson being the most notable—but the driving force behind deism was to apply Reason to religion rather than to advance to a position of aggressive atheism. Deism was an effort to cleanse theology of encrusted superstition and supernaturalism, to purify and update religious doctrines that they might be in closer harmony with the secular knowledge of the day. Deism did not aim, then, at denying God, God's universe, or God's law.

Among the orthodox the Enlightenment did not pass without leaving its traces. Just how the rationalism of the eighteenth century both transformed and divided Calvinists in the New World is treated in Section Two of this book.

In the years of ferment after 1763 the colonial churches and their ministers (with the exception of the Anglican establishment) largely tended to side with the colonists in revolt. Since the revolutionaries directed their efforts primarily at dissolving the chains of Empire rather than radicalizing the social order at home, the churches in most instances were rarely subject to attack. Thus the majority of the clergy, fearing no general threat to the religious *status quo*, could and did aid the colonial cause. What was more, the arguments for revolution often paralleled (perhaps even parroted) traditional themes of religious thought. Especially in New England were the ministers outspoken in their opposition to English tyranny, and the churches of the region reverberated with sermons encouraging the congregations to resist royal authority. Unlike the French experience after 1789, the course of revolution in America never moved in the direction of a fierce attack upon all theology and an assault upon all religious institutions. There were, to be sure, efforts, only partially successful, to disestablish the official ties between church and state, symbolized by the passage of the Virginia Statute of Religious Liberty. But the movement toward the separation of church and state was motivated by the Enlightenment idea of truth, even religious truth, emerging from competition in the free forum of ideas.

Despite some variations, then, the assumptions of the European Enlightenment found ready acceptance in the New World. In the years after 1763 the American colonists eagerly set the social philosophy of the Age of Reason to work in justifying their revolution and in providing the framework within which new constitutions were conceived and debated. The conjunction of the

[5] Louis Hartz, *The Liberal Tradition in America* (New York, 1955), p. 36.

intellectual movement known as the American Enlightenment and the political events of the American Revolution raises, however, a fundamental question for the intellectual historian. Were the events of the years 1763–1789 in some way caused by the ideas of the American Enlightenment, or were the ideas of the Age of Reason employed only to rationalize actions that were caused essentially by social, economic, and political factors?

The article by Gordon S. Wood (page 155) details the controversy, as it applies to the historiography of the American Revolution, between the materialists and their opponents, the idealists. The idealists, who believe in the primacy of ideas as sources of human behavior, are engaged, as Wood indicates, "in a phase of writing about the Revolution in which the thought of the Revolutionaries, rather than their social and economic interests, has become the major focus of research and analysis."

But Wood repudiates both materialist and the idealist philosophies as exclusive alternatives for intellectual history. Rather, he attempts to resolve the argument by establishing the value of both approaches as valid and necessary. In fact, it is Wood's position that the two alternatives are actually complementary—that a study of ideas enhances our understanding of what contemporaries perceived as happening in their time, just as a study of social, economic, or political factors provides the historical context within which certain ideas come to have specific meaning. Wood insists that to understand the Revolution and the constitution-making that followed in its wake all angles of historical vision (social, economic, political, *and* intellectual) must be combined before we can make any claim to comprehension.

In the last analysis all social theory reflects a view of human nature because the private person and the public citizen are inextricably intertwined. Although eighteenth-century philosophers did not attain unanimity in their view of the essential nature of man, they did agree that the basic components of human nature could be discovered by science. The eighteenth-century philosophers "scientifically" discovered that society was natural to man. They were not so sure that government, the organization of society into the body politic, was necessarily natural, but they were convinced that man had been designed to live in company with his fellows with or without a formal political system. The notion that man had from the first lived in collective groups or associations gave rise to the widely shared belief that originally man had lived without controls in a state of nature, free of all restraints except those imposed by the law of nature. Whether this state of nature was a heaven or a hell, however, divided the social theorists, and the division followed the logic of their conceptions of the moral nature of man. Those who chose to posit that human nature was essentially good and reasonable tended to extol the state of nature. Those who calculated that at his core man was evil and passionate were relieved that the state of nature had been supplanted by the political state.

In the history of English social theory—that body of social thought upon which the English colonists in the New World were most dependent—

John Locke and Thomas Hobbes represented the two contrasting modes of evaluating human nature and the society of the state of nature. Hobbes' portrayal of the way in which human nature operated in the freedom of the natural state was at best uncomplimentary to man and at worst a frightening picture of immoral chaos. In the state of nature, thought Hobbes, the actions of men were determined by the sensations of pleasure and pain. What gave pleasure was sought and what produced pain avoided. No morality other than the ethics of hedonism existed, and since men were bound to come into conflict with one another as they scrambled after pleasure, the state of nature, in Hobbes' famous phrase, was "a war of all against all." To escape these intolerable conditions man quit the state of nature and formed a social compact that he might enjoy the peace and security possible only when authority to regulate and control human passions had been granted to a government. From his description of man's nature Hobbes concluded that government should not be free and democratic but total and authoritarian. While the American social theorists of the eighteenth century were fully familiar with the Hobbesian philosophy, his pessimism did not fit their mood nor did his justification of absolutism sit well with colonists engaged in conducting a revolution against the "tyranny" of the Mother Country.

John Locke was more congenial and more influential among the intellectuals of the American Enlightenment. Unlike Hobbes, Locke contended that man was endowed by nature with reason, that the knowledge of morality was innate, and that man possessed a moral sense even in the state of nature. Such being the case, the state of nature in the Lockean analysis was a relatively benign condition of existence. All men in the state of nature were equal in their natural rights, defined by Locke as the rights to life, liberty, and property, and a modicum of order was created without the benefit of government. Locke took pains to deny what Hobbes had affirmed, that the state of nature was a state of war. In his *Second Treatise of Government* Locke argued that "here we have the plain difference between the state of nature and the state of war which, however some men have confounded, are as far distant as a state of peace, goodwill, mutual assistance and preservation, and a state of enmity, malice, violence, and mutual destruction are one from another." But if the natural state was so pleasant, how could Locke explain the logic that convinced man to sacrifice the freedom of the state of nature for the constraints of the civil state? Locke faced this issue by explaining that the state of nature was not Utopia; he indicated that there were certain "inconveniences" to life in the state of nature. As Locke portrayed the situation:

If man in the state of nature be so free, as had been said, if he be absolute lord of his own person and possessions, equal to the greatest, and subject to nobody, why will he part with his freedom, why will he give up his empire and subject himself to the dominion and control of any other power? To which it is obvious to answer that though in the state of nature he has such a right, yet the enjoyment of it is very uncertain and constantly exposed to the invasion of others; for all being kings as much as he, every man his equal, and the greater part no strict observers of equity and justice, the enjoyment of the property he has in this state is very unsafe, very unsecure. This makes him willing to quit a condition which, however free, is full of fears and continual dangers; and it is not without reason that he seeks out and is willing to join in society with others who are already united, or have a mind to unite for the mutual preservation of their lives, liberties, and estates, which I call by the general name "property."

The civil state, government, is instituted according to Locke in order that the majority of men may gain a greater security in the enjoyment of their natural rights. In exchange for perfect equality and natural freedom man gained in the protection afforded those rights which remained to him even in the civil state.

One of the crucial rights which men retained in the Lockean philosophy was the right of revolution. Since government had been founded on the basis of a social contract (here Locke and Hobbes were in agreement), both rulers and ruled had mutual obligations. Should the rulers act in ways to subvert the contract, should rulers seek to infringe the natural rights adhering to the individual *qua* individual, should rulers attempt to impose a tyranny be exceeding their authority as granted in the compact, the ruled had a right to rise up in rebellion, depose the despots, and reestablish the balance of rights and obligations between governor and governed inherent in the contract.

Locke's optimism and his justification for revolution entered the mainstream of American social thought in the eighteenth century for several reasons. Locke was the English social philosopher *par excellence*, and the majority of colonists were English by heritage and by culture. Locke seemed to explain the desirability for the genesis of the civil state from the state of nature in a manner satisfying to the colonists, who lived terrifyingly close to a frontier wilderness that threatened to engulf the narrow fringe of civilization and established government. Furthermore, Locke was himself a central figure in the Enlightenment, as committed as any of its partisans to the trinity of nature, reason, and science. Lastly, and perhaps most importantly, Locke provided the colonists with a usable rationale for their revolution against the tyranny of King George III. By 1776 the Lockean philosophy was so much a part of the colonial perspective that Jefferson believed that the assumptions of the Declaration of Independence— a most Lockean document —were universally shared by Americans. Commenting on the Declaration toward the close of his life, Jefferson stoutly contended that it was written "Not to find out new principles, or new arguments, never before thought of, not merely to say things which had never been said before; but to place before mankind the common sense of the subject, in terms so plain and firm as to command their assent, and to justify ourselves in the independent stand we are compelled to take."[6]

As recent scholarship has amply documented, Locke was not the only English source from which the colonists derived the social philosophy of the Revolution. Equally important was a group of radical, dissenting thinkers of eighteenth-century England collectively known as the Commonwealthmen. While the Commonwealthmen shared with Locke a belief in natural rights and the social compact, they were more solicitous of protecting the liberty of the individual under government than even Locke had been. At the heart of the position of the Commonwealthmen was the desire for the maximum of individual liberty consistent with civil government. But, skeptics all, the Commonwealthmen postulated a constant struggle between the liberty of the people and the power of the rulers. Those who held political power, even political power constitutionally granted, were inexorably tempted to expand their authority at the expense of the people's liberty. The genius of the English constitution, according to the Commonwealthmen, was the balance it ordained between King, Lords, and Commons. With power distributed among the three components of government, no one segment could attain the upper hand and threaten liberty. By the mid-eighteenth century, however, many American colonists and even some English observers had reached the conclusion that corruption was rampant in the Mother Country, that political chicanery had unbalanced the constitutional distribution of power, and that as a result the King had gained control over Lords and Commons. Tyranny, many thought, was near at hand, and events from 1763 to 1776 only served to confirm the colonists in their suspicions. The social theory of the Common-wealthmen functioned to alert the colonists to the danger that power always threatened liberty; it alerted them to the possibility that the English King might be conspiring to deprive them of their rights as Englishmen; and, seeing in the efforts of England to tax the colonies after 1763 proof of the conspiracy, they declared their independence in 1776, sustained in their revolution by the writings of John Locke (page 168).

The revolution presented a novel task to American social theorists. Locke and the Commonwealthmen had served well to rationalize the destruction of the imperial government, but now the colonists had to construct new governments upon the ruins of the old. Confronted with the happy prospect of erecting a new political order, the Americans relied in part on their past experience and in part on the political science of the European Enlightenment.

Buoyed by the faith that every aspect of human behavior could be investigated scientifically, eighteenth-century philosophers devoted a considerable amount of time and energy to the science of government and politics. Their generally accepted findings were both absolutist and relativist. That is,

[6] Thomas Jefferson to Richard Henry Lee, May 18, 1825, in Koch and Peden *The Life and Writings of Jefferson*, p. 719.

the political scientists of the Age of Reason were sure that they had discovered laws that obtained in all situations, universally, but the applications
of those laws were subject to qualifications of specific time and historical place.

Montesquieu was an important source of intellectual stimulus for American social philosophers as they struggled to create a series of wholly original
social compacts. The French *philosophe* had taught that there existed three
absolute forms of government: despotism, monarchy, and republicanism.
Montesquieu further calculated that each form of government was actuated by
a specific principle: for monarchy the principle was honor, for despotism, fear,
and for republicanism, virtue. Montesquieu understood that every state was
an admixture of these forms and principles. Thus he concluded that every
workable system was one in which the three forms of government were
properly balanced. But the particular circumstances of time and place always
influenced the balance of forms and principles that was appropriate to a given
society. Physical factors, like the soil or climate, just as surely as "moral"
factors, like religion or social customs, set the limits within which suitable
governments could be devised. Failure to take these variables into account,
Montesquieu warned, inevitably led to governmental decay, collapse, revolution, and tyranny.

With the accepted wisdom of Enlightenment political sociology as their
guide, the American constitution-makers were prepared to pose and answer a
difficult but necessary set of questions. What were the special characteristics
of the American physical environment to which the new governments must be
adapted? What were the special characteristics of the American social environment which would determine the best mixture of governmental principles? What were the special characteristics of the American people which
would set the limits of governmental possibilities? As Americans pondered
these questions, they reached sufficient consensus to make the founding of new
governments possible, but they never did reach a unanimity that could end all
controversy. The selections from the writings of the Founding Fathers consequently point up areas of both agreement and dispute.

One subject of general agreement was that in the former English colonies
of the New World the economic and class distinctions of the Old World were
nonexistent. American society was a society of equals not only in theoretical
natural rights but in the attainment of material prosperity as well. Addition-
ally, the Founding Fathers reasoned, the recognized equality of American life
fostered public virtue, restrained the evil desire for private power within
manageable limits, and thus encouraged the maximum enjoyment of liberty.
Such being the case, they concluded that only a republican form of government was appropriate to American conditions. Note that the social theorists
of the American Enlightenment did not advocate that the new constitutions
should reflect simple democracy, for as that term was understood in the
eighteenth century it meant a system of government in which all the people
participated directly in the decision-making process, a proposition that the
Age of Reason thought preposterous. But a republic was feasible and desir-

able, for republicanism meant a government the authority of which was derived from the sovereign people who elected representatives to conduct the business of state.

If the constitution-makers agreed that republicanism was the proper form of the new American governments, they were not in similar concert respecting the problem of what institutional structures would best insure republicanism. They were at odds, that is, as to how the various elements of government could be most wisely balanced. For republicanism, whatever its attraction, suffered, as all eighteenth-century thinkers acknowledged, from an inherent tendency to degenerate into tyranny or anarchy. From their study of history, especially the history of the Greek and Roman republics, from their healthy draughts at the European fountain of political science, the Founding Fathers knew that the specific danger of republicanism was instability. The curb on instability was the very principle of republicanism, the virtue of the people, but should the citizenry somehow lose their virtue, the republic would be cast into a maelstrom of factionalism wherein each of the segments of society would seek its own gain at the expense of the general welfare. And the end result of factional contentiousness could be predicted: either the bickering would be ended by enthroning a tyranny, whether of the one, the few, or the many, or government would dissolve into anarchy, a condition in which no citizen receives the protection of the state, and thus the natural rights of all men are lost in the sea of controversy.

The different views of the Founding Fathers on how to escape either tyranny or anarchy in the American republic, a disparity reflected in the documents below, ultimately centered upon each men's faith or lack of faith in the virtue of the people and the efficiency of the established government. One must keep in mind that attitudes on these subjects changed over time. For instance, John Adams, who was optimistic about the virtuous character of New England as a source for sustaining republicanism in 1776 (page 172) had become less sanguine by the late 1780's (page 173) and had grown positively pessimistic by 1800 when he was relieved of his presidential duties by his former friend and colleague, Thomas Jefferson, who retained throughout his lifetime a roseate image of the mass of humanity (pages 186, 187, 188).

John Adams, New England lawyer and Revolutionary leader, doubted that a perfectly equalitarian society was possible. Adams perceived that even if material goods and economic rewards were equitably distributed, an aristocracy of talents inevitably resulted from the fact that nature distributed virtue and intelligence unequally among men. Adams, lacking the faith of some of his contemporaries that lands in the west would preserve economic equality for the foreseeable future, cautioned that the majority must constantly guard against the emergence of an artificial aristocratic minority. An artificial aristocracy, as Adams pointed out to John Taylor, philosopher and Virginia planter, was one created by human devices and not by the operations of natural law (pages 175, 176). Adams distrusted both groups of aristocrats, although he recognized the positive social value of the natural aristocracy.

But Adams feared that whenever, wherever, and for whatever reasons any aristocracy existed it would seek to enlarge its power at the expense of the liberty of others.

The characteristic note that Adams sounded in all his writings on social theory and constitutional structure was the necessity for a balance of forces (pages 177–185). Adams had no passion for majoritarianism, for the majority could act just as tyrannically as the minority. Conceiving of every society and every political entity as a collection of clashing interest groups, Adams was preoccupied with ways and means of weighing one group interest against another. Only in this manner, he maintained, could the freedom of all be insured. Adams thus helped forge a constitution for Massachusetts which theoretically protected the rights of the majority against the interest of the minority, the prerogatives of the legislature against encroachment on behalf of the executive, the interests of the poor against the gouging of the rich. As Adams informed Thomas Jefferson: "You [Jefferson] are afraid of the one—I, of the few . . . You are Apprehensive of Monarchy; I, of Aristocracy." And Adams might well have added that he remained skeptical of the representative democracy towards which the United States was moving in the first decade of the nineteenth century.

Adams was correct: Thomas Jefferson did have a greater fear of the one than the few. Although Adams and Jefferson concurred that every society produced a natural aristocracy, Jefferson wished to nurture and cultivate that aristocracy in a way that Adams thought dangerous. Rather than balance the natural aristocracy with a particular countervailing force, Jefferson would have educated and trained, at government expense if necessary, those blessed by nature with superior abilities, for they were the natural leaders of society (pages 189, 191). But the Virginia lawyer had less faith in the few—including the natural aristocrats—than he had in the many. More enthusiastic than Adams about the nature of human nature, Jefferson approached the typical nineteenth-century belief in majoritarian democracy (pages 192, 193). His trust in the majority was sustained by what he conceived to be the special qualities of the American environment. Jefferson subscribed wholeheartedly to the doctrine of agrarianism—the notion that those who worked the soil were the most virtuous, independent, and moral men on the face of the earth (page 194). Since the majority of Americans in the eighteenth century were yeomen farmers, Jefferson was reassured that his reliance on the virtue of the majority was underwritten by its occupational situation. As long as the majority of citizens remained yeomen farmers, a condition Jefferson, like Franklin, thought guaranteed by virgin lands to the west, just so long could one have confidence in the ultimate "rightness" of decisions made by that majority.

Furthermore, as a by-product of his trust in the natural wisdom of the bulk of men, Jefferson preferred to leave men as unhampered in their individual actions as feasible. Some power must be relegated by the individual to the state, but that power should always be limited and circumscribed. In a letter to Madison, Jefferson confessed that "I am not a friend to a very energetic government. It is always oppressive."[7] Jefferson summarized his desire for a negative state that exercised a minimum of functions in his first inaugural address (page 195).

One last comparison between Jefferson and Adams as social philosophers is appropriate. Adams' desire to balance the interests of society accorded perfectly with the eighteenth century's aesthetic appreciation of order, stability, and equilibrium. Society, to the mind of Adams, should resemble the formal gardens of an English country house, each shrub planted in perfect relation to every other. Social upheaval, political conflict, and the raucous noise of the multitudes participating in frequent elections annoyed Adams, because these events upset the balance of forces created by a good constitution. Jefferson, on the other hand, foreshadowed the aesthetic outlook of nineteenth-century romanticism which celebrated movement, tension, and the unpredictability of the emotions. Jefferson knew that society must change, that governmental structures convenient for one generation must not bind the generations that followed, and that only by keeping the government attuned to newly emergent social needs could the happiness of the social whole be preserved. Jefferson, then, looked forward to "a little rebellion, now and then" (page 198). His ability to alter course with fluctuations in the winds of social change gave a tone of pragmatic realism to Jefferson's policies as President that was often lacking in the more doctrinaire attitudes of the Adams administration.

James Scanlan's essay, "*The Federalist* and Human Nature" (page 200), by means of an intensive analysis of the psychological presuppositions upon which the defense of the Constitution relied, indicates that Jefferson was not an isolated pragmatist among his generation. Perhaps somewhat more pessimistic than Jefferson respecting the nature of human nature, the Founding Fathers struggled conscientiously to erect a form of government that recognized both human strength and weakness. That the Constitution of 1787 remains the basic document of the American political system attests to their lasting achievement.

James Madison, close friend and political ally of Thomas Jefferson, penned in *The Federalist* No. 10 (page 211), one of the great landmarks of American social thought in the eighteenth century. Madison's perspective is best described as realistic. He did not unqualifiedly place his trust in the majority to rule with justice, because he acknowledged that the majority could just as effectively trample on the rights of the minority as the minority could tyrannize the majority. Neither did Madison have much faith that the virtue of the people would prevent the outbreak of factionalism presumably endemic in republics. Factionalism had already proceeded too far by 1788 for Madison to hope that Americans were immune from the disease. The issue, then, that Madison addressed in *The Federalist* No. 10

[7] Thomas Jefferson to James Madison, November 13, 1787 in Koch and Peden, *The Life and Writings of Jefferson*, p. 440.

was to demonstrate that the new Constitution was so constructed as to preclude simultaneously the tyranny of the majority and the chaos of factionalism. He also sought to refute the doctrine of Montesquieu that a republic could avert factionalism only when limited in population and extent of territory, for under such conditions the unity of interests among the people would guarantee that division need not arise.

Madison managed to resolve all problems by holding first that the disease of factionalism could not ever be completely cured, because "The latent causes of faction are ... sown in the nature of man." Therefore, the judicious course was to deal directly with the effects of the disease. And this, Madison advocated, was precisely what the Constitution was designed to do. By establishing a representative republic, the Constitution would insure that the most virtuous men were elected to office, men not subject to temporary passions or parochial interests. By forming a federated republic, the Constitution would insure that local matters would be handled by the state governments, limiting the national government to exclusive concern with issues of the general welfare. Lastly, with an insight still relevant to the present state of political life in the United States, Madison argued that a republic established over a large extent of territory would insure that a multitude of factions would appear, that competition among them would tend to neutralize the power of any one, and that in this manner the minority would be protected in its rights, especially the right to have its property free from expropriation by the majority. Madison's insight, comments Edmund S. Morgan, "was the most fruitful intellectual achievement of the Revolutionary period ... It gave Madison and his colleagues at Philadelphia the courage to attempt a republican government for the whole nation ... [And] the character of American politics from 1789 to the present day has borne out Madison's observation: majorities in the United States have been composed of such a variety of interests that they have seldom proved oppressive, and the national government has been a stronger bulwark of freedom than the state governments."[8]

In a brief three decades (1763–1789) Americans had constructed from borrowed materials a radical critique of relations between the colonies and Mother Country, declared their separation, successfully concluded a war of revolution, and refashioned their political system on the basis of ideas which were drawn from the special conditions of their New World environment and experience. It was a proud record. As the new government took its seat at New York in 1789, it could rest confident that its structure had been defined and defended not by European models but by an American science of politics. In its first stages imitative and derivative, the American Enlightenment had now attained maturity, sophistication, and even a degree of intellectual independence.

[8] Edmund S. Morgan, "The American Revolution Considered as an Intellectual Movement," in Arthur M. Schlesinger, Jr. and Morton White, eds. *Paths of American Thought* (Boston, 1963), p. 32.

Interpretation

1 / Gordon S. Wood
Rhetoric and Reality in the American Revolution

(1966)

If any catch phrase is to characterize the work being done on the American Revolution by this generation of historians, it will probably be "the American Revolution considered as an intellectual movement." For we now seem to be fully involved in a phase of writing about the Revolution in which the thought of the Revolutionaries, rather than their social and economic interests, has become the major focus of research and analysis. This recent emphasis on ideas is not of course new, and indeed right from the beginning it has characterized almost all our attempts to understand the Revolution. The ideas of a period which Samuel Eliot Morison and Harold Laski once described as, next to the English revolutionary decades of the seventeenth century, the most fruitful era in the history of Western political thought could never be completely ignored in any phase of our history writing.

It has not been simply the inherent importance of the Revolutionary ideas, those "great principles of freedom," that has continually attracted the attention of historians. It has been rather the unusual nature of the Revolution and the constant need to explain what on the face of it seems inexplicable that has compelled almost all interpreters of the Revolution, including the participants themselves, to stress its predominantly intellectual character and hence its uniqueness among Western revolutions. Within the context of Revolutionary historiography the one great effort to disparage the significance of ideas in the Revolution—an effort which dominated our history writing in the first half of the twentieth century—becomes something of an anomaly, a temporary aberration into a deterministic social and economic explanation from which we have been retreating for the past two decades. Since roughly the end of World War II we have witnessed a resumed and increasingly heightened insistence on the primary significance of conscious beliefs, and particularly of

Gordon S. Wood, "Rhetoric and Reality in the American Revolution," *The William and Mary Quarterly*, 3rd ser., XXIII (1966), pp. 3–32. Reprinted without footnotes by permission of the author.

constitutional principles, in explaining what once again has become the unique character of the American Revolution. In the hands of idealist-minded historians the thought and principles of the Americans have consequently come to repossess that explanative force which the previous generation of materialist-minded historians had tried to locate in the social structure.

Indeed, our renewed insistence on the importance of ideas in explaining the Revolution has now attained a level of fullness and sophistication never before achieved, with the consequence that the economic and social approach of the previous generation of behaviorist historians has never seemed more anomalous and irrelevant than it does at present. Yet paradoxically it may be that this preoccupation with the explanatory power of the Revolutionary ideas has become so intensive and so refined, assumed such a character, that the apparently discredited social and economic approach of an earlier generation has at the same time never seemed more attractive and relevant. In other words, we may be approaching a crucial juncture in our writing about the Revolution where idealism and behaviorism meet.

It was the Revolutionaries themselves who first described the peculiar character of what they had been involved in. The Revolution, as those who took stock at the end of three decades of revolutionary activity noted, was not "one of those events which strikes the public eye in the subversions of laws which have usually attended the revolutions of governments." Because it did not seem to have been a typical revolution, the sources of its force and its momentum appeared strangely unaccountable. "In other revolutions, the sword has been drawn by the arm of offended freedom, under an oppression that threatened the vital powers of society." But this seemed hardly true of the American Revolution. There was none of the legendary tyranny that had so often driven desperate peoples into revolution. The Americans were not an oppressed people; they had no crushing imperial shackles to throw off. In fact, the Americans knew they were probably freer and less burdened with cumbersome feudal and monarchical restraints than any part of mankind in the eighteenth century. To its victims, the Tories, the Revolution was truly incomprehensible. Never in history, said Daniel Leonard, had there been so much rebellion with so "little real cause." It was, wrote Peter Oliver, "the most wanton and unnatural rebellion that ever existed.". . .

The same logic that drove the participants to view the Revolution as peculiarly intellectual also compelled Moses Coit Tyler, writing at the end of the nineteenth century, to describe the American Revolution as "preeminently a revolution caused by ideas, and pivoted on ideas." That ideas played a part in all revolutions Tyler readily admitted. But in most revolutions, like that of the French, ideas had been perceived and acted upon only when the social reality had caught up with them, only when the ideas had been given meaning and force by long-experienced "real evils." The American Revolution, said Tyler, had been different: it was directed "not against tyranny inflicted, but only against tyranny anticipated." The Americans revolted not out of actual suffering but out of reasoned principle. "Hence, more than with most other epochs of revolutionary strife, our epoch of revolutionary strife was a strife of ideas: a long warfare of political logic; a succession of annual campaigns in which the marshalling of arguments not only preceded the marshalling of armies, but often exceeded them in impression upon the final result."

It is in this historiographical context developed by the end of the nineteenth century, this constant and at times extravagant emphasis on the idealism of the Revolution, that the true radical quality of the Progressive generation's interpretation of the Revolution becomes so vividly apparent. For the work of these Progressive historians was grounded in a social and economic explanation of the Revolutionary era that explicitly rejected the causal importance of ideas. These historians could scarcely have avoided the general intellectual climate of the first part of the twentieth century which regarded ideas as suspect. By absorbing the diffused thinking of Marx and Freud and the assumptions of behaviorist psychology, men had come to conceive of ideas as ideologies or rationalizations, as masks obscuring the underlying interests and drives that actually determined social behavior. For too long, it seemed, philosophers had reified thought, detaching ideas from the material conditions that produced them and investing them with an independent will that was somehow alone responsible for the determination of events. As Charles Beard pointed out in his introduction to the 1935 edition of *An Economic Interpretation of the Constitution,* previous historians of the Constitution had assumed that ideas were "entities, particularities, or forces, apparently independent of all earthly considerations coming under the head of 'economic.'" It was Beard's aim, as it was the aim of many of his contemporaries, to bring into historical consideration "those realistic features of economic conflict, stress, and strain" which previous interpreters of the Revolution had largely ignored. The product of this aim was a generation or more of historical writing about the Revolutionary period (of which Beard's was but the most famous expression) that sought to explain the Revolution and the formation of the Constitution in terms of socio-economic relationships and interests rather than in terms of ideas.

Curiously, the consequence of this reversal of historical approaches was not the destruction of the old-fashioned conception of the nature of ideas. As Marx had said, he intended only to put Hegel's head in its rightful place; he had no desire to cut it off. Ideas as rationalization, as ideology, remained— still distinct entities set in opposition to interests, now however lacking any deep causal significance, becoming merely a covering superstructure for the underlying and determinative social reality. Ideas therefore could still be the subject of historical investigation, as long as one kept them in their proper place, interesting no doubt in their own right but not actually counting for much in the movement of events . . .

Bringing to their studies of the Revolution similar assumptions about the nature of ideas, some [Progressive historians] went on to expose starkly the implications of those assumptions. When the entire body of Revolutionary thinking was examined, these historians could not avoid being struck by its generally bombastic and overwrought quality. The ideas expressed seemed so inflated, such obvious exaggerations of reality, that they could scarcely be taken seriously. The Tories were all "wretched hirelings, and execrable parricides"; George III, the "tyrant of the earth," a "monster in human form"; the British soldiers, "a mercenary, licentious rabble of banditti," intending to "tear the bowels and vitals of their brave but peaceable fellow subjects, and *to wash the ground with a profusion of innocent blood.*" Such extravagant language, it seemed, could be nothing but calculated deception, at best an obvious distortion of fact, designed to incite and mold a revolutionary fervor. "The stigmatizing of British policy as 'tyranny,' 'oppression' and 'slavery,'" wrote Arthur M. Schlesinger, the dean of the Progressive historians, "had little or no objective reality, at least prior to the Intolerable Acts, but ceaseless repetition of the charge kept emotions at fever pitch."

Indeed, so grandiose, so overdrawn, it seemed, were the ideas that the historians were necessarily led to ask not whether such ideas were valid but why men should have expressed them. It was not the content of such ideas but the function that was really interesting. The revolutionary rhetoric, the profusion of sermons, pamphlets, and articles in the patriotic cause, could best be examined as propaganda, that is, as a concerted and self-conscious effort by agitators to manipulate and shape public opinion. Because of the Progressive historians' view of the Revolution as the movement of class minorities bent on promoting particular social and economic interests, the conception of propaganda was crucial to their explanation of what seemed to be a revolutionary consensus. Through the use of ideas in provoking hatred and influencing opinion and creating at least "an appearance of unity," the influence of a minority of agitators was out of all proportion to their number. The Revolution thus became a display of extraordinary skillfulness in the manipulation of public opinion. In fact, wrote Schlesinger, "no disaffected element in history has ever risen more splendidly to the occasion."...

With this conception of ideas as weapons shrewdly used by designing propagandists, it was inevitable that the thought of the Revolutionaries should have been denigrated. The Revolutionaries became by implication hypocritical demagogues, "adroitly tailoring their arguments to changing conditions." Their political thinking appeared to possess neither consistency nor significance. "At best," said Schlesinger in an early summary of his interpretation, "an exposition of the political theories of the anti-parliamentary party is an account of their retreat from one strategic position to another." So the Whigs moved, it was strongly suggested, easily if not frivolously from a defense of charter rights, to the rights of Englishmen, and finally to the rights of man, as each position was exposed and became untenable. In short, concluded Schlesinger, the Revolution could never be understood if it were regarded "as a great forensic controversy over abstract governmental rights."

It is essentially on this point of intellectual consistency that Edmund S. Morgan has fastened for the past decade and a half in an attempt to bring down the entire interpretive framework of the socio-economic argument. If it could be shown that the thinking of the Revolutionaries was not inconsistent after all, that the Whigs did not actually skip from one constitutional notion to the next, then the imputation of Whig frivolity and hypocrisy would lose its force. This was a central intention of Morgan's study of the political thought surrounding the Stamp Act. As Morgan himself has noted and others have repeated, "In the last analysis the significance of the Stamp Act crisis lies in the emergence, not of leaders and methods and organizations, but of well-defined constitutional principles." As early as 1765 the Whigs "laid down the line on which Americans stood until they cut their connections with England. Consistently from 1765 to 1776 they denied the authority of Parliament to tax them externally or internally; consistently they affirmed their willingness to submit to whatever legislation Parliament should enact for the supervision of the empire as a whole." This consistency thus becomes, as one scholar's survey of the current interpretation puts it, "an indication of American devotion to principle."

It seemed clear once again after Morgan's study that the Americans were more sincerely attached to constitutional principles than the behaviorist historians had supposed, and that their ideas could not be viewed as simply manipulated propaganda. Consequently the cogency of the Progressive historians' interpretation was weakened if not unhinged. And as the evidence against viewing the Revolution as rooted in internal class conflict continued to mount from various directions, it appeared more and more comprehensible to accept the old-fashioned notion that the Revolution was after all the consequence of "a great forensic controversy over abstract governmental rights." There was, it seemed, no deprived and depressed populace yearning for a participation in politics that had long been denied; no coherent merchant class victimizing a mass of insolvent debtors; no seething discontent with the British mercantile system; no privileged aristocracy, protected by law, anxiously and insecurely holding power against a clamoring democracy. There was, in short, no internal class upheaval in the Revolution.

If the Revolution was not to become virtually incomprehensible, it must have been the result of what the American Whigs always contended it was— a dispute between Mother Country and colonies over constitutional liberties. By concentrating on the immediate events of the decade leading up to independence, the historians of the 1950's have necessarily fled from the economic and social determinism of the Progressive historians. And by emphasizing the consistency and devotion with which Americans held their constitutional beliefs they have once again focused on what seems to be the extraordinary intellectuality of the American Revolution and hence its uniqueness among Western revolutions. This interpretation, which, as Jack P. Greene notes, "may appropriately be styled neo-whig," has turned the Revolution into a rationally conservative movement, involving mainly a constitutional defense of existing political liberties against the abrupt and unexpected provocations of the British government after 1760 . . .

In a different way Bernard Bailyn in a recent article has clarified and reinforced this revived idealistic interpretation of the Revolution. The accumulative influence of much of the latest historical writing on the character of eighteenth-century American society has led Bailyn to the same insight expressed by Samuel Williams in 1794. What made the Revolution truly revolutionary was not the wholesale disruption of social groups and political institutions, for compared to other revolutions such disruption was slight; rather it was the fundamental alteration in the Americans' structure of values, the way they looked at themselves and their institutions. Bailyn has seized on this basic intellectual shift as a means of explaining the apparent contradiction between the seriousness with which the Americans took their revolutionary ideas and the absence of radical social and institutional change. The Revolution, argues Bailyn, was not so much the transformation as the realization of American society.

The Americans had been gradually and unwittingly preparing themselves for such a mental revolution since they first came to the New World in the seventeenth century. The substantive changes in American society had taken place in the course of the previous century, slowly, often imperceptibly, as a series of small piecemeal deviations from what was regarded by most Englishmen as the accepted orthodoxy in society, state, and religion. What the Revolution marked, so to speak, was the point when the Americans suddenly blinked and saw their society, its changes, its differences, in a new perspective. Their deviation from European standards, their lack of an established church and a titled aristocracy, their apparent rusticity and general equality, now became desirable, even necessary, elements in the maintenance of their society and politics. The comprehending and justifying, the endowing with high moral purpose, of these confusing and disturbing social and political divergences, Bailyn concludes, was the American Revolution.

Bailyn's more recent investigation of the rich pamphlet literature of the decades before Independence has filled out and refined his idealist interpretation, confirming him in his "rather old-fashioned view that the American Revolution was above all else an ideological-constitutional struggle and not primarily a controversy between social groups undertaken to force changes in the organization of society." While Bailyn's book-length introduction to the first of a multivolumed edition of Revolutionary pamphlets makes no effort to stress the conservative character of the Revolution and indeed emphasizes (in contrast to the earlier article) its radicalism and the dynamic and transforming rather than the rationalizing and declarative quality of Whig thought, it nevertheless represents the culmination of the idealist approach to the history of the Revolution. For "above all else," argues Bailyn, it was the Americans' world-view, the peculiar bundle of notions and beliefs they put together during the imperial debate, "that in the end propelled them into revolution." Through his study of the Whig pamphlets Bailyn became convinced "that the fear of a comprehensive conspiracy against liberty throughout the English-speaking world—a conspiracy believed to have been nourished in corruption, and of which, it was felt, oppression in America was only the most immediately visible part—lay at the heart of the revolutionary movement." No one of the various acts and measures of the British government after 1763 could by itself have provoked the extreme and violent response of the American Whigs. But when linked together they formed in the minds of the Americans, imbued with a particular historical understanding of what constituted tyranny, an extensive and frightening program designed to enslave the New World . . .

Labeling the recent historical interpretations of the Revolution as "neo-Whig" is indeed appropriate, for, as Page Smith has pointed out, "After a century and a half of progress in historical scholarship, in research techniques, in tools and methods, we have found our way to the interpretation held, substantially, by those historians who themselves participated in or lived through the era of the Revolution." By describing the Revolution as a conservative, principled defense of American freedom against the provocations of the English government, the neo-Whig historians have come full circle to the position of the Revolutionaries themselves and to the interpretation of the first generation of historians. Indeed, as a consequence of this historical atavism, praise for the contemporary or early historians has become increasingly common.

But to say "that the Whig interpretation of the American Revolution may not be as dead as some historians would have us believe" is perhaps less to commend the work of David Ramsay and George Bancroft than to indict the approach of recent historians. However necessary and rewarding the neo-Whig histories have been, they present us with only a partial perspective on the Revolution. The neo-Whig interpretation is intrinsically polemical; however subtly presented, it aims to justify the Revolution. It therefore cannot accommodate a totally différent, an opposing, perspective, a Tory view of the Revolution. It is for this reason that the recent publication of Peter Oliver's "Origin and Progress of the American Rebellion" is of major significance, for it offers us—"by attacking the hallowed traditions of the revolution, challenging the motives of the founding fathers, and depicting revolution as passion, plotting, and violence"—an explanation of what happened quite different from what we have been recently accustomed to. Oliver's vivid portrait of the Revolutionaries with his accent on their vicious emotions and interests seriously disturbs the present Whiggish interpretation of the Revolution. It is not that Oliver's description of, say, John Adams as madly ambitious and consumingly resentful is any more correct than Adam's own description of himself as a virtuous and patriotic defender of liberty against tyranny. Both interpretations of Adams are in a sense right, but neither can comprehend the other because each is preoccupied with seemingly contradictory sets of motives. Indeed, it is really these two interpretations that have divided historians of the Revolution ever since.

Any intellectually satisfying explanation of the Revolution must encompass the Tory perspective as well as the Whig, for if we are compelled to take sides and choose between opposing motives—unconscious or avowed, passion or principle, greed or liberty—we will be endlessly caught up in the polemics of the participants themselves. We must, in other words, eventually dissolve the distinction between conscious and unconscious motives, between the Revolutionaries' stated intentions and their supposedly hidden needs and desires, a dissolution that involves somehow relating beliefs and ideas to the social world in which they operate. If we are to understand the causes of the Revolution we must therefore ultimately transcend this problem of motivation. But this we can never do as long as we attempt to explain the Revolution mainly in terms of the intentions of the participants. It is not that men's motives are unimportant; they indeed make events, including revolutions. But the purposes of men, especially in a revolution, are so numerous, so varied, and so contradictory that their complex interaction produces results that no one intended or could even foresee. It is this interaction and these results that recent historians are referring to when they speak so disparagingly of those "underlying determinants" and "impersonal and inexorable forces" bringing on the Revolution. Historical explanation which does not account for these "forces," which, in other words, relies simply on understanding the conscious intentions of the actors, will thus be limited. This preoccupation with men's purposes was what restricted the perspectives of the contemporaneous Whig and Tory interpretations; and it is still the weakness of the neo-Whig histories, and indeed of any interpretation which attempts to explain the events of the Revolution by discovering the calculations from which individuals supposed themselves to have acted . .

By implying that certain declared rational purposes are by themselves an adequate explanation for the Americans' revolt, in other words that the Revolution was really nothing more than a contest over constitutional principles, the neo-Whig historians have not only threatened to deny what we have learned of human psychology in the twentieth century, but they have also in fact failed to exploit fully the terms of their own idealist approach by not taking into account all of what the Americans believed and said. Whatever the deficiencies and misunderstandings of the role of ideals in human behavior present in the propagandist studies of the 1930's, these studies did for the first time attempt to deal with the entirety and complexity of American Revolutionary thought—to explain not only all the well-reasoned notions of law and liberty that were so familiar but, more important, all the irrational and hysterical beliefs that had been so long neglected. Indeed, it was the patent absurdity and implausibility of much of what the Americans said that lent credence and persuasiveness to their mistrustful approach to the ideas. Once this exaggerated and fanatical rhetoric was uncovered by the

Progressive historians, it should not have subsequently been ignored—no matter how much it may have impugned the reasonableness of the American response. No widely expressed ideas can be dismissed out of hand by the historian.

In his recent analysis of Revolutionary thinking Bernard Bailyn has avoided the neo-Whig tendency to distort the historical reconstruction of the American mind. By comprehending "the assumptions, beliefs, and ideas that lay behind the manifest events of the time," Bailyn has attempted to get inside the Whigs' mind, and to experience vicariously all of what they thought and felt, both their rational constitutional beliefs and their hysterical and emotional ideas as well. The inflammatory phrases, "slavery," "corruption," "conspiracy," that most historians had either ignored or readily dismissed as propaganda, took on a new significance for Bailyn. He came "to suspect that they meant something very real to both the writers and their readers: that there were real fears, real anxieties, a sense of real danger behind these phrases, and not merely the desire to influence by rhetoric and propaganda the inert minds of an otherwise passive populace." No part of American thinking, Bailyn suggests—not the widespread belief in a ministerial conspiracy, not the hostile and vicious indictments of individuals, not the fear of corruption and the hope for regeneration, not any of the violent, seemingly absurd distortions and falsifications of what we now believe to be true, in short, none of the frenzied rhetoric—can be safely ignored by the historian seeking to understand the causes of the Revolution.

Bailyn's study, however, represents something other than a more complete and uncorrupted version of the common idealist interpretations of the Revolution. By viewing from the "interior" the Revolutionary pamphlets, which were "to an unusual degree, *explanatory*," revealing "not merely positions taken but the reasons why positions were taken," Bailyn like any idealist historian has sought to discover the motives the participants themselves gave for their actions, to re-enact their thinking at crucial moments, and thereby to recapture some of the "unpredictable reality" of the Revolution. But for Bailyn the very unpredictability of the reality he has disclosed has undermined the idealist obsession with explaining why, in the participants' own estimation, they acted as they did. Ideas emerge as more than explanatory devices, as more than indicators of motives. They become as well objects for analysis in and for themselves, historical events in their own right to be treated as other historical events are treated. Although Bailyn has examined the Revolutionary ideas subjectively from the inside, he has also analyzed them objectively from the outside . . .

In his study of the Revolutionary ideas Bailyn has come to an opposite conclusion: ideas counted for a great deal, not only being responsible for the Revolution but also for transforming the character of American society. Yet in his hands ideas lose that static quality they have commonly had for the Whig historians . . . For Bailyn the ideas of the Revolutionaries take on an elusive and unmanageable quality, a dynamic self-intensifying character that transcended the intentions and desires of any of the historical participants. By emphasizing how the thought of the colonists was "strangely reshaped, turned in unfamiliar directions," by describing how the Americans "indeliberately, half-knowingly" groped toward "conclusions they could not themselves clearly perceive," by demonstrating how new beliefs and hence new actions were the responses not to desire but to the logic of developing situations, Bailyn has wrested the explanation of the Revolution out of the realm of motivation in which the neo-Whig historians had confined it.

With this kind of approach to ideas, the degree of consistency and devotion to principles become less important, and indeed the major issues of motivation and responsibility over which historians have disagreed become largely irrelevant. Action becomes not the product of rational and conscious calculation but of dimly perceived and rapidly changing thoughts and situations, "where the familiar meaning of ideas and words faded away into confusion, and leaders felt themselves peering into a haze, seeking to bring shifting conceptions somehow into focus." Men become more the victims than the manipulators of their ideas, as their thought unfolds in ways few anticipated, "rapid, irreversible, and irresistible," creating new problems, new considerations, new ideas, which have their own unforeseen implications. In this kind of atmosphere the Revolution, not at first desired by the Americans, takes on something of an inevitable character, moving through a process of escalation into levels few had intended or perceived. It no longer makes sense to assign motives or responsibility to particular individuals for the totality of what happened. Men were involved in a complicated web of phenomena, ideas, and situations, from which in retrospect escape seems impossible.

By seeking to uncover the motives of the Americans expressed in the Revolutionary pamphlets, Bailyn has ended by demonstrating the autonomy of ideas as phenomena, where the ideas operate, as it were, over the heads of the participants, taking them in directions no one could have foreseen. His discussion of Revolutionary thought thus represents a move back to a deterministic approach to the Revolution, a determinism, however, which is different from that which the neo-Whig historians have so recently and self-consciously abandoned. Yet while the suggested determinism is thoroughly idealist—indeed never before has the force of ideas in bringing on the Revolution been so emphatically put—its implications are not. By helping to purge our writing about the Revolution of its concentration on constitutional principles and its stifling judicial-like preoccupation with motivation and responsibility, the study serves to open the way for new questions and new appraisals. In fact, it is out of the very completeness of his idealist interpretation, out of his exposition of the extraordinary nature—the very dynamism and emotionalism—of the Americans' thought that we have the evidence for an entirely different, a behaviorist, perspective on the causes of the American

Revolution. Bailyn's book-length introduction to his edition of Revolutionary pamphlets is therefore not only a point of fulfillment for the idealist approach to the Revolution, it is also a point of departure for a new look at the social sources of the Revolution.

It seems clear that historians of eighteenth-century America and the Revolution cannot ignore the force of ideas in history to the extent that Namier and his students have done in their investigations of eighteenth-century English politics. This is not to say, however, that the Namier approach to English politics has been crucially limiting and distorting. Rather it may suggest that the Namier denigration of ideas and principles is inapplicable for American politics because the American social situation in which ideas operated was very different from that of eighteenth-century England. It may be that ideas are less meaningful to a people in a socially stable situation. Only when ideas have become stereotyped reflexes do evasion and hypocrisy ... become significant. Only in a relatively settled society does ideology become a kind of habit, a bundle of widely shared and instinctive conventions, offering ready-made explanations for men who are not being compelled to ask any serious questions. Conversely, it is perhaps only in a relatively unsettled, disordered society, where the questions come faster than men's answers, that ideas become truly vital and creative.

Paradoxically it may be the very vitality of the Americans' ideas, then, that suggests the need to examine the circumstances in which they flourished. Since ideas and beliefs are ways of perceiving and explaining the world, the nature of the ideas expressed is determined as much by the character of the world being confronted as by the internal development of inherited and borrowed conceptions. Out of the multitude of inherited and transmitted ideas available in the eighteenth century, Americans selected and emphasized those which seemed to make meaningful what was happening to them ... There was always, in Max Weber's term, some sort of elective affinity between the Americans' interests and their beliefs, and without that affinity their ideas would not have possessed the peculiar character and persuasiveness they did. Only the most revolutionary social needs and circumstances could have sustained such revolutionary ideas.

When the ideas of the Americans are examined comprehensively, when all of the Whig rhetoric, irrational as well as rational, is taken into account, one cannot but be struck by the predominant characteristics of fear and frenzy, the exaggerations and the enthusiasm, the general sense of social corruption and disorder out of which would be born a new world of benevolence and harmony where Americans would become the "eminent examples of every divine and social virtue." As Bailyn and the propaganda studies have amply shown, there is simply too much fanatical and millennial thinking even by the best minds that must be explained before we can characterize the Americans' ideas as peculiarly rational and legalistic and thus view the Revolution as merely a conservative defense of constitutional liberties ...

The ideas of the Americans seem, in fact, to form what can only be called a revolutionary syndrome. If we were to confine ourselves to examining the Revolutionary rhetoric alone, apart from what happened politically or social-ly, it would be virtually impossible to distinguish the American Revolution from any other revolution in modern Western history. In the kinds of ideas expressed the American Revolution is remarkably similar to the seventeenth-century Puritan Revolution and to the eighteenth-century French Revolution: the same general disgust with a chaotic and corrupt world, the same anxious and angry bombast, the same excited fears of conspiracies by depraved men, the same utopian hopes for the construction of a new and virtuous order. It was not that this syndrome of ideas was simply transmitted from one genera-tion or from one people to another. It was rather perhaps that similar, though hardly identical, social situations called forth within the limitations of in-herited and available conceptions similar modes of expression. Although we need to know much more about the sociology of revolutions and collective movements, it does seem possible that particular patterns of thought, particu-lar forms of expression, correspond to certain basic social experiences. There may be, in other words, typical modes of expression, typical kinds of beliefs and values, characterizing a revolutionary situation, at least within roughly similar Western societies. Indeed, the types of ideas manifested may be the best way of identifying a collective movement as a revolution. As one student of revolutions writes, "It is on the basis of a knowledge of men's beliefs that we can distinguish their behaviour from riot, rebellion or insanity."

It is thus the very nature of the Americans' rhetoric—its obsession with corruption and disorder, its hostile and conspiratorial outlook, and its millennial vision of a regenerated society—that reveals as nothing else apparently can the American Revolution as a true revolution with its sources lying deep in the social structure. For this kind of frenzied rhetoric could spring only from the most severe sorts of social strain. The grandiose and feverish language of the Americans was indeed the natural, even the inevitable, expression of a people caught up in a revolutionary situation, deeply alienated from the existing sources of authority and vehemently involved in a basic reconstruction of their political and social order. The hysteria of the Amer-icans' thinking was but a measure of the intensity of their revolutionary passions. Undoubtedly the growing American alienation from British author-ity contributed greatly to this revolutionary situation. Yet the very weakness of the British imperial system and the accumulating ferocity of American antagonism to it suggests that other sources of social strain were being fed into the revolutionary movement. It may be that the Progressive historians in their preoccupation with internal social problems were more right than we have recently been willing to grant. It would be repeating their mistake, however, to expect this internal strain necessarily to take the form of coherent class conflict or overt social disruption. The sources of revolutionary social stress may have been much more subtle but no less severe . . .

It is through the Whigs' ideas, then, that we may be led back to take up where the Progressive historians left off in their investigation of the internal social sources of the Revolution. By working through the ideas—by reading them imaginatively and relating them to the objective social world they both reflected and confronted—we may be able to eliminate the unrewarding distinction between conscious and unconscious motives, and eventually thereby to combine a Whig with a Tory, an idealist with a behaviorist, interpretation. For the ideas, the rhetoric, of the Americans were never obscuring but remarkably revealing of their deepest interests and passions. What they expressed may not have been for the most part factually true, but it was always psychologically true. In this sense their rhetoric was never detached from the social and political reality; and indeed it becomes the best entry into an understanding of that reality. Their repeated overstatements of reality, their incessant talk of "tyranny" when there seems to have been no real oppression, their obsession with "virtue," and "luxury," and "corruption," their devotion to "liberty" and "equality"—all these notions were neither manipulated propaganda nor borrowed empty abstractions, but ideas with real personal and social significance for those who used them. Propaganda could never move men to revolution. No popular leader, as John Adams put it, has ever been able "to persuade a large people, for any length of time together, to think themselves wronged, injured, and oppressed, unless they really were, and saw and felt it to be so." The ideas had relevance; the sense of oppression and injury, although often displaced onto the imperial system, was nonetheless real. It was indeed the meaningfulness of the connection between what the Americans said and what they felt that gave the ideas their propulsive force and their overwhelming persuasiveness.

It is precisely the remarkable revolutionary character of the Americans' ideas now being revealed by historians that best indicates that something profoundly unsettling was going on in the society, that raises the question, as it did for the Progressive historians, why the Americans should have expressed such thoughts. With their crude conception of propaganda the Progressive historians at least attempted to grapple with the problem. Since we cannot regard the ideas of the Revolutionaries as simply propaganda, the question still remains to be answered . . . Precisely because they sought to understand both the Revolutionary ideas and American society, the behaviorist historians of the Progressive generation, for all of their crude conceptualizations, their obsession with "class" and hidden economic interests, and their treatment of ideas as propaganda, have still offered us an explanation of the Revolutionary era so powerful and so comprehensive that no purely intellectual interpretation will ever replace it.

Documents

■ The Argument for Revolution

2 / Samuel Adams
The Rights of the Colonists

(1772)

The Committee appointed by the Town the second Instant "to State the Rights of the Colonists and of this Province in particular, as Men, as Christians, and as Subjects; to communicate and publish the same to the several Towns in this Province and to the World as the sense of this Town with the Infringements and Violations thereof that have been, or from Time to Time may be made. Also requesting of each Town a free Communication of their Sentiments Reported . . .

1st. Natural Rights of the Colonists as Men.—

Among the Natural Rights of the Colonists are these First, a Right to *Life;* Secondly to *Liberty;* thirdly to *Property;* together with the Right to support and defend them in the best manner they can—Those are evident Branches of, rather than deductions from the Duty of Self Preservation, commonly called the first Law of Nature—

All Men have a Right to remain in a State of Nature as long as they please: And in case of intollerable Oppression, Civil or Religious, to leave the Society they belong to, and enter into another.—

When Men enter into Society, it is by voluntary consent; and they have a right to demand and insist upon the performance of such conditions, And previous limitations as form an equitable *original compact.*—

Every natural Right not expressly given up or from the nature of a Social Compact necessarily ceded remains.—

All positive and civil laws, should conform as far as possible, to the Law of natural reason and equity. . . .

The natural liberty of Men by entring into society is abridg'd or restrained so far only as is necessary for the Great end of Society the best good of the whole—

Samuel Adams, "The Rights of the Colonists," adopted by the Town of Boston, November 20, 1772 from Harry Alonzo Cushing (ed.), *The Writings of Samuel Adams,* II (G.P. Putnam's, New York, 1906), pp. 350–359.

In the state of nature, every man is under God, Judge and sole Judge, of his own rights and the injuries done him: By entering into society, he agrees to an Arbiter or indifferent Judge between him and his neighbours; but he no more renounces his original right, than by taking a cause out of the ordinary course of law, and leaving the decision to Referees or indifferent Arbitrations. In the last case he must pay the Referees for time and trouble; he should be also willing to pay his Just quota for the support of government, the law and constitution; the end of which is to furnish indifferent and impartial Judges in all cases that may happen, whether civil ecclesiastical, marine or military.—

"The natural liberty of man is to be free from any superior power on earth, and not to be under the will or legislative authority of man; but only to have the law of nature for his rule."—

In the state of nature men may as the *Patriarchs* did, employ hired servants for the defence of their lives, liberty and property: and they should pay them reasonable wages. Government was instituted for the purposes of common defence; and those who hold the reins of government have an equitable natural right to an honourable support from the same principle "that the labourer is worthy of his hire" but then the same community which they serve, ought to be assessors of their pay: Governors have no right to seek what they please; by this, instead of being content with the station assigned them, that of honourable servants of the society, they would soon become Absolute masters, Despots, and Tyrants. Hence as a private man has a right to say, what wages he will give in his private affairs, so has a Community to determine what they will give and grant of their Substance, for the Administration of publick affairs. And in both cases more are ready generally to offer their Service at the proposed and stipulated price, than are able and willing to perform their duty.—

In short it is the greatest absurdity to suppose it in the power of one or any number of men at the entering into society, to renounce their essential natural rights, or the means of preserving those rights when the great end of civil government from the very nature of its institution is for the support, protection and defence of those very rights: the principal of which as is before observed, are life liberty and property. If men through fear, fraud or mistake, should *in terms* renounce and give up any essential natural right, the eternal law of reason and the great end of society, would absolutely vacate such renunciation; the right to freedom being *the gift* of God Almighty, it is not in the power of Man to alienate this gift, and voluntarily become a slave . . .

3d. *The Rights of the Colonists as Subjects*

A Common Wealth or state is a body politick or civil society of men, united together to promote their mutual safety and prosperity, by means of their union.

The *absolute Rights* of Englishmen, and all freemen in or out of Civil society, are principally, *personal security personal liberty* and *private property*.

All Persons born in the British American Colonies are by the laws of God and nature, and by the Common law of England, *exclusive of all charters from the Crown*, well Entitled, and by the Acts of the British Parliament are declared to be entitled to all the natural essential, inherent & inseperable Rights Liberties and Privileges of Subjects born in Great Britain, or within the Realm. Among those Rights are the following; which no men or body of men, consistently with their own rights as men and citizens or members of society, can for themselves give up, or take away from others

First, "The first fundamental positive law of all Commonwealths or States, is the establishing the legislative power; as the first fundamental *natural* law also, which is to govern even the legislative power itself, is the preservation of the Society."

Secondly, The Legislative has no right to absolute arbitrary power over the lives and fortunes of the people: Nor can mortals assume a prerogative, not only too high for men, but for Angels; and therefore reserved for the exercise of the *Deity* alone . . .

Thirdly, The supreme power cannot Justly take from any man, any part of his property without his consent, in person or by his Representative.—

These are some of the first principles of natural law & Justice, and the great Barriers of all free states, and of the British Constitution in particular. It is utterly irreconcileable to these principles, and to many other fundamental maxims of the common law, common sense and reason, that a British house of commons, should have a right, at pleasure, to give and grant the property of the Colonists. That these Colonists are well entitled to all the essential rights, liberties and privileges of men and freemen, born in Britain, is manifest, not only from the Colony charter, in general, but acts of the British Parliament . . . Now what liberty can there be, where property is taken away without consent? Can it be said with any colour of truth and Justice, that this Continent of three thousand miles in length, and of a breadth as yet unexplored, in which however, its supposed, there are five millions of people, has the least voice, vote or influence in the decisions of the British Parliament? Have they, all together, any more right or power to return a single number to that house of commons, who have not inadvertently, but deliberately assumed a power to dispose of their lives, Liberties and properties, then to choose an Emperor of China! Had the Colonists a right to return members to the british parliament, it would only be hurtfull; as from their local situation and circumstances it is impossible they should be ever truly and properly represented there. The inhabitants of this country in all probability in a few years will be more numerous, than those of Great Britain and Ireland together; yet it is absurdly expected by the promoters of the present measures, that these, with their posterity to all generations, should be easy while their property, shall be disposed of by a house of commons at three thousand miles distant from them; and who cannot be supposed to have the least care or concern for their real interest: Who have not only no natural care for their interest, but must be *in effect* bribed against it; as every burden they lay on the colonists is so much saved or gained to themselves . . . The Colonists have been branded with the odious names of traitors and rebels, only for complaining of their grievances; How long such treatment will, or ought to be born is submitted.

■ John Adams On Human Nature

3 / John Adams
Letter to Mercy Warren

(1776)

. . . The form of government which you admire, when its principles are pure, is admirable; indeed, it is productive of everything which is great and excellent among men. But its principles are as easily destroyed as human nature is corrupted. Such a government is only to be supported by pure religion or austere morals. Public virtue cannot exist in a nation without private, and public virtue is the only foundation of republics. There must be a positive passion for the public good, the public interest, honor, power, and glory, established in the minds of the people, or there can be no republican government, nor any real liberty; and this public passion must be superior to all private passions. Men must be ready, they must pride themselves, and be happy to sacrifice their private pleasures, passions, and interests, nay, their private friendships and dearest connections, when they stand in competition with the rights of society.

Is there in the world a nation which deserved this character? There have been several, but they are no more. Our dear Americans perhaps have as much of it as any nation now existing, and New England perhaps has more than the rest of America. But I have seen all along my life such selfishness and littleness even in New England that I sometimes tremble to think that, although we are engaged in the best cause that ever employed the human heart, yet the prospect of success is doubtful, not for want of power or of wisdom, but of virtue.

John Adams to Mercy Warren, April 16, 1776 from Adrienne Koch and William Peden (eds.), *The Selected Writings of John and John Quincy Adams* (Alfred Knopf, 1946), pp. 57–58.

4 / John Adams
Discourses on Davila

(1790)

Men, in their primitive conditions, however savage, were undoubtedly gregarious; and they continue to be social, not only in every stage of civilization, but in every possible situation in which they can be placed. As nature intended them for society, she has furnished them with passions, appetites, and propensities, as well as a variety of faculties, calculated both for their individual enjoyment, and to render them useful to each other in their social connections. There is none among them more essential or remarkable, than the *passion for distinction*. A desire to be observed, considered, esteemed, praised, beloved, and admired by his fellows, is one of the earliest, as well as keenest dispositions discovered in the heart of man. If any one should doubt the existence of this propensity, let him go and attentively observe the journeymen and apprentices in the first workshop, or the oarsmen in a cockboat, a family or a neighborhood, the inhabitants of a house or the crew of a ship, a school or a college, a city or a village, a savage or civilized people, a hospital or a church, the bar or the exchange, a camp or a court. Wherever men, women, or children, are to be found, whether they be old or young, rich or poor, high or low, wise or foolish, ignorant or learned, every individual is seen to be strongly actuated by a desire to be seen, heard, talked of, approved and respected, by the people about him, and within his knowledge.

A regard to the sentiments of mankind concerning him, and to their dispositions towards him, every man feels within himself; and if he has reflected, and tried experiments, he has found, that no exertion of his reason, no effort of his will, can wholly divest him of it. In proportion to our affection for the notice of others is our aversion to their neglect; the stronger the desire of the esteem of the public, the more powerful the aversion to their disapprobation; the more exalted the wish for admiration, the more invincible the abhorrence of contempt. Every man not only desires the consideration of others, but he frequently compares himself with others, his friends or his enemies; and in proportion as he exults when he perceives that he has more of it than they, he feels a keener affliction when he sees that one or more of them, are more respected than himself.

This passion, while it is simply a desire to excel another, by fair industry in the search of truth, and the practice of virtue, is properly called *Emulation*. When it aims at power, as a means of distinction, it is *Ambition*. When it is in a situation to suggest the sentiments of fear and apprehension, that another,

John Adams, "Discourses on Davila" (1790), from Charles Francis Adams (ed.), *The Life and Works of John Adams*, VI (Boston, 1851), pp. 232–234.

who is now inferior, will become superior, it is denominated *Jealousy*. When it is in a state of mortification, at the superiority of another, and desires to bring him down to our level, or to depress him below us, it is properly called *Envy*. When it deceives a man into a belief of false professions of esteem or admiration, or into a false opinion of his importance in the judgment of the world, it is *Vanity*. These observations alone would be sufficient to show, that this propensity, in all its branches, is a principal source of the virtues and vices, the happiness and misery of human life; and that the history of mankind is little more than a simple narration of its operation and effects.

There is in human nature, it is true, simple *Benevolence*, or an affection for the good of others; but alone it is not a balance for the selfish affections. Nature then has kindly added to benevolence, the desire of reputation, in order to make us good members of society ... Nature has sanctioned the law of self-preservation by rewards and punishments. The rewards of selfish activity are life and health; the punishments of negligence and indolence are want, disease, and death. Each individual, it is true, should consider, that nature has enjoined the same law on his neighbor, and therefore a respect for the authority of nature would oblige him to respect the rights of others as much as his own. But reasoning as abstruse, though as simple as this, would not occur to all men. The same nature therefore has imposed another law, that of promoting the good, as well as respecting the rights of mankind, and has sanctioned it by other rewards and punishments. The rewards in this case, in this life, are *esteem* and *admiration* of others; the punishments are *neglect* and *contempt*; nor may any one imagine that these are not as real as the others. The desire of the esteem of others is as real a want of nature as hunger; and the neglect and contempt of the world as severe a pain as the gout or stone. It sooner and oftener produces despair, and a detestation of existence; of equal importance to individuals, to families and to nations. It is a principal end of government to regulate this passion, which in its turn becomes a principal means of government. It is the only adequate instrument of order and subordination in society, and alone commands effectual obedience to laws, since without it neither human reason, nor standing armies, would ever produce that great effect.

■ On Natural and Artificial Aristocracies

(1814)

By *natural aristocracy*, in general, may be understood those superiorities of influence in society which grow out of the constitution of human nature. By *artificial aristocracy*, those inequalities of weight and superiorities of influence which are created and established by civil laws. Terms must be defined before we can reason. By aristocracy, I understand all those men who can command, influence, or procure more than an average of votes; by an aristocrat, every man who can and will influence one man to vote besides himself. Few men will deny that there is a natural aristocracy of virtues and talents in every nation and in every party, in every city and village. Inequalities are a part of the natural history of man.

That all men are born to equal rights is true. Every being has a right to his own, as clear, as moral, as sacred, as any other being has. This is as indubitable as a moral government in the universe. But to teach that all men are born with equal powers and faculties, to equal influence in society, to equal property and advantages through life, is as gross a fraud, as glaring an imposition on the credulity of the people, as ever was practised by monks, by Druids, by Brahmins, by priests of the immortal Lama, or by the self-styled philosophers of the French revolution.

John Adams to John Taylor, April 15, 1814 from Charles Francis Adams (ed.), *The Life and Works of John Adams*, VI (Boston, 1851), pp. 451–452, 453–454.

6 / John Adams
Letter to Thomas Jefferson

(1813)

"Nobility in Men is worth as much as it is in Horses Asses or Rams: but the meanest blooded Puppy, in the World, if he gets a little money, is as good a man as the best of them." Yet Birth and Wealth together have prevailed over Virtue and Talents in all ages. The Many, will acknowledge no other "αριστοι" [Ruler]. Your Experience of this Truth, will not much differ from that of your old Friend . . .

John Adams to Thomas Jefferson, July 9, 1813 from Lester J. Cappon (ed.), *The Adams-Jefferson Letters*, II (University of North Carolina Press, Chapel Hill, for The Institute of Early American History and Culture, 1959), p. 352. Reprinted by permission of the publisher.

■ On the Necessity for Constitutional Balance

7 / John Adams
Defense of the Constitutions

(1787)

The United States of America have exhibited, perhaps, the first example of governments erected on the simple principles of nature; and if men are now sufficiently enlightened to disabuse themselves of artifice, imposture, hypocrisy, and superstition, they will consider this event as an era in their history. Although the detail of the formation of the American governments is at present little known or regarded either in Europe or in America, it may hereafter become an object of curiosity. It will never be pretended that any persons employed in that service had interviews with the gods, or were in any degree under the inspiration of Heaven, more than those at work upon ships or houses, or laboring in merchandise or agriculture; it will forever be acknowledged that these governments were contrived merely by the use of reason and the senses . . .

Neither the people, nor their conventions, committees, or sub-committees, considered legislation in any other light than as ordinary arts and sciences, only more important. Called without expectation, and compelled without previous inclination, though undoubtedly at the best period of time, both for England and America, suddenly to erect new systems of laws for their future government, they adopted the method of a wise architect, in erecting a new palace for the residence of his sovereign. They determined to consult Vitruvius, Palladio, and all other writers of reputation in the art; to examine the most celebrated buildings, whether they remain entire or in ruins; to compare these with the principles of writers; and to inquire how far both the theories and models were founded in nature, or created by fancy; and when this was done, so far as their circumstances would allow, to adopt the advantages and reject the inconveniences of all. Unembarrassed by attachments to noble families, hereditary lines and successions, or any considerations of royal blood, even the pious mystery of holy oil had no more influence than that other

John Adams, "Preface to A Defense of the Constitutions of Government of the United States of America" (1787), from Charles Francis Adams (ed.), *The Life and Works of John Adams*, IV (Boston, 1851), pp. 292–294.

one of holy water. The people were universally too enlightened to be imposed on by artifice; and their leaders, or more properly followers, were men of too much honor to attempt it. Thirteen governments thus founded on the natural authority of the people alone, without a pretence of miracle or mystery, and which are destined to spread over the northern part of that whole quarter of the globe, are a great point gained in favor of the rights of mankind. The experiment is made, and has completely succeeded; it can no longer be called in question, whether authority in magistrates and obedience of citizens can be grounded on reason, morality, and the Christian religion, without the monkery of priests, or the knavery of politicians. As the writer was personally acquainted with most of the gentlemen in each of the states, who had the principal share in the first draughts, the following work was really written to lay before the public a specimen of that kind of reading and reasoning which produced the American constitutions.

8 / John Adams
Thoughts on Government

(1776)

MY DEAR SIR,—If I was equal to the task of forming a plan for the government of a colony, I should be flattered with your request, and very happy to comply with it; because, as the divine science of politics is the science of social happiness, and the blessings of society depend entirely on the constitutions of government, which are generally institutions that last for many generations, there can be no employment more agreeable to a benevolent mind than a research after the best.

Pope flattered tyrants too much when he said,

> "For forms of government let fools contest,
> That which is best administered is best."

Nothing can be more fallacious than this. But poets read history to collect flowers, not fruits; they attend to fanciful images, not the effects of social institutions. Nothing is more certain, from the history of nations and nature of man, than that some forms of government are better fitted for being well administered than others.

We ought to consider what is the end of government, before we determine which is the best form. Upon this point all speculative politicians will agree,

John Adams, "Thoughts on Government" (1776), from Charles Francis Adams (ed.), *The Life and Works of John Adams*, IV (Boston, 1851), pp. 193–200, addressed to George Wythe of Virginia.

that the happiness of society is the end of government, as all divines and moral philosophers will agree that the happiness of the individual is the end of man. From this principle it will follow, that the form of government which communicates ease, comfort, security, or, in one word, happiness, to the greatest number of persons, and in the greatest degree, is the best.

All sober inquirers after truth, ancient and modern, pagan and Christian, have declared that the happiness of man, as well as his dignity, consists in virtue. Confucius, Zoroaster, Socrates, Mahomet, not to mention authorities really sacred, have agreed in this.

If there is a form of government, then, whose principle and foundation is virtue, will not every sober man acknowledge it better calculated to promote the general happiness than any other form?

Fear is the foundation of most governments; but it is so sordid and brutal a passion, and renders men in whose breasts it predominates so stupid and miserable, that Americans will not be likely to approve of any political institution which is founded on it.

Honor is truly sacred, but holds a lower rank in the scale of moral excellence than virtue. Indeed, the former is but a part of the latter, and consequently has not equal pretensions to support a frame of government productive of human happiness.

The foundation of every government is some principle or passion in the minds of the people. The noblest principles and most generous affections in our nature, then, have the fairest chance to support the noblest and most generous models of government.

A man must be indifferent to the sneers of modern Englishmen, to mention in their company the names of Sidney, Harrington, Locke, Milton, Nedham, Neville, Burnet, and Hoadly. No small fortitude is necessary to confess that one has read them. The wretched condition of this country, however, for ten or fifteen years past, has frequently reminded me of their principles and reasonings. They will convince any candid mind, that there is no good government but what is republican. That the only valuable part of the British constitution is so; because the very definition of a republic is "an empire of laws, and not of men." That, as a republic is the best of governments, so that particular arrangement of the powers of society, or, in other words, that form of government which is best contrived to secure an impartial and exact execution of the laws, is the best of republics.

Of republics there is an inexhaustible variety, because the possible combinations of the powers of society are capable of innumerable variations.

As good government is an empire of laws, how shall your laws be made? In a large society, inhabiting an extensive country, it is impossible that the whole should assemble to make laws. The first necessary step, then, is to depute power from the many to a few of the most wise and good. But by what rules shall you choose your representatives? Agree upon the number and qualifications of persons who shall have the benefit of choosing, or annex this privilege to the inhabitants of a certain extent of ground.

The principal difficulty lies, and the greatest care should be employed, in constituting this representative assembly. It should be in miniature an exact portrait of the people at large. It should think, feel, reason, and act like them. That it may be the interest of this assembly to do strict justice at all times, it should be an equal representation, or, in other words, equal interests among the people should have equal interests in it. Great care should be taken to effect this, and to prevent unfair, partial, and corrupt elections. Such regulations, however, may be better made in times of greater tranquillity than the present; and they will spring up themselves naturally, when all the powers of government come to be in the hands of the people's friends. At present, it will be safest to proceed in all established modes, to which the people have been familiarized by habit.

A representation of the people in one assembly being obtained, a question arises, whether all the powers of government, legislative, executive, and judicial, shall be left in this body? I think a people cannot be long free, nor ever happy, whose government is in one assembly. My reasons for this opinion are as follow:

1. A single assembly is liable to all the vices, follies, and frailties of an individual; subject to fits of humor, starts of passion, flights of enthusiasm, partialities, or prejudice, and consequently productive of hasty results and absurd judgments. And all these errors ought to be corrected and defects supplied by some controlling power.

2. A single assembly is apt to be avaricious, and in time will not scruple to exempt itself from burdens, which it will lay, without compunction, on its constituents.

3. A single assembly is apt to grow ambitious, and after a time will not hesitate to vote itself perpetual. This was one fault of the Long Parliament; but more remarkably of Holland, whose assembly first voted themselves from annual to septennial, then for life, and after a course of years, that all vacancies happening by death or otherwise, should be filled by themselves, without any application to constituents at all.

4. A representative assembly, although extremely well qualified, and absolutely necessary, as a branch of the legislative, is unfit to exercise the executive power, for want of two essential properties, secrecy and despatch.

5. A representative assembly is still less qualified for the judicial power, because it is too numerous, too slow, and too little skilled in the laws.

6. Because a single assembly, possessed of all the powers of government, would make arbitrary laws for their own interest, execute all laws arbitrarily for their own interest, and adjudge all controversies in their own favor.

But shall the whole power of legislation rest in one assembly? Most of the foregoing reasons apply equally to prove that the legislative power ought to be more complex; to which we may add, that if the legislative power is wholly in one assembly, and the executive in another, or in a single person, these two powers will oppose and encroach upon each other, until the contest shall end in war, and the whole power, legislative and executive, be usurped by the strongest.

The judicial power, in such case, could not mediate, or hold the balance between the two contending powers, because the legislative would undermine it. And this shows the necessity, too, of giving the executive power a negative upon the legislative, otherwise this will be continually encroaching upon that.

To avoid these dangers, let a distinct assembly be constituted, as a mediator between the two extreme branches of the legislature, that which represents the people, and that which is vested with the executive power.

Let the representative assembly then elect by ballot, from among themselves or their constituents, or both, a distinct assembly, which, for the sake of perspicuity, we will call a council. It may consist of any number you please, say twenty or thirty, and should have a free and independent exercise of its judgment, and consequently a negative voice in the legislature.

These two bodies, thus constituted, and made integral parts of the legislature, let them unite, and by joint ballot choose a governor, who, after being stripped of most of those badges of domination, called prerogatives, should have a free and independent exercise of his judgment, and be made also an integral part of the legislature. This, I know, is liable to objections; and, if you please, you may make him only president of the council, as in Connecticut. But as the governor is to be invested with the executive power, with consent of council, I think he ought to have a negative upon the legislative. If he is annually elective, as he ought to be, he will always have so much reverence and affection for the people, their representatives and counsellors, that, although you give him an independent exercise of his judgment, he will seldom use it in opposition to the two houses, except in cases the public utility of which would be conspicuous; and some such cases would happen.

The dignity and stability of government in all its branches, the morals of the people, and every blessing of society depend so much upon an upright and skilful administration of justice, that the judicial power ought to be distinct from both the legislative and executive, and independent upon both, that so it may be a check upon both, as both should be checks upon that. The judges, therefore, should be always men of learning and experience in the laws, of exemplary morals, great patience, calmness, coolness and attention. Their minds should not be distracted with jarring interests; they should not be dependent upon any man, or body of men. To these ends, they should hold estates for life in their offices; or, in other words, their commissions should be during good behavior, and their salaries ascertained and established by law. For misbehavior, the grand inquest of the colony, the house of representatives, should impeach them before the governor and council, where they should have time and opportunity to make their defence; but, if convicted, should be removed from their offices, and subjected to such other punishment as shall be thought proper.

A constitution founded on these principles introduces knowledge among the people, and inspires them with a conscious dignity becoming freemen; a general emulation takes place, which causes good humor, sociability, good manners, and good morals to be general. That elevation of sentiment inspired by such a government, makes the common people brave and enterprising. That ambition which is inspired by it makes them sober, industrious, and frugal. You will find among them some elegance, perhaps, but more solidity; a little pleasure, but a great deal of business; some politeness, but more civility. If you compare such a country with the regions of domination, whether monarchical or aristocratical, you will fancy yourself in Arcadia or Elysium.

9 / John Adams
Defense of the Constitutions

(1787)

There can be no free government without a democratical branch in the constitution ... If there is one certain truth to be collected from the history of all ages, it is this; that the people's rights and liberties, and the democratical mixture in a constitution, can never be preserved without a strong executive, or, in other words, without separating the executive from the legislative power. If the executive power, or any considerable part of it, is left in the hands either of an aristocratical or a democratical assembly, it will corrupt the legislature as necessarily as rust corrupts iron, or as arsenic poisons the human body; and when the legislature is corrupted, the people are undone.

The rich, the well-born, and the able, acquire an influence among the people that will soon be too much for simple honesty and plain sense, in a house of representatives. The most illustrious of them must, therefore, be separated from the mass, and placed by themselves in a senate; this is, to all honest and useful intents, an ostracism. A member of a senate, of immense

John Adams, "Preface to A Defense of the Constitutions of Government of the United States of America" (1787), from Charles Francis Adams (ed.), *The Life and Works of John Adams*, IV (Boston, 1851), pp. 289–291.

wealth, the most respected birth, and transcendent abilities, has no influence in the nation, in comparison of what he would have in a single representative assembly. When a senate exists, the most powerful man in the state may be safely admitted into the house of representatives, because the people have it in their power to remove him into the senate as soon as his influence becomes dangerous. The senate becomes the great object of ambition; and the richest and the most sagacious wish to merit an advancement to it by services to the public in the house. When he has obtained the object of his wishes, you may still hope for the benefits of his exertions, without dreading his passions; for the executive power being in other hands, he has lost much of his influence with the people, and can govern very few votes more than his own among the senators.

10 / John Adams
Discourses on Davila

(1790)

The great question will forever remain, *who shall work?* Our species cannot all be idle. Leisure for study must ever be the portion of a few. The number employed in government must forever be very small... As rest is rapture to the weary man, those who labor little will always be envied by those who labor much, though the latter in reality be probably the most enviable. With all the encouragements, public and private, which can ever be given to general education, and it is scarcely possible they should be too many or too great, the laboring part of the people can never be learned. The controversy between the rich and the poor, the laborious and the idle, the learned and the ignorant, distinctions as old as the creation, and as extensive as the globe, distinctions which no art or policy, no degree of virtue or philosophy can ever wholly destroy, will continue, and rivalries will spring out of them. These parties will be represented in the legislature, and must be balanced, or one will oppress the other. There will never probably be found any other mode of establishing such an equilibrium, than by constituting the representation of each an independent branch of the legislature, and an independent executive authority, such as that in our government, to be a third branch and a mediator or an arbitrator between them. Property must be secured, or liberty cannot exist. But if unlimited or unbalanced power of disposing property, be put into the hands of those who have no property, France will find, as we have found,

---

John Adams, "Discourses on Davila" (1790), from Charles Francis Adams (ed.), *The Life and Works of John Adams*, VI (Boston, 1851), pp. 279–281.

the lamb committed to the custody of the wolf. In such a case, all the pathetic exhortations and addresses of the national assembly to the people, to respect property, will be regarded no more than the warbles of the songsters of the forest. The great art of lawgiving consists in balancing the poor against the rich in the legislature, and in constituting the legislative a perfect balance against the executive power, at the same time that no individual or party can become its rival. The essence of a free government consists in an effectual control of rivalries. The executive and the legislative powers are natural rivals; and if each has not an effectual control over the other, the weaker will ever be the lamb in the paws of the wolf. The nation which will not adopt an equilibrium of power must adopt a despotism. There is no other alternative. Rivalries must be controlled, or they will throw all things into confusion; and there is nothing but despotism or a balance of power which can control them. Even in the simple monarchies, the nobility and the judicatures constitute a balance, though a very imperfect one, against the royalties.

11 / John Adams
Letter to Thomas Jefferson

(1787)

DEAR SIR

The Project of a new Constitution, has Objections against it, to which I find it difficult to reconcile my self, but I am so unfortunate as to differ somewhat from you in the Articles, according to your last kind Letter.

You are afraid of the one—I, of the few. We agree perfectly that the many should have a full fair and perfect Representation.—You are Apprehensive of Monarchy; I, of Aristocracy. I would therefore have given more Power to the President and less to the Senate. The Nomination and Appointment to all offices I would have given to the President, assisted only by a Privy Council of his own Creation, but not a Vote or Voice would I have given to the Senate or any Senator, unless he were of the Privy Council. Fraction and Distraction are the sure and certain Consequence of giving to a Senate a vote in the distribution of offices.

You are apprehensive the President when once chosen, will be chosen again and again as long as he lives. So much the better as it appears to me. —You are apprehensive of foreign Interference, Intrigue, Influence. So am I.—But, as often as Elections happen, the danger of foreign Influence recurs. The less frequently they happen the less danger.—And if the Same Man may be chosen again, it is probable he will be, and the danger of foreign Influence will be less. Foreigners, seeing little Prospect will have less Courage for Enterprize.

Elections, my dear sir, Elections to offices which are great objects of Ambition, I look at with terror. Experiments of this kind have been so often tryed, and so universally found productive of Horrors, that there is great Reason to dread them.

John Adams to Thomas Jefferson, December 6, 1787 from Lester J. Cappon (ed.), *The Adams-Jefferson Letters*, I (University of North Carolina Press, Chapel Hill, for The Institute of Early American History and Culture, 1959), pp. 213–214. Reprinted by permission of the publisher.

■ Thomas Jefferson On Human Nature

12 / Thomas Jefferson
Letter to DuPont de Nemours

(1816)

We consider society as one of the natural wants with which man has been created; that he has been endowed with faculties and qualities to effect its satisfaction by concurrence of others having the same want; that when by the exercise of these faculties he has procured a state of society, it is one of his acquisitions which he has a right to regulate and controul, jointly, indeed with all those who have concurred in the procurement, whom he cannot exclude from its use or direction more than they him. We think experience has proved it safer, for the mass of individuals composing the society, to reserve to themselves personally the exercise of all rightful powers to which they are competent, and to delegate those to which they are not competent to deputies named, and removable for unfaithful conduct, by themselves immediately. Hence with us, the people (by which is meant the mass of individuals composing the society) being competent to judge of facts occurring in ordinary life, they have retained the functions of judges of facts, under the name of jurors; but being unqualified for the management of affairs requiring intelligence above the common level, yet competent judges of human character, they chuse for their management representatives, some by themselves immediately, others by electors chosen by themselves . . .

We both consider the people as our children, and love them with parental affection. But you love them as infants whom you are afraid to trust without nurses, and I as adults, whom I freely leave to self government . . . Enlighten the people generally, and tyranny and oppressions of body and mind will vanish like evil spirits at the dawn of day. Altho' I do not, with some enthusiasts, believe that the human condition will ever advance to such a state of perfection as that there shall no longer be pain or vice in the world, yet I believe it susceptible of much improvement, and, most of all, in matters of government and religion; and that the diffusion of knowledge among the people is to be the instrument by which it is to be effected.

Thomas Jefferson to DuPont de Nemours, April 24, 1816 from Gilbert Chinard (ed.), *The Correspondence of Jefferson and DuPont de Nemours*, I (The Johns Hopkins Press, Baltimore, 1931), pp. 256–259. Reprinted by permission of the publisher.

13 / Thomas Jefferson
Letter to Peter Carr

(1787)

Moral Philosophy. I think it lost time to attend lectures on this branch. He who made us would have been a pitiful bungler, if he had made the rules of our moral conduct a matter of science. For one man of science, there are thousands who are not. What would have become of them? Man was destined for society. His morality, therefore, was to be formed to this object. He was endowed with a sense of right and wrong, merely relative to this. This sense is as much a part of his nature, as the sense of hearing, seeing, feeling; it is the true foundation of morality, and not the $\tau o \ \kappa \alpha \lambda o \nu$,[1] truth, &c., as fanciful writers have imagined. The moral sense, or conscience is as much a part of man as his leg or arm. It is given to all human beings in a stronger or weaker degree, as force of members is given them in a greater or less degree. It may be strengthened by exercise, as may any particular limb of the body. This sense is submitted, indeed, in some degree, to the guidance of reason; but it is a small stock which is required for this: even a less one than what we call common sense. State a moral case to a ploughman and a professor. The former will decide it as well, and often better than the latter, because he has not been led astray by artificial rules. In this branch, therefore, read good books, because they will encourage, as well as direct your feelings.

Thomas Jefferson to Peter Carr, August 10, 1787 from Adrienne Koch and William Peden (eds.), *The Life and Selected Writings of Thomas Jefferson* (Random House, 1944), pp. 430–431.

[1] The beautiful.

14 / Thomas Jefferson
Letter to Francis W. Gilmer

(1816)

Assuming the fact, that the earth has been created in time, and consequently
the dogma of final causes, we yield, of course, to this short syllogism. Man
was created for social intercourse; but social intercourse cannot be maintained without a sense of justice; then man must have been created with a
sense of justice. There is an error into which most of the speculators on
government have fallen, and which the well-known state of society of our
Indians ought, before now, to have corrected. In their hypothesis of the
origin of government, they suppose it to have commenced in the patriarchal
or monarchical form. Our Indians are evidently in that state of nature which
has passed the association of a single family; and not yet submitted to the
authority of positive laws, or of any acknowledged magistrate. Every man,
with them, is perfectly free to follow his own inclinations. But if, in doing this,
he violates the rights of another, if the case be slight, he is punished by the
disesteem of his society, or, as we say, by public opinion; if serious, he is
tomahawked as a dangerous enemy. Their leaders conduct them by the
influence of their character only; and they follow, or not, as they please,
him of whose character for wisdom or war they have the highest opinion.
Hence the origin of the parties among them adhering to different leaders,
and governed by their advice, not by their command. The Cherokees, the
only tribe I know to be contemplating the establishment of regular laws,
magistrates, and government, propose a government of representatives,
elected from every town. But of all things, they least think of subjecting themselves to the will of one man. This, the only instance of actual fact within
our knowledge, will be then a beginning by republican, and not by patriarchal
or monarchical government, as speculative writers have generally conjectured.

Thomas Jefferson to Francis W. Gilmer, June 7, 1816 from Albert Ellery Bergh
(ed.), *The Writings of Thomas Jefferson*, XV (The Thomas Jefferson Memorial Association, Washington, D.C., 1903), pp. 23–27.

■ On Natural and Artificial Aristocracies

15 / Thomas Jefferson
Letter to John Adams

(1813)

. . . I agree with you that there is a natural aristocracy among men. The grounds of this are virtue and talents. Formerly, bodily powers gave place among the aristoi. But since the invention of gunpowder has armed the weak as well as the strong with missile death, bodily strength, like beauty, good humor, politeness and other accomplishments, has become but an auxiliary ground of distinction. There is also an artificial aristocracy, founded on wealth and birth, without either virtue or talents; for with these it would belong to the first class. The natural aristocracy I consider as the most precious gift of nature, for the instruction, the trusts, and government of society. And indeed, it would have been inconsistent in creation to have formed man for the social state, and not to have provided virtue and wisdom enough to manage the concerns of the society. May we not even say, that that form of government is the best, which provides the most effectually for a pure selection of these natural aristoi into the offices of government? The artificial aristocracy is a mischievous ingredient in government, and provision should be made to prevent its ascendency . . .

On the question, What is the best provision, you and I differ; but we differ as rational friends, using the free exercise of our own reason, and mutually indulging it's errors. *You* think it best to put the Pseudo-aristoi into a separate chamber of legislation where they may be hindered from doing mischief by their coordinate branches, and where also they may be a protection to wealth against the Agrarian and plundering enterprises of the Majority of the people. I think that to give them power in order to prevent them from doing mischief, is arming them for it, and increasing instead of remedying the evil. For if the coordinate branches can arrest their action, so may they that of the co-ordinates. Mischief may be done negatively as well as positively . . .

I think the best remedy is exactly that provided by all our constitutions, to leave to the citizens the free election and separation of the aristoi from

Thomas Jefferson to John Adams, October 28, 1813 from Adrienne Koch and William Peden (eds.), *The Life and Selected Writings of Thomas Jefferson* (Random House, 1944), pp. 632–634.

the pseudo-aristoi, of the wheat from the chaff. In general they will elect the real good and wise. In some instances, wealth may corrupt, and birth blind them; but not in sufficient degree to endanger the society . . .

But even in Europe a change has sensibly taken place in the mind of man. Science had liberated the ideas of those who read and reflect, and the American example had kindled feelings of right in the people. An insurrection has consequently begun, of science, talents, and courage, against rank and birth, which have fallen into contempt. It has failed in its first effort, because the mobs of the cities, the instrument used for its accomplishment, debased by ignorance, poverty, and vice, could not be restrained to rational action. But the world will recover from the panic of this first catastrophe. Science is progressive, and talents and enterprise on the alert. Resort may be had to the people of the country, a more governable power from their principles and subordination; and rank, and birth, and tinsel-aristocracy will finally shrink into insignificance, even there.

■ On Education

16 / Thomas Jefferson
Notes on Virginia

(1782)

As soon as they [students] are of sufficient age, it is supposed they will be sent on from the grammar schools to the university, which constitutes our third and last stage, there to study those sciences which may be adapted to their views. By that part of our plan which prescribes the selection of the youths of genius from among the classes of the poor, we hope to avail the State of those talents which nature has sown as liberally among the poor as the rich, but which perish without use, if not sought for and cultivated. But of the views of this law none is more important, none more legitimate, than that of rendering the people the safe, as they are the ultimate, guardians of their own liberty. For this purpose the reading in the first stage, where *they* will receive their whole education, is proposed, as has been said, to be chiefly historical. History, by apprizing them of the past, will enable them to judge of the future; it will avail them of the experience of other times and other nations; it will qualify them as judges of the actions and designs of men; it will enable them to know ambition under every disguise it may assume; and knowing it, to defeat its views. In every government on earth is some trace of human weakness, some germ of corruption and degeneracy, which cunning will discover, and wickedness insensibly open, cultivate and improve. Every government degenerates when trusted to the rulers of the people alone. The people themselves therefore are its only safe depositories. And to render even them safe, their minds must be improved to a certain degree. This indeed is not all that is necessary, though it be essentially necessary. An amendment of our constitution must here come in aid of the public education.

Thomas Jefferson, *Notes on Virginia* (1782) from Adrienne Koch and William Peden (eds.), *The Life and Selected Writings of Thomas Jefferson* (Random House, 1944), p. 265.

17 / Opinion upon the question whether the President should veto the Bill, declaring that the seat of government shall be transferred to the Potomac

(1790)

Every man, and every body of men on earth, possesses [sic] the right of self-government. They receive it with their being from the hand of nature. Individuals exercise it by their single will; collections of men by that of their majority; for the law of the majority is the natural law of every society of men. When a certain description of men are to transact together a particular business, the times and places of their meeting and separating, depend on their own will; they make a part of the natural right of self-government. This, like all other natural rights, may be abridged or modified in its exercise by their own consent, or by the law of those who depute them, if they meet in the right of others; but as far as it is not abridged or modified, they retain it as a natural right and may exercise them in what form they please, either exclusively by themselves, or in association with others, or by others altogether as they shall agree.

_____

Thomas Jefferson, "Opinion upon the question whether the President should veto the Bill, declaring that the seat of government shall be transferred to the Potomac" (July 15, 1790), from Adrienne Koch and William Peden (eds.), *The Life and Selected Writings of Thomas Jefferson* (Random House, 1944), p. 316.

18 / Thomas Jefferson
Letter to Col. Edward Carrington

(1787)

... The tumults in America I expected would have produced in Europe an unfavorable opinion of our political state. But it has not. On the contrary, the small effect of these tumults seems to have given more confidence in the firmness of our governments. The interposition of the people themselves on the side of government has had a great effect on the opinion here. I am persuaded myself that the good sense of the people will always be found to be the best army. They may be led astray for a moment, but will soon correct themselves. The people are the only censors of their governors; and even their errors will tend to keep these to the true principles of their institution. To punish these errors too severely would be to suppress the only safeguard of the public liberty. The way to prevent these irregular interpositions of the people, is to give them full information of their affairs through the channel of the public papers, and to contrive that those papers should penetrate the whole mass of the people. The basis of our governments being the opinion of the people, the very first object should be to keep that right; and were it left to me to decide whether we should have a government without newspapers, or newspapers without a government, I should not hesitate a moment to prefer the latter.

Thomas Jefferson to Colonel Edward Carrington, January 16, 1787 from Adrienne Koch and William Peden (eds.), *The Life and Selected Writings of Thomas Jefferson* (Random House, 1944), pp. 411–412.

19 / Thomas Jefferson
Notes on Virginia

(1782)

The political economists of Europe have established it as a principle, that every State should endeavor to manufacture for itself; and this principle, like many others, we transfer to America, without calculating the difference of circumstance which should often produce a difference of result. In Europe the lands are either cultivated, or locked up against the cultivator. Manufacture must therefore be resorted to of necessity not of choice, to support the surplus of their people. But we have an immensity of land courting the industry of the husbandman. Is it best then that all our citizens should be employed in its improvement, or that one half should be called off from that to exercise manufactures and handicraft arts for the other? Those who labor in the earth are the chosen people of God, if ever He had a chosen people, whose breasts He has made His peculiar deposit for substantial and genuine virtue. It is the focus in which he keeps alive that sacred fire, which otherwise might escape from the face of the earth. Corruption of morals in the mass of cultivators is a phenomenon of which no age nor nation has furnished an example. It is the mark set on those who, not looking up to heaven, to their own soil and industry, as does the husbandman, for their subsistence, depend for it on casualties and caprice of customers. Dependence begets subservience and venality, suffocates the germ of virtue, and prepares fit tools for the designs of ambition. This, the natural progress and consequence of the arts, has sometimes perhaps been retarded by accidental circumstances; but, generally speaking, the proportion which the aggregate of the other classes of citizens bears in any State to that of its husbandmen, is the proportion of its unsound to its healthy parts, and is a good enough barometer whereby to measure its degree of corruption. While we have land to labor then, let us never wish to see our citizens occupied at a workbench, or twirling a distaff. Carpenters, masons, smiths, are wanting in husbandry;

Thomas Jefferson, *Notes on Virginia* (1782) from Adrienne Koch and William Peden (eds.), *The Life and Selected Writings of Thomas Jefferson* (Random House, 1944), pp. 279–281.

but, for the general operations of manufacture, let our workshops remain in Europe. It is better to carry provisions and materials to workmen there, than bring them to the provisions and materials, and with them their manners and principles. The loss by the transportation of commodities across the Atlantic will be made up in happiness and permanence of government. The mobs of great cities add just so much to the support of pure government, as sores do to the strength of the human body. It is the manners and spirit of a people which preserve a republic in vigor. A degeneracy in these is a canker which soon eats to the heart of its laws and constitution.

■ Jefferson and the Concept of the Negative State

20 / Thomas Jefferson
First Inaugural Address

(1801)

During the contest of opinion through which we have passed, the animation of discussion and of exertions has sometimes worn an aspect which might impose on strangers unused to think freely and to speak and to write what they think; but this being now decided by the voice of the nation, announced according to the rules of the constitution, all will, of course, arrange themselves under the will of the law, and unite in common efforts for the common good. All, too, will bear in mind this sacred principle, that though the will of the majority is in all cases to prevail, that will, to be rightful, must be reasonable; that the minority possess their equal rights, which equal laws must protect, and to violate which would be oppression. Let us, then, fellow citizens, unite with one heart and one mind. Let us restore to social intercourse that harmony and affection without which liberty and even life itself are but dreary things. And let us reflect that having banished from our land

Thomas Jefferson, "First Inaugural Address" (March 4, 1801) from Adrienne Koch and William Peden (eds.), *The Life and Selected Writings of Thomas Jefferson* (Random House, 1944), pp. 321–325.

that religious intolerance under which mankind so long bled and suffered, we have yet gained little if we countenance a political intolerance as despotic, as wicked, and capable of as bitter and bloody persecutions. During the throes and convulsions of the ancient world, during the agonizing spasms of infuriated man, seeking through blood and slaughter his long-lost liberty, it was not wonderful that the agitations of the billows should reach even this distant and peaceful shore; that this should be more felt and feared by some and less by others; that this should divide opinions as to measures of safety. But every difference of opinion is not a difference of principle. We have called by different names brethren of the same principle. We are all republicans—we are federalists. If there be any among us who would wish to dissolve this Union or to change its republican form, let them stand undisturbed as monuments of the safety with which error of opinion may be tolerated where reason is left free to combat it. I know, indeed, that some honest men fear that a republican government cannot be strong; that this government is not strong enough. But would the honest patriot, in the full tide of successful experiment, abandon a government which has so far kept us free and firm, on the theoretic and visionary fear that this government, the world's best hope, may by possibility want energy to preserve itself? I trust not. I believe this, on the contrary, the strongest government on earth. I believe it is the only one where every man, at the call of the laws, would fly to the standard of the law, and would meet invasions of the public order as his own personal concern. Sometimes it is said that man cannot be trusted with the government of himself. Can he, then, be trusted with the government of others? Or have we found angels in the forms of kings to govern him? Let history answer this question.

Let us, then, with courage and confidence pursue our own federal and republican principles, our attachment to our union and representative government. Kindly separated by nature and a wide ocean from the exterminating havoc of one quarter of the globe; too high-minded to endure the degradations of the others; possessing a chosen country, with room enough for our descendants to the hundredth and thousandth generation; entertaining a due sense of our equal right to the use of our own faculties, to the acquisitions of our industry, to honor and confidence from our fellow citizens, resulting not from birth but from our actions and their sense of them; enlightened by a benign religion, professed, indeed, and practiced in various forms, yet all of them including honesty, truth, temperance, gratitude, and the love of man; acknowledging and adoring an overruling Providence, which by all its dispensations proves that it delights in the happiness of man here and his greater happiness hereafter; with all these blessings, what more is necessary to make us a happy and prosperous people? Still one thing more, fellow citizens—a wise and frugal government, which shall restrain men from injuring one another, which shall leave them otherwise free to regulate their own pursuits of industry and improvement, and shall not take from the mouth of labor the bread it has earned. This is the sum of good government, and this is necessary to close the circle of our felicities.

About to enter, fellow citizens, on the exercise of duties which comprehend everything dear and valuable to you, it is proper that you should understand what I deem the essential principles of our government, and consequently those which ought to shape its administration. I will compress them within the narrowest compass they will bear, stating the general principle, but not all its limitations. Equal and exact justice to all men, of whatever state or persuasion, religious or political; peace, commerce, and honest friendship, with all nations—entangling alliances with none; the support of the state governments in all their rights, as the most competent administrations for our domestic concerns and the surest bulwarks against antirepublican tendencies; the preservation of the general government in its whole constitutional vigor, as the sheet anchor of our peace at home and safety abroad; a jealous care of the right of election by the people—a mild and safe corrective of abuses which are lopped by the sword of the revolution where peaceable remedies are unprovided; absolute acquiescence in the decisions of the majority—the vital principle of republics, from which there is no appeal but to force, the vital principle and immediate parent of despotism; a well-disciplined militia—our best reliance in peace and for the first moments of war, till regulars may relieve them; the supremacy of the civil over the military authority; economy in the public expense, that labor may be lightly burdened; the honest payment of our debts and sacred preservation of the public faith; encouragement of agriculture, and of commerce as its handmaid; the diffusion of information and the arraignment of all abuses at the bar of public reason; freedom of religion; freedom of the press; freedom of person under the protection of the habeas corpus; and trial by juries impartially selected—these principles form the bright constellation which has gone before us, and guided our steps through an age of revolution and reformation. The wisdom of our sages and the blood of our heroes have been devoted to their attainment. They should be the creed of our political faith—the text of civil instruction—the touchstone by which to try the services of those we trust; and should we wander from them in moments of error or alarm, let us hasten to retrace our steps and to regain the road which alone leads to peace, liberty, and safety.

21 / Thomas Jefferson
Letter to Samuel Kercheval

(1816)

... I am not among those who fear the people. They, and not the rich, are our dependence for continued freedom. And to preserve their independence, we must not let our rulers load us with perpetual debt. We must make our election between *economy and liberty*, or *profusion and servitude.* If we run into such debts, as that we must be taxed in our meat and in our drink, in our necessaries and our comforts, in our labors and our amusements, for our callings and our creeds, as the people of England are, our people, like them, must come to labor sixteen hours in the twenty-four, give the earnings of fifteen of these to the government for their debts and daily expenses; and the sixteenth being insufficient to afford us bread, we must live, as they now do, on oatmeal and potatoes; have no time to think, no means of calling the mismanagers to account; but be glad to obtain subsistence by hiring ourselves to rivet their chains on the necks of our fellow sufferers. Our land-holders, too, like theirs, retaining indeed the title and stewardship of estates called theirs, but held really in trust for the treasury, must wander, like theirs, in foreign countries, and be contented with penury, obscurity, exile, and the glory of the nation. This example reads to us the salutary lesson, that private fortunes are destroyed by public as well as by private extravagance. And this is the tendency of all human governments. A departure from principle in one instance becomes a precedent for a second; that second for a third; and so on, till the bulk of the society is reduced to be mere automatons of misery, to have no sensibilities left but for sinning and suffering. Then begins, indeed, the *bellum omnium in omnia*, which some philosophers observing to be so general in this world, have mistaken it for the natural, instead of the abusive state of man. And the fore horse of this frightful team is public debt. Taxation follows that, and in its train wretchedness and oppression.

Some men look at constitutions with sanctimonious reverence, and deem them like the ark of the covenant, too sacred to be touched. They ascribe to

Thomas Jefferson to Samuel Kercheval, July 12, 1816 from Adrienne Koch and William Peden (eds.), *The Life and Selected Writings of Thomas Jefferson* (Random House, 1944), pp. 673–676.

the men of the preceding age a wisdom more than human, and suppose what they did to be beyond amendment. I knew that age well; I belonged to it, and labored with it. It deserved well of its country. It was very like the present, but without the experience of the present; and forty years of experience in government is worth a century of bookreading; and this they would say themselves, were they to rise from the dead. I am certainly not an advocate for frequent and untried changes in laws and constitutions. I think moderate imperfections had better be borne with; because, when once known, we accommodate ourselves to them, and find practical means of correcting their ill effects. But I know also, that laws and institutions must go hand in hand with the progress of the human mind. As that becomes more developed, more enlightened, as new discoveries are made, new truths disclosed, and manners and opinions change with the change of circumstances, institutions must advance also, and keep pace with the times. We might as well require a man to wear still the coat which fitted him when a boy, as civilized society to remain ever under the regimen of their barbarous ancestors . . . Each generation is as independent of the one preceding, as that was of all which had gone before. It has then, like them, a right to choose for itself the form of government it believes most promotive of its own happiness; consequently, to accommodate to the circumstances in which it finds itself, that received from its predecessors; and it is for the peace and good of mankind, that a solemn opportunity of doing this every nineteen or twenty years, should be provided by the Constitution; so that it may be handed on, with periodical repairs, from generation to generation, to the end of time, if anything human can so long endure. This corporeal globe, and everything upon it, belong to its present corporeal inhabitants, during their generation. They alone have a right to direct what is the concern of themselves alone, and to declare the law of that direction; and this declaration can only be made by their majority.

22 / James Scanlan
The Federalist and Human Nature

(1959)

Students of American political theory find themselves in general agreement concerning the character and significance of their most celebrated document, *The Federalist*. Few deny that this series of essays in support of the Constitution by Alexander Hamilton, James Madison, and John Jay represents a substantial contribution to the literature of political theory. The nature of the contribution is also well established. *The Federalist*, it is agreed, is a skillful exposition of the principles of constitutional republicanism—an exposition not haphazard or fanciful, but controlled by constant reference to the capacities and limitations of the political animal. The latter point is often emphasized; Benjamin F. Wright states: "The aspect of *The Federalist* which is of universal applicability is . . . its recognition of the importance of human nature in politics, together with its remarkably penetrating analysis of the motives and the behavior of men in a free society." Finally, there is agreement on the general outlines of this theory of human nature. The authors of *The Federalist*, it is said, were decidedly "realistic," brooking no illusions of the inherent goodness or rationality of man, but holding firm to "a conception of human corruptibility." The adjective most often employed is "pessimistic."

Attempts to delineate *The Federalist*'s pessimism more precisely, however, not only generate disagreement but actually raise serious questions as to the ultimate value of *The Federalist* as a theoretical contribution. It is sometimes suggested, for example, that *The Federalist*'s gloominess is radical and far-reaching: that in its view "men are not to be trusted with power because they are selfish, passionate, full of whims, caprices, and prejudices," and human rationality is so weak as to be politically negligible. But if the work really incorporates what has been called "the Hamiltonian concept of total human depravity," the spectacle it presents is plainly in-

James Scanlan, "*The Federalist* and Human Nature," *The Review of Politics*, XXI (1959), pp. 657–677. Reprinted without footnotes by permission of the publisher.

congruous: for *The Federalist* consists from beginning to end of closely-reasoned arguments, defending a system of government said to be grounded on the will of the people and operated by human beings. How can intellectually feeble humanity understand or be moved by elaborate reasoning, and how can a morally feeble humanity safely be given political power? On this interpretation it would seem that the political conclusions of *The Federalist* are at odds with its psychological premises; the work is theoretically schizophrenic, and the justification for esteeming it as an enduring contribution is no longer clear.

In recent years attempts have been made to avoid this apparent contradiction between *The Federalist's* purposes and its theory of human nature, by tempering the theory. Thus E. M. Burns writes of Madison: "Contrary to the usual opinion Madison did not always look at mankind with such a jaundiced eye. He did not really believe in the *total* depravity of man's political nature." Sometimes it is suggested that the authors simply engaged in occasional "departures" from their otherwise complete pessimism, such as Hamilton's willingness to trust the executive and judiciary. The more usual view, however, is that the authors' undoubted pessimism is consistently moderate—that, with respect to the intellectual and moral capabilities of mankind, they were neither visionary nor despairing. "The major premise of the book," according to Wright, "is that men, or at least Americans, are sufficiently rational to make self-government practicable." This view is well summarized by Neal Riemer, referring to the thought of Madison as expressed in *The Federalist*:

> The total effect is a balanced picture of man, the only basis for a constructive, creative, and enduring political theory. Face up to the worst without abandoning hope for the best—this would be Madison's motto . . . Pessimism and optimism combine to vitalize and energize the republican experiment . . . The success of Madison's theory is, in large part, based upon this sound concept of man.

Men are not *so* irrational or *so* evil as to be incapable of listening to reason or ruling themselves.

Doubtless this view offers a more fruitful approach to a sound understanding of *The Federalist*, but it cannot be taken as the statement of a functioning theory of human nature. To assert simply that men are both good and bad, partly but not completely rational, explains nothing. Such a view can hardly be regarded as a theoretical source, ground, or test of political doctrines, for it has no specific implications. In what respects and to what degree is human depravity less than total? When is it reasonable and when is it unreasonable to count on the goodness and intelligence of man? . . .

In short, *The Federalist*'s theory of human nature, if it amounts to no more than the general assertion of a moderate pessimism as described above, is theoretically functionless. Suspicion arises that the authors' frequent appeals to the nature of man are largely *ad hoc*, and that there is little real connection between *The Federalist*'s political conclusions and the principles of human nature in which they are supposedly grounded.

These disagreements and doubts can be resolved only by a closer examination of *The Federalist*'s many actual references to the characteristics of men in a political context. Sustained investigation has been discouraged, perhaps, by the apparent casualness and simplicity of the authors' presentation, tempting commentators to make equally casual and simple generalizations, and to assume that richness of underlying principles is not to be found in the work. Actually *The Federalist* contains a more complex, fully-developed, and consistent "theory of human nature" than is usually suspected, and this theory does function in such a way as to give the work a truly remarkable theoretical coherence. Closer examination of the theory and its functions makes possible a more adequate understanding and appreciation of *The Federalist*.

In judging a plan of government, the authors of *The Federalist* consider "human nature" because the acceptance and successful operation of any system of government depends in countless ways upon human *action*. For the proposed Constitution to prosper, an intricate network of supporting actions is required; and for the Constitution to promote the public good, some of the possible actions of men must be encouraged and others discouraged. What is the assurance that *this* constitution will foster the proper actions? According to the authors, we must look to the prevailing internal causes or motives of human action, "the true springs by which human conduct is actuated," to determine whether suggested political arrangements will have desirable results in action. We must ask whether institutions are designed so that men, motivated as they are, will accept and operate them, and so that they will counteract those motives of men which are socially dangerous.

The authors of *The Federalist*, then, commit themselves to a program of judging projected institutions by examining the motives of men. Consequently, what confronts us in *The Federalist* is not so much a comprehensive theory of "human nature" as a theory of "*human motivation*," related to political action. Given their overriding practical aims, the authors do not expound this theory systematically, or often make it explicit; and it is impossible to determine the exact extent to which the theory was clearly adumbrated in their own minds. Nevertheless, there is hardly a paper which does not mention motives in some guise—sometimes as "motives," more often as "springs," "impulses," "inclinations," "inducements," "dispositions," "propensities," or "humours." Kinds of motives are distinguished, roughly but with general consistency; their relationships and different degrees of efficacy are indicated; and the elements of the theory are deliberately marshalled in support of political doctrines. Simply on the basis of the number and variety of applications demanded of this theory, *The Federalist* must be accounted one of the most comprehensive treatments of political motivation in existence.

Three general varieties of motives are distinguished by the authors of *The Federalist*. Though an occasional usage blurs the lines between the different categories, this division is maintained throughout the work, by each of its three authors.

First, there are motives of *passion*. The authors do not directly discuss the nature or exact psychological operation of passions. But there is abundant evidence in *The Federalist* that they consider passions as emotional states which can determine action. "Passion," without qualification, is mentioned very frequently as a source of human action, as in the expressions "stimulated by some irregular passion" and "actuated by some . . . impulse of passion." "Feelings" and "sentiments," terms which seem to be mild or honorific substitutes for "passions," occur in the same connection. More specifically, individual passions such as ambition, envy, fear, jealousy, family affection, love of country, and many others, are referred to continually as actual or possible motives of men in given situations.

Second, there are what may be called (to have a ready label) motives of *reason and virtue*. Again it cannot be said that this is a category of motives explicitly defined and analyzed by the authors. Yet they frequently suggest that there are objective rational and moral standards which can be perceived by man, and that the mere apprehension of these standards can function as a motive to action . . . In some places reason as a motivating factor is explicitly distinguished from passion. From these and other passages, such as Hamilton's reference to "minds animated and guided by superior virtue," we may conclude that the authors of *The Federalist* believed men can be moved to action by dispassionate concern for what is reasonable and right. This is not to say that such motives are powerful; but it cannot be denied that the authors recognized their existence.

Third, there are motives of *interest*. "Immediate interests," says Hamilton, have an "active and imperious control over human conduct"; and this point is echoed again and again in such expressions as "our interests prompt us" and "the temptation of interest." That the authors of *The Federalist* regard interests as motives distinguishable from passions, is clear from the fact that they often refer to motives of both sorts in the same context: thus they speak of groups of men "actuated by some common impulse of passion, or of interest"; and Hamilton discusses situations in which passions, as motives to action, are at variance with interests. Similarly, interests are distinguished from motives of reason and virtue . . . As with the other two classes of motives, however, it is easier to see that the authors of *The Federalist* persist in identifying interest as a separate motivational category than it is to discover the exact dimensions of the category. But it is possible to formulate an account of their ordinary use of the term. Action motivated by interest, in the authors' typical usage, is action expected by the agent to have some identifiable *result* which will be *beneficial* or *advantageous* to him. Presumably the action may, at the same time, proceed from an emotional state of the agent, and be in formal accord with objective standards of rationality and virtue; but only insofar as the agent is influenced by an expectation of some consequent benefit or advantage is the action motivated by interest.

These usages are further exhibited in subordinate distinctions which the authors employ. Within the categories of passion and interest, further divisions of motives are made. Thus there is a distinction between what may be called *amicable* and *antagonistic* passions—or, as the authors most often view them, between passions which promote harmony and passions which promote hostility among men . . . On the other side, there are references to "angry and malignant passions" and "unfriendly passions"; Hamilton supplies a partial list of these when he speaks of "the impulses of rage, resentment, jealousy, avarice, and of other irregular and violent propensities."

But the authors divide interests more deliberately, by differentiating kinds of benefits and advantages which are important in the analysis of political motivation. Two such distinctions are particularly critical.

One is a distinction between *true* and *immediate* interests. True interests are those which, objectively and in the long run, are of greatest importance to the individual: that is, permanent benefits, comprehensive benefits, and benefits which are ultimate or distant results of present action. As might be expected, the authors argue that adoption of the Constitution will bring benefits of this sort. Immediate interests, on the other hand, are any benefits which pertain directly to the individual's present situation, and for that reason most easily gain his attention. Property owners, according to Madison, have an "immediate interest" in securing a low rate of taxation on their property; and Hamilton finds that the "immediate interests" of the States, under the Articles of Confederation, led them to ignore Union requisitions. An interest, of course, may be both true and immediate. But the authors make the distinction because they find that very often this is not the case: in a given situation, immediate interests may be of no great or lasting importance, and are likely to conflict with true interests.

The second distinction is between *common* and *personal* interests. Common interests are those which the individual or group shares with the other members of the community or nation: the benefit or advantage in this case accrues more or less equally to all . . . Personal interests, on the other hand, are those interests of an individual or group which are not common to all members of the community, and for this reason are called "particular," "partial," and "private" by the authors. The benefit is that of one individual or group and not of another; the advantage is that of one individual or group over another.

Given these subdivisions of interests, the authors of *The Federalist* proceed to a more detailed and concrete development of the categories of immediate and personal interests. Care is taken to specify the content of typical interests, that is, the actual benefits or advantages which are most likely to affect men, giving rise to politically noteworthy motives. Thus immediate and personal interests are almost invariably traced to possessions, or potential possessions, which concern the economic or political advantage of the individual; and possessions of various types are distinguished. But the present account has been carried far enough to identify the chief materials employed by the authors in constructing a theory of motivation for political use: three basic types of motives to which men are susceptible, with subordinate divisions, particularly in the case of interests, which allow greater accuracy of analysis. Since this catalogue is presumably exhaustive, any action in a political context must be traceable to one or more of these three sources.

Once the types of motives are distinguished, what additional knowledge of motivation is necessary for judging a plan of government? Primarily, a knowledge of the relative efficacy of motives of different types. If motives differ in force, and if these differences are discoverable and systematic, it will be possible to estimate the workability of suggested political arrangements. A given motive cannot be counted upon to produce some desired action if stronger motives oppose it. Political arrangements which depend for their success upon the weaker motives of men cannot be considered practical.

According to the authors of *The Federalist*, the whole history of mankind gives evidence that motives do differ in force, in ways which can easily be described. The authors do not, of course, systematically estimate the efficacy of motives of each distinguishable group, or arrange all groups in a graduated series. Motives of some types, such as amicable passions and true interests, for example, are never brought into direct comparison with each other in *The Federalist*. But the authors do make many clear comparisons of stronger and weaker motives. Motives of some types are consistently linked, as being practically equal in degree of force; and others are consistently distinguished, as differing in force. The frequent comparisons and contrasts which the authors make may be summed up conveniently in the form of two generalizations, or principles of the relative efficacy of motives, to which the authors may be said to adhere. These principles, though qualified by other considerations, as we shall see, constitute the core of the theory of human motivation employed in *The Federalist*.

First, *antagonistic passions and immediate interests have greater efficacy than true interests and motives of reason and virtue*. The former are more dependable sources of action. When an individual is in a situation where motives of these two sorts conflict, the former will usually overpower the latter.

We saw that Hamilton distrusted treaties "which have no other sanction than the obligations of good faith, and which oppose general considerations of peace and justice to the impulse of any immediate interest or passion." The point is a general one, brought out in many instances in *The Federalist*. "Why has government been instituted at all?" Hamilton asks; and he answers: "Because the passions of men will not conform to the dictates of reason and justice, without constraint." Madison remarks that no man is allowed to be a judge in his own cause, "because his interest would certainly bias his judgment, and, not improbably, corrupt his integrity."...

Second, *antagonistic passions and personal interests have greater efficacy than amicable passions and common interests.* As above, where motives of the two sorts conflict, the former will predominate.

This principle, too, is illustrated in many contexts in *The Federalist*, but it appears most prominently in the argument for a strong Union. According to Hamilton, the parts of America will not cooperate effectively if concerted action is voluntary; this was shown under the Articles of Confederation:

> There was a time when we were told ... that a sense of common interest would preside over the conduct of the respective members, and would beget a full compliance with all the constitutional requisitions of the Union.... [This shows] an ignorance of the true springs by which human conduct is actuated.

Nor can harmony be preserved in America by the establishment of three or four smaller confederacies: "Envy and jealousy would soon extinguish confidence and affection, and the partial interests of each confederacy, instead of the general interests of all America, would be the only objects of their policy and pursuits." Whether the parts of America are independent States or a few confederacies, frequent and violent conflicts can be expected; in spite of common interests, "motives for such conflicts" will not be wanting. Even the adjectives which the authors employ in these discussions reveal the relative efficacy of motives: amicable tendencies, for example, are "mild," while antagonistic tendencies are "fiery" and "violent."

To the extent that the two principles bear on motives of interest, they reflect the authors' repeated suggestions that personal interests are stronger than common interests, and immediate interests stronger than true interests. Perhaps Hamilton has both these phenomena in mind when he refers to "a known fact in human nature, that its affections are commonly weak in proportion to the distance or diffusiveness of the object"—a fact which is exhibited, Hamilton notes, in the greater attachment of a man to his family than to his neighborhood, to his neighborhood than to his community, and so on. This passage would seem to allow further discriminations of degree among motives of interest, along lines which we might suspect: the less distant a benefit or advantage, and the less diffuse or widely shared, the stronger will be the motive. In another interesting passage Hamilton implies that the question of the *immediacy* of an interest is more important than the question of its personal or common character: "Where there is an *immediate* common interest," he states, "we may safely count upon its operation." Other things being equal, however, it is simply a fact that men are more concerned with their private benefit, their advantage in the sense of superiority or ascendancy over other human beings, than in the benefits they share with others.

The two principles which have been stated must be regarded as supplemented and qualified by additional facts concerning human motivation which the authors of *The Federalist* draw upon. There are other factors, for example, which have some effect upon the degree of efficacy of motives. According to Hamilton, it is "a general principle of human nature" that the strength of an individual's interest in any possession is proportional to the security of the tenure by which the possession is held; and this "principle" has important practical application in some of Hamilton's arguments concerning the powers of the executive and the judiciary. Again, Hamilton and Madison agree that men acting in groups are even more susceptible to antagonistic passions and personal interests, and less susceptible to motives of reason and virtue, than are men acting as individuals—a point which Madison expresses forcefully: "Had every Athenian citizen been a Socrates, every Athenian assembly would still have been a mob." But perhaps the most important qualification of the two major principles is an admission, often stated in *The Federalist*, that some individuals differ from the majority in their susceptibility to motives of the various types. Specifically, there are some men in whom motives of reason and virtue are actually stronger than motives of passion and interest. According to Hamilton, "there are men who could neither be distressed nor won into a sacrifice of their duty"; these are the "minds animated and guided by superior virtue," mentioned above. Their number is not great; a stern regard for duty, Hamilton says, is "the growth of few soils." But the existence of such individuals is taken as a fact by the authors of *The Federalist*, and enters into their reasoning in certain contexts. There is no indication that such "exceptions" to their major principles offered the authors any embarrassment: they clearly share with Hume and many other thinkers the assumption that in the realm of human nature, principles of absolute universality and precision will rarely be found.

How, then, shall we describe the over-all character and bearing of *The Federalist*'s theory of "human nature," or human motivation? Men are not radically or intrinsically depraved, though neither are they by nature angels. All men are susceptible to motives of various sorts—good and bad, selfish and unselfish. Motives, however, may have different degrees of efficacy: taking the human race as a whole, it is obvious that some motives operate more consistently and powerfully than others. Many factors affect the efficacy of motives, and the science of human motivation is not sufficiently exact to evaluate and relate all these factors precisely. But on the whole the stronger forces which affect human action are antagonistic passions and immediate and personal interests; the weaker are amicable passions, true and common interests, and motives of reason and virtue. It is true that in some individuals this pattern is altered or reversed; but they are few, and political thinking must emphasize the strongest motives of the majority of men. In general we must count on men following the lines of their immediate and personal interests, and even being powerfully moved by "angry sentiments." To make political plans which assume that motives of other sorts will often prevail is, in Hamilton's words, "to calculate on the weaker springs of the human character."...

It now remains to be seen that the theory of motivation we have attributed to the authors of *The Federalist* has a theoretical function—that it is in fact systematically and fruitfully used in their political reasoning.

The authors of *The Federalist* were recommending the Constitution to an audience all or most of whom, it is to be assumed, were capable of seeing beyond immediate and personal interests, and being influenced, at least in some degree, by considerations of the objective value of a proposed system of government. Some members of their audience, indeed, would be powerfully moved by such considerations. Consequently the authors attempt not only to praise the Constitution but to *justify* it as providing an adequate system of government for America. Once committed to an exercise in justification, they cannot escape theorizing: they must find and utilize principles of judgment appropriate to politics, and develop lines of connection between these principles and the actual provisions of the Constitution. In short, they must formulate a political philosophy of sufficient power and scope to handle the complexities of the plan of government they are attempting to justify.

The authors' chief method of justification consists in showing that the Constitution contains solutions to all of the important problems of political organization. But what are these problems, and what are the criteria for their adequate solution? It is here that the authors' theory of motivation comes into play: the theory of motivation is used both to identify significant political problems and to support the particular solutions which, in the authors' opinion, were incorporated in the Constitution. Other basic principles to which the authors are committed, such as the political ideals of republicanism and federalism, only define in very general terms the sort of political system which should be established. The principles of motivation make possible the more specific treatment of problems which must be met and solved in constructing a sound federal republic.

The political problems discussed in *The Federalist* are of course very numerous. With respect to the internal organization of government, however, there are three pervasive problems which may be considered absolutely fundamental in *The Federalist*'s analysis, and which the authors formulate by reference to human motivation: (1) In any political system, the immediate and personal interests of the rulers may be opposed to the interests of the ruled, and may motivate the rulers to use their power for oppression. (2) In a federal system, where political power is shared by two orders of government, state and federal, the members of each government will have opposed interests which may motivate them to attempt to encroach on the power of the other. (3) In a republic, where the majority possesses ultimate political power, the interests of the majority may be opposed to the interests of a minority, and may motivate the majority to use its power for oppression. In each case, the possibility of predicting the strength of immediate and personal interests (supported, of course, by less predictable emotional antagonisms) leads to the recognition of a danger point. The properly constructed federal republic is one in which these dangers are eliminated or controlled: the practical problem in each case is to devise safeguards for the threatened individuals and groups.

The authors argue that effective safeguards are incorporated in the Constitution, and they support their arguments by appealing to what they consider to be appropriate criteria. Proposed political arrangements must, for example, be consistent with the ideals of federalism and republicanism. But other conditions must also be satisfied. In each area of potential conflict, the danger arises when individuals or groups are able to act on certain motives. The authors find, consequently, that proper safeguards will be established if two conditions are fulfilled in each area. First, wherever possible, and to whatever extent possible, *the power or opportunity to act must be withheld from those who might act on motives productive of conflict and oppression.* Second, where power cannot be withheld—because, for example, withholding it would be inconsistent with the intrinsic requirements of federal, republican government —*those who are invested with power should have, or be provided with, strong motives to use it properly.* If the political system can be organized in such a way that no individuals or groups will have *both* strong antagonistic motives *and* the power to act on them, solutions to all the above problems will be achieved.

In *The Federalist*, solutions are set forth in the form of doctrines which state how the above criteria may be fulfilled; and it is shown that practical arrangements to carry these doctrines into effect are prescribed by the Constitution, or will inevitably result from its adoption . . .

The problem of majority oppression receives its central treatment in Madison's famous discussion of "faction." The problem is seen to be important largely because of the known efficacy of motives of certain sorts. Madison, in fact, defines "faction" by reference to shared motives: "By a faction, I understand a number of citizens, whether amounting to a majority or minority of the whole, who are united and actuated by some common impulse of passion, or of interest, adverse to the rights of other citizens, or to the permanent and aggregate interests of the community." Given a *majority* so motivated, how can the rights of the minority be preserved in a republic? The great desideratum, according to Madison, is to achieve simultaneously two seemingly inconsistent goals: "To secure the public good and private rights against the danger of such a faction, and at the same time to preserve the spirit and the form of popular government." Madison finds, however, that it is possible to state conditions for the joint realization of these goals—conditions concerning, of course, the *motives* and the *power* of the majority:

By what means is this object attainable? Evidently by one of two only. Either the existence of the same passion or interest in a majority at the same time must be prevented, or the majority, having such coexistent passion or interest, must be rendered, by their number and local situation, unable to concert and carry into effect schemes of oppression. If the impulse and the opportunity be suffered to coincide, we well know that neither moral nor religious motives can be relied on as an adequate control.

As is well known, Madison proceeds to argue that both of these conditions will be fulfilled in America united under the Constitution. Should a majority have a common factious motive, their very numbers and the large area over which they will be distributed will make it difficult for them to "concert and execute their plans of oppression." But further, there is reason to believe that no majority so motivated can arise in the new nation: in a large society encompassing many distinct parties and interests, the peculiarities of individual group interests must be abandoned or seriously modified in the process of majority formation and action. The result, according to Madison, is that "a coalition of a majority of the whole society could seldom take place on any other principles than those of justice and the general good." Thus Madison seeks to maintain that the possession of power will coincide with motives to use it properly; very probably, in his opinion, the *only* motives common to the different groups comprising any practicable majority will coincide with the public good . . .

The political theory of *The Federalist* reaches far beyond the points here chosen for brief elaboration, but its many ramifications do not destroy its unity. *The Federalist* is a record of accomplishments in political theorizing with a given starting-point—a determination to ground political speculation on any other principles than those of justice and the general good." Thus ideals and psychological premises. The psychological premises do not imply that men are hopelessly "irrational," implacably selfish or hostile, or incapable of self-government. They do suggest that any attempt to establish a sound system of government is fraught with difficult problems. But the same psychological premises lead to an intelligent recognition and understanding of the problems, and to insight into the conditions for their solution.

Document

23 / James Madison
The Federalist No. 10

(1787)

To the People of the State of New York:

Among the numerous advantages promised by a well-constructed Union, none deserves to be more accurately developed than its tendency to break and control the violence of faction. The friend of popular governments never finds himself so much alarmed for their character and fate, as when he contemplates their propensity to this dangerous vice. He will not fail, therefore, to set a due value on any plan which, without violating the principles to which he is attached, provides a proper cure for it. The instability, injustice, and confusion introduced into the public councils, have, in truth, been the mortal diseases under which popular governments have everywhere perished; as they continue to be the favorite and fruitful topics from which the adversaries to liberty derive their most specious declamations. The valuable improvements made by the American constitutions on the popular models, both ancient and modern, cannot certainly be too much admired; but it would be an unwarrantable partiality, to contend that they have as effectually obviated the danger on this side, as was wished and expected. Complaints are everywhere heard from our most considerate and virtuous citizens, equally the friends of public and private faith, and of public and personal liberty, that our governments are too unstable, that the public good is disregarded in the conflicts of rival parties, and that measures are too often decided, not according to the rules of justice and the rights of the minor party, but by the superior force of an interested and overbearing majority. However anxiously we may wish that these complaints had no foundation, the evidence of known facts will not permit us to deny that they are in some degree true. It will be found, indeed, on a candid review of our situation, that some of the distresses under which we labor have been erroneously charged on the operation of our governments; but it will be found, at the same time, that other causes will not alone account for many of our heaviest misfortunes; and, particularly, for that prevailing and increasing distrust of public engagements, and alarm for private rights, which are echoed

The Federalist. (ed.) Henry Cabot Lodge (New York & London: G. P. Putnam's Sons, 1888).

from one end of the continent to the other. These must be chiefly, if not wholly, effects of the unsteadiness and injustice with which a factious spirit has tainted our public administrations.

By a faction, I understand a number of citizens, whether amounting to a majority or minority of the whole, who are united and actuated by some common impulse of passion, or of interest, adverse to the rights of other citizens, or to the permanent and aggregate interests of the community.

There are two methods of curing the mischiefs of faction: the one, by removing its causes; the other, by controlling its effects.

There are again two methods of removing the causes of faction: the one, by destroying the liberty which is essential to its existence; the other, by giving to every citizen the same opinions, the same passions, and the same interests.

It could never be more truly said than of the first remedy, that it was worse than the disease. Liberty is to faction what air is to fire, an aliment without which it instantly expires. But it could not be less folly to abolish liberty, which is essential to political life, because it nourishes faction, than it would be to wish the annihilation of air, which is essential to animal life, because it imparts to fire its destructive agency.

The second expedient is as impracticable as the first would be unwise. As long as the reason of man continues fallible, and he is at liberty to exercise it, different opinions will be formed. As long as the connection subsists between his reason and his self-love, his opinions and his passions will have a reciprocal influence on each other; and the former will be objects to which the latter will attach themselves. The diversity in the faculties of men, from which the rights of property originate, is not less an insuperable obstacle to a uniformity of interests. The protection of these faculties is the first object of government. From the protection of different and unequal faculties of acquiring property, the possession of different degrees and kinds of property immediately results; and from the influence of these on the sentiments and views of the respective proprietors, ensues a division of the society into different interests and parties.

The latent causes of faction are thus sown in the nature of man; and we see them everywhere brought into different degrees of activity, according to the different circumstances of civil society. A zeal for different opinions concerning religion, concerning government, and many other points, as well of speculation as of practice; an attachment to different leaders ambitiously contending for pre-eminence and power; or to persons of other descriptions whose fortunes have been interesting to the human passions, have, in turn, divided mankind into parties, inflamed them with mutual animosity, and rendered them much more disposed to vex and oppress each other than to co-operate for their common good. So strong is this propensity of mankind to fall into mutual animosities, that where no substantial occasion presents itself, the most frivolous and fanciful distinctions have been sufficient to kindle their unfriendly passions and excite their most violent conflicts. But the most common and durable source of factions has been the various and unequal distribution of property. Those who hold and those who are without property have ever formed distinct interests in society. Those who are creditors, and those who are debtors, fall under a like discrimination. A landed interest, a manufacturing interst, a mercantile interest, a moneyed interest, with many lesser interests, grow up of necessity in civilized nations, and divide them into different classes, actuated by different sentiments and views. The regulation of these various and interfering interests forms the principal task of modern legislation, and involves the spirit of party and faction in the necessary and ordinary operations of the government.

No man is allowed to be a judge in his own cause, because his interest would certainly bias his judgment, and, not improbably, corrupt his integrity. With equal, nay with greater reason, a body of men are unfit to be both judges and parties at the same time; yet what are many of the most important acts of legislation, but so many judicial determinations, not indeed concerning the rights of single persons, but concerning the rights of large bodies of citizens? And what are the different classes of legislators but advocates and parties to the causes which they determine? Is a law proposed concerning private debts? It is a question to which the creditors are parties on one side and the debtors on the other. Justice ought to hold the balance between them. Yet the parties are, and must be, themselves the judges; and the most numerous party, or, in other words, the most powerful faction must be expected to prevail. Shall domestic manufactures be encouraged, and in what degree, by restrictions on foreign manufactures? are questions which would be differently decided by the landed and the manufacturing classes, and probably by neither with a sole regard to justice and the public good. The apportionment of taxes on the various descriptions of property is an act which seems to require the most exact impartiality; yet there is, perhaps, no legislative act in which greater opportunity and temptation are given to a predominant party to trample on the rules of justice. Every shilling with which they overburden the inferior number, is a shilling saved to their own pockets.

It is in vain to say that enlightened statesmen will be able to adjust these clashing interests, and render them all subservient to the public good. Enlightened statesmen will not always be at the helm. Nor, in many cases, can such an adjustment be made at all without taking into view indirect and remote considerations, which will rarely prevail over the immediate interest which one party may find in disregarding the rights of another or the good of the whole.

The inference to which we are brought is, that the *causes* of faction cannot be removed, and that relief is only to be sought in the means of controlling its *effects*.

If a faction consists of less than a majority, relief is supplied by the republican principle, which enables the majority to defeat its sinister views by regular vote. It may clog the administration, it may convulse the society; but it will be unable to execute and mask its violence under the forms of the Constitution. When a majority is included in a faction, the form of popular government, on the other hand, enables it to sacrifice to its ruling passion or interest both the public good and the rights of other citizens. To secure the public good and private rights against the danger of such a faction, and at the same time to preserve the spirit and the form of popular government, is then the great object to which our inquiries are directed. Let me add that it is the great desideratum by which this form of government can be rescued from the opprobrium under which it has so long labored, and be recommended to the esteem and adoption of mankind.

By what means is this object attainable? Evidently by one of two only. Either the existence of the same passion or interest in a majority at the same time must be prevented, or the majority, having such coexistent passion or interest, must be rendered, by their number and local situation, unable to concert and carry into effect schemes of oppression. If the impulse and the opportunity be suffered to coincide, we well know that neither moral nor religious motives can be relied on as an adequate control. They are not found to be such on the injustice and violence of individuals, and lose their efficacy in proportion to the number combined together, that is, in proportion as their efficacy becomes needful.

From this view of the subject it may be concluded that a pure democracy, by which I mean a society consisting of a small number of citizens, who assemble and administer the government in person, can admit of no cure for the mischiefs of faction. A common passion or interest will, in almost every case, be felt by a majority of the whole; a communication and concert result from the form of government itself; and there is nothing to check the inducements to sacrifice the weaker party or an obnoxious individual. Hence it is that such democracies have ever been spectacles of turbulence and contention; have ever been found incompatible with personal security or the rights of property; and have in general been as short in their lives as they have been violent in their deaths. Theoretic politicians, who have patronized this species of government, have erroneously supposed that by reducing mankind to a perfect equality in their political rights, they would, at the same time, be perfectly equalized and assimilated in their possessions, their opinions, and their passions.

A republic, by which I mean a government in which the scheme of representation takes place, opens a different prospect, and promises the cure for which we are seeking. Let us examine the points in which it varies from pure democracy, and we shall comprehend both the nature of the cure and the efficacy which it must derive from the Union.

The two great points of difference between a democracy and a republic are: first, the delegation of the government, in the latter, to a small number of citizens elected by the rest; secondly, the greater number of citizens, and greater sphere of country, over which the latter may be extended.

The effect of the first difference is, on the one hand, to refine and enlarge the public views, by passing them through the medium of a chosen body of citizens, whose wisdom may best discern the true interest of their country, and whose patriotism and love of justice will be least likely to sacrifice it to temporary or partial considerations. Under such a regulation, it may well happen that the public voice, pronounced by the representatives of the people, will be more consonant to the public good than if pronounced by the people themselves, convened for the purpose. On the other hand, the effect may be inverted. Men of factious tempers, of local prejudices, or of sinister designs, may, by intrigue, by corruption, or by other means, first obtain the suffrages, and then betray the interests, of the people. The question resulting is, whether small or extensive republics are more favorable to the election of proper guardians of the public weal; and it is clearly decided in favor of the latter by two obvious considerations:

In the first place, it is to be remarked that, however small the republic may be, the representatives must be raised to a certain number, in order to guard against the cabals of a few; and that, however large it may be, they must be limited to a certain number, in order to guard against the confusion of a multitude. Hence, the number of representatives in the two cases not being in proportion to that of the two constituents, and being proportionally greater in the small republic, it follows that, if the proportion of fit characters be not less in the large than in the small republic, the former will present a greater option, and consequently a greater probability of a fit choice.

In the next place, as each representative will be chosen by a greater number of citizens in the large than in the small republic, it will be more difficult for unworthy candidates to practise with success the vicious arts by which elections are too often carried; and the suffrages of the people being more free, will be more likely to centre in men who possess the most attractive merit and the most diffusive and established characters.

It must be confessed that in this, as in most other cases, there is a mean, on both sides of which inconveniences will be found to lie. By enlarging too much the number of electors, you render the representative too little acquainted with all their local circumstances and lesser interests; as by reducing it too much, you render him unduly attached to these, and too little fit to comprehend and pursue great and national objects. The federal Constitution forms a happy combination in this respect; the great and aggregate interests being referred to the national, the local and particular to the State legislatures.

The other point of difference is, the greater number of citizens and extent of territory which may be brought within the compass of republican than of democratic government; and it is this circumstance principally which renders factious combinations less to be dreaded in the former than in the latter. The smaller the society, the fewer probably will be the distinct parties and interests composing it; the fewer the distinct parties and interests, the more frequently will a majority be found of the same party; and the smaller the number of individuals composing a majority, and the smaller the compass within which they are placed, the more easily will they concert and execute their plans of oppression. Extend the sphere and you take in a greater variety of parties and interests; you make it less probable that a majority of the whole will have a common motive to invade the rights of other citizens; or if such a common motive exists, it will be more difficult for all who feel it to discover their own strength, and to act in unison with each other. Besides other impediments, it may be remarked that, where there is a consciousness of unjust or dishonorable purposes, communication is always checked by distrust in proportion to the number whose concurrence is necessary.

Hence, it clearly appears, that the same advantage which a republic has over a democracy, in controlling the effects of faction, is enjoyed by a large over a small republic,—is enjoyed by the Union over the States composing it. Does the advantage consist in the substitution of representatives whose enlightened views and virtuous sentiments render them superior to local prejudices and to schemes of injustice? It will not be denied that the representation of the Union will be most likely to possess these requisite endowments. Does it consist in the greater security afforded by a greater variety of parties, against the event of any one party being able to outnumber and oppress the rest? In an equal degree does the increased variety of parties comprised within the Union, increase this security. Does it, in fine, consist in the greater obstacles opposed to the concert and accomplishment of the secret wishes of an unjust and interested majority? Here, again, the extent of the Union gives it the most palpable advantage.

The influence of factious leaders may kindle a flame within their particular States, but will be unable to spread a general conflagration through the other States. A religious sect may degenerate into a political faction in a part of the Confederacy; but the variety of sects dispersed over the entire face of it must secure the national councils against any danger from that source. A rage for paper money, for an abolition of debts, for an equal division of property, or for any other improper or wicked project, will be less apt to pervade the whole body of the Union than a particular member of it; in the same proportion as such a malady is more likely to taint a particular county or district, than an entire State.

In the extent and proper structure of the Union, therefore, we behold a republican remedy for the diseases most incident to republican government. And according to the degree of pleasure and pride we feel in being republicans, ought to be our zeal in cherishing the spirit and supporting the character of Federalists.

Publius

Suggested Reading

*Bailyn, Bernard. *The Ideological Origins of the American Revolution* (Cambridge: Belknap Press of Harvard University Press, 1967).

*Bailyn, Bernard. *The Origins of American Politics* (New York: Alfred A. Knopf, 1968).

*Becker, Carl. *The Heavenly City of the Eighteenth-Century Philosophers* (New Haven: Yale University Press, 1932).

*Boorstin, Daniel J. *The Lost World of Thomas Jefferson* (New York: Henry Holt, 1948).

*Cassirer, Ernst. *The Philosophy of the Enlightenment* (Princeton: Princeton University Press, 1951).

*Chinard, Gilbert. *Thomas Jefferson: The Apostle of Americanism* (Ann Arbor: University of Michigan Press, 1957).

*Colbourn, H. Trevor. *The Lamp of Experience: Whig History and the Intellectual Origins of the American Revolution* (Chapel Hill: University of North Carolina Press, 1965).

*Conner, Paul W. *Poor Richard's Politicks: Benjamin Franklin and His New American Order* (New York: Oxford University Press, 1965).

*Gay, Peter. *The Enlightenment: An Interpretation*, 2 vols. (New York: Alfred A. Knopf, 1967, 1969).

*Haraszti, Zoltan. *John Adams and the Prophets of Progress* (Cambridge: Harvard University Press, 1952).

*Hofstadter, Richard. *The Idea of a Party System: The Rise of Legitimate Opposition in the United States, 1780–1840* (Berkeley and Los Angeles: University of California Press, 1969). Chs. 1 and 2.

*Koch, Adrienne. *Power, Morals, and The Founding Fathers* (Ithaca: Great Seal Books Inc., 1961).

*Koch, Adrienne. *Jefferson and Madison: The Great Collaboration* (New York: Alfred A. Knopf, 1950).

*Lynd, Staughton. *Intellectual Origins of American Radicalism* (New York: Pantheon Books, 1968). Chs. 1–3.

Morgan, Edmund S. "The American Revolution Considered as an Intellectual Movement," in Arthur M. Schlesinger, Jr., and Morton White, eds., *Paths of American Thought* (Boston: Houghton Mifflin, 1963).

Morgan, Edmund S. "The Puritan Ethic and the American Revolution," *William and Mary Quarterly*, 3rd series, XXIV, 1967, pp. 3–43.

*Palmer, R. R. *The Age of the Democratic Revolution: A Political History of Europe and America, 1760–1800* (Princeton: Princeton University Press, 1959).

*Robbins, Caroline. *The Eighteenth-Century Commonwealthmen: Studies in the Transmission, Development, and Circumstances of English Liberal Thought* *from the Restoration of Charless II until the War with the Thirteen Colonies* (Cambridge: Harvard University Press, 1959).

*Rossiter, Clinton. *Seedtime of the Republic: The Origin of the American Tradition of Political Liberty* (New York: Harcourt Brace, 1953).

*Stourzh, Gerald. *Alexander Hamilton and the Idea of Republican Government* (Stanford, California: Stanford University Press, 1970).

*Wiltse, Charles M. *The Jeffersonian Tradition in American Democracy* (Chapel Hill: University of North Carolina Press, 1935).

*Wood, Gordon. *The Creation of the American Republic, 1776–1787* (Chapel Hill: University of North Carolina Press, 1969).

* Available in paperback edition.

Section Four
The Emergence of American Nationalism

PETER MARSHALL

Contents

Introduction

"When I was young," John Adams recalled, as he exchanged with Thomas Jefferson memories of the changes that they had seen and wrought, "the Summum Bonum in Massachusetts, was to be worth ten thousand pounds Sterling, ride in a Chariot, be Colonel of a Regiment of Militia and hold a seat in His Majesty's Council. No Mans Imagination aspired to any thing higher beneath the Skies."[1] The reasons which led the colonists to abandon this set of limited aims and transform themselves into Americans of altogether more ambitious purpose are not easy to describe. Although the American Revolution established a precedent of universal significance by its inauguration of successful national rejection of imperial rule, the movement lacked those elements which are conventionally considered proof of a distinctive identity. Differences existed in matters of race, language, religion, law, social and economic structure, between the societies of Britain and her American colonies, but both governors and governed preferred for the most part to lay stress on similarities. The growth of conflicts after 1763 stimulated an awareness of distinctions, but the colonists' case stressed the role of Providence, the constitutional rights of Americans as Englishmen, the maintenance of American virtue against the corruptions of English government and society rather than a need to acknowledge the existence of two separate nations.

In the years before 1776 contemporaries noted, and historians have confirmed, the piecemeal growth of a colonial sense of divergence, increasingly termed American, from British patterns of life and thought. It was impossible to be certain of the consequences this development would bring. Andrew Burnaby, an Anglican clergyman who traveled in 1759 from Virginia to New Hampshire, noted many examples of incipient division but felt that lack of colonial unity would ensure a continuance of imperial control (p. 229). A decade later, Philip Freneau and Hugh Henry Brackenridge would conclude

---

[1] Adams to Jefferson, Nov. 15, 1813. *The Adams-Jefferson Letters*, Lester J. Cappon (ed.), (Chapel Hill, 1959), II, p. 402.

their Princeton Commencement poem with an expression of exuberant confidence in an American future (p. 232). Youthful idealism marched in step with deductions drawn from political conflict: the specific grievances of Boston were seen to be caused by the incompatibility of British intentions and American rights (p. 233). Prior to the Revolution, American society had made considerable progress in its move away from its British origins.

Few saw or wished that this rift should become fundamental. As Max Savelle has concluded, "American nationalism of 1770 was not a nationalism of independence. It was a nationalism that expected to find self-expression within the framework of the Empire."[2] This hope vanished reluctantly, its futility exposed by Englishmen as well as by Americans: none excelled Thomas Paine in the ferocity of his denunciation of a corrupt empire. Even after *Common Sense* he devoted a pamphlet to refuting the belief, still widely prevalent, that the quarrel could be resolved by a return to the conditions of 1763 (p. 236). The war years were not marked by precise definition of patriotic and nationalist goals, with the result that the recognition of political independence in 1783 left many questions concerning the nature of the new nation unresolved. Merrill Jensen has provided a sympathetic survey of the cultural achievements which marked the period of Confederation (p. 240). In the absence of self-evident contrasts to distinguish the United States from other English-speaking societies, historians, as David D. Van Tassel indicates, proved particularly useful as guides to the pattern of events which had led to independence (p. 244).

The Republic's politicians, deeply divided though they were on specific issues, shared a commitment to the maintenance and growth of the new nation. *The Federalist Papers* opened with an appeal to Americans to reject solutions which would destroy national unity (p. 247). Alexander Hamilton urged the necessity of developing manufactures as an economic means to the same end (p. 249). Jefferson, the Revolution's principal ideologue, offered American achievements as an example to other nations (p. 252). In the course of time and for widely differing reasons awareness grew of the unique nature of the American experiment.

Yet, as Hans Kohn points out (p. 254), the *idea* of American nationalism was for many years more evident than the *reality* of its existence. From the appearance in 1782 of St. Jean de Crèvecoeur's *Letters of an American Farmer*, in which was posed the famous question, "What is the American, this new man?," generations of observers, both from home and abroad, addressed themselves to the definition and description of the peculiar characteristics of the new nation. The inability of even the most skilled and perceptive of foreign observers to provide more than an interim assessment of the individual quality of the national stance suggests in itself a distinguishing feature of

[2] Max Savelle, *Seeds of Liberty: The Genesis of the American Mind* (New York, 1948), p. 582.

American nationalism: while drawing deeply, as would European nationalist movements, on historic expressions of origins and development, it differed in an equally stressed conviction that the future would display its full purpose and magnitude. Prospect vied with achievement as themes proper for the expression of American nationalism.

The elements to which the exponents of American nationalism made recourse were not, in themselves, unusual or absent from contemporary nationalist movements in Europe. Their distinction resided in a particular conjunction of beliefs which in other nations would be separately held, and in an application of concepts which circumstance would adapt into very different forms in Europe. When Perry Miller alludes to "the theme, *the* American theme, of Nature versus civilization"[3] he refers not to a unique idea, but to the mode of its expression and employment. In the period between the Revolution and the Jacksonian era American nationalism evolved through reference to real, or imagined, examples of historical endeavor, the justifications offered by the achievements and expectations of material developments, and the spiritual challenges evoked by the process of confronting and subduing nature.

Many observers of nineteenth-century America would comment on the mingling of material growth and idealistic intentions: Timothy Dwight, of Yale, New England, and the United States, could conclude that material and religious progress might emanate in widening circles from the societies to which he adhered, ultimately to embark on the task of international advancement and enlightenment. His travels through New England and New York provided evidence that this process had substantially commenced (p. 258). Daniel Webster's oration on the completion, in 1843, of the Bunker Hill monument, could hardly fail to dwell on the achievements of the Revolution and of its leader. It emphasized the ability of the New World to produce "the colossal grandeur of the character and life of Washington," and asserted that the obligations of the United States to Europe, accumulated on account of inherited institutions, had long since been repaid in both moral and material terms (p. 261).

The death of Andrew Jackson appeared to numerous orators both to snap the final thread which linked contemporaries with the Revolutionary generation and to provide a fitting occasion for the review of the achievements of the nation, its particular distinction, and its rise to unchallenged eminence in the international order. Hendrick B. Wright expressed general sentiments when he linked the international and historical stature of the authors of Independence with the "republican simplicity" they nevertheless maintained as embodiments of the national character. Jackson's life constituted an indelible and unblemished record of the course of American moral and geographical progress, and offered incontrovertible testimony to the stature

[3] Perry Miller, *Errand Into the Wilderness* (Cambridge, 1956), p. 205.

of a unique national achievement which, because of its democratic origins, represented the virtues of an entire people (p. 264).

To John William Ward (p. 268), Andrew Jackson exemplifies symbolically the forces and events which had combined, by the 1840's, to permit the United States to contrast its national experience with that of the rest of the world. The victory at New Orleans had contributed a confirmation of American independence which continually improved in the telling. The events of Jackson's life marched concurrently with the growth of the United States, and the sources of his glory could be seen as immanent traits of the directing powers of the nation. Nature, Providence, and Will were to be regarded as the forces which directed the national mission, and which justified its political purposes, economic policies, expansionist ambitions, and rejection of the past. Jackson, therefore, was far more than a personal participant in the creation of American nationalism: his life demonstrated the rise to primacy of its directing concepts.

As the Revolution had, in certain respects, marked the distance that existed between the achievement of political and of cultural independence, so the first half of the nineteenth century illustrated a comparable gap between the ideas and institutions of American nationalism. The accoutrements and symbols of national identity were acquired in haphazard fashion. National holidays were, until the Civil War, limited to the celebration of the Fourth of July and Washington's birthday. The design of the Stars and Stripes was not finally settled until 1818, and then had to wait a further sixteen years for adoption as the emblem of the army; similar uncertainty and delay were to be found in the adoption of a national anthem since the "Star Spangled Banner" grew but slowly in popularity after the War of 1812 and "My Country 'Tis of Thee" could find no more inspired setting than the tune of "God Save the King." Symbols and stereotypes fared somewhat better: the American eagle became a popular alternative to the English lion, and the initial personification of the United States as Brother Jonathan gave ground to Uncle Sam, who is noted to have first appeared in 1813. Apart from the initial flurry of conscious efforts to rid the new nation of its colonial origins, the process of establishing popular forms of national identity seems to have been left largely to chance and occasion.

The inculcation of nationalism cannot, however, be regarded in the same light. The content and use of educational materials were closely scrutinized in endeavors to ensure that children were well acquainted with national qualities and events. School texts were designed to inculcate American virtues, and educational systems were urged to ensure that provision be made for the study of the Constitution which had nurtured them. Massachusetts and Vermont set the example, in 1827, of enacting into law requirements for the study and teaching of American history. Beyond the bounds of the schoolroom architecture and painting testified to the presence of a distinctive nationalism, while George Bancroft, the most respected historian of his age, set out to trace in ten volumes the steps by which Providence had conducted the United States to its present happiness and glory. It was impossible for an American in the first decades of the nineteenth century to overlook the manifestations of a nationalism which, created and developed as a united response to the claims and pretensions of another continent, would, in 1861, face its gravest and most unexpected test from within.

(1775)

Having traveled over so large a tract of this vast continent, before I bid a final farewell to it I must beg the reader's indulgence while I stop for a moment and as it were from the top of a high eminence take one general retrospective look at the whole. An idea, strange as it is visionary, has entered into the minds of the generality of mankind that empire is traveling westward, and every one is looking forward with eager and impatient expectation to that destined moment when America is to give law to the rest of the world. But if ever an idea was illusory and fallacious, I will venture to predict that this will be so.

America is formed for happiness, but not for empire: in a course of 1200 miles I did not see a single object that solicited charity, but I saw insuperable causes of weakness, which will necessarily prevent its being a potent state.

Our colonies may be distinguished into the southern and northern, separated from each other by the Susquehanna and that imaginary line which divides Maryland from Pennsylvania.

The southern colonies have so many inherent causes of weakness that they never can possess any real strength. The climate operates very powerfully upon them, and renders them indolent, inactive, and unenterprising; this is visible in every line of their character. I myself have been a spectator, and it is not an uncommon sight, of a man in the vigor of life, lying upon a couch, and a female slave standing over him, wafting off the flies and fanning him, while he took his repose.

The southern colonies (Maryland, which is the smallest and most inconsiderable, alone excepted) will never be thickly seated. For as they are not confined within determinate limits, but extend to the westward indefinitely, men, sooner than apply to laborious occupations—occupations militating with their dispositions and generally considered too as the inheritance and badge of slavery—will gradually retire westward, and settle upon fresh lands which are said also to be more fertile, where, by the servitude of a Negro or two, they may enjoy all the satisfaction of an easy and indolent independency. Hence the lands upon the coast will of course remain thin of inhabitants.

Andrew Burnaby, *Travels Through the Middle Settlements in North America* (2nd ed., London, 1775), pp. 154–62. Spelling and punctuation revised.

The mode of cultivation by slavery is another insurmountable cause of weakness. The number of Negroes in the southern colonies is upon the whole nearly equal, if not superior, to that of the white men, and they propagate and increase even faster. Their condition is truly pitiable: their labor excessively hard, their diet poor and scanty, their treatment cruel and oppressive. They cannot therefore but be a subject of terror to those who so inhumanly tyrannize over them.

The Indians near the frontiers are a still further formidable cause of subjection. The southern Indians are numerous and are governed by a sounder policy than formerly; experience has taught them wisdom. They never make war with the colonists without carrying terror and devastation along with them. They sometimes break up entire counties together. Such is the state of the southern colonies.

The northern colonies are of stronger stamina, but they have other difficulties and disadvantages to struggle with, not less arduous or more easy to be surmounted than what have been already mentioned. Their limits being defined, they will undoubtedly become exceedingly populous. For though men will readily retire back towards the frontiers of their own colony, yet they will not so easily be induced to settle beyond them, where different laws and politics prevail and where, in short, they are a different people, But in proportion to want of territory, if we consider the proposition in a general and abstract light, will be want of power. But the northern colonies have still more positive and real disadvantages to contend with. They are composed of people of different nations, different manners, different religions, and different languages. They have a mutual jealousy of each other, fomented by considerations of interest, power, and ascendency. Religious zeal too, like a smothered fire, is secretly burning in the hearts of the different sectaries that inhabit them, and were it not restrained by laws and superior authority, would soon burst out into a flame of universal persecution. Even the peaceable Quakers struggle hard for pre-eminence and evince in a very striking manner that the passions of mankind are much stronger than any principles of religion.

The colonies, therefore, separately considered, are internally weak. But it may be supposed, that by a union or coalition they would become strong and formidable. But a union seems almost impossible. One founded in dominion or power is morally so, for, were not England to interfere, the colonies themselves so well understand the policy of preserving a balance that, I think, they would not be idle spectators were any one of them to endeavor to subjugate its next neighbor. Indeed, it appears to me a very doubtful point, even supposing all the colonies of America to be united under one head, whether it would be possible to keep in due order and government so wide and extended an empire, the difficulties of communication, of intercourse, of correspondence, and all other circumstances considered.

A voluntary association or coalition, at least a permanent one, is almost as difficult to be supposed, for fire and water are not more heterogeneous than the different colonies in North America. Nothing can exceed the jealousy and emulation which they possess in regard to each other. The inhabitants of Pennsylvania and New York have an inexhaustible source of animosity in their jealousy for the trade of the Jerseys. Massachusetts Bay and Rhode Island are not less interested in that of Connecticut. The West Indies are a common subject of emulation to them all. Even the limits and boundaries of each colony are a constant source of litigation. In short, such is the difference of character, of manners, of religion, of interest of the different colonies that I think, if I am not wholly ignorant of the human mind, were they left to themselves, there would soon be a civil war from one end of the continent to the other, while the Indians and Negroes would, with better reason, impatiently watch the opportunity of exterminating them all together.

After all, however, supposing what I firmly believe will never take place, a permanent union or alliance of all the colonies, yet it could not be effectual or productive of the event supposed. For such is the extent of coast settled by the American colonies that it can never be defended but by a maritime power. America must first be mistress of the sea before she can be independent, or mistress of herself. Suppose the colonies ever so populous, suppose them capable of maintaining 100,000 men constantly in arms (a supposition in the highest degree extravagant), yet half a dozen frigates would, with ease, ravage and lay waste the whole country from end to end without a possibility of their being able to prevent it. The country is so intersected by rivers, rivers of such magnitude as to render it impossible to build bridges over them, that all communication is in a manner cut off. An army under such circumstances could never act to any purpose or effect; its operations would be totally frustrated.

Further, a great part of the opulence and power of America depends upon her fisheries and her commerce with the West Indies; she cannot subsist without them. But these would be entirely at the mercy of that power which might have the sovereignty of the seas. I conclude therefore that England, so long as she maintains her superiority in that respect, will also possess a superiority in America. But the moment she loses the empire of the one, she will be deprived of the sovereignty of the other. For were that empire to be held by France, Holland, or any other power, America, I will venture to foretell, will be annexed to it. New establishments formed in the interior parts of America will not come under this predicament. I should therefore think it the best policy to enlarge the present colonies, but not to establish fresh ones. For to suppose interior colonies to be of use to the mother country by being a check upon those already settled is to suppose what is contrary to experience and the nature of things, viz., that men removed beyond the reach of power will be subordinate to it.

2 / Philip Freneau and Hugh Henry Brackenridge
A Poem on the Rising Glory of America

(1771)

And when a train of rolling years are past,
(So sung the exil'd seer in Patmos isle)
A new Jerusalem, sent down from heaven,
Shall grace our happy earth—perhaps this land,
Whose ample breast shall then receive, tho' late,
Myriads of saints, with their immortal king,
To live and reign on earth a thousand years,
Thence called *Millennium*. Paradise anew
Shall flourish, by no second Adam lost.
No dangerous tree with deadly fruit shall grow,
No tempting serpent to allure the soul
From native innocence. A *Canaan* here,
Another *Canaan* shall excel the old,
And from a fairer *Pisgah's* top be seen.
No thistle here, nor thorn, nor briar shall spring,
Earth's curse before: the lion and the lamb,
In mutual friendship link'd, shall browse the shrub,
And timorous deer with soften'd tygers stray
O'er mead, or lofty hill, or grassy plain:
Another Jordan's stream shall glide along,
And Siloah's brook in circling eddies flow:
Groves shall adorn their verdant banks, on which
The happy people, free from toils and death,
Shall find secure repose. No fierce disease,
No fevers, slow consumption, ghastly plague,
(Fate's ancient ministers) again proclaim
Perpetual war with man: fair fruits shall bloom,
Fair to the eye, and grateful to the taste;
Nature's loud storms be hush'd, and seas no more
Rage hostile to mankind—and, worse than all,
The fiercer passions of the human breast
Shall kindle up to deeds of death no more,
But all subside in universal peace.
                    Such days the world,
And such, AMERICA, thou first shalt have,
When ages, yet to come, have run their round,
And future years of bliss alone remain.

Philip Freneau and Hugh Henry Brackenridge, *A Poem on the Rising Glory of America*, Princeton Commencement Poem, 1771.

3 / Instructions from the Town of Boston to Their Representatives

(1770)

Gentlemen,

The town of Boston, by their late choice of you to represent them, in the ensuing general court, have given strong proof of their confidence in your abilities and integrity. For no period, since the perilous times of our venerable fathers, has worn a more gloomy and alarming aspect. Unwarrantable and arbitrary exactions made upon the people, trade expiring, grievances, murmurs, and discontents, convulsing every part of the British empire, forbode a day of trail, in which, under GOD, nothing but stern virtue and inflexible fortitude can save us from a rapacious and miserable destruction. A series of occurrences, many recent events, and especially the late journals of the house of lords, afford good reason to believe, that a deep-laid and desperate plan of imperial despotism has been laid and partly executed, for the extinction of all civil liberty:—and from a gradual sapping the grand foundation, from a subtle undermining the main pillars, breaking the strong bulwarks, destroying the principal ramparts and battlements, the august, and once revered fortress of English freedom—that admirable work of ages—the British constitution—seems just tottering into fatal and inevitable ruin. The dreadful catastrophe threatens universal havock, and presents an awful warning to hazard all, if peradventure, we, in these distant confines of the earth, may prevent being totally overwhelmed and buried under the ruins of our most established rights. For many years past, we have, with sorrow, beheld the approaching conflict; various have been the causes which pressed on this decisive period; and every thing now conspires to prompt a full exertion of our utmost vigilance, wisdom, and firmness:—and as the exigencies of the times require, not only the refined abilities of true policy, but the more martial virtues, conduct, valour, and intrepidity; so, gentlemen, in giving you our suffrages, at this election, we have devolved upon you a most important trust; to discharge which, we doubt not, you will summon up the whole united faculties of both mind and body.

We decline, gentlemen, a minute detail of many momentous concernments, relative to which, it is believed, no instructions need be given; but we shall express our thoughts on such matters, as, we suppose, you will choose to have our explicit sentiments . . .

The despicable situation of our provincial militia, you will make the object of your peculiar attention, and as it is apparent, from what putrid source this decline of military emulation hath flowed, we press, that such

Reprinted from Thomas Hutchinson, *The History of the Colony and Province of Massachusetts-Bay*, (ed.) John Hutchinson (London, 1828), pp. 508–509, 513–515.

animated steps may be taken, as shall speedily remove this just reproach from the land. When every method is obstinately pursued to enervate with foreign luxuries, every artifice practised to corrupt, in order to enslave; when we are denied a free, constitutional exercise of our rights, as men and citizens; when high-handed invasions are made on our property, and audacious attempts to intimidate not only from resistance, but complaint; surely the constitutional watchmen and sentinels of our liberties are asleep upon their stations, or traitors to the main body, if they do not rouse and rescue from this insidious plot.

As a voluntary and laudable renunciation of a baneful commerce has naturally occasioned a general stagnation of trade; and as the true riches of a people are numbers and industry, we warmly recommend to you such measures, as will tend to increase population, encourage industry, and promote our own manufactures; and as this is a very pacifick political device for the defeat of our malicious foes, we presume it may be less obnoxious to the virulent slander of ministerial dependants:—but these salutary methods of genuine policy ought never to exclude or supersede the more open, manly, bold, and pertinacious exertions for our freedom.

One of the most weighty matters, which attracts our affection, and lies deep in the heart of every sensible and honest American, is the firm and lasting union of the colonies: there is no one point which ought more to engage your affectionate zeal. Our enemies, well knowing the consequence of this great acquisition, have bent their whole force to render it abortive. Without the least foundation, jealousies have been insidiously infused, diabolical falsehoods forged, idle tales propagated, little discords fomented; and every engine, that fraud could invent, and hardy villains manage, has been set to work, in order to retard, if not utterly overthrow, this desirable attainment. But all hath not done. The eyes of our worthy brethren, through the continent, are open.—Yet as we know the plotting malice, inveteracy, and indefatigable labour of the desperately wicked, we strongly inculcate, that you be zealous to keep up a cordial intercourse with our sister colonies; and, as our interests are so apparently inseparable, nothing but an intimate communion is requisite to cement our political and natural attachment.

We have, for a long time, beheld, with grief and astonishment, the unwarrantable practice of ministerial instructions to the commanders-in-chief of this province. It is high time, gentlemen, for this matter to be searched into and remedied.

Such an enormous stretch of power, if much longer unchecked, will eventually annihilate the essentials of all civil liberty. It is repugnant to the very first principle of true government, (which was alone instituted for the good of the governed,) that a remote power, not only much disconnected, but often different in interest, should undertake, at pleasure, to control, nay command, in affairs of the last moment, for the benefit and relief of the people: —a power, three thousand transmarine miles distant, not only ignorant of our true welfare, but, if perchance discovered, interested to oppose it; not only attempting to oppress, but actually oppressing;—that such a power should be allowed, wantonly, to proscribe patricians and plobeians;—at will, to fix the residence of our parliament; to order that parliament when, and how to proceed, and where to retire; at one time to forbid the best improvement of our own produce; at another time, effectually to force us to purchase foreign merchandise;—again, as it were, sword in hand, to demand our property; and, anon, to forbid our own disposal of a certain part of it:—these are doctrines and political solecisms, which may take root and spring up, under the meridian of modern Rome; but we trust in GOD, will not flourish in the soil and climate of British America. We, therefore, strictly charge you, not to grant any supplies to the instruments of government, if, through their defect, or misapplication, the grand ends, for which we support and obey our rulers, are not accomplished . . .

Our choice of you, gentlemen, to represent us, at this hazardous juncture, is a sufficient evidence of our great dependence on your wise, honest and steady conduct:—we, therefore, leave all other matters to your best discretion and judgment, till we shall see fit to give further instructions:—we greatly confide, that you will bear in strong remembrance, the hardships and sufferings of our pious fathers to find out and purchase this remote asylum from ecclesiastical persecution and civil tyranny; that, inspired, by their glorious example, you will vigorously repel, even unto the uttermost, the insults and violences of internal and external enemies to our peace. We remind you, that the further nations recede and give way to the gigantic strides of any powerful despot, the more rapidly will the fiend advance to spread wide desolation;—and then should an attempt be made to stay his ravaging progress—"the dogs of war, let loose and hot for blood,—rush on to waste and havock." *Obsta principiis* is the maxim to be held in view: it is now no time to halt between two opinions: the demands of fraud, violence, and usurpation are insatiable: it is, therefore, no season to stand listening to subtle allurements, deceitful cajolings, or formidable threatenings; We, therefore, enjoin you, at all hazards to deport (as we rely your own hearts will stimulate) like the faithful representatives of a freeborn, awakened, and determined people;—who, being impregnated with the spirit of liberty in conception, and nurtured in principles of freedom from their infancy, are resolved to breathe the same celestial æther, till summoned to resign the heavenly flame by that omnipotent GOD who gave it.

4 / Thomas Paine
A Dialogue

(1776)

Delegate. Welcome to this retreat, my good friend. If I mistake not, I now see the ghost of the brave General Montgomery.

General Montgomery. I am glad to see you. I still love liberty and America, and the contemplation of the future greatness of this continent now forms a large share of my present happiness. I am here upon an important errand, to warn you against listening to terms of accommodation from the court of Britain.

Del. I shall be happy in receiving instruction from you in the present trying exigency of our public affairs. But suppose the terms you speak of should be just and honorable?

Gen. Mont. How can you expect these, after the king has proclaimed you rebels from the throne, and after both Houses of Parliament have resolved to support him in carrying on a war against you? No, I see no offers from Great Britain but of PARDON. The very word is an insult upon our cause. To whom is pardon offered?—to virtuous freemen. For what?—for flying arms in defence of the rights of humanity: And from whom do these offers come?— From a ROYAL CRIMINAL. You have furnished me with a new reason for triumphing in my death, for I had rather have it said that I died by his vengeance, than lived by his mercy.

Del. But you think nothing of the destructive consequences of war. How many cities must be reduced to ashes! how many families must be ruined! and how many widows and orphans must be made, should the present war be continued any longer with Great Britain.

Gen. Mont. I think of nothing but the destructive consequences of slavery. The calamities of war are transitory and confined in their effects. But the calamities of slavery are extensive and lasting in their operation. I love mankind as well as you, and I could never restrain a tear when my love of justice has obliged me to shed the blood of a fellow creature. It is my humanity that makes me urge you against a reconciliation with Great Britain, for if this takes place, nothing can prevent the American colonies from being the seat of war as often as the king of Great Britain renews his quarrels with any of the colonies, or with any of the belligerent powers of Europe.

Thomas Paine, *A Dialogue Between the Ghost of General Montgomery just arrived from the Elysian Fields; and an American Delegate, in a Wood near Philadelphia* (Philadelphia, 1776).

Del. I tremble at the doctrine you have advanced. I see you are for the independence of the colonies of Great Britain.

Gen. Mont. I am for permanent liberty, peace and security to the American colonies.

Del. These can only be maintained by placing the colonies in the situation they were in the year 1763.

Gen. Mont. And is no satisfaction to be made to the colonies for the blood and treasure they have expended in resisting the arms of Great Britain? Who can soften the prejudices of the king—the Parliament—and the nation, each of whom will be averse to maintain a peace with you in proportion to the advantages you have gained over them? Who shall make restitution to the widows—the mothers—and the children of the men who have been slain by their arms? Can no hand wield the sceptre of government in America except that which has been stained with the blood of your countrymen? For my part if I thought this continent would ever acknowledge the sovereignty of the crown of Britain again, I should forever lament the day in which I offered up my life for its salvation.

Del. You should distinguish between the king and his ministers.

Gen. Mont. I live in a world where all political superstition is done away. The king is the author of all the measures carried on against America. The influence of bad ministers is no better apology for these measures, than the influences of bad company is for a murderer, who expiates his crimes under a gallows. You all complain of the corruption of the Parliament, and of the venality of the nation, and yet you forget that the crown is the source of them both. You shun the streams, and yet you are willing to sit down at the very fountain of corruption and venality.

Del. Our distance and charters will protect us from the influence of the crown.

Gen. Mont. Your distance will only render your danger more imminent, and your ruin more irretrievable. Charters are no restraints against the lust of power. The only reason why you have escaped so long is, because the treasure of the nation has been employed for these fifty years in buying up the virtue of Britain and Ireland. Hereafter the reduction of the representatives of the people of America will be the only aim of administration should you continue to be connected with them.

Del. But I foresee many evils from the independence of the colonies. Our trade will be ruined from the want of a navy to protect it. Each colony will put in its claim for superiority, and we shall have domestic wars without end.

Gen. Mont. As I now know that Divine Providence intends this country to be the asylum of persecuted virtue from every quarter of the globe, so I think your trade will be the vehicle that will convey it to you. Heaven has furnished you with greater resources for a navy than any nation in the world. Nothing but an ignorance of your strength could have led you to sacrifice your trade for the protection of a foreign navy. A freedom from the restraints of the acts of navigation I foresee will produce such immense addition to the wealth of this country that posterity will wonder that ever you thought your present trade worth its protection. As to the supposed contentions between sister colonies, they have no foundation in truth. But supposing they have, will delaying the independence of the colonies 50 years prevent them? No—the weakness of the colonies, which at first produced their union, will always preserve it, 'till it shall be their interest to be separated. Had the colony of Massachusett's Bay been possessed of the military resources which it would probably have had 50 years hence, would she have held out the signal of distress to her sister colonies, upon the news of the Boston Port Bill! No—she would have withstood all the power of Britain alone, and afterwards the neutral colonies might have shared the fate of the colony of Canada. Moreover, had the connection with Great Britain been continued 50 years longer, the progress of British laws, customs and manners (now totally corrupted) would have been such that the colonies would have been prepared to welcome slavery. But had it been otherwise, they must have asserted their independence with arms. This is nearly done already. It will be cruel to bequeath another contest to your posterity.

Del. But I dread all innovations in governments. They are very dangerous things.

Gen. Mont. The revolution, which gave a temporary stability to the liberties of Britain, was an innovation in government, and yet no ill consequences have arisen from it. Innovations are dangerous only as they shake the prejudices of a people; but there are now, I believe, but few prejudices to be found in this country, in favor of the old connection with Great Britain. I except those men only who are under the influence of their passions and offices.

Del. But is it not most natural for us to wish for a connection with a people who speak the same language with us, and possess the same laws, religion and forms of government with ourselves?

Gen. Mont. The immortal Montesquieu says, that nations should form alliances with those nations only which are as unlike to themselves as possible in religion, laws and manners, if they mean to preserve their own constitutions. Your dependence upon the crown is no advantage, but rather an injury to the people of Britain, as it increases the power and influence of the King. The people are benefited only by your trade, and this they may have after you are independent of the crown. Should you be disposed to forgive the king and the nation for attempting to enslave you, they will never forgive you for having baffled them in the attempt.

Del. But we have many friends in both Houses of Parliament.

Gen. Mont. You mean the ministry have many enemies in Parliament who connect the cause of America with their clamors at the door of administration. Lord Chatham's conciliatory bill would have ruined you more effectually than Lord North's motion. The Marquis of Rockingham was the author of the declaratory bill. Mr. Wilkes has added infamy to the weakness of your cause, and the Duke of Grafton and Lord Lyttleton have rendered the minority Junto, if possible, more contemptible than ever.

Del. But if we become independent we shall become a commonwealth.

Gen. Mont. I maintain that it is your interest to be independent of Great Britain, but I do not recommend any new form or government to you. I should think it strange that a people who have virtue enough to defend themselves against the most powerful nation in the world should want wisdom to contrive a perfect and free form of government. You have been kept in subjection to the crown of Britain by a miracle. Your liberties have hitherto been suspended by a thread. Your connection with Great Britain is unnatural and unnecessary. All the wheels of a government should move within itself. I would only beg leave to observe to you, that monarchy and aristocracy have in all ages been the vehicles of slavery.

Del. Our governments will want force and authority if we become independent of Great Britain.

Gen. Mont. I beg leave to contradict that assertion. No royal edicts or acts of assembly have ever been more faithfully or universally obeyed than the resolves of the Congress. I admire the virtue of the colonies, and did not some of them still hang upon the haggard breasts of Great Britain, I should think the time now come in which they had virtue enough to be happy under any form of government. Remember that it is in a commonwealth only that you can expect to find every man a patriot or a hero. Aristides, Epaminondas, Pericles, Scipio, Camillus and a thousand other illustrious Grecian and Roman heroes, would never have astonished the world with their names, had they lived under royal governments.

Del. Will not a Declaration of Independence lessen the number of our friends, and increase the rage of our enemies in Britain?

Gen. Mont. Your friends (as you call them) are too few—too divided—and too interested to help you. And as for your enemies, they have done their worst. They have called upon Russians—Hanoverians—Hessians—Canadians—savages and Negroes to assist them in burning your towns—desolating your country—and in butchering your wives and children. You have nothing further to fear from them. Go, then, and awaken the Congress to a sense of their importance; you have no time to lose. France waits for nothing but a declaration of your independence to revenge the injuries they sustained from Britain in the last war. But I forbear to reason any further with you. The decree is finally gone forth. Britain and America are now distinct empires. Your country teems with patriots—heroes—and legislators, who are impatient to burst forth into light and importance. Hereafter your achievements shall no more swell the page of British history. God will not excite the attention of all Europe—of the whole world—nay of angels themselves to the present controversy for nothing. The inhabitants of heaven long to see the ark finished, in which all the liberty and true religion of the world are to be deposited. The day in which the colonies declare their independence will be a jubilee to Hampden—Sidney—Russell—Warren—Gardiner—Macpherson—Cheeseman, and all the other heroes who have offered themselves as sacrifices upon the altar of liberty. It was no small mortification to me when I fell upon the Plains of Abraham, to reflect that I did not expire like the brave General Wolfe, in the arms of victory. But I now no longer envy him his glory. I would rather die in *attempting* to obtain permanent freedom for a handful of people, than survive a conquest which would serve only to extend the empire of despotism. A band of heroes now beckon to me. I can only add that America is the theater where human nature will *soon* receive its greatest military, civil, and literary honors.

5 / Merrill Jensen
The Spirit of the New Nation

(1950)

The spirit and faith of the new nation were expressed variously, but no expression was more obvious and popular than that to be found in Fourth of July celebrations. In 1783 a Charleston paper reported: "Yesterday, the 4th of July, afforded a spectacle equally awful and grand. The inhabitants of the whole continent of America, eagerly devoted in commemorating the anniversary of the greatest revolution that ever took place—the expulsion of tyranny and slavery, and the introduction of freedom, happiness, and independency, throughout the greatest continent in the world."[1] Four years later, after a celebration of the eleventh anniversary of the Declaration of

Merrill Jensen, *The New Nation*, pp. 88–92. Copyright 1950 by Alfred A. Knopf, Inc. Reprinted by permission of the publisher.
[1] *South Carolina Gazette, and General Advertiser*, 5th July 1783.

Independence, a Boston paper declared that the Revolution "has not only given the blessing of freedom to this western world; but has enlightened nearly all Europe, with respect to the natural rights of mankind."[2]

The news of Yorktown in 1781 had barely reached New England before doughty Timothy Dwight preached a sermon in which he summed up the experience of the past, the problems of the present, and the hopes for the future. His text was from Isaiah: "to the islands he will repay recompense . . ." The Lord had humbled Britain for her cruelties in India and America, and Yorktown was the crowning victory. But the Americans had sins too: dissipation of thought, prostitution of reason, contempt for religion, disdain of virtue, deliberation in vice, and universal levity and corruption of soul. Skepticism was growing everywhere. But there is progress in knowledge. The present century is the most enlightened of any. The growth of knowledge has shown the ridiculousness of "popish ceremonial" and the folly of prescribing creeds. Even war may be ended, and kings walk in the way of science. As a result of "the convulsion," the American Revolution, "the world hath seen for the first time an extensive empire founded on the only just basis, the free and general choice of the inhibitants." In America the rights of human nature are unfolded. The church is free from control. Here society is friendly to genius. The "convulsion" has awakened a disposition to freedom of inquiry and to independence of decision. We may therefore hope for great advances in political and natural science and a most noble progress in theology. We may soon have arts hitherto without name and sciences besides electricity "deriving their birth from American genius." To this disposition we may soon owe new, improving, and enrapturing ideas of human nature and duty. "May we not in a word expect from this disposition a depth of research, a candor of debate, and a friendliness to truth, which shall exhibit a contrast to former prejudices, begin a new era in the progress of science, and attemper the mind to the easiest reception of the grace of gospel."[3]

Dwight's prophecies were echoed by many another, particularly in the rapidly growing number of newspapers. One writer said that the United States was "like the sun rising with brilliant radiance from the eastern ocean . . . in the infancy of their power, emerging from the tumultuous sea of warfare, and shining in the cultivation of arts and sciences. Genius is now fostered by the charitable hand of public munificence; and the man of invention reaps the benefit of his ingenuity. The states in general vie with each other in the encouragement and patronage of learning, and the polite arts."[4] Still another writer declared that it was difficult to conceive of the greatness or importance

[2] *Massachusetts Centinel*, 14 July 1787.

[3] *A Sermon Preached at Northampton on the Twenty-Eighth of November 1781 Occasioned by the Capture of the British Army Under the Command of Earl Cornwallis* (Hartford, n.d.).

[4] *Massachusetts Centinel*, 27 March 1784.

of North America within a century or two. "Agriculture, the basis of a nation's greatness," will probably "be raised to its pinnacle of perfection and its attendant, commerce, will so agreeably and usefully employ mankind, that wars will be forgotten, nations by a free intercourse with this vast and fertile continent, will again become brothers, and no longer treat each other as savages and monsters. The iron generations will verge to decay. . . . " To the west lies land of "inexpressible beauty and fertility." There the trees are greater, there the rivers and streams fall into that "grand repository of a thousand streams the far famed Mississippi . . . this prince of rivers, in comparison of whom the Nile is but a rivulet, and the Danube a mere ditch . . ."[5]

America's vastness was a continuous source of pride and wonder. Everything is on a larger plan than on the "eastern" continent. The mountains are a third larger and higher, the rivers and lakes are larger, and the five Great Lakes are like so many Baltics and Mediterraneans. It is reasonable to suppose that the sentiments of the mind bear some relation to the objects around it. Philosophers and poets declare that the natural course of improvement will lead to universal civilization and social happiness and that the millennium may actually commence in the territories of the United States. Here everything, like its mountains and rivers, is on a more liberal plan. "And this seems to be the reason why this country is reserved to be the last and greatest theater for the improvement of mankind, that the productions of nature, and the expansion of the human mind, should unite in completing the perfection of civil government and the happiness of society." The greatness of genius and the liberality of sentiment in America are such as no nation has ever equaled. "Many of the useful arts of life, as well as various branches of philosophy, such as electricity, mechanicks and astronomy, have received more improvements from our countrymen than they have from all Europe during the present century."[6]

Not only was America already the center of learning in the eyes of some of its citizens, it was to be a refuge for the oppressed of the world. The independency of the United States was in no one instance a greater blessing to the world "than in its being the asylum whither the indigent and oppressed, whom the lawless hand of European despotism would crush to the earth, can find succour and protection, and join common fellowship in a country,

> Where happy millions their own fields possess,
> No tyrant awes them, and no lords oppress,"[7]

By 1786 the boasts and prophecies were bolstered by assertions of achievements. Franklin's philosophy was declared to have the unrivaled admiration of every country in Europe. The "moral scrutinies" of Jonathan Edwards had

---

[5] *Ibid.*, 11 Dec. 1784.

[6] *Massachusetts Centinel*, 25 Feb. 1786.

[7] *Pennsylvania Gazette*, 5 Oct. 1785.

the applause of most Protestant countries, even of those opposed to his opinions. "The quadrant, injuriously called Hadley's, was the invention of Mr. Godfrey of Philadelphia; mercurial inoculation was the discovery of the late Dr. Muirson . . ." Trumbull's *M'Fingal* was ranked along with *Hudibras* by the English reviewers. The painters Copley and West found little competition, even in Europe. The memorials of Congress were classed in Europe along with the best of their kind ever published. European praise of our military and political characters renders "our own applauses totally unnecessary to their glory. Of no other nation can so honorable things be mentioned, at so early a period of their existence."[8]

The following year "An Essay on American Genius" declared that the time had come to explode the European creed that "we are infantile in our acquisitions and savage in our manners; because we are inhabitants of a New World, lately occupied by a race of savages." The writer then proceeded to review the achievements of living Americans. He pointed to Ramsay's history of the Revolution in South Carolina as an example and urged further writing on the military history of the Revolution. The writer's main concern, however, was with the fine arts. Americans have a strong talent for painting. Benjamin West of Philadelphia is one of "the first historical painters of the age." John Singleton Copley of Boston, "in the same walk of genius, is not spoken of as second to any of the profession." John Trumbull of Connecticut, though a younger man, has "exhibited the happiest dispositions . . ."

Yet the writer of the essay was forced to admit that "the age of ultimate refinement in America is yet to arrive." Most of the painters he had named could not have attained their fame and wealth if they had remained in America. Too much money was spent on vulgar amusement and some pains should be taken to "lead the taste of the nation to substitute, instead of the vulgar enjoyments of cock-fighting, gambling, and tavern haunting, pleasures of a more refined and innocent nature." He was convinced, however, that there was much less gaming, dissipation, and tavern haunting than before the war and that the future progress of wealth and population would be a source of improvement in "music, architecture, gardening, sculpture, and other elegant arts." As an example he pointed to the progress of poetry despite "many disadvantages, and notwithstanding some ungracious insinuations to the contrary . . ." Perhaps the poets living in Connecticut were equal to any then writing. At least the question might be appealed to the "bar of critical taste." Joel Barlow's *Vision of Columbus* was in press, and when published it would give the "reader of discernment an exalted idea of American genius and refinement."[9]

Such boastfulness was the result of a pride that was not without solid foundation, a foundation that was laid by American writers, who, with great

[8] *Ibid.*, 17 May 1786.
[9] *The New Haven Gazette and the Connecticut Magazine*, 1 Feb. 1787.

effort and little profit, sought to tell the story of the movement of which they had been a part and to give character to the new nation which they had helped create.

6 / David D. Van Tassel
The Revolution: National Historical Writing, 1774–1800

(1960)

David Ramsay's second history [*History of the American Revolution*] met with an enthusiastic reception. The *Columbian* hailed it and declared that Ramsay's book was one step more in the realization of "that independence, which for some years after the termination of the late arduous conflict with Britain, existed only in name." Other historians quickly followed Ramsay's lead. Jedidiah Morse included a history of the war in his geography and wrote a *History of America in Two Books*. In 1787, Noah Webster had added a history of the revolution to his *An American Selection of Readings*. Textbook histories began to appear, and one author, Richard Snowden, wrote of the revolution in biblical style. All echoed the same theme.

That theme was the nationalists' story of the past, a defense of the revolution and support of the standing order, which became the American interpretation of the revolutionary period. The nationalists' defense of the revolution did not differ greatly from the early propaganda of the war, Paine's letter to Abbé Raynal, or Gordon's history, although with the passage of time they magnified its importance to mankind. "The American cause," Morse declared, was "the cause of liberty," and the struggle for the rights of Englishmen became, upon closer inspection, a fight for the natural rights of mankind whose "legitimate freedom" did not rest upon "the almes . . . of princes." Webster told the rising generation, called by John Adams the most important generation in the history of the world, that "Lexington opened the first scene of the great drama, which . . . exhibited the most illustrious characters and events, and closed with a revolution, equally glorious for the actors and important in its consequences to the human race."

The conditions of America and the wise colonial policy of Great Britain had promoted the growth of "a love of liberty and a quick sense of injury" among the colonists. Nevertheless, the nationalists demonstrated that the British colonials had been loyal and happy because "they shared in every privilege belonging to . . . [England's] native sons [and] but slightly felt

---

David D. Van Tassel, *Recording America's Past* (Chicago: The University of Chicago Press, 1960). Copyright © by The University of Chicago. Reprinted, without footnotes, by permission of the publisher.

the inconveniences of subordination" until 1764, when British colonial policy changed. The colonies objected to the "new" principle of taxation and to the mode of collection, considered "an unconstitutional and oppressive innovation." The colonists used every argument, every peaceful means, to dissuade the British ministers from their tyrannical course, until the hard-pressed Americans were convinced that they could not do otherwise—they must resort to force in order to preserve their freedom. In this interpretation, certainly most of the early revolutionaries agreed with the nationalists.

All the same, the nationalists had forced a constitution upon a reluctant people. Historians such as Ramsay and Webster saw that a necessary part of their task was to encourage "habits of obedience" and submission to the new government. They knew that "to overset an established government unhinges many of those principles which bind individuals to each other." Not only had the United States "overset an established government" but had made the right to do so a cornerstone of the Republic. The problem of the historian was to reconcile the Declaration of Independence, a revolutionary document successfully setting forth and sanctioning unsettling principles, with the hope of stability and permanence provided by the Constitution.

Ramsay, Webster, and Morse, as well as other Americans who wrote histories during the early years of the Republic, attempted to make the revolution a symbol of national unity and to demonstrate that the Constitution was the most natural and perfect embodiment of the purposes of the war. "The act of independence," Ramsay wrote, "did not hold out to the world thirteen sovereign states, but a common sovereignty of the whole of their united capacity." These historians often wrote and sometimes tried to prove that the revolution was a war of all true Americans for their natural rights of life, liberty, and property, carried on not by mobs, but by an "enlightened, virtuous, substantial body of uncorrupted citizens." Unity was a product of the revolution. A Continental Army and a Continental Congress, Ramsay pointed out, were the beginnings of unity. Individuals from both the army and the Congress "desseminated principles of union . . . and a foundation was laid for the establishment of a nation . . ." Nationalist historians did not disparage or belittle the role of the early revolutionary leaders; they adopted them and failed to mention the strife of internal politics. One historian went so far as to publish in the 1790's a refutation of the claims of a British author who hinted at disunity in the American government during the Revolutionary War.

After showing that the revolution had established a great precedent for unified action and playing down any discord or neglecting it entirely, the nationalist historians moved on to write of the ratification of the Constitution. Jedidiah Morse in his history omitted the Confederation interlude, allowing his readers to believe that the Constitution came directly out of the revolution. Other historians acknowledged the Confederation as an amateurish experiment in government that led to disrespect abroad and chaos at home and could protect neither life, liberty, nor property, the objectives of the revolution.

A concept of history current in the new nation fortified the nationalist interpretation and supplied a firm ideological basis for the Federalist form of government. The idea of historical cycles was not new to eighteenth-century Americans; it had been seen in the popular works of David Hume and in those of some of the classical historians, but only after the revolution did it become all-pervasive in American historical writings. In 1787, John Quincy Adams summarized this philosophy and applied it to the United States: "There is never a rising or meridian without a setting sun.—We it is true have happily passed the dangerous period of infancy;—we are rising into youth and man-hood, with encouraging prospects. But let us remember we shall fall . . . into the decline and infirmities of old age." Ministers in their sermons, politicians in their orations, authors and historians in their works, all expressed the same idea.

The cyclical concept of history stemmed from a belief in a mechanical universe and the eternal sameness of human nature. Nations adhered to fixed laws, as did physical and organic bodies. Wrote Noah Webster: "Every person tolerably well versed in history, knows that nations are often compared to individuals and to vegetables, in their progress from their origin to maturity and decay." Moreover, "the resemblance is fair and just." Human nature, like basic elements in chemistry, was the common denominator. Man might differ in his capacities and faculties, but the same "passions" always actuated him. The identification of the passions included in elemental nature varied with the writer—ambition, lust, greed—any of which, if unchecked, threat-ened to become a destroyer of organized society. And, like a chemical element, basic human nature reacted to the same forces of history in the same way. The people of nations "in the early stages of their existence . . . are usually industrious and frugal . . . active and hardy, united and brave. Their feeble, exposed, and necessitous condition in some sort forced upon them this conduct and these habits." Although practice of virtue brings a young nation to a pros-perous and flourishing maturity, its downfall begins inexorably with its suc-cess. "Prosperity inflates and debauches." The passions of "pride and avarice," "idleness and sensuality," are unloosed and bring about the ruin and destruction of the nation.

This was the pattern of history which Ramsay, Webster, Morse, and other American historians at the close of the eighteenth century believed most truly represented ascertainable facts. All American colonial history pointed to the possibility of an empire. Independence was the first step, and the second was the establishment of a government which would hold in check the passions of men, "to retard, if possible, and not accelerate the progress of corruption."

By 1800 the Revolutionary War no longer represented to Americans the revolt of thirteen separate colonies against imperial injustice; instead, it was the birth struggle of a new republic and a symbol of national unity. "Its records," said one writer speaking before the Massachusetts Historical Society, "ought to be sacredly preserved." The Revolutionary War was considered the noblest moment of our national glory. When the Jeffersonians came into power they would try to capture the past from the Federalists, but they would not attempt to change the national interpretation of the revolution and the Constitution. The victors of the revolution were the nationalist historians who called for the erection of a granite monument and thereon carved its story.

7 / John Jay
Federalist Paper No. 2

(1787)

To the People of the State of New York:

When the people of America reflect that they are now called upon to decide a question, which, in its consequences, must prove one of the most important that ever engaged their attention, the propriety of their taking a very comprehensive, as well as a very serious, view of it, will be evident.

Nothing is more certain than the indispensable necessity of government, and it is equally undeniable, that whenever and however it is instituted, the people must cede to it some of their natural rights in order to vest it with requisite powers. It is well worthy of consideration therefore, whether it would conduce more to the interest of the people of America that they should, to all general purposes, be one nation, under one federal government, or that they should divide themselves into separate confederacies, and give to the head of each the same kind of powers which they are advised to place in one national government.

It has until lately been a received and uncontradicted opinion that the prosperity of the people of America depended on their continuing firmly united, and the wishes, prayers, and efforts of our best and wisest citizens have been constantly directed to that object. But politicians now appear, who insist that this opinion is erroneous, and that instead of looking for safety and happiness in union, we ought to seek it in a division of the States into distinct confederacies or sovereignties. However extraordinary this new doctrine may appear, it nevertheless has its advocates; and certain characters who were much opposed to it formerly, are at present of the number. Whatever may be the arguments or inducements which have wrought this change in the sentiments and declarations of these gentlemen, it certainly would not be wise in the people at large to adopt these new political tenets without being fully convinced that they are founded in truth and sound policy.

The Federalist (Washington & London, 1901), I, pp. 14–17.

It has often given me pleasure to observe that independent America was not composed of detached and distant territories, but that one connected, fertile, widespreading country was the portion of our western sons of liberty. Providence has in a particular manner blessed it with a variety of soils and productions, and watered it with innumerable streams, for the delight and accommodation of its inhabitants. A succession of navigable waters forms a kind of chain round its borders, as if to bind it together; while the most noble rivers in the world, running at convenient distances, present them with highways for the easy communication of friendly aids, and the mutual transportation and exchange of their various commodities.

With equal pleasure I have as often taken notice that Providence has been pleased to give this one connected country to one united people—a people descended from the same ancestors, speaking the same language, professing the same religion, attached to the same principles of government, very similar in their manners and customs, and who, by their joint counsels, arms, and efforts, fighting side by side throughout a long and bloody war, have nobly established general liberty and independence.

This country and this people seem to have been made for each other, and it appears as if it was the design of Providence, that an inheritance so proper and convenient for a band of brethren, united to each other by the strongest ties, should never be split into a number of unsocial, jealous, and alien sovereignties.

Similar sentiments have hitherto prevailed among all orders and denominations of men among us. To all general purposes we have uniformly been one people; each individual citizen everywhere enjoying the same national rights, privileges, and protection. As a nation we have made peace and war; as a nation we have vanquished our common enemies; as a nation we have formed alliances, and made treaties, and entered into various compacts and conventions with foreign states.

A strong sense of the value and blessings of union induced the people, at a very early period, to institute a federal government to preserve and perpetuate it. They formed it almost as soon as they had a political existence; nay, at a time when their habitations were in flames, when many of their citizens were bleeding, and when the progress of hostility and desolation left little room for those calm and mature inquiries and reflections which must ever precede the formation of a wise and well-balanced government for a free people. It is not to be wondered at, that a government instituted in times so inauspicious, should on experiment be found greatly deficient and inadequate to the purpose it was intended to answer.

This intelligent people perceived and regretted these defects. Still continuing no less attached to union than enamored of liberty, they observed the danger which immediately threatened the former and more remotely the latter; and being pursuaded that ample security for both could only be found in a national government more wisely framed, they as with one voice, convened the late convention at Philadelphia, to take that important subject under consideration.

This convention composed of men who possessed the confidence of the people, and many of whom had become highly distinguished by their patriotism, virtue and wisdom, in times which tried the minds and hearts of men, undertook the arduous task. In the mild season of peace, with minds unoccupied by other subjects, they passed many months in cool, uninterrupted, and daily consultation; and finally, without having been awed by power, or influenced by any passions except love for their country, they presented and recommended to the people the plan produced by their joint and very unanimous councils . . .

8 / Alexander Hamilton
Report on the Subject of Manufactures

(1791)

Not only the wealth, but the independence and security of a country, appear to be materially connected with the prosperity of manufactures. Every nation, with a view of these great objects, ought to endeavor to possess within itself, all the essentials of national supply. These comprise the means of subsistence, habitation, clothing, and defence.

The possession of these is necessary to the perfection of the body politic; to the safety as well as to the welfare of the society. The want of either is the want of an important organ of political life and motion; and in the various crises which await a State, it must severely feel the effects of any such deficiency. The extreme embarrassments of the United States, during the late war, from an incapacity of supplying themselves, are still matter of keen recollection; a future war might be expected again to exemplify the mischiefs and dangers of a situation, to which that incapacity is still, in too great a degree, applicable, unless changed by timely and vigorous exertion. To effect this change, as fast as shall be prudent, merits all the attention and all the zeal of our public councils: 'tis the next great work to be accomplished.

The want of a navy, to protect our external commerce, as long as it shall continue, must render it a peculiarly precarious reliance for the supply of essential articles, and must serve to strengthen prodigiously the arguments in favor of manufactures.

To these general considerations are added some of a more particular nature.

Alexander Hamilton, *Report on the Subject of Manufactures* (1791).

Our distance from Europe, the great fountain of manufactured supply, subjects us, in the existing state of things, to inconvenience and loss, in two ways.

The bulkiness of those commodities, which are the chief productions of the soil, necessarily impose very heavy charges on their transportation to distant markets. These charges, in the cases in which the nations to whom our products are sent, maintain a competition in the supply of their own markets, principally fall upon us, and form material deductions from the primitive value of the articles furnished. The charges on manufactured supplies, brought from Europe, are greatly enhanced by the same circumstances of distance. These charges, again, in the cases in which our own industry maintains no competition in our own markets, also principally fall upon us, and are an additional cause of extraordinary deduction from the primitive value of our own products; these being the materials of exchange for the foreign fabrics which we consume.

The equality and moderation of individual property, and the growing settlements of new districts, occasion, in this country an unusual demand for coarse manufactures; the charges of which being greater in proportion to their greater bulk, augment the disadvantage which has been just described.

As, in most countries, domestic supplies maintain a very considerable competition with such foreign productions of the soil as are imported for sale, if the extensive establishment of manufactories in the United States does not create a similar competition in respect to manufactured articles, it appears to be clearly deducible, from the considerations which have been mentioned, that they must sustain a double loss in their exchanges with foreign nations, strongly conducive to an unfavorable balance of trade, and very prejudicial to their interests.

These disadvantages press, with no small weight, on the landed interest of the country. In seasons of peace, they cause a serious deduction from the intrinsic value of the products of the soil. In the time of war, which should either involve ourselves, or another nation possessing a considerable share of our carrying trade, the charges on the transportation of our commodities, bulky as most of them are, could hardly fail to prove a grievous burthen to the farmer, while obliged to depend, in so great a degree as he now does, upon foreign markets, for the vent of the surplus of his labor.

As far as the prosperity of the fisheries of the United States is impeded by the want of an adequate market, there arises another special reason for desiring the extension of manufactures. Besides the fish, which, in many places, would be likely to make a part of the subsistence of the persons employed, it is known that the oils, bones, and skins, of marine animals, are of extensive use in various manufactures. Hence, the prospect of an additional demand for the produce of the fisheries.

One more point of view only remains, in which to consider the expediency of encouraging manufactures in the United States.

It is not uncommon to meet with an opinion, that, though the promoting of manufactures may be the interest of a part of the Union, it is contrary to that of another part. The Northern and Southern regions are sometimes represented as having adverse interests in this respect. Those are called manufacturing, these agricultural States; and a species of opposition is imagined to subsist between the manufacturing and agricultural interests.

This idea of an opposition between those two interests, is the common error of the early periods of every country, but experience gradually dissipates it. Indeed, they are perceived so often to succor and befriend each other, that they come at length to be considered as one—a supposition which has been frequently abused, and is not universally true. Particular encouragements of particular manufactures may be of a nature to sacrifice the interests of land holders to those of manufacturers; but it is nevertheless a maxim, well established by experience, and generally acknowledged, where there has been sufficient experience, that the aggregate prosperity of manufactures and the aggregate prosperity of agriculture are intimately connected. In the course of the discussion which has had place, various weighty considerations have been adduced, operating in support of that maxim. Perhaps the superior steadiness of the demand of a domestic market, for the surplus of produce of the soil, is, alone, a convincing argument of its truth.

Ideas of a contrariety of interests between the Northern and Southern regions of the Union are, in the main, as unfounded as they are mischievous. The diversity of circumstances, on which such contrariety is usually predicated, authorizes directly contrary conclusion. Mutual wants constitute one of the strongest links of political connexion, and the extent of these bears a natural proportion to the diversity in the means of mutual supply.

Suggestions of an opposite complexion are ever to be deplored, as unfriendly to the steady pursuit of one great common cause, and to the perfect harmony of all the parts.

In proportion as the mind is accustomed to trace the intimate connexion of interest which subsists between all the parts of a society, united under the same government, the infinite variety of channels will serve to circulate the prosperity of each, to and through the rest—in that proportion will it be little apt to be disturbed by solicitudes and apprehensions, which originate in local discriminations.

It is a truth, as important as it is agreeable, and one to which it is not easy to imagine exceptions, that every thing tending to establish substantial and permanent order in the affairs of a country, to increase the total mass of industry and opulence, is ultimately beneficial to every part of it. On the credit of this great truth, an acquiescence may safely be accorded, from every quarter, to all institutions and arrangements which promise a confirmation of public order and an augmentation of national resource.

But there are more particular considerations which serve to fortify the idea that the encouragement of manufactures is the interest of all parts of the Union. If the Northern and Middle States should be the principal scenes of such establishments, they would immediately benefit the more Southern, by creating a demand for productions, some of which they have in common with the other States, and others, which are either peculiar to them, or more abundant, or of better quality, than elsewhere. These productions, principally, are timber, flax, hemp, cotton, wool, raw silk, indigo, iron, lead, furs, hides, skins, and coals; of these articles, cotton and indigo are peculiar to the Southern States, as are, hitherto, lead and coal; flax and hemp are, or may be, raised in greater abundance there, than in the more Northern States; and the wool of Virginia is said to be of better quality than that of any other State—a circumstance rendered the more probable, by the reflection, that Virginia embraces the same latitudes with the finest wool countries of Europe. The climate of the South is also better adapted to the production of silk.

The extensive cultivation of cotton, can, perhaps, hardly be expected but from the previous establishment of domestic manufactories of the article; and the surest encouragement and vent for the others, would result from similar establishments in respect to them.

9 / Thomas Jefferson
Letter to John Adams

(1813)

At the first session of our legislature after the Declaration of Independence, we passed a law abolishing entails. And this was followed by one abolishing the privilege of primogeniture, and dividing the lands of intestates equally among all their children, or other representatives. These laws, drawn by myself, laid the ax to the foot of pseudo-aristocracy. And had another which I prepared been adopted by the legislature, our work would have been complete. It was a bill for the more general diffusion of learning. This proposed to divide every county into wards of five or six miles square, like your townships; to establish in each ward a free school for reading, writing and common arithmetic; to provide for the annual selection of the best subjects from these schools, who might receive, at the public expense, a higher degree of education at a district school; and from these district schools to select a certain number of the most promising subjects, to be completed at an University, where all the useful sciences should be taught. Worth and genius would thus have been sought out from every condition of life, and completely prepared by education for defeating the competition of wealth and birth for public trusts. My proposition had, for a further object, to impart to these

Paul Leicester Ford (ed.), *The Writings of Thomas Jefferson*, XI (New York and London, 1905), pp. 346–50. Letter dated October 28, 1813.

wards those portions of self-government for which they are best qualified, by confiding to them the care of their poor, their roads, police, elections, the nomination of jurors, administration of justice in small cases, elementary exercises of militia; in short, to have made them little republics . . . The law for religious freedom, which made a part of this system, having put down the aristocracy of the clergy, and restored to the citizen the freedom of the mind, and those of entails and descents nurturing an equality of condition among them, this on education would have raised the mass of the people to the high ground of moral respectability necessary to their own safety, and to orderly government; and would have completed the great object of qualifying them to select the veritable *aristoi*, for the trusts of government, to the exclusion of the pseudalists . . . Although this law has not yet been acted on but in a small and inefficient degree, it is still considered as before the legislature, with other bills of the revised code, not yet taken up, and I have great hope that some patriotic spirit will, at a favorable moment, call it up, and make it the key-stone of the arch of our government.

With respect to aristocracy, we should further consider, that before the establishment of the American States, nothing was known to history but the man of the old world, crowded within limits either small or overcharged, and steeped in the vices which that situation generates. A government adapted to such men would be one thing; but a very different one, that for the man of these States. Here every one may have land to labor for himself, if he chooses; or, preferring the exercise of any other industry, may exact for it such compensation as not only to afford a comfortable subsistence, but wherewith to provide for a cessation from labor in old age. Every one, by his property, or by his satisfactory situation, is interested in the support of law and order. And such men may safely and advantageously reserve to themselves a wholesome control over their public affairs, and a degree of freedom, which, in the hands of the *canaille* of the cities of Europe, would be instantly perverted to the demolition and destruction of everything public and private. The history of the last twenty-five years of France, and of the last forty years in America, nay of its last two hundred years, proves the truth of both parts of this observation.

But even in Europe a change has sensibly taken place in the mind of man. Science had liberated the ideas of those who read and reflect, and the American example had kindled feelings of right in the people. An insurrection has consequently begun, of science, talents, and courage, against rank and birth, which have fallen into contempt. It has failed in its first effort, because the mobs of the cities, the instrument used for its accomplishment, debased by ignorance, poverty and vice, could not be restrained to rational action. But the world will recover from the panic of this first catastrophe. Science is progressive, and talents and enterprise on the alert. Resort may be had to the people of the country, a more governable power from their principles and subordination; and rank, and birth, and tinsel-aristocracy will finally shrink into insignificance, even there. This, however, we have no right to meddle with. It suffices for us, if the moral and physical condition of our own citizens qualifies them to select the able and good for the direction of their government, with a recurrence of elections at such short periods as will enable them to displace an unfaithful servant, before the mischief he meditates may be irremediable.

I have thus stated my opinion on a point on which we differ, not with a view to controversy, for we are both too old to change opinions which are the result of a long life of inquiry and reflection; but on the suggestions of a former letter of yours, that we ought not to die before we have explained ourselves to each other. We acted in perfect harmony, through a long and perilous contest for our liberty and independence. A constitution has been acquired, which, though neither of us thinks perfect, yet both consider as competent to render our fellow citizens the happiest and the securest on whom the sun has ever shone. If we do not think exactly alike as to its imperfections, it matters little to our country, which, after devoting to it long lives of disinterested labor, we have delivered over to our successors in life, who will be able to take care of it and of themselves.

10 / Hans Kohn
The Stream of American Nationalism

(1956)

The rising stream of American nationalism, which was yet barely discernible in American life in the 1760's, was fed from two sources: the English national consciousness which had developed in the seventeenth century and, transplanted to the New World, had found there a propitious soil for its growth; and the natural rights idea which the age of Enlightenment had sent across the ocean in the eighteenth century. These sources mingled their waters, often so that they became indistinguishable. No contradiction was felt between the two positions. One and the same man, one and the same declaration or manifesto, could adduce both, either at different times or even in the same sentence. Alexander Hamilton, one of the foremost exponents of the English tradition theory, wrote in his first pamphlet, "A Full Vindication" (1774), when he was still a student at King's College in New York: "The sacred rights of mankind are not to be rummaged for among old parchments or musty records. They are written, as with a sunbeam, in the whole volume of human

Hans Kohn, *The Idea of Nationalism* (New York: The Macmillan Company, 1956). Copyright 1944 by Hans Kohn. Reprinted without footnotes by permission of the publisher.

nature, by the hand of divinity itself." On the other hand, Thomas Jefferson, whose great service to the cause of American nationalism was his reinterpretation of the American Revolution in the light of natural rights, wrote in August, 1776, to Edmund Pendleton, "Are we not the better for what we have hitherto abolished of the feudal system? Has not every restitution of the ancient Saxon laws had happy effects? Is it not better now that we return at once into that happy system of our ancestors, the wisest & most perfect ever yet devised by the wit of man, as it stood before the 8th century?" . . .

As soon as the waters of American nationalism began to flow freely, the two sources of the British tradition and of natural rights were indistinguishably mingled. A member of the Continental Congress on September 5, 1774, spoke of "the unalienable and inestimable inheritance, which we derive from nature, the constitution of Britain, and the privileges warranted to us in the charter of the province." He was not conscious that he had treated elements of a vastly different and historically even antagonistic background as one and the same; in the living stream of history they had fused into a new reality. Samuel Adams' plea may sound confused, if viewed from its historical origins; it sounded convincing to many of his contemporaries, not only in the colonies but also in England. "It is the glory of the British Prince and the happiness of all his subjects that their constitution hath its foundations in the immutable laws of nature, and as the supreme legislature as well as the supreme executive derives its authority from the constitution, it should seem that no laws can be made or executed that are repugnant to any essential law in nature." In the resolutions of the House of Representatives of Massachusetts on October 29, 1765—proposed by Samuel Adams, who had been elected a month earlier to the House—the strictest allegiance to the King and the greatest veneration for the Parliament were expressed, but at the same time "there are certain essential rights of the British Constitution of government, which are founded in the law of God and nature, and are the common rights of mankind;—therefore, Resolved, That the inhabitants of this Province are unalienably entitled to those essential rights in common with all men: and that no law of society can, consistent with the law of God and nature, divest them of those rights." The emphasis upon the rational, universal, and natural rights character of the movement of the colonists came above all from Englishmen, from Thomas Paine, Richard Price, and Joseph Priestley, who disregarded the British constitutional aspect and gave to the American struggle a more democratic interpretation and a universal appeal. It was in that light that the conflict was viewed and interpreted in Europe, especially in France.

These were the sources from which the welling stream of American national consciousness was to be fed. But by the middle of the seventies this stream was by no means a mighty current watering and fertilizing American life. To many contemporaries it appeared rather as a thin trickle which might at any moment dry up. For the growth of a national consciousness is a long process with many retrogressions and retardations, spurred on in the excitement of great political issues, wars and revolutions, and losing impetus in the slow-moving course of "normal" times. There seemed little in the seventies upon which to build a new nation. There was no territorial unity, the different colonies and settlements being widely separated not only geographically, but also historically and intellectually. There was no unity of will or purpose; many people in the colonies, especially among the educated classes and the older age groups, clung firmly to their British nationality. They rejected not only the incipient nationalism of the Revolution but also what they regarded as its anti-liberal character, its destruction of those liberties which had been the pride of the British tradition. They saw it in "the barbarian rule of frantic folly, and lawless ambition—freedom of speech suppressed, liberty of press destroyed, voice of truth silenced, a lawless power depriving men of their natural rights." The struggle against Britain was in their eyes a fratricidal undertaking, the success of which might endanger the most precious heritage of the American settlers: their connection with the mother country, their membership in a great and liberal empire which was the envy of mankind, admired both for its strength and for its progressive freedom—an empire in which America might have to play a role of yet unpredictable grandeur. Daniel Leonard even foresaw a time when a future English king would cross the Atlantic Ocean, when North America would become the center of the Empire and rule Great Britain by an American Parliament. None of the commonly adduced objective factors of nationhood separated the Loyalists from the rebels who called themselves "patriots." They were united by common descent, common language, common traditions, and common territory. Nothing separated them but an idea . . .

No sense of loyalty to America filled the hearts of the colonists before the Revolution. America as a political concept, as a center of allegiance, did not exist. Loyalty belonged to Great Britain and to the individual colonies or settlements. While there was little or no feeling of strangeness or hostility against Great Britain among the colonists, there was much mutual jealousy and violent prejudice in the relations of the colonies to one another. Their commercial and economic competition was as bitter as their distrust and dislike . . .

The opinion of the most eminent American[s] of that time was shared by a competent English observer, the well known economist Josiah Tucker, one of the earliest advocates of the separation of the colonies from the mother country. "The mutual antipathies and clashing interests of the Americans, their difference of governments, habitudes and manners indicate that they will have no centre of union and no common interests. They never can be united into one compact empire under any species of government whatever; a disunited people till the end of time, suspicious and distrustful of each other, they will be divided into little commonwealths according to natural bound-aries, by great bays of the sea and by vast rivers, lakes and ridges of mountains." . . .

The new Constitution was a great step forward on the road to nationhood. The traditionally strong isolationism of the thirteen states had been overcome, a new foundation for peace and security, for economic prosperity and thriving commerce, had been created. An example had been set, not only in the republican form of government but in its federative character, which combined a far-reaching independence of historical, parochial entities with the existence of a strong central authority for common concerns, the number and extent of which would naturally grow with the development of communications and intercourse. The Constitution and the Bill of Rights have remained the unshakable foundations of the new nation. They have drawn their strength not from their legal character but from the ideas which they expressed. In spite of their imperfections they have withstood the test of time better than any other constitution on earth, for during the past one hundred and fifty years all other nations have changed theirs repeatedly. The American constitutional laws of 1789 have lasted because the idea for which they stand was so intimately welded with the existence of the American nation that without the idea there would have been no nation. It was the idea which gave to Americans that unity and strength which built the nation. With all its vigorous political and economic aspects, American nationalism nevertheless has been primarily an ideological nationalism, the embodiment of an idea, which, though geographically and historically located in the United States, was a universal idea, the most vital and enduring legacy of the eighteenth century.

Among the realities of national life, the image which a nation forms of itself, and in which it mirrors itself is one of the most important. Perhaps only slightly less important is the reflection produced by foreign observers and the image thus formed by other nations, for the original image and its reflection shape and influence each other. Though the reality, in many ways, does not correspond to the image, falls far short of its ideal perfection, and often contradicts it in the countless and conflicting trends of the complex actuality, nevertheless this image, woven of elements of reality, tradition, imagination, and aspiration, is one of the most formative agents in national character. It molds national life; it acts at least as a constant brake, if not always as an impelling force. Thomas Jefferson recognized it clearly in a letter to Joseph Priestley: "It is certain that though written constitutions may be violated in moments of passion or delusion, yet they furnish a text to which those who are watchful may again rally and recall the people; they fix too for the people the principles of their political creed." Nations like America which have not been rooted for many centuries in a circumscribed soil or nourished by common ancient traditions stemming from the belief in common descent over a long period live even more by the force of their national image or idea. The territory of the United States was not circumscribed; in spite of Noah Webster's efforts the country never developed a language of its own; Negroes and Jews, German Lutherans and Latin Catholics, participated in the Revolutionary War and fought for the American Nation; the national idea alone could serve as a foundation and a tie.

At the end of the eighteenth century the conception which the most enlightened European nations formed of the new American nation was not fundamentally different from the Americans' idea of themselves, except that it was even more removed from the actual struggles of daily reality, even more deeply immersed in the philosophical ideal of the century. America appeared as a symbol of liberty and "natural" virtue, a land in whose vast open spaces the natural order could become creative, unhampered by the traditions and superstitions of past ages. Far-off America seemed a sanctuary for the truly philosophical attitude, a refuge for all those who longed for the rule of nature. Jacques Pierre Brissot, the leading Girondist in France, praised the United States as a land of regeneration and moral reform. This interpretation abroad reacted upon America's own conception—the more so because it gladly conceded the leadership of America on humanity's road to the future. *Ex occidente lux;* not only did the "ball of empire" seem to roll over to the western world, but also the center of mankind seemed to shift to the West. In truth, this keen flight of imagination had not the slightest backing in fact: for a very long time to come, culturally and politically, the young nation remained on the outskirts of the civilized world. Nevertheless something fundamentally new and of immense importance had happened. For the first time a nation had arisen on the basis of the truths held "to be self-evident, that all men are created equal, that they are endowed by their Creator with certain unalienable Rights, that among those are Life, Liberty and the Pursuit of Happiness"—truths which the nation could not give up without destroying its own foundation. Through all the many sermons, articles, and poems, with their empty bombast, their rhetorical unctuosity, and their tribute paid to the tastes of the times, through all the political struggles and economic maneuvers of petty men and greedy leaders, the American idea lived on, disfigured and sometimes obliterated, and yet struggling for its self-realization.

11 / Timothy Dwight
Prospects of the United States

(1822)

Almost all our institutions, perhaps all which deserve to be permanent, have with as much regularity as seems compatible with the present state of mankind been in a course of improvement. Manners, laws, learning, and in some respects religion may be justly considered as being *now* progressive. The

Timothy Dwight, *Travels; in New-England and New-York,* IV (New Haven, 1822), pp. pp. 522–524. Reprinted with spelling, punctuation, and capitalization modernized.

mechanical, manufacturing, and liberal arts, literature, and science are at the present time advanced, upon the whole, beyond any preceding attainments. Agriculture and domestic economy are better understood and more skillfully pursued. Roads, bridges, and canals are multiplied, and constructed in a better manner. The number of schools and colleges is increasing, and those which already exist are more successfully directed. Judicial proceedings are daily becoming more accurate, and more conformed to the best principles of legal science; and political measures, although for some time past in a state of deterioration, are yet teaching us several valuable lessons, out of which improvement will one day spring. In spite of the pride of self-consistency, it is now acknowledged by those who are most opposed to making the acknowledgment that a navy is the proper means of our defense and safety; that our principal harbors ought to be fortified; that our form of government is ill suited to offensive war; and that for defraying the expenses of war, taxes are indispensable. We are also learning, though it must be confessed by slower degrees, that we are not so much wiser and better than the rest of mankind as many of our people have heretofore believed or at least professed to believe. Persons of this cast are beginning to suspect that modesty is one excellence of the human character, and a proof of other excellencies, and that boasting furnishes fewer and smaller claims to respect than they have been accustomed to imagine. This melioration of our character will undoubtedly make a slow progress, yet I believe it is really progressive. The religious part of the community also are evidently assuming a higher character. A catholicism, heretofore not generally cherished by religious men, a catholicism real and evangelical, far removed from that gross indifference to truth and falsehood, to right and wrong, so often boasted of under the sacred name of catholicism, is fostered and exercised extensively by men of real piety. The "tithing of mint, anise, and cummin" makes a less, and "judgment, mercy, and faith" make a much more prominent appearance on the roll of Christian attributes. The minds of good men are becoming more expansive; their prejudices are beginning to disappear; and the benevolence of the Gospel is exhibiting itself in its own proper character with vigor and success. Seen in a light more its own, and operating in a manner more suited to its nature, it is claiming higher respect from mankind and daily finds its claims more and more readily acknowledged. The world, bad as it is, is willing that Christians, in some modes at least, should do good: and to do good has, to a considerable extent, become their favorite and even their acknowledged employment.

With all these objects in view, you will suffer me to indulge the feelings of an American while I contemplate the prospect which futurity presents concerning my country. Permit me to remind you of the extent of these states: the climate, the soil, the productions, the population; the character of the inhabitants; their arts, commerce, education, learning, science, freedom, laws, manners, morals and religion. Let me bring to your recollection the rapid progress of our population, the progressive state in which most of the articles which I have recited actually exist at the present time, and the promise which they give of superior advancement. With these objects in contemplation, a traveler passing through the countries which I have described, surveying the scenes which they everywhere present to his eye, and remembering within how short a period and amid how many difficulties they have been raised up in a howling wilderness, will think it no extravagance of imagination to believe that throughout this vast empire, villages innumerable will everywhere speedily adorn its surface with the same beauty and cheerfulness which he beholds around him. To these he will add the flourishing towns and splendid cities which not only the shore of the ocean, but the numerous lakes and rivers, will in the interior see rising on their borders, the seats of various useful manufactures and of an inland commerce resembling and excelling that of the Chinese empire. Everywhere he will foresee neat schoolhouses stationed at little distances, diffusing each over its proper circle the education necessary to every human being, and contributing to create a new national character by elevating the minds of those of whom the great body of every nation is formed. To these his fancy will add, at distances somewhat greater, the vast collection of superior schools communicating more extensive information to a multitude, less indeed, but still very great. Within every twenty thousand square miles, his mind will easily station a college, where literature and science will shed their light upon a number of votaries sufficiently great to perform all the kinds of human business which demand extensive information. Nor will he hesitate, since he sees the work already begun, to fix here and there seats of professional science, in which shall be taught whatever is known by man concerning medicine, law, policy, and religion; or to superadd those national institutions designed not so much to teach as to advance the knowledge of man. From what he has already seen, he will easily anticipate the rise of temples consecrated to the worship of God, diffusing, like so many stars, light and splendor over the whole horizon of his view. In these temples a hundred thousand enlightened ministers of the Gospel may be fairly supposed to teach the way of life through the Redeemer of mankind to an equal number of congregations, containing at least as many millions of worshippers; of human beings worshipping, not the idol Fo, nor Juggernaut, nor Jupiter, nor the sun, nor Osiris, but JEHOVAH. The ministers intended will be such as are enlightened by learning and science, and by the beams of the Sun of Righteousness; and will illuminate the mass of inhabitants, in most lands and ages covered by the clouds of ignorance, but here enjoying the means of that education which is indispensable to all men, and sufficient to raise them to the proper character of intelligent beings.

12 / Daniel Webster
The Completion of the Bunker Hill Monument

(1843)

Few topics are more inviting, or more fit for philosophical discussion, than the effect on the happiness of mankind of institutions founded upon these principles; or, in other words, the influence of the New World upon the Old.

Her obligations to Europe for science and art, laws, literature, and manners, America acknowledges as she ought, with respect and gratitude. The people of the United States, descendants of the English stock, grateful for the treasures of knowledge derived from their English ancestors, admit also, with thanks and filial regard, that among those ancestors, under the culture of Hampden and Sydney and other assiduous friends, that seed of popular liberty first germinated, which on our soil has shot up to its full height, until its branches overshadow all the land.

But America has not failed to make returns. If she has not wholly cancelled the obligation, or equalled it by others of like weight, she has, at least, made respectable advances towards repaying the debt. And she admits, that, standing in the midst of civilized nations, and in a civilized age, a nation among nations, there is a high part which she is expected to act, for the general advancement of human interests and human welfare.

American mines have filled the mints of Europe with the precious metals. The productions of the American soil and climate have poured out their abundance of luxuries for the tables of the rich, and of necessaries for the sustenance of the poor. Birds and animals of beauty and value have been added to the European stocks; and transplantations from the unequalled riches of our forests have mingled themselves profusely with the elms, and ashes, and Druidical oaks of England.

America has made contributions to Europe far more important. Who can estimate the amount, or the value, of the augmentation of the commerce of the world that has resulted from America? Who can imagine to himself what would now be the shock to the Eastern Continent, if the Atlantic were no longer traversable, or if there were no longer American productions, or American markets?

But America exercises influences, or holds out examples, for the consideration of the Old World, of a much higher, because they are of a moral and political character.

America has furnished to Europe proof of the fact, that popular institutions, founded on equality and the principle of representation, are capable of

Daniel Webster, "The Completion of the Bunker Hill Monument: An Address delivered on Bunker Hill, on the 17th of June, 1843." Reprinted from *The Works of Daniel Webster*, 7th ed. (Boston: Little, Brown & Co., 1853), I, pp. 103–107.

maintaining governments, able to secure the rights of person, property, and reputation.

America has proved that it is practicable to elevate the mass of man-kind—that portion which in Europe is called the laboring, or lower class,—to raise them to self-respect, to make them competent to act a part in the great right and great duty of self-government; and she has proved that this may be done by education and the diffusion of knowledge. She holds out an example, a thousand times more encouraging than ever was presented before, to those nine tenths of the human race who are born without hereditary fortune or hereditary rank.

America has furnished to the world the character of Washington! And if our American institutions had done nothing else, that alone would have entitled them to the respect of mankind.

Washington! "First in war, first in peace, and first in the hearts of his countrymen!" Washington is all our own! The enthusiastic veneration and regard in which the people of the United States hold him prove them to be worthy of such a countryman; while his reputation abroad reflects the highest honor on his country. I would cheerfully put the question today to the intelligence of Europe and the world, what character of the century, upon the whole, stands out in the relief of history, most pure, most respect-able, most sublime; and I doubt not, that, by a suffrage approaching to una-nimity, the answer would be Washington!

The structure now standing before us, by its uprightness, its solidity, its durability, is no unfit emblem of his character. His public virtues and public principles were as firm as the earth on which it stands; his personal motives, as pure as the serene heaven in which its summit is lost. But, indeed, though a fit, it is an inadequate emblem. Towering high above the column which our hands have builded, beheld, not by the inhabitants of a single city or a single State, but by all the families of man, ascends the colossal grandeur of the character and life of Washington. In all the constituents of the one, in all the acts of the other, in all its titles to immortal love, admiration, and renown, it is an American production. It is the embodiment and vindication of our Transatlantic liberty. Born upon our soil, of parents also born upon it; never for a moment having had sight of the Old World; instructed, according to the modes of his time, only in the spare, plain, but wholesome elementary knowledge which our institutions provide for the children of the people; growing up beneath and penetrated by the genuine influences of American society; living from infancy to manhood and age amidst our expanding, but not luxurious civilization; partaking in our great destiny of labor, our long contest with unreclaimed nature and uncivilized man, our agony of glory, the war of Independence, our great victory of peace, the formation of the Union, and the establishment of the Constitution; he is all, all our own! Washington is ours. That crowded and glorious life,

"Where multitudes of virtues passed along,
Each pressing foremost, in the mighty throng
Ambitious to be seen, then making room
For great multitudes that were to come,"

that life was the life of an American citizen.

I claim him for America. In all the perils, in every darkened moment of the state, in the midst of the reproaches of enemies and the misgiving of friends, I turn to that transcendent name for courage and for consolation. To him who denies or doubts whether our fervid liberty can be combined with law, with order, with the security of property, with the pursuits and advancement of happiness; to him who denies that our forms of government are capable of producing exaltation of soul, and the passion of true glory; to him who denies that we have contributed any thing to the stock of great lessons and great examples;—to all these I reply by pointing to Washington!

And now, friends and fellow-citizens, it is time to bring this discourse to a close.

We have indulged in gratifying recollections of the past, in the prosperity and pleasures of the present, and in high hopes for the future. But let us remember that we have duties and obligations to perform, corresponding to the blessings which we enjoy. Let us remember the trust, the sacred trust, attaching to the rich inheritance which we have received from our fathers. Let us feel our personal responsibility, to the full extent of our power and influence, for the preservation of the principles of civil and religious liberty. And let us remember that it is only religion, and morals, and knowledge, that can make men respectable and happy, under any form of government. Let us hold fast the great truth, that communities are responsible, as well as individuals; that no government is respectable, which is not just; that without unspotted purity of public faith, without sacred public principle, fidelity, and honor, no mere forms of government, no machinery of laws, can give dignity to political society. In our day and generation let us seek to raise and improve the moral sentiment, so that we may look, not for a degraded, but for an elevated and improved future. And when both we and our children shall have been consigned to the house appointed for all living, may love of country and pride of country glow with equal fervor among those to whom our names and our blood shall have descended! And then, when honored and decrepit age shall lean against the base of this monument, and troops of ingenuous youth shall be gathered round it, and when the one shall speak to the other of its objects, the purposes of its construction, and the great and glorious events with which it is connected, there shall rise from every youthful breast the ejaculation, "Thank God, I—I also—AM AN AMERICAN!"

13 / Hendrick B. Wright
Eulogy for Andrew Jackson

(1845)

The same patriotism which kindled up the hearts of the colonists in 1776, to a blaze, was equally manifest in 1812, and the sons of the heroes of the former war proved conclusively that their ancestors' blood coursed through their veins . . . Probably among them all, this spirit was not more manifest than in the exalted character whose death had brought us together on this occasion. Because, however much the nation may be divided as to some of the leading measures of his administration, and the effect they are to produce hereafter—there is but *one opinion* as to his long and successful career as a soldier. And that opinion is recorded deep and lasting on the hearts of his grateful countrymen—an opinion that finds a ready response on every tongue—that the laurels that covered the brow of the hero, and which will grow green for ever—were the honest reward of true merit, and about which there is no dispute. This feature in the life of Andrew Jackson, together with all others, has now become a part, and an important part of the history of the age in which he lived—and let me say, there are few indeed, during that time, who will occupy so full a page. Nor will I confine the assertion I have made to the narrow limits of the lines which designate the width and breadth of the United States of America—no indeed. His fame as a great captain, and most accomplished and brave soldier has extended "to the utmost limits of the civilized world." And by common consent, in all nations, professing civilization, the name of Andrew Jackson will be classed among the most distinguished generals of ancient or modern history.

. . . now that the head of the hero and statesman is laid low, I feel as though, having undertaken to speak his eulogy, I would be derelict in my duty to the *dead*, as well as the *living*, were I not to speak openly, and in defence of the character of this man, who has commanded the public eye, and public attention, for more than half a century. It is seldom, indeed, the country goes into mourning at the decease of her sons. Now and then, the death of a distinguished and illustrious man produces a universal shock, and reaches the hearts of the *whole* people, but it is indeed seldom. There are few men, who, by their public acts and private virtues, can become familiar to twenty millions of inhabitants. Within the limits of our own knowledge, few and far between, have been the occasions that have thrown the black pall of grief over the whole land. In the enumeration of the deaths of Washington,

Hendrick B. Wright, "Eulogy Delivered at Wilkesbarre, Pa., July 4, 1845." Reprinted from B. M. Dusenbery, comp., *Monument to the Memory of General Andrew Jackson . . .* (Philadelphia: James A. Bell, 1846), pp. 237–238, 245–248.

Adams, Jefferson, La Fayette, Harrison, and Jackson, we have them all. All told in this brief catalogue. The feeling of deep regret, and the public sorrow in each case, showed that these patriots had a deep hold on the affections not only of the American people, but through the civilized world; wherever a bosom throbbed for universal freedom. What a proud and enviable distinction! What a rich and glorious renown! The lives of these glorious men have been the theme of history, and the inspiration of song, the models after which the most profound statesmen of Europe have copied, and copied largely. Think you not that the most humble devotee at liberty's shrine in the isles of Greece, down-trodden, forsaken, obliterated Poland, or the Alpine hills of frozen Switzerland, has not heard of the acts and deeds of these Anglo-Americans—has not studied *their* creed with the same devotion he did the book of his religion!

Nor has their fame been confined to the pale of civilized life—it has entered the tents of savage and barbarous hordes: it has rung in the ear of the swarthy Moor, the black and ill-favoured African, and the despised and beastly inhabitant of the South Sea Islands. To their fame, it is not in the power of man, civilized or barbarous, to set up a barrier; it pervades the space of "the great globe itself," and is eternal as the vast and heaving ocean!

But the history of Andrew Jackson establishes two points beyond disputation. The first, that true merit, sooner or later, meets a suitable reward—the second, that the oft-repeated charge that republics do not reward men who have served their country faithfully, is an idle and empty allegation, meaning nothing.

We all know the fact that the distinguished individuals I have named, enjoyed the principal posts of honour and trust in the Union, and that they have been the unsought and unsolicited offering of a grateful people. Their services in the cabinet and in the field, have, time and time again, been rewarded by all those tokens of the popular will, which could satisfy the largest and greatest ambition.

It was the fortune of Jackson to go through all the inferior grades in the councils of state, to the exalted post of president of the Union—and it was all gratuitous—conferred upon the man because of his merits and deserving. The duties, too, he discharged with an eye single to the prosperity and happiness of the people.

Connected with his life and history, there is a moral lesson, imposing as it is grand. To the youth of the country, it is a volume written in letters of gold, and establishes a precedent for imitation, that is beyond price. It points to the great highway of fame and distinction—it tells him that the man who honestly serves his country, in whatever position it may be his fortune to be cast, will as surely bring down upon him the gratitude of that country, as the fulfilment of prophecy. In this land of equal rights, the humblest youth, with honesty, talents, and perseverance to recommend him, enjoys the same opportunities with the high-born and the wealthy, for political honours. The first blow at

Lexington, in the revolutionary struggle, not only knocked to atoms the bonds and fetters of Great Britain, but also all the orders and tiles of nobility—levelled the political condition of the American colonies to a common standard, and made merit, in the place of hereditary fortune, the republican test. Who would have even conjectured, at that early day, that a young man of the tender age of fourteen years, a captive in the British camp, but who had the courage and bravery, unarmed, to face the same weapon which had already drank the blood of an only brother, rather than stoop to the menial service of becoming the boot-black of an English officer—would be at the head of the grandest government on the face of the earth? An orphan child, unprotected, without friends, without influence. It is this trait in the features of a popular government, that truly makes it the *grandest* in the world. In following the course of that young man, we find him, when the war is over, pursuing the profession of law—representing his state in the nation's councils—upon the bench—again, at the head of the American troops, pushing on to glorious victory—and finally, the chief executive officer of the United States of America. What a theme for contemplation—what a subject for thought! Let the young man who is ambitious for durable fame, read and reflect upon the noble example which he will find in the life of Andrew Jackson. Let him believe that the gigantic obstacles that lie between him and the summit of his hopes and anticipations, will vanish like snow-flakes beneath the rays of the sun, by labour—temperance—perseverance, and virtue.

There is no ordinary obstacle that can thwart or defeat a well-directed and prudent ambition—momentary it may be, but the courage and determination of the human heart are not easily foiled, and when a point is fixed in the distance, it is almost invariably attained. The subject of our discourse is full proof of the position, and the experience of every day's life confirms it.

The American presidents were all "self-made men"—by perseverance, they were elevated to a point of political prominence, which is above and beyond all others. Let the proud motto of our flag be engraved upon the heart of the American youth: "Virtue, Liberty, and Independence," and the perpetuity of that government, which our ancestors regarded as an "experiment," will be certain. And the illustrious hero of New Orleans, by his acts and deeds—by his habits and conduct, has been among the foremost of those who have given a character and tone to our country, that have placed her high upon the great scroll of nations. Let those who would share his honours, imitate his example.

But the voice of wisdom, and patriotism, and advice, from the Hermitage, is hushed—hushed in the deep silence that pervades the grave. That voice which was so powerful and overruling in the affairs of state, has ceased, and the pulse of that heart, which beat quick and strong amidst the shouts of victory on the plains of Orleans, has also ceased for ever.

Full of years, full of honours, and full of gratitude to the great Father of the Universe, the sage has gone to test the realities of that holy religion, without which, the pomp and pageantry of this world is but the dust of the balance; which was his solace upon earth, and the hope of a glorious inheritance in Heaven—

> "How sleep the brave who sink to rest
> With all their country's wishes blest!"

The great valley of the Mississippi contains his sepulchre. That vast region, destined to become the seat of populated millions, contains his funeral pile. Think you not that the consecrated ground that covers the bones of the hero will not become a modern Mecca, where the foot of the pilgrim will pause on his route to his new home in the far and boundless West, and his eye drop a tear upon the tomb of the brave? His warm heart will gush with sympathies once kindred with the inanimate dust that lies beneath it. Virginia has her Mount Vernon, and her Monticello; New England is the repository of the remains of the compeers of Washington and Jefferson; Tennessee has her Hermitage!—as if the decrees of fate had ordained that the ashes of the immortal founders of this giant government should commingle with the soil that drank the first blood of the Revolution, as well as *that* of our second independence. Let this be the symbol of the mystic tie that shall bind us stronger and stronger together in the union of our confederation. That the wayward, the weak, the vacillating, in whichever part of the land he shall be, may be brought to a sense of duty to the cause of popular right, by casting his eye over the registered marble that covers the last relics of the mighty dead. Think ye that the iron nerve of treason could remain unsubdued at the base of the mausoleum of Washington, or Adams, or Jefferson, or Jackson? Nay! at such a spectacle, if there be a second Arnold, his brain would reel to and fro, as did that of the Babylonian monarch at the feast when the solitary finger upon the wall wrote the awful characters of his destiny.

We have paid this day, the last solemn rites in honourable testimony of the distinguished man whose death brought us together. To you, fellow-citizens, who have joined in the exercises of this occasion, allow me, if it be not arrogance, to thank you in the name of the friends of the departed hero and statesman—in the name of the people of the Union—and in the name of every human creature whose heart throbs for universal freedom throughout the civilized world.

14 / John William Ward
Extending the Area of Freedom

(1955)

The idea that America was destined to extend the area of freedom represents a union under the aegis of providence of two separate ideas, democracy and expansion. In the eighteenth century no organic connection was perceived between democracy and the government of the United States; democracy as a way of life was considered to be a universal ideal, not the special property of the new nation. Although America was generally held to be an example to the rest of the world, it was not felt that democracy could prosper under American auspices alone nor that, as a corollary, the spread of freedom necessarily entailed the territorial expansion of the United States. In addition to the absence of a logical connection between democracy and American expansion, a further obstacle blocked the union of the two ideas. From Montesquieu, political theorists in the United States derived the belief that democratic government could thrive only in small states and that by centrifugal force large states would disintegrate politically. The fear of extended territory was quieted by stressing the representative character of American democracy and by asserting that the creation of many sectional interests would result in their counterbalancing one another, thus extending in an unforeseen direction Montesquieu's famous balance of power scheme for maintaining republican government. The image of "a constellation of suns," used by the editor of the *Illinois Gazette* to convey the idea of the light spread by the American example, easily allowed the inclusion of more suns to increase the radiance spread by the new world. The tragedian (and Jacksonian), Edwin Forrest, in his Fourth of July Oration at New York in 1838, said that the experience of our fathers now stands as "the mark and model of the world ... New stars [i.e. new states], from year to year, emerging with perfect radiance in the western horizon, have increased the benignant splendor of that constellation which now shines the political guiding light of the world." The additional wattage which Forrest's simile makes possible is the imaginative equivalent of O'Sullivan's flat assertion that since America has been chosen by God to be the depository of freedom nothing must stand in the way of its development.

From the time John Winthrop aboard the *Arbella* told his fellow voyagers that "wee must Consider that we shall be as a Citty vpon a Hill, the eies of all people are vppon vs," Americans were intensely aware of the universal import of their experiment in the new world. In 1828, William

John William Ward, *Andrew Jackson: Symbol for an Age (1815–1845)*. Copyright 1955 by John William Ward. Reprinted by permission of Oxford University Press, Inc. Footnotes omitted by permission.

Plumer echoed the Puritan phrase, saying that "our American Republic exists not for herself alone. She is a city set upon a hill which cannot be hid, a beacon kindled upon a mountain top."

The United States, in its experiment of republican freedom, was constantly compared to a city or a column set upon a hill, a beacon or a guiding light, a constellation of stars or suns in the west. The connotations of such metaphors are, of course, the same as the cosmic imagery which so abundantly clustered about the symbol of Andrew Jackson. Felix Grundy, in a speech in 1840, demonstrated quite clearly how Andrew Jackson was used to implement a belief long part of the American tradition.

> I *have* seen [said Grundy] a light arise in the West; and so brilliant was it, that it dimmed and obscured all the lesser lights around it; it ascended higher and higher, until it reached the meridian; there it remained stationary for a time [!]; so effulgent was it, that it irradiated this whole continent; its rays crossed the Atlantic and penetrated the courts and palaces of kings, and influenced their councils; it was seen and felt wherever civilized man dwelt. But that light is fast descending in the West; it has almost reached the horizon, and will soon be beyond the sight of mortals. Mr. President, you and I shall never see its like again; we are too old. Such lights do not visit our earth but at rare and long intervals. I need not say to the Senate, or to this audience, that the individual I have described . . . is Andrew Jackson, the pride and glory of our country.

The idea of America as example served a developing nationalism in two ways. It made American isolation morally acceptable. It supported nearly any self-seeking national program by phrasing it in terms of the highest international altruism. Andrew Jackson represented both aspects in his own proper person. He symbolized the special concern of providence for America which is the basic assumption of the various ideas grouped under the term, manifest destiny. Also, the presentation of Jackson as a child of nature embodied the concept which made it seem feasible and even necessary that America cut itself off from Europe. Lastly, it was Jackson himself who pointed out to his contemporaries how they could justify their acquisitiveness by subsuming it under the divine plan of providence manifestly indicated for all to see in the configurations of new world geography, so that nature and providence were intertwined at every turn. God was, as O'Sullivan reminded his readers, the "God of nature and of nations."

As America turned, after the War of 1812, to its own development it was not willing to conceive of its isolationist ideal in egoistic terms. The Republic was still regarded as an international force by virtue of its influence. When a Fourth of July orator described his audience to themselves as "but the favoured instruments of Heaven" he also made clear that "we are responsible not only to our own country . . . but to every other country of this globe, and all its present and all its future inhabitants." Echoing Jefferson, who had said, "It is impossible not to be sensible that we are acting for all mankind," a less literate American wrote to his son in Congress, "You must not loose sight that you are ligislating for a great Nation whose Decisions may be a president [precedent] for ages to come." By a neat dialectic, isolationism took on the aura of internationalism by the leavening influence America's example was to have in the world. An editorial in the *National Intelligencer* made the point by drawing upon classical mechanics: "'Give me a place to stand on,' said the ancient Mathematician, 'and I will move the World.' This place, in the ideal world of politics, the founders of the United States discovered."

The belief that America existed as an example for the rest of the world not only provided an account of America's place in the community of nations but made it possible for Americans to perceive national selfishness as international good will. In 1825 it was pointed out that America "has left to other empires to do but half what she has done—and with a selfishness that may be forgiven, she has reserved to herself the reward of her valour and her toils, while to all mankind she has given, freely given, the benefit of her example." In the 'thirties, the *New-York American* closed an editorial called "The Influence and Example of the United States" with the assertion that "it is in this way, by her moral influence and example . . . that America may and does repay her debt to Europe." In the 'forties, a literal minded Iowa editor even made the concrete proposal that America repudiate its debts to Europe on the ground that Europe was sufficiently recompensed by having been allowed to assist in the spread of the American example. Even as a debtor nation, the United States had no sense that it might be other than first in the world community.

The special mission assigned America by providence to show the way to the rest of the world not only supported a repudiation of debts owed Europe, it supported a repudiation of Europe itself. If America was elected to point the way for the unregenerate to political salvation, then it behooved her to preserve her purity by avoiding the contamination of Europe, which was after all, as the *Illinois Gazette* had observed, a "fallen world." Richard B. Lee, in an address in which he traced the whole course of American history, ended by alluding to the inland empire, "equal in extent to that of imperial Rome."

We shall need [said Lee] little or no connection, even in commerce, with foreign countries, if we improve the vast resources of our own . . . And is it not worthy of consideration, whether the diminution of our intercourse with foreign nations, whose modes and notions of government, and whose manners are so different from our own, would not have the most salutary tendency in preserving untainted the industrious habits, and the pure and manly virtues of our citizens, and thereby perpetuating to the most remote future ages the happiness and freedom which we possess . . . "Oh, yet happiest, if we seek no happier state / And know to know no more."

Lee's address presents a clear statement of the economic basis of America's self-absorption. Present also is the article of faith, observed already in characterizations of Jackson, which made it possible to dispense with the old world. Europe was corrupt and could contribute nothing of value to the United States. Nature, as raw material, made economic isolation seem possible; nature, as the fount of wisdom, made intellectual isolation seem acceptable. As one orator put it, America had rescued "that vestal fire of liberty ... from the sickening depravity of the Stuarts, to be rekindled amid the primeval forests" and it was her duty to nurse the flame which "is yet to illumine every region of the world." The stress was on the present and future; the past was rejected as a fallen world of sickening depravity. The rejection of the past was an integral part of the concept of manifest destiny and was implicit in the care providence bestowed on America. When John L. O'Sullivan first hit upon the slogan of manifest destiny, he wrote:

What friend of human liberty, civilization, and refinement, can cast his view over the past history of the monarchies and aristocracies of antiquity, and not deplore that they ever existed ...

America is destined for better deeds ... We have no interest in the scenes of antiquity, only as lessons of avoidance of nearly all their examples. The expansive future is our arena, and for our history. We are entering on its untrodden space with the truths of God in our minds, beneficent objects in our hearts, and with a clear conscience unsullied by the past ...

O'Sullivan's next paragraph states that the United States is "destined to manifest" the design of providence in the world and deplores the vestigial remains of European habits that still persist in this country.

But [he continues] with all the retrograde tendencies of our laws, our judicature, our colleges, our literature, still they are compelled to follow the mighty impulse of the age; they are carried onward by the increasing tide of progress; and though they cast many a longing look behind, they cannot stay the glorious movement of the masses, nor induce them to venerate the rubbish, the prejudices, the superstitions of other times and other lands, the theocracy of priests, the divine right of kings, the aristocracy of blood, the metaphysics of colleges, the irrational stuff of law libraries. Already the brightest hopes of philanthropy, the most enlarged speculations of true philosophy, are inspired by the indications perceptible amongst the mechanical and agricultural population. There, with predominating influence, beats the vigorous national heart of America, propelling onward the march of the multitude, propagating and extending, through the present and the future, the powerful purpose of soul, which in the seventeenth century, sought a refuge among savages, and reared in the wilderness the sacred altars of intellectual freedom. This was the seed that produced individual equality, and political liberty, as its natural fruit; and this is our true nationality.

For a people who believed that they had been chosen by God for the preservation of liberty and that the hut in the primitive forest was the seed of republican government, Andrew Jackson provided one conjunction that wedded the two ideas. God and nature watched over the unique course of America's destiny; both were symbolized in the figure of Andrew Jackson.

Postscript

American Nationalism as an Exertion of the Spirit

America's remarkable economic growth and continental expansion during the first half of the nineteenth century helped define the identity of the emergent nation. Yet in themselves material and territorial factors did not perfectly solve the problem of achieving nationality. The Revolution had been ambiguous on the point of nationalism, as was the post-Revolutionary experience of a people who were not at all certain that they were really "one nation." If, as some contemporary observers and later historians have suggested, Nature made Americans, what would Americans make of Nature? Could the national character be based on material accomplishments alone? Such questions troubled countless nineteenth-century thinkers who knew that the nationality of the New World Republic, unlike that of many Old World countries, was experimental, that it had to be *invented* or *contrived*, and that it rested on nothing more secure than the moral and patriotic commitment of the people themselves. To ensure that commitment, supernatural assistance was invoked. As Perry Miller has observed, "The most utilitarian conquest known to history had somehow to be viewed not as inspired by a calculus of rising land values and investments but (despite the orgies of speculation) as an immense exertion of the spirit."[1] The development of American nationalism, as an exertion of the spirit, was marked by the construction of an ideology which mingled religious, institutional, and historical components to present a symbolic representation of a Republic unique in virtue, watched over by Providence, and blessed with institutions which citizens should respect as works of God and man.

A nation whose Constitution had ordained the separation of Church and State encountered no difficulties in ascribing mundane achievements to divine intercession. Innumerable addresses and sermons interpreted the progress and fortunate condition of the United States as the work of Providence. Individuals and institutions had protected the nation as instruments of God's particular benevolence. It is tempting, but by no means beyond

---

[1] Perry Miller, *Errand into the Wilderness* (Cambridge, 1956), p. 207.

dispute, to link this emphasis upon Providence, perhaps *the* theme most commonly employed in explanations of unique blessings bestowed upon Americans, with the Providence which gave shape and meaning to the lives of seventeenth-century Puritans. In the course of two centuries, however, the concept of Providence had undergone change. To the Puritans, Providence signified the unpredictable, perhaps inexplicable, intervention of God, whether in the form of disasters or deliverances, punishments or answers to prayer. By the nineteenth century, Providence had been stripped of its theological subtleties and reduced to a notion of protective care. Believers could clearly discern the operations of Providence through the smoke of the Industrial Revolution. Thus the Reverend H. W. Bellows did not doubt that the purpose of recent inventions was the maintenance of national unity. "May we not feel that steam in its application as a motive power was discovered with express reference to our enormous rivers and lakes? ... Was not the railroad expressly invented to hold together in its vast iron cleats our broad and otherwise unbound country, threatening to fall to pieces by its own weight?"[2] As proofs accumulated of America's protection by Providence, so the element of religious uncertainty diminished: the way was cleared for an acceptance of Manifest Destiny.

Religious sentiment colored attitudes towards the political institutions of the United States. In 1861 Owen Lovejoy remarked that the concept of the Union, the Constitution, and the flag constituted "a sort of trinity, to which the American people pay political homage and worship." Lovejoy, then a congressman, formerly a clergymen, might be accused of confusing the language of his two professions, but Emerson too had declared that "The Union is part of the religion of this people."[3] The Declaration of Independence, the Constitution, and the Union were expounded and lauded in language more appropriate to religious fervor than to legal argument, unless both approaches could be fused by the patriotic orators like Daniel Webster. By the middle of the nineteenth century American nationalism was linked irrevocably with reverence towards political and constitutional procedures which, sixty years before, had been acknowledged as experiments, but which had now become nothing less than a "sacred" trust.

As with institutions, so with events and heroes: the realities of the Revolution gave way to the celebration of its peerless purity. George Washington was the first of its heroes to be placed beyond the reach of criticism, whether by the simple hagiography of Parson Weems, the measured praise of John Marshall, or adoption as a national symbol for political purposes, as the Federalists between 1809 and 1824 fostered Washington Benevolent Societies which engaged in patriotic demonstrations bearing relics of the departed

[2] Paul Nagel, *One Nation Indivisible* (New York, 1964), pp. 179–180.
[3] *Ibid.*, pp. 145, 210.

leader.[4] The 1832 centenary of Washington's birth offered a further opportunity for orators throughout the nation to compare the achievements of a matchless life with the needs and aspirations of the present. Six years earlier, exactly on the fiftieth anniversary of the Declaration of Independence, Thomas Jefferson and John Adams had died. The date and simultaneity of their passing, severing the last great links with the generation of '76, filled Americans with wonder. Out of this dramatic coincidence they created a "fable of the republic" that brought them into a "community of loyalty and belief, and turned the nation's loss into a triumph ... Providence, Union, Heritage: these were three of the emotion-laden ideas composing the patriotic faith. In the 'double apotheosis' of 1826 they were confirmed with awesome finality ..."[5] President John Quincy Adams officially proclaimed the event as further proof of the nation's blessing by Providence. It was a sign of divine approval, a formal close to a period of political strife long since abandoned by the two statesmen, a human end to a generation whose virtues and achievements would be cherished by Americans. America now possessed a richly peopled past and had acquired the symbolic accoutrements of nationalism.

Selected Additional Reading

Bailyn, Bernard. *The Ideological Origins of the American Revolution* (Cambridge, Mass., 1967).

Boorstin, Daniel J. *The Americans: The Colonial Experience* (New York: Random House, 1958).

Boorstin, Daniel J. *The Americans: The National Experience* (New York, 1965).

Colbourn, H. Trevor. *The Lamp of Experience: Whig History and the Intellectual Origins of the American Revolution* (Chapel Hill, 1965).

Curti, Merle. *The Roots of American Loyalty* (New York, 1946).

Davies, Wallace. *Patriotism on Parade* (Cambridge, Mass., 1955).

Hindle, Brooke. *The Pursuit of Science in Revolutionary America, 1735–1789* (Chapel Hill, 1956).

Kohn, Hans. *American Nationalism: An Interpretative Essay* (New York, 1957).

[4] David Hackett Fischer, *The Revolution of American Conservatism* (New York, 1965), pp. 110–128.
[5] Merrill D. Peterson, *The Jeffersonian Image in the American Mind* (New York, 1960), p. 5.

Kraus, Michael. *The Atlantic Civilization: Eighteenth-Century Origins* (Ithaca, N.Y., 1949).

Merritt, Richard L. *Symbols of American Community, 1735–1775* (New Haven & London: Yale University Press, 1966).

Nye, Russel B. *This Almost Chosen People* (East Lansing: Michigan State University Press, 1966).

Palmer, Robert R. *The Age of the Democratic Revolution: A Political History of Europe and America*, 2 vols. (Princeton, 1959, 1964).

Savelle, Max. *Seeds of Liberty: The Genesis of the American Mind* (New York, 1948).

Somkin, Fred. *The Unquiet Eagle: Memory and Desire in the Idea of American Freedom, 1815–1860* (Ithaca: Cornell University Press, 1967).

Spencer, Benjamin. *The Quest for Nationality: An American Literary Campaign* (Syracuse, N.Y., 1957).

Tuveson, Ernest Lee. *Redeemer Nation: The Idea of America's Millennial Role* (Chicago: University of Chicago Press, 1968).

Varg, Paul A. "The Advent of Nationalism, 1758–1776," *American Quarterly*, XVI (1964), 169–181.

Section Five
Perfectionist Social Thought in the Jacksonian Era

EDWARD PESSEN

Contents

Introduction

Lust for gain and material accumulation preoccupied Americans, according to most of the Europeans who visited the United States during the Jacksonian era. Worship of the dollar was held to be the true American religion not by Europeans alone. The Emersonian comment that "things are in the saddle and ride mankind," like similar critiques voiced by other members of his circle and by James Fenimore Cooper, indicated that at least some reflective persons not only held aloof from the era's frenzied competition for wealth but that they regarded it with misgivings as well. Relatively rare, such skepticism was characteristic of men unusually sensitive or possessed of strong religious convictions.

When they did denounce materialism, most Protestant leaders managed to do so without casting blame on any social institution. To the prophet of the new evangelicalism, Charles Grandison Finney, or to the more orthodox divine, Lyman Beecher, or to the lay leaders of the variegated "Benevolent Empire," excessive concern with worldly goods was a *universal* fault, attributable to human weakness rather than to a deficient social order. The disease was to be exorcised through prayer, by vigorous participation in Christian worship, or by joining with others to promote the influence and extend the reach of biblical teachings. It must have been a source of much gratification to the wealthy merchants active in these diverse Protestant movements to learn that fighting the devil required renunciation neither of one's own worldly goods nor of the system which had made possible their accumulation and their subsequent transmission to one's offspring.

Another Protestant viewpoint—inevitably a minority viewpoint—held otherwise. A small number of zealots attributed excessive materialism more to the corrupting influence of a capitalistic society than to innate human flaws. Private property and a family system which was designed above all to confine wealth to one's own were the fundamental sources of selfishness. New sects emerged during the era, organized around such beliefs. The most interesting of these religious analogues to the Brook Farm and other Fourierist or socialist groups which established "backwoods utopias" during the period was the Perfectionist group of John Humphrey Noyes and his followers, in Oneida, New York.

If Oneida was—and for that matter continues to be—a source of intense curiosity primarily because of its marital arrangements, that fact tells more about the prurient interest of observers and critics than it does about Noyes and his fellow Perfectionists. John Humphrey Noyes was capable of publishing an amazingly frank and charmingly unblushing account of precisely how "male continence" could be maintained without undue deprivation of sensual pleasure. As Whitney R. Cross has pointed out, this community showed both by word and deed that the "complex marriage" it practiced catered not to the sensual desires of its members so much as to their religious and social ideology. Repudiation of the traditional private family was part of an indivisible struggle waged against the forces that bred selfishness, and formed a companion tactic to the renunciation of private property, the devotion to honest work and frank criticism, and, above all, the dedication to the teachings of Jesus Christ and the Bible, that were required of every member of the community. Oneida's rejection of private property was based on the clear language of scripture, which had proclaimed that on the day of Pentecost true believers regarded all their possessions not as their own but as the common property of all.

Secular dissenters attacked private property for other reasons. They repudiated it not for its effects on human character and values but for the physical misery it was believed to cause. In contrast to moralists who seemed to believe Jacksonian America was in danger of losing its soul precisely because so much of its population was gaining the world, a few dissenters charged that most people here suffered under severe material deprivation due primarily to the institution of private property.

Secular perfectionists were divided as were their religious brethren. The "Utopians," drawing heavily on European socialist doctrines, particularly those preached by Charles Fourier, established their model communities, evidently hopeful that the superior social organization and more attractive ways of meeting human needs would attract converts and imitators. (Such things are impossible to prove, yet one wonders about the extent to which leaders and followers both fled to "experimental" communities not so much to inspire others as to please themselves, "doing their own thing" by escaping a competitive society they could no longer accept emotionally.) Others, such as the leaders of the Working Men's movement, remained in this world, propagandizing not with their feet or the power of example, but by written and spoken appeals for a renovated society. As befitted social critics more concerned with what they said than with what they did, the laborites were quite explicit in explaining the social ills besetting the country. They depicted an inegalitarian society whose social injustice was camouflaged by the artful rhetoric of Jacksonian demagogues falsely claiming to be friends of the common man.

The Jacksonian era's reputation for equality and social fluidity would make it appear that the social critics, blinded by their preoccupation with the sordid or by the neuroses that at times afflict inveterate naysayers, were simply unable to see the happy setting discerned by more balanced and therefore more accurate observers. Yet much evidence has been adduced by scholars lately, supplementing earlier hints, that challenges the roseate version of American society in the Jacksonian era.[1] The labor critics, if they forbore to dwell on the smiling aspects that so many others noted, drew attention to a darker side that was by no means merely imaginary.

Some admirers of the Jacksonian Democrats have contended that some of their leaders, too, were radical: witness the Bank Veto message or the decision written by the Jacksonian Chief Justice of the Supreme Court in the famous *Charles River* case. Thus, there was nothing new or unique contributed by the labor radicals. Other modern critics, evidently unhappy at the suggestion that influential American labor leaders were truly radical at any time in our history, have drawn the comforting conclusion that the alleged labor "radicalism" could not have been what it seemed, in view of the fact that major party spokesmen shared similar viewpoints. The fact is, however, that the Working Men's denunciation of American society *was* unique. The "radical" Jacksonian propagandists such as George Bancroft, William Gouge, Roger B. Taney and Amos Kendall, did not attack private property, for all the flamboyance of their rhetoric. Jackson party "radicals" did not denounce the American party system in general; they did not denounce their own party in particular as a great "humbug," as did the labor leaders. The advocacy by the latter of one or another form of socialism was hardly the same thing as the vague praise of "honest labor" and "opportunity" indulged in by Andrew Jackson and his followers. The views of the labor critics were indeed radical, in the classic meaning of that term, calling as they did for the pulling down of the characteristic institutions of a capitalistic society.

Secular and spiritual perfectionists did not agree in all particulars. Unlike the spiritual dissenters, secular radicals would not tamper with the institution of the family. Where the labor critics stressed material inequality as the chief

---

[1] Among these studies are Stuart Blumin, "Mobility in a Nineteenth-Century American City: Philadelphia, 1820–1860," (University of Pennsylvania Doctoral Dissertation, 1968); Raymond A. Mohl, "Poverty in Early America, A Reappraisal: The Case of 18th-Century New York City," *New York History*, L (January 1969); Douglas T. Miller, *Jacksonian Aristocracy: Class and Democracy in New York 1830–1860* (New York, 1967); Miller, "Immigration and Social Stratification in Pre-Civil War New York," *New York History*, XLIX (April 1968), pp. 157–168; Richard C. Wade, *The Urban Frontier: The Rise of Western Cities, 1790–1830* (Cambridge, 1959), ch. 4, 7; Edward Pessen, *Jacksonian America: Society, Personality, and Politics* (Homewood, 1969), ch. 3; and Pessen, "Did Fortunes Rise and Fall Mercurially in Antebellum America? The Tale of Two Cities: Boston and New York." *Journal of Social History*, V (Summer 1971), pp. 339–357.

evil flowing from private property, the religious radicals focused on the moral deterioration it allegedly caused. The spiritual perfectionists acted out their social vision rather than merely urging others to follow it. The chief difference concerned ideology. Rappites, Zoarites, Shakers, as well as the Oneida community, regarded their movements as essentially religious in character. If the actual rules underlying work and distribution in their communities were similar to those called for by Robert Dale Owen's "federative system" or by Thomas Skidmore's scheme, to the religious zealots, unlike the secular, socialism or communitarianism was a mere technique to be created only because it was most conducive to achieving the great end in view: the spiritual regeneration of the individual.

Yet if their ultimate goals and values differed, the critics of worldly and otherworldly persuasion agreed that the society should be rebuilt from the ground up. Some intellectual historians would call attention to another similarity. The theories, whether of secular or religious perfectionism, emanated from above, from their leaders rather than their memberships. The fact hardly constitutes elitism. The masses lacked the knowledge and the leisure required to create new social programs or to modify plans put forward earlier. If social theories are to be subjected to a quantitative test, the important number would appear to be not how many authors but rather how many followers they had. A more valuable test would combine quantitative with qualitative factors. If perfectionism was very much a minority movement during the age of speculation, it was nevertheless a significant reflection of actual inequities then present in American society and of the sense of alienation these induced, as much for their moral as for their material consequences.

Like so many other zealots in the era, John Humphrey Noyes, the leader of the Oneida Community, was a child of New England and its anti-latitudinarian moral atmosphere. Diverted from his earlier study of the law by the effects of a revival meeting he attended in Putney, Vermont, in 1831, Noyes became a Perfectionist, believing that the Second Advent had occurred at the time of the destruction of Jerusalem and that a life without sin was required of those who would be "Christian in the highest sense of the word." Although Noyes and his followers were preoccupied with what to others might appear to be fine points of theology, Oneida's interest to the world at large derived not from its religious concepts but from its social arrangements. Regarded by the Perfectionists themselves as the means of exorcising the twin sins of selfishness and greed, these arrangements took the form of communal work, living, and marriage.

Commencement of Practical Communism

Perfectionism assumed the form of association first at Putney, Vt., in a small circle of the immediate connections of J. H. Noyes. His wife (whose original name was Harriet A. Holton), and several members of his father's family being associated with him in religious faith, and in the business of editing and printing, adopted, or rather naturally fell into, the principle of community of interests. From 1840 to 1847 there was a gradual accession of members, till the family numbered nearly forty. During the same period all the leading principles of the present social theory of the Oneida Community were worked out theoretically and practically; and, step by step, the school advanced from community of faith to community of property, community of households, community of affections.

Organization of the Oneida Community

The village of Putney was at first considerably excited on account of the religious doctrines of the new society, and afterward still more disturbed by the development of its social principles; and the little band was finally com-

---

Reprinted from *Hand-Book of the Oneida Community with a Sketch of its Founder and an Outline of its Constitution and Doctrines* (1867).

pelled to seek a new location for the Community school. On the same day that the exodus from Putney commenced (Nov. 26, 1847), practical movements were being made by Perfectionists of the same faith toward the formation of a Community at Oneida, Madison County, N. Y. The Putney exiles joined these brethren, and on the first day of the following March the Oneida Community was fully organized. Other smaller Communities have since been established at Wallingford and at New Haven, Conn., in New York city, and at Willow Place near Oneida.

The Pentecostal Model

These Communities are organized after the model exhibited to the world on the day of Pentecost: "The multitude of them that believed were of one heart and of one soul; neither said any of them that aught of the things which he possessed was his own, but they had all things common." There is free interchange of men and means between the different Communities, and no accounts (except for purposes of information) are kept between the several Communities, or the members of the same Community. Their constitution and by-laws are not written instruments, but principles wrought out and embodied in customs and institutions. The general character of the government is similar to that of a family. Indeed, the Community organization began as a family, and has grown as a family, with this important difference, that in the original compact between Mr. Noyes and his wife, they mutually agreed not to be exclusively devoted to each other, but to receive others into their unity. Under this compact the original duality has been gradually increased until it embraces about 300 souls. When prudent persons intend marriage, they first seek acquaintance with each other, and endeavor to ascertain whether they are adapted to make each other happy—whether, in short, they love each other well enough to commit themselves to each other "for better or for worse." Thus it is in joining the Communities: all permanent connections are preceded by acquaintance, and take place as the result of affection and deliberate consultation. And as the original compact admits of a plurality of partners to the same marriage, so the effort and aim of the original pair has been to multiply the fathers and mothers of the Communities—to educate and encourage others to fill their places as guides and counselors; and they have so far succeeded, that their personal presence is not regarded as essential to the harmonious development of associative life.

Means of Government

The measures relied upon for good government, in these Community families are, first, *daily evening meetings*, which all are expected to attend, and in which religious, social and business matters are freely discussed; and secondly, *the system of mutual criticism.* This system takes the place of backbiting in ordinary society, and is regarded as one of the greatest means of improvement and fellowship. All of the members are accustomed to voluntarily invite the benefit of criticism from time to time. Sometimes persons are criticised by the entire family; at other times by a committee of six, eight, twelve, or more, selected by themselves from among those best acquainted with them, and best able to do justice to their character. In these criticisms the most perfect sincerity is expected; and in practical experience it is found best for the subject to receive his criticism without replying.—There is little danger that the general verdict in respect to his character will be unjust. This ordinance is far from agreeable to those whose egotism and vanity are stronger than their love of truth. It is an ordeal which reveals insincerity and selfishness; but it also often takes the form of commendation, and reveals hidden virtues as well as secret faults. It is always acceptable to those who wish to see themselves as others see them.

These two agencies, viz. daily evening meetings and criticism, are found quite adequate to the maintenance of good order and government in the Communities. Those who join the Communities understanding their principles, and afterward prove refractory and inharmonic, and also those who come into the Communities in childhood, and afterwards develop characters antagonistic to the general spirit, and refuse to yield to the governmental agencies mentioned, either voluntarily withdraw or are expelled. Only one case of expulsion has, however, been recorded.

Business Organization

The organization by which the business of the Oneida Community is managed is simple and easily explained. The first great wheel of the machine is the weekly meeting of the Business Board, comprising the heads of industrial departments and such others as choose to attend its sessions. It might be called a board of directors. Its officers are a chairman, whose duty it is to preside at the deliberations of the Board, and a secretary, who preserves a record of the proceedings. All the members of the Community are free to participate in the deliberations of this Board, and it is a limited body only because all who are not especially interested in managing, generally choose to stay away. The report of the secretary is read to the entire Community on the evening following the session of the Board, and opportunity is then given for discussion of any measure resolved upon by the Board; and business matters are frequently referred for discussion and decision by the Board to the general meeting; so that constant communication is kept up between the Board and the mass of the Community. There are no secret sessions. Everything is free, open, democratic. In the early spring of each year a special session of the Business Board is called for maturing plans of a business campaign, and for organizing

the forces of the season. Previous to the meeting a conspicuous bulletin in-
vites every one to hand in a written slip, stating what department of business
he would like to engage in, etc. An organizing committee is appointed at this
annual meeting who select foremen for the different departments of business,
and apportion the help, keeping in view as much as possible the expressed
choice of individuals. Their plan is submitted to the Board for approval or
amendment, and also to the family in general assembly. Still further, a standing committee is appointed at the annual meeting, consisting of two or three
persons of approved judgment, whose duty it is to have a general oversight
of all the businesses, and transfer hands from one department to another,
as the fluctuations of business or the improvement of individuals may
require.

The women also have a similar organization for the management of their
particular departments of business.

In determining upon any course of action or policy, *unanimity* is always
sought by committees, by the Business Board, and by the Community. All
consider themselves as one party, and intend to act together or not at all. This
principle is illustrated in the working of juries. It forms part of the constitution of the Community. If there are serious objections to any proposed
measure, action is delayed until the objections are removed. The majority
never go ahead leaving a grumbling minority behind. This principle is found
compatible with prompt action and the transaction of large and complicated
business.

The Social Organization

This aspect of the Oneida Community and its branches, and the intercourse
of the sexes, are also easily explained and readily understood. In the first
place, the Communities believe, contrary to the theory of the novelists and
others, that the affections can be controlled and guided, and that they will
produce far better results when rightly controlled and rightly guided than
if left to take care of themselves without restraint. They entirely reject the
idea that love is an inevitable and uncontrollable fatality, which must have its
own course. They believe the whole matter of love and its expression should
be subject to enlightened self-control, and should be managed for the greatest
good. In the Communities it is under the special supervision of the fathers and
mothers, or, in other words, of the wisest and best members, and is often
under discussion in the evening meetings, and is also subordinate to the institution of criticism. The fathers and mothers are guided in their management by certain general principles, which have been worked out, and are well
understood in the Communities. One is termed the principle of the ascending
fellowship. It is regarded as better for the young of both sexes to associate
in love with persons older than themselves, and, if possible, with those who

are spiritual and have been some time in the school of self-control, and who are thus able to make love safe and edifying. This is only another form of the popular principle of contrasts. It is well understood by physiologists, that it is undesirable for persons of similar characters and temperaments to mate together. Communists have discovered that it is not desirable for two inexperienced and unspiritual persons to rush into fellowship with each other; that it is far better for both to associate with persons of mature character and sound sense.

Another general principle well understood in the Communities, is, that it is not desirable for two persons, whatever may be their standing, to become exclusively attached to each other—to worship and idolize each other—however popular this experience may be with sentimental people generally. They regard exclusive, idolatrous attachment as unhealthy and pernicious wherever it may exist. The Communities insist that the heart should be kept free to love all the true and worthy, and should never be contracted with exclusiveness or idolatry, or purely selfish love in any form.

Another principle, well known and carried out in the Communities, is, that *persons shall not be obliged to receive under any circumstances the attention of those whom they do not like*. They abhor rapes, whether committed under the cover of marriage or elsewhere. The Communities are pledged to protect all their members from disagreeable social approaches. Every woman is free to refuse every man's attentions.

Still another principle is, that it is best for men in their approaches to women, to invite personal interviews through the intervention of a third party, for two important reasons: viz., first, that the matter may be brought in some measure under the inspection of the Community; and, secondly, that the women may decline proposals, if they choose, without embarrassment or restraint.

Under the operation of these general principles, but little difficulty attends the practical carrying out of the social theory of the Communities. As fast as the members become enlightened, they *govern themselves* by these very principles. The great aim is to teach every one self-control. This leads to the greatest happiness in love, and the greatest good to all.

Sexual freedom in the Communities is subject to the general restriction prescribed by the doctrine of *Male Continence*; i.e., all men are expected to make it a point of honor to refrain from the propagative part of sexual intercourse, except when propagation is intended and provided for by due consultation with the Community and with the other party concerned.

But little practical advance has been made in the direction of propagation. The Community is waiting for light; but in the meantime holds firmly that this is one of the most important interests of society, and should not be left to blind chance or selfish, uncivilized passion, but should be placed under the control of scientific guidance, equal at least to that which is applied to perfecting the breeds of valuable animals.

Children's Department

The children of the Community are cared for in the following manner: During the period of nursing, the mother devotes herself to her child as much as she pleases; has a room to herself, and assistants, if she wishes. When the child is weaned, say at the age of a year or fifteen months, it is placed in the general nursery or children's department. This is an establishment separate from the main household, but in close communication with it, and always open to mothers, and to all who choose to visit it. The mother, on weaning her child, generally takes her turn for a while in the children's department as assistant. Children remain in this establishment under the care of men and women selected for their skill in managing the young, till the age of twelve or fourteen. The smallest children eat in the nursery at a table by themselves. The rest eat at the general table with the family. All attend school, and are taught to read, write, etc.

Religious Belief

The Communists have no formal creed, but are firmly and unanimously attached to the Bible, as the textbook of the Spirit of truth; to Jesus Christ, as the eternal Son of God; to the Apostles and Primitive Church, as the exponents of the everlasting Gospel. Their belief is, that the second advent of Christ took place at the period of the destruction of Jerusalem; that at that time there was a primary resurrection and judgment in the spiritual world; that the final kingdom of God then began in the heavens; that the manifestation of that kingdom in the visible world is now approaching; that its approach is ushering in the second and final resurrection and judgment; that a church on earth is now rising to meet the approaching kingdom in the heavens, and to become its duplicate and representative; that inspiration, or open communication with God and the heavens, involving perfect holiness, is the element of connection between the church on earth and the church in the heavens, and the power by which the kingdom of God is to be established and reign in the world.

Complex Functions

From what has been said it will readily appear that the Community combines in one organization the various functions of education, religion, industry, and domestic life. These in ordinary society are separated. The church is in one place, the school in another, the workshop in a third, and the family is apart from them all. In Communism these various interests are consolidated and interlocked; and their benefits, instead of having to be sought for abroad, are brought to all the members of the society within the limits of that one best locality, home.

Applications for Membership

These are abundant; but few, however, of those who apply are considered ready to enter the society, and are generally advised to study more thoroughly its character and principles before attempting a permanent junction. No one is considered fit for membership who has not previously commended himself as earnestly devoted to the same objects the Communities have in view. Those who really love the principles of the society are certain to attract the fellowship of its members wherever they are, and so become virtually identified with them, whether they come into formal connection with them or not. Persons, on actually joining the Oneida Community or any of its branches, are expected to sign the following document:

"On the admission of any member, all property belonging to him or her becomes the property of the Community. A record of the estimated amount will be kept, and in case of the subsequent withdrawal of the member, the Community, according to its practice heretofore, will refund the property or an equivalent amount. This practice, however, stands on the ground, not of obligation, but of expediency and liberality; and the time and manner of refunding must be trusted to the discretion of the Community. While a person remains a member, his subsistence and education in the Community are held to be just equivalents for his labor; and no accounts are kept between him and the Community, and no claim of wages accrues to him in case of subsequent withdrawal."

Those who brought no property into the Community, if they withdraw honorably, are given a good outfit of clothing and a sum of money not exceeding one hundred dollars.

No Place for Selfish Persons

Of course in Communities, where the members are sincerely devoted to such principles as have been described, poverty, oppression, and crime must be unknown. There can be no rich unless all are rich. There can be no poor unless all are poor. Every one will be respected according to his worth. Individual happiness will be found in seeking the general happiness and good of all. In the words of a Communistic writer: "There is here the largest liberty for love and generosity, but no liberty for selfishness and seeking one's own. If a person can find gratification in the public service and the prosperity of the whole, then a Commune is exactly his place. But those who enter with their eye mainly on private luxury and pleasure-seeking, are courting special disappointment. True Communism has nothing for them but arrest and crucifixion until their motive is changed. The freedom to enjoy, which it is supposed must exist in such a state of society, has its counterpart in the renunciation of all selfish aims."

Financial Experience and Conditions

The Communities have not made the accumulation of wealth a primary object. They care not for money, except as it enables them to publish what they consider the truth, and to embody their ideal of a true life. The Community at Oneida was not, for the first eight years of its existence, self-support-ing, owing to many causes, such as the lack of well-organized businesses, the printing of a free paper, extortions of seceders, outside enemies, etc.; but since 1857 there has been a gradual improvement in its circumstances. The Indian log-hut and unpainted wooden dwellings of the first year were early replaced by commodious wooden structures, to which are now added substantial brick houses. Their domain now comprises over 500 acres of well-cultivated land. The orchards, vineyards, and gardens cover about 50 acres. Much attention is given to the cultivation of grapes, strawberries, and other small fruits. Four hundred bushels of strawberries and eight tons of grapes have been harvested in a single season.

To the single water-power originally purchased, two others have been added, and a large proportion of the Community members are employed in the different mechanical branches carried on. Beside the ordinary businesses of carpentry, blacksmithing, shoemaking, tailoring, dentistry, etc., there is a large satchel factory on the site of the old Indian sawmill. At another location there is an iron foundry and sawmill. At another there are large machine shops and extensive trapworks, where are annually made many thousands of Newhouse's celebrated steel traps, known among all trappers from Maine to Oregon and from the Hudson Bay to Texas. Here, also, are the Community silk-works, which employ thirty hands in the manufacture of sewing-silk. At still another place the business of fruit preserving is carried on. The fruits, vegetables, and jellies here put up are in such repute as causes the demand for them to generally exceed the supply. Several other branches of manufactures are carried on, such as the making of tin cans, hop-stoves, bag-frames, window-caps, etc. The earnings of the Community for the last ten years have averaged $18,000 a year, clear of expenses.

Woman's Position in the Community

In this connection it may be remarked, that two of the leading businesses of the Community are superintended by women, viz., satchel-making, and fruit-preserving. Women also keep the accounts of the Community, and are found well adapted to this employment. The sexes freely mingle in many departments of industry, and women enjoy many privileges denied them in ordinary society. They are at least relieved from household drudgery, and from the curse of excessive and undesired propagation, and allowed a fair chance with their brothers in education and labor.

About Labor

Compulsory labor is neither sought nor permitted in the Communities. The aim is to make labor attractive, and a means of improvement; and this is found compatible with good and industrious habits. The members occasionally exchange employments, and many who brought a single trade into the society, are now equally proficient in many others. Mr. Noyes, the leader, has chosen an exceedingly varied course of service during his life in the Community, having worked as a farmer, gardener, brick mason, job printer, bag maker, tinker, editor, steward, blacksmith, trapper, etc., and been active in starting several of the most profitable businesses of the Community. In the department of trapmaking, he has originated several mechanical improvements of great service.

The Communities furnish employment to many who have not yet learned that they can do better than to work for wages. More than eighty outside helpers are at present on the pay-roll of the Oneida Community.

Education

The Communists think much of integral education, and consider a knowledge of the practical arts not less important than the wisdom gained from books, and the culture of the heart and social character as most essential. But facilities for acquiring a good book education are allotted to all—to the old as well as the young. Persons of three-score and ten are seen as enthusiastically devoted to self-improvement as the young and middle-aged. It is in contemplation to establish at some future day a Community University, wherein all sciences shall be taught to persons of both sexes and of all ages; and the surplus income of the Oneida Community and its branches, whatever it may be, will be devoted to this enterprise and other like objects of improvement.

Diet and Dress

Tobacco and ardent spirits are not used in the Communities; neither are tea and coffee. The members are not Grahamites, yet use little meat, preferring fruit and a farinaceous diet. The short dress has been worn by the Community women since the summer of 1848; and it is supposed that the style originated at Oneida.

2 / Whitney R. Cross
The Social Blueprint of Spiritual Perfectionism

(1950)

Whitney R. Cross's brilliant book has reminded students of history that during the Jacksonian era western New York State and nearby New England formed a "psychic highway," regularly traversed by movements that combined religious zeal with social crusading. No one has better understood the relationship between the unique theological concepts and social practices that were at the heart of the Oneida and the other Perfectionist communities which took the road of community based on discipline, rather than the path of pure individualism taken by some religious Perfectionists.

The two bands of enthusiasts emerging from ultraism in the late thirties both continued during the early forties their quest for the regeneration of American society. The greater depths of economic depression at the beginning of the new decade made both alike concentrate their energies anew and hasten their steps. As their pace increased, however, their ways diverged ever farther. The group traveling to the right sought an escapist's short cut to the millennium, looking to supernatural forces for miraculous change. The crowd going left, having departed from the literal rendition of their religious tradition, could make a somewhat more realistic approach to the problems of this world. In their view, too, the millennium would come immediately, but it would be a Utopia built by mortal hand and brain, of earthly materials, established in the midst of contemporary society.

Moreover, when once the former ultraists journeying on the leftward branch progressed beyond the confines of orthodoxy, they found a goodly company of strangers going their way. In their new assault on the evils of the world they were joined by others who had never been religious enthusiasts. For revival religion, even at its height, had never obtained complete sway in western New York. Freethinkers had for a few years even supported a periodical in the enthusiastic city of Rochester![1] Masonry had discovered many champions who became distrustful of all movements toward churchly influence in politics or personal mores. Most persistently aggressive of the enemies of revivalism and all its works had been the flourishing Universalist Church.

Students of American culture and church historians alike have quite

Whitney R. Cross, *The Burned-Over District: The Social and Intellectual History of Enthusiastic Religion in Western New York, 1800–1850.* Copyright 1950 by Cornell University. Reprinted by permission of Cornell University Press.
[1] *Liberal Advocate* (Rochester), 1832–1833.

neglected the Universalists, and the oversight seems to be a serious one. They greatly exceeded the Unitarians in their area of effective influence and may have been more numerous as well. Their impact upon reform movements and upon the growth of modern religious attitudes might prove to be greater than that of either the Unitarians or the freethinkers. And their less sophisticated, more homely warfare upon the forces fettering the American mind might be demonstrated to have equaled the influence of the transcendentalist philosophers. In the Burned-over District, at least, they played a highly significant role, and no hint appears to suggest that they behaved abnormally in this one region.

The Universalists, like the orthodox Yorkers, were good Yankees. They had the tender conscience, the intense concern for the community, the preoccupation with a perfected society, long grown in the Puritan tradition. But their generously conceived heaven had room for sinner as well as saint. Christ had died to atone for the original sin of all men. Regeneration, then, could be no Heavenly miracle, sorting the saved from the damned, but rather betokened a growth in morality which could as well be gradual as instantaneous. Such a theology might easily accord with the opinion, as orthodox doctrine did not, that evil was the consequence more of social maladjustment than of individual sin.

Zealous reformers these liberals were, but in a sharply different style from the ultraists. Much as they hated Negro bondage, they considered abolitionists to be fanatics and believed that slavery must be handled by practical remedies looking to the benefit of southern whites as well as blacks. No more temperate group inhabited western New York, but none fought more bitterly the organized temperance societies with their petty tyrannies. Often in this region aligned with both Masons and Democrats, Universalists attacked debtor prisons, blue laws, the inequities suffered by workingmen, capital punishment, and extortion by land speculators, while they fumed over revivals, anti-Catholicism, and dictatorial benevolent societies of all types.[2]

Orestes Brownson, for one, journeyed while in this area from the bosom of Universalism into a temporary alliance with the "infidel" Workingmen of New York City, where he espoused programs of economic and political change designed to bring about fundamental alterations in American society as a whole.[3] His reaction was not strange, but only rather more extreme than that of his fellows. Many of his upstate companions followed Robert Owen's ventures with keen interest, and some nearly established a com-

---

[2] [George Rogers], *Memoranda of the Experience, Labors, and Travels of a Universalist Preacher*, etc. (n.p., 1846), 353 ff.; *Gospel Advocate* (Buffalo), V (Feb. 24, 1827), 62; *Evangelical Magazine and Gospel Advocate* (Utica), II (Feb. 5, 1831), 42, III (May 12, Aug. 11, 1832), 147, 254, V (Oct. 11, 1834), 326.

[3] Arthur M. Schlesinger, Jr., *Orestes A. Brownson, A Pilgrim's Progress* (Boston, 1939), 13–27.

munity similar to New Harmony in all but religious orientation, at Williamsville, near Buffalo, in 1827. The largest periodical of the sect in the region carried an editorial in 1837 entitled "Science and Christianity," which could almost as well have been written a hundred years later.[4]

The Universalists acquired recruits in increasing numbers through the thirties, as people became satiated with protracted meetings and revivals. More important, they provided a leadership in reform for others beyond their church membership: disillusioned revivalists and enthusiastic reformers who had outgrown their original religious inspiration. Universalists usually led in taking up the new intellectual currents introduced from Europe and in adapting them to the needs of liberal reform. They acquired in turn from their new allies attitudes originally grown in ultraism: a goodly dose of one-ideaism to make them risk all on one panacea at a time, and a strong tendency, novel with these liberals, to seek the ideal, absolute form of their single obsession rather than to follow the rule of expediency in all things. Perhaps the broader tendencies of the age operated in the same direction.

With the encouragement of Universalists and other liberals, a series of new ideas spread about during the late thirties and early forties. Phrenology, mesmerism, land reform, Fourierist communism, and Swedenborgianism all helped to direct Burned-over District enthusiasm into new channels. None of these had any peculiar development in this single region, though all prevailed more in the Northeast than elsewhere in the country. But all worked themselves into the point of view of the liberal type of thinkers in this area and persisted for several years.

At least one phrenologist was lecturing in western New York in 1836, and LaRoy Sunderland of *Zion's Watchman* probably became a "phrenopathist" and then a mesmerist before his partner, George Storrs, became a Millerite. Interest in this fad seems first to have reached epidemic proportions, however, with the tour of the Scotch lecturer, George Combe, begun in 1837. Following the canal line, he attracted large audiences at least in Syracuse and Buffalo and even found a few societies organized to sponsor him. Clerical opposition he found so strong as to discourage the naturally eager sympathy of physicians and other liberal thinkers.[5] But the Universalist press gave him prompt and hearty support, as did the Noyes perfectionists and many former ultraists. The *Baptist Register* admitted debates on the subject, but with a pronounced editorial frown. Orson Fowler, founder of the Fowler and Wells publishing house, destined to become a mainstay of this movement and others of related nature, grew up in western New York and began his career as a phrenological lecturer in the region early in the history of the cause.

---

[4] *Gospel Advocate*, V (June 23, 1827), 198, VI (March 1, 1828), 73; *Evangelical Magazine*, VIII (Aug. 18, 1837), 262.

[5] George Combe, *Notes on the United States of America during a Phrenological Visit in 1838–1839–1840* (2 vols.; Philadelphia, 1841), I, 148, 170, II, 70–84.

Phrenology paraded as a science based on natural law. No doubt many of its popularizers were ill-equipped to deal even with pseudo science; but however much imagination flourished in the propagator or credulity in his audience, the belief definitely discouraged supernatural interpretations of human conduct. As one man reported to George Combe, sinners had according to this system to be deemed "unfortunate rather than criminal: as 'moral patients' . . . rather than fit subjects for punitive justice."[6] Possibly this fad of pseudoscientific nature did as much as geology or biology to undermine revealed religion.

Soon after the first phrenologists entered western New York, mesmerism began to rouse a similar curiosity among the same groups of people. To some folk mesmeric trances appeared to be a species of magic or trickery; to others reared in superstition they seemed the work of departed spirits. Others thought that the phenomena of the trance revealed hidden powers in stronger minds which could prevail over weaker ones. The more intellectually sophisticated considered mesmerism to be a new revelation, "opening a passage from the highest point of physical science, into spiritual philosophy"; a "connecting link between the sciences which treat of those subtler powers of nature . . . and the science of life, animal and eternal." Like phrenology, it seemed "a foundation on which a form of society might be built which would result in the regeneration of the whole human family."[7]

Both of these pseudo sciences reinforced Universalist religious doctrines and suggested that natural laws rather than whimsical miracles embodied God's purposes for humanity. They also stimulated speculations about the constitution of the human mind and its correspondence with the similarly constituted universe. Persons thinking along these lines quite as a matter of course extended their search to discover the laws of social organization which related to the nature of the individual and the universe. The severe depression of the early forties served to focus attention upon economic subjects, particularly land reform and communism. For the liberal reformers these two causes temporarily provided a sociology to match the supposed sciences of phrenology and mesmerism.

George and Frederick Evans had come to western New York from England in 1820, bent on developing their interests in free thought, land reform, and communism. They joined in the Workingmen's and antimonopoly movements of the early thirties and studied the communism of Robert Owen and the Shakers. George edited a journal at Ithaca for a time before he joined the New York City radicals and founded the *Workingman's Advocate* in the metropolis. By the forties he was the leading land reformer in the country. Frederick

---

[6] *Ibid.*, I, 131.

[7] Mary B. A. King, *Looking Backward* (New York, 1870), 170; John H. Noyes, *The Berean: A Manual for the Help of Those Who Seek the Faith of the Primitive Church* (Putney, Vt., 1847), 65; H. J. Seymour, Westmoreland, in *Spiritual Magazine* (Putney, Vt.), II (Aug. 15, 1847), 109.

joined the Shakers and rose to leadership of that church in the same decade.[8] Possibly these two brothers had roused some early upstate support for their ideas; the agrarian agitations of the mid-thirties in the Hudson Valley would seem to indicate a persevering concern with problems of land ownership.

Yet neither the "agrarian" socialist land reform notions of the New York City labor radicals in the thirties, nor George Evans's "national" reform of the forties which anticipated the homestead system, seem to have appealed widely in upstate New York. The one was perhaps too drastic a plan for farmer landowners, and the other may have seemed geographically remote to a long-settled people. Or possibly the historians of land policy have paid insufficient attention to the ideological aspects of their subject to realize the possible connection in people's minds between rent wars and home-steading theories.[9] Perhaps a genuine interest in the subject did exist here, which has merely not been discovered.

Such a hypothesis would explain Gerrit Smith's otherwise paradoxical advocacy of land reform. He not only donated a large number of virtually worthless plots on the fringes of the Adirondacks to help support free Negroes but also during his term in Congress sponsored bills for the free distribution of western land. Of course Smith may have been a rare exception, not the mouthpiece of a general concern. He may have been prodded into his attitude by Beriah Green, who wrote him about banking monopolies in 1840, or by his conservative uncle, Daniel Cady, who taunted him for his deep concern for poor blackfolk while, as the greatest landholder in the state of New York, he contributed to the poverty of white folk.[10]

Probably land reform of other sorts appealed less than might have been the case in this region, in part because communal ownership proved to be a much more entertaining subject for speculation. Ordinary folk knew enough of the technicalities of land ownership, in an area whose apportionment of real estate had been substantially accomplished, to prevent the growth of unrealistic dreams along that line. A scheme to avoid the pitfalls of private ownership was far more appealing. The pitfalls of communal arrangements being unknown to most men, their imagination could soar unrestrained as they contemplated the Fourierist plans.

Though pleasantly mysterious, however, communism was not inordinately strange to the Burned-over District. Most people by the early forties must have had some slight cognizance of Jemima Wilkinson's New Jerusalem and of the several Shaker colonies in the state. Liberals, at least, had interested

[8] Marguerite F. Melcher, *The Shaker Adventure* (Princeton, 1941), 157, 178, 179, 275–278; Arthur M. Schlesinger, Jr., *The Age of Jackson* (Boston, 1945), 182, and *passim*.

[9] Paul D. Evans, *The Holland Land Company* (Buffalo, 1924), and David M. Ellis, *Landlords and Farmers in the Hudson-Mohawk Region* (Ithaca, 1946), fail to approach this angle of the subject.

[10] Ralph V. Harlow, *Gerrit Smith, Philanthropist and Reformer* (New York, 1939), 31–32, 242–257.

themselves in New Harmony and in Fanny Wright's project at Nashoba. A number in the region maintained contact with the developing ideas of John Humphrey Noyes, and many no doubt had some knowledge of the Mormon United Order.

Liberals in the region thus had ample preparation when in the depth of the depression the theories of Fourier began to receive extensive publicity. Albert Brisbane, a product of the locality, gave the movement its initial impetus in the *New York Tribune* and also lectured at Utica, Syracuse, Seneca Falls, and Rochester. Dr. Alexander Theller, a filibuster in the 1837 Canadian Rebellion, Edwin Stillman, a former Noyes perfectionist, and one Theron C. Leland spread the doctrine from Rochester, while a lawyer named Alonzo Watson roused interest about Watertown. A convention at Rochester in August, 1843, gathered together several hundred delegates and launched the active organization of phalanxes in the area.[11]

The agitation quickly reached the proportions and acquired many of the characteristics of a religious revival. By April, 1844, nine units were contemplated within fifty miles of Batavia, and Leland estimated that twenty thousand persons west of Rochester awaited opportunity to enter communities. Farther east the enthusiasm was probably little less intense. The Watertown area started a phalanx in the spring, and others in central New York made plans which failed to reach maturity.[12]

Several members of the Throop family, spread over Madison and Cortland counties, led one such venture. Their comments indicate the kind of people the movement attracted and the style of their thoughts. The family were abolitionists, Washingtonian temperance advocates, lawyers and teachers by profession, students of phrenology, physiology, and anatomy, opponents of "sectarian" religion, and devout, though liberal, Episcopalians. DeWitt Throop, of Sherburne, entitled one two-hour lecture, "The destiny of Man + the means God has provided for raising man to his proper station." His brother, George, of Preston Corners, grew "stronger and stronger in the belief that if it is not the true system which God designed for the human species ... it is a great improvement on the present Isolated system." George delighted to see "such a man as G. Smith throw off the shakles [*sic*] + Expose ... the hypocrisy of the churches. ... I hate *Bigotry*. ... I want a faith the bow of whose promise embraces the children of every clime, country + tongue upon one Broad + general Basis of Philanthropy." Brother William, of East Hamilton, presided over the founding of a Hamilton Fourier

[11] Arthur E. Bestor, Jr., "American Phalanxes: A Study of Fourierist Socialism in the United States (with Special Reference to the Movement in Western New York)" (2 vols.; MS at Yale University, 1938), 25, 26, 30, 38, 46, 64, 68, 69, 85, and *passim*. This is a thorough and dependable study to which I am indebted more heavily than specific citations can suggest. George W. Noyes, ed., *John Humphrey Noyes, The Putney Community* (Oneida, 1931), 160; John H. Noyes, *History of American Socialisms* (Philadelphia, 1870), 268–272.

[12] Noyes, *Socialisms*, 268; see map, p. 300.

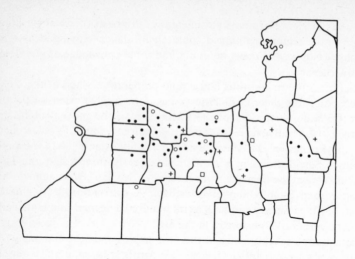

○   Phalanxes
□   Other communities
+   Villages with a convention or society
•   Villages exhibiting interest

Association in December, 1843. He reported a month later the abolition, Washingtonian, and Fourier meetings he attended, "all in one sense aiming at the same great center." "First make all *sober* then equal + the Philosophy of Fourier carried out will do the rest." A disagreement over the appraisal of the proposed site of the community set the Hamilton scheme at rest, but George took comfort that "in the hearts they have acknowledged the doctrine to be true . . . It is the grand and Angelic theme comeing [*sic*] down to suffering humanity. . . ."[13]

No community achieved actual establishment on the Fourierist plan in this central New York area, but that the doctrine appealed widely is witnessed by reports in 1847. Farther west and north, phalanxes had by this time risen and fallen, leaving a lingering disillusionment; but Cayuga, Onondaga, Oneida, Cortland, and Madison counties appeared to two New England itinerants to be a superb field for cultivation. The farmers of the vicinity listened eagerly, and antirenters and "national" reformers thereabouts would make powerful

[13] D. D. W. C. Throop, Sherburne, Aug. 7, 1843, to George, George A. Throop, Preston, Oct. 4, 1843, to DeWitt, William H. Throop, East Hamilton, Jan. 7, 1844, George, March 17, 1844, to DeWitt, George A. Throop Papers, Cornell Collection of Regional History.

allies. Here was "more wealth, refinement, freedom of thought, general intelligence ... , than among either our village or farming population in New England." Utica and Kings Ferry, on Cayuga Lake, had active associations, trembling on the verge of community-founding.[14]

But it was the earlier flush of enthusiasm about Rochester that yielded five of the six Fourierist colonies in upstate New York. All commenced in the spring of 1844, as did the sixth, near Watertown. The five lay in a wide circle about the city on the Genesee: Clarkson, a few miles west on the Lake Ontario shore; Mixville, about fifty miles up the river valley; Bloomfield, twenty miles to the southeast; Ontario, between Canandaigua and Manchester; and Sodus, on the lake shore, thirty miles east.

These western New York phalanxes, like the rest of the forty-odd of their type in the United States, had brief careers, wherein an early excess of fervor led to extreme disillusionment. By 1847 Rochester was the least receptive spot in the state for lecturers on association, and most of the area to the west was little less hostile. During their short history, however, the communities founded here demonstrated a certain similarity to the region's religious ventures, beyond their waxing and waning emotions. The American Industrial Union, a confederation of the six colonies in New York State, was the only effective co-ordinating organization to appear among all the communist projects of the period.[15] The Yankee Yorkers, fundamentalist or liberal, habitually formulated their plans in large, orderly designs, with mechanisms meant to function for all of society whenever it might be converted to the panacea of the moment.

All sorts and conditions of people seem to have joined the communal experiments. One of the chief reasons for the broader appeal of Fourierism, compared with Owenite communism in the twenties, was the lack in the later variety of any pronounced religious skepticism. Liberals in religion and urban residents no doubt led the movement. Universalists and Quakers probably participated more fully than the members of any other church, and capital to inaugurate the colonies probably came largely from an urban middle class. But a majority of the residents seems to have been farmers and laborers, and no class lines are featured in the literature of the movement. Many of the members had served apprenticeship in the religion-dominated reform movements of temperance, abolition, or perfectionism. Probably more of them entered the venture out of need than out of principle. Indeed, though the plans of the Burned-over District phalansteries were hastily drawn and certainly in some cases economically unsound, the more serious difficulty seems to have been the incompatibility of liberal and orthodox groups within

[14] *Harbinger* (New York and Boston), V (July 24, Sept. 18, Oct. 9, 16, 1847), 98, 235–240, 304.

[15] *Harbinger*, V (Oct. 23, 1847), 317; Bestor, "Phalanxes," 81; Noyes, *Socialisms*, 272–275.

the communities. At least, a schism in the Sodus colony over the question of Sabbath observance preceded and brought on its most pronounced economic difficulties.[16]

A seventh and independent colony in the region, located near Skaneateles, lasted three years and apparently had a degree of economic success. John A. Collins, formerly a Massachusetts Antislavery Society agent, was its prime mover. The experiment was nearer to the Owenite than the Fourierist type, with a prejudice against religion which the *Harbinger* considered its most serious error. With total community of goods, a "no-government, or non-resistance principle," and "the largest liberty . . . [and] the broadest principle of democratic equality," the venture nevertheless failed, because, according to its founder, its principles were "false in theory and pernicious in their practical tendencies. They might . . . do very well if men were angels, and angels Gods; but human nature is too low, too selfish and too ignorant for relations so exalted."[17]

Yet another community distinct from the phalanxes was planted near Buffalo in 1842 by the Amana Inspirationists from Germany. This one, like several other religious communisms of foreign sectarians, had a lengthy and successful history, though it removed to Iowa in 1854. But its foreign origin and separate development remove it from direct relationship with causes native to Burned-over District society.

Most famous of all early American socialisms was John Humphrey Noyes's Oneida Community. This, too, was primarily a religious enterprise, not to be confused with the Fourierist projects. Noyes acknowledged his indebtedness both to the Shakers and the Fourierists, but these examples only supplemented his original concept of primitive Christian communism. Oneida was remarkable both for the scale and perseverance of its economic success, and for its unique combination of religious, economic, and social beliefs. It deserves more extensive study than it has yet received, and far more than the proportions of this investigation allow. But its history must at least be sketched and its leading principles summarized in order to clarify its position among the other religious movements of the region. Indeed, it is veritably the keystone in the arch of Burned-over District history, demonstrating the connection between the enthusiasms of the right and those of the left.

Noyes's colony gathered at Putney, Vermont, in the early forties. A nucleus of his own family and several neighbors was swelled by persons like George and Mary Cragin who fled the licentiousness of the New York perfectionists. The group's religious services began in 1840, and three years later

[16] Bestor, "Phalanxes," 4–14, 49–53, 99, 109–111, 218–221; *Harbinger*, I (Sept. 27, 1845), 247, 254, II (Jan. 31, 1846), 126; *Western Luminary* (Rochester), IV (Nov. 29, 1845), 379.

[17] *Harbinger*, I (Sept. 27, 1845), 253; *Friends Weekly Intelligencer* (Philadelphia), III (Aug. 29, 1846), 172; *Communitist* (Skaneateles Community, Mottville), I, no. 25 (May 21, 1845).

a financial partnership commenced among four couples. The estates of John's father and his wife's grandfather, rather large for the times, fortunately made available in the same years nearly thirty thousand dollars and several properties. Other associates added smaller amounts to form a joint-stock company, superseding the partnership, in March, 1845. On November 6, 1846, the band adopted a set of principles for social union, declaring a total communism under God, through the lieutenancy of John Noyes. The Cragins and Noyes's at the same time joined in one family and three other couples composed a second home. These two households amalgamated the following spring.[18]

But staid Vermont could not tolerate complex marriage. Two sympathizers apparently turned renegade and advertised the communal proceedings in the village. In October, 1847, Noyes suffered arrest on charges of "adultery and *fornication.*" A month later he forfeited his bond and departed from his home state, leaving thirty-one adults and fourteen children to straggle after him into central New York. Meanwhile, the New York perfectionists, who for a decade had been looking increasingly to Noyes's leadership, had begun to prepare a refuge at Oneida.[19]

Both Noyes himself and George Cragin as his representative had made periodic tours in the more westerly region for several years, working to unify the various cults with similar notions. After several preliminary consultations, conventions met at Lairdsville, Oneida County, and Genoa, Cayuga County, in September, 1847. At the first meeting, Noyes laid bare the full extent of practice in marital communism at Putney and received a pledge of support from thirty-six New York State delegates. At the second, a committee was selected to plan a community here on the Putney model.

Jonathan Burt of Chittenango had recently undertaken purchase of a forty-acre timber lot and mill site in the newly opened Oneida Indian Reservation. Five families who had come together near Hamilton joined Burt, just as Noyes was fleeing Vermont. Another group had formed at Oneida Depot and now purchased adjacent land. Small colonies from Lairdsville and Syracuse followed suit. Thus about as many Yorkers as Vermonters participated in founding the new community. The first issue of the *Spiritual Magazine* at the new location recorded sixty-five members. By January 1, 1849, the number had risen to eighty-seven, and in another year it had doubled this figure.[20]

With a decade of thought and planning, several years of experience, and relatively abundant resources, Oneida Community was launched with

[18] Noyes, *Putney Community*, 46–74, 201, 205, 206; Pierrepont Noyes, *My Father's House, An Oneida Boyhood* (New York, 1937), 5.

[19] Noyes, *Putney Community*, 282, 283, 302, 393; Rev. Hubbard Eastman, *Noyesism Unveiled: A History of the Sect Self-Styled Perfectionists*, etc. (Brattleboro, Vt., 1849), 36.

[20] *Spirtual Magazine*, II (Aug. 5, 1848), 200; *First Annual Report of the Oneida Association*, etc. (Oneida Reserve, 1849), 1; *Second Report* (1850), 1.

steam already at full pressure and paddle wheels turning full speed ahead. The canny Yankee acumen of its founder augured well for its material prosperity, and good fortune conspired to bring as an early convert Sewall Newhouse, the inventor of the era's best small animal trap.

Perhaps because he had never concerned himself primarily with ideal economic conceptions, Noyes did not aim to accomplish any particular degree of self-sufficiency in the colony and never suffered from the agrarian emphasis of many Utopian socialists. Trap manufacturing brought prosperity and silver plate production continued it to modern times. No other American communism enjoyed such an economic success. Shakerism was self-destructive and had passed its peak. The Mormons had yet to reach theirs, but at no time did they make their United Order into a full communism. All the Owenite, Fourierist, and spiritualist colonies experienced sudden and early collapse. Several religious communities of European origin did succeed and persist on a small scale, by practically isolating themselves from American society, but none approached in prosperity or in significance the adventure of the perfectionists in central New York.

But economic matters were incidental to the original colony. Noyes stated the philosophy of the community in this fashion:

> Our warfare is an assertion of human rights; first the right of man to be governed by God and to live in the social state of heaven; second the right of woman to dispose of her sexual nature by attraction instead of by law and routine and to bear children only when she chooses; third, the right of all to diminish the labors and increase the advantages of life by association.[21]

The primary aim, then, was religious. Unlike Owen and Fourier, Noyes believed with the evangelists that personal sanctification must precede social regeneration. Or at least, as he came to modify his original position, the two must go on together.

The Oneida members thought of themselves as saints, purified by repeated, intense religious experiences and disciplined by a prolonged search for true righteousness. They were a Bible congregation, the only genuine descendants of the original primitive Christian church. Secure as they were in sinlessness, moreover, they had progressed beyond any need for literal adherence to Scripture. The letter of the Bible was a mere preliminary instruction for the unsaved and striving multitudes. Their standard of perfection, by contrast, was a progressive, not a fixed measure. They sought absolute fellowship between men and total love of God, but what kind of behavior met these tests in ideal fashion might change on an ascending scale as they grew in capacity and judgment. Sinless perfection did not mean the end of spiritual growth.

Had such flexible standards of ideal conduct remained open to the vagaries

[21] J. H. Noyes, Jan. 21, 1848, in Noyes, *Putney Community*, 368.

of individual interpretation, Oneida's history would indeed have been as brief as that of the secular communities, and of the other perfectionists beyond the Noyes group. But the colony emphasized its organization; and organization meant the unquestioned acceptance by all associates of John Noyes's discipleship to God.[22] The enterprise was, at least in theory, a thoroughly dictatorial theocracy. Yet it utilized democratic procedures, and no trustworthy source indicates any tyrannical action by the leader. Noyes must have been tactful and persuasive as well as firm and righteous. The extraordinary success of the community is almost exclusively attributable to the singularly large mold of its founder's character. He must surely be ranked as one of the geniuses of his generation.

Even saints secure from sin were not proof against the minor frictions which in other communities developed into great controversies. But Noyes solved this problem satisfactorily. A system of "mutual criticism" kept irritations at a minimum and renewed dedication to higher spirituality. Like the other distinctive practices of Oneida, this ritual began at Putney on a small scale, after lengthy preparation. The germ of the idea had come from Noyes's membership in the Brethren Society of Andover Seminary.

> Love for the truth and for one another had been nurtured and strengthened till it could bear any strain. We could receive criticism kindly and give it without fear of offending ... We had studied the Bible systematically for ten years, and were trying to express our conclusions in appropriate external forms.

Like the Catholic confessional, mutual criticism apparently utilized as a religious ordinance an inborn need for release from the conscience, placing upon a perpetual basis the satisfied feeling of redemption which orthodox Protestantism had to realize irregularly in periodic revivals. One member, who in the process "felt as though he were being dissected with a knife...," testified, "These things are all true, but they are gone, they are washed away."[23]

The perfectionist religion of Oneida, though it developed directly from the ultraism of the thirties, did not continue the emphasis upon reform movements which others derived from the same impulse. The conclusions of Noyes on this subject, as on many others, developed in the direction of antirevivalistic attitudes. He felt that temperance reformers were trying to enforce a non-Biblical morality. The abstinence pledge, furthermore, was an artificial device calculated to eliminate evil without piety, when the real sin was not alcohol but rather "a disease of the drunkard's heart." Temperance could be a problem in political economy, but not legitimately a religious

---

[22] J. H. Noyes, Nov. 11, 1847, to Mary J. [Noyes] Mead, Noyes, *Putney Community*, 298.
[23] From *Mutual Criticism* (1849, 1876), in Noyes, *Putney Community*, 100, 101.

question. The signing of the pledge, moreover, confirmed "the self-com-
placency that is natural to men who have reformed themselves." All the
reformers refused "to recognize the principle that every valuable form of
outward amelioration holds a secondary and dependent relation to Spiritual
Life."[24]

In many ways, Oneida Community developed a balanced philosophy which
co-ordinated the best elements from the diverse theories of social regeneration of liberals and ultraists. Viewing these opposite appproaches, Noyes
concluded:

> A millennium arranged in accordance only with either of the two . . . would
> be decidedly *simplistic* (to borrow a word from our friends of the Har-
> binger.) The great ideas of both must be *combined* in the right proportions,
> and in one living organization, before the Kingdom of Heaven can come.[25]

Persons perpetually sanctified, near to the heavenly state of being, could
scarcely be expected to share the physical and mental ills common to sinful
humanity. By implication, perfectionism demanded a belief in faith healing,
and Noyes was not the man to stop short of a logical absolute. Thus Putney and
Oneida folk provided a precedent for Christian Science.

As early as 1838, the *Witness* carried an article on victory over death.
Elaborate testimony was gathered at Putney to demonstrate that Noyes and
Mary Cragin saved one Harriet Hall, pronounced incurable by doctors, to live
thirty years longer at Oneida. An attempt to heal the tuberculosis of a young
woman, however, was a total failure, only to be explained by her own and
her neighbors' lack of faith. Repercussions of this episode contributed to the
hostility which produced the hegira from Vermont. In New York, George W.
Robinson testified to the cessation of his own multitudinous infirmities upon
his conversion in 1845, and Horace Burt, Jonathan's brother, removed from
an asylum at Worcester, Massachusetts, had his evil spirit conquered and
tamed by Noyes in 1849.[26]

Most interesting and distinctive of the Oneida practices, however, was the
sexual communism, instituted originally on religious grounds and perpetuated by social justifications. Like many of the other sexual experiments of the
period, complex marriage started because intensely spiritual people discovered an incompatibility between absolute good will among all regenerate
beings and the exclusive attachments of a man and woman physically and
legally bound together.

Noyes recognized the danger of perverted solutions of this problem. He
held himself aloof from the early perfectionist experiments in spiritual wifery

---

[24] *Spiritual Magazine*, I (April 15, 1846), 19, II (May 15, June 1, 1847), 9, 24–26.

[25] *Ibid.*, I (Jan. 15, 1847), 161–162.

[26] E. Douglas Branch, *The Sentimental Years, 1836–1860* (New York, 1934), 353; Noyes,
Putney Community, 63, 240–273; *Perfectionist* (Putney, Vt.), V (March 22, 1845), 4;
Spiritual Magazine, II (Oct. 15, 1849), 280–282.

and constantly warned of the consequent evils. He held the strayed sheep in abhorrence but apparently was ready to pardon upon evidence that one had been an innocent accomplice or had undergone a change of principle. George and Mary Cragin had had extensive experience in religious adultery but became pillars of the community. The Belchertown, Massachusetts, cult was by 1843 held in high repute by Noyes. A substantial number of once-errant central New Yorkers eventually became members of Oneida Community.

The difference between complex marriage at Oneida and the looseness Noyes disapproved may seem insignificant to the casual modern observer, but it was great in the eyes of the community. Complex marriage was "organized" instead of fortuituous: in other words, it came under Noyes's direct supervision. More important, it was inspired by "true spirituality." "Whoever meddles with the affairs of the inner sanctuary ... [otherwise motivated] will plunge himself into consuming fire."[27]

Total sanctification should precede freedom of association. This, at least, was the original belief. When no significant tokens appeared of the final physical resurrection among the saints which Noyes expected, he

> perceived for the first time that there was interaction between life and environment; that increased life tended to improve environment, and improved environment to increase life. He therefore announced his belief that Complex Marriage was one of the means by which the resurrection power would be let into the world.

He always maintained that "the Putney Community instead of causing the flood [of spiritual wifery] built the ark, and that it set about the work not a moment too soon."[28]

Noyes was an omnivorous student and inclined to experiment. Robert Dale Owen's *Moral Physiology* began his interest in birth control. This concern became an obsession when his wife lost four out of five babies through premature births in the first six years of their marriage. Lengthy thought and experiment recommended the practice of male continence as the basis of a unique practice of selective breeding, carried on at Oneida for at least twenty years.

> So long as the amative and propagative functions are confounded sexual communion carries with it physical consequences that take it out of the category of purely social acts ... But let the act of fellowship stand by itself and sexual communion differs only by its superior intensity and beauty from other acts of love. The self-control, retention of life and ascent out of sensuality that must result from making freedom of love a bounty on the chastening of physical indulgence will elevate the race to new vigor and nobility.

[27] From *Bible Communism*, in Noyes, *Putney Community*, 122.
[28] Noyes, *Putney Community*, 194–195.

> Male continence ... opens the way for scientific propagation. We are not opposed to procreation. ... But we are in favor of intelligent, well-ordered procreation. The time will come when scientific combination will be freely and successfully applied to human generation.[29]

The time Noyes spoke of may never come, but it is difficult to escape a degree of sympathy with his purposes. No one with an appreciation of the last century's advance in genetics and the merest concern over the present difficulties of an apparently perverse human race can consistently call the sexual experiments of the Oneida Community less than noble in aim. In this respect as in others, the Oneida beliefs demonstrated the way in which essentially rational attitudes could develop out of a background of revival religion. The tendency is only more sharply defined here than in the companion movements stemming from ultraism.

John Humphrey Noyes and his fellows concerned themselves only with their own perfection, not with making over the world about them. But this attitude did not betoken total indifference to the salvation of society in general. Like the Fourierists and the transcendentalists, they believed that the good example of the absolute ideal, however small its embodiment, would be the most persuasive propaganda. Once men knew the nature of righteousness, they could not but follow automatically. Noyes never doubted that the community was constantly "growing in confidence, and love, and assurance that God will give us the kingdom."

> What if there is not another bright spot in the wide world, and what if this is a very small one? Turn your eye toward it when you are tired of looking into chaos, and you will catch a glimpse of a better world.[30]

3 / Robert Dale Owen
A Plan for the Good Society

(1830)

Robert Dale Owen's diverse careers spanned much of the nineteenth century. Owen was an active figure in the New York City Working Men's movement early in the Jacksonian era, convinced that he possessed the panaceas certain to end not only the misery of the laboring classes but the unhappiness of the better sort as well. In this phase of his life, Owen was a pioneer advocate

[29] *Witness* (Ithaca, Putney, Vt.), 1 (Sept. 23, 1837), 22; Noyes, *Putney Community.* 114.

[30] J. H. Noyes to G. W. Robinson, in Noyes, *Putney Community,* 193.

Robert Dale Owen, "Wealth and Misery," *Working Man's Advocate* (New York), May 1, 8, and 15, 1830. The first edition of this tract was published by Owen in *The New Harmony Gazette,* November, December, 1826. As the text indicates, by 1830 he had significantly modified his original plan.

of birth control and state-controlled boarding schools, measures designed to enhance the material and moral situations of have-nots. As the following passage indicates, he also believed that society's economic institutions had to be transformed.

We are a prosperous nation. Riches are increasing in our hands. We possess the means, or we are rapidly acquiring them, to produce 40 times as much wealth as our ancestors did. But embarked as we are with all this abundant wealth in the ocean of commerce, whither is our course? The very gale of plenty that fills our sails is bearing us along the hidden shoals and engulfing breakers—England's vessel is aground amongst them already. If we would escape her fate, let us put about the helm while we may.

To speak without a metaphor—let us enquire what system of distribution adapted to the present state of science and commerce, may beneficially supersede the distribution of commerce.

It appears that we are wealthy; that, as a nation, we possess abundantly the means of continuing and increasing our wealth; and that the only real difficulty before us in our progress to permanent affluence is removed, so soon as the problem is solved: how to distribute wealth in such a manner, that the surplus produce of our producer may always procure him a just share of the surplus of his neighbors.

Let us see whether we shall derive, in the solution of this great problem, any assistance from considering the effects produced in a large family, acting on the second plan we supposed possible (namely, the *federative* system), by a gradual increase of productive power.

This system presupposes a common stock into which each producer puts the articles of wealth he creates, so soon as they are created, and from which he draws articles of necessity and comfort, as he requires them. So long, therefore, as this general magazine is kept fully supplied, there *can* be no want or distress among the producers.

Now there might possibly have been some difficulty in obtaining supplies during a period of comparative adversity; that is, while production was difficult, and the demand was, therefore, beyond the supply. But in a period of *prosperity*, that is, when the world's powers of production are increasing to forty-fold, at least, what they were formerly, there can be no possible difficulty in supplying most abundantly the family storehouse; seeing that one-fortieth part of the labor our ancestors must have expended to obtain this object, will suffice in our days. It appears, then, at first sight, that the *federative* system of distribution is excellently adapted to a family producing all the articles of wealth and abundance.

We have traced the results produced by the introduction of scientific power in aid of a family whose produce was distributed under the commercial system. Let us examine what effects follow this same gradual increase of power under the *federative* system.

The first effect is to overstock the commercial storehouse. Well, no one need starve surely on that account; on the contrary, there is an opportunity of increasing the supply of comforts to each producer, if such increase be desired, or to lay up an extra stock in case of the failure of crops and other unforeseen accidents; or to exchange the useless surplus for foreign articles of wealth, if the family desire them. It is true that men cannot use more than a certain quantity of wealth, domestic and foreign, with benefit to themselves, nor accumulate beyond a certain quantity of produce with advantage, or indeed, with any possibility of preserving it from decay: and therefore it must be admitted that without any additional exertion on the part of the family, the increase of mechanical power would at last fairly oversupply their ware- houses, so that they know not what to do with so abundant a surplus, as in England at present. And what then? Why, the remedy for this mighty evil is self-evident, and most easy and pleasant of practice, a remedy to which no one probably will object. *Let the family relax its exertions and shorten its hours of labor.* This is the only natural result produced by superabundance.

Can such a remedy be applied under the individual commercial system? Evidently not: each man must push on to increase his production, regardless of the consequences to society, or else competition will leave him behind to starve.

Now, scientific power must continue and must increase: to desire that it should not, would be to wish for a gradual sinking back into ignorance and barbarism. The supply must continue to exceed the demand: to desire that it should not, would be to wish for a relapse into adversity and indigence.

But if productive power must increase, and the supply must exceed the demand, *then the world must sooner or later, adopt some system of distribution, that, like the federative system, can bear abundance and prosperity.* At present, the greatest misfortune that can befall a commercial nation, is to attain wealth and plenty.

The United States are rapidly approaching to both. "And yet at the present moment," it will be said, "we are truly prosperous. Our condition resembles not that of Britain: no one need starve here who deserves to be industrious. Our present situation, therefore, is proof of the benefits *we* derive from commerce."

True: but, is it possible that our present resources should remain station- ary? No, nor do we desire it: they will increase, and fortunately so. What then? We shall soon rival Great Britain in all her production. And then? Then we shall be able to supply all our own wants, and become perfectly in- dependent, if we choose to be so, of all foreign supplies. —And afterwards? —Afterwards we may proceed to supply other nations, and spread the pro- duction of our country over all the civilized world. What then? — Must we stop here? Is there no analogy to light our steps further into futurity? There is: Britain has passed on before us, and already obtained what we anticipate. She has oversupplied herself and all her neighbors, and sent the produce of her industry to the furthest countries on the globe. And what then? She has become a national Tantalus, tormented by the display of abundance she may not use and expiring beside streams of plenty she cannot enjoy.

If a fate like this be our object, let us proceed in our present course. We have all the advantages Great Britain ever had, and many more too: we have a liberal government, light taxes, security at home, increasing markets abroad—everything in our favor; and we shall soon attain this envied situation—then to reflect that we have been toiling in vain—and to discover that the same commerce which *once* raised us from indigence and adversity, now ruins us in prosperity and amidst abundance.

[The following passages were added by Owen in May, 1830.]

The foregoing articles were written more than three years ago. Three years' experience has only strengthened my conviction, that the present competitive commercial system cannot go on, without a continual increase to national distress; but that experience has also somewhat shaken my faith in the practicability of introducing the community system among the adults of the present generation.

I see as clearly as I saw three years ago, that some great change must be made: I see even more clearly than I did then, that this country is every year, sinking deeper and deeper in the miseries which commerce extracts from our production. I see that the present commercial system will not bear prosperity; that, while it lasts, industry actually works to its own destruction, by producing until its abundant product deprives it of employment. I see that the numerous modern powers of production *might be* a blessing, and that they *are* a curse. I see that machinery, instead of aiding the laborer, is brought into the market against him; and that it thus reduces his wages and injures his situation.

I see also that the cooperative system of labor, according to which each man works to supply a common storehouse, instead of working to supply a capricious market, is an effectual remedy for all this. I see that in a community of united labor and expenditure, an overstocked market would be a real blessing, and every mechanical improvement a positive gain to the whole.

But I do *not* see, as I once thought I did, that men, in their present habits and education, are sufficiently disinterested in motive, sufficiently social in feeling, and sufficiently accommodating in disposition, to unite harmoniously as equal members of a common society, whence individual interest is banished. I do not see that the public good is a sufficiently powerful motive to replace, in ill-trained minds, the spur of individual competition. I do not see that antisocial habits can be suddenly laid aside by a body of adults, in whom they have grown with their growth and strengthened with their strength. I wish I could see and believe all this, for then I should perceive how the present state of things might be immediately and most essentially improved; but I do not.

All that, three years ago, I anticipated regarding the commercial depression of the country has been realized. The same causes which ground England's laborers to the dust, have already produced similar effects here: not indeed to the same extent, because we have freer institutions and lighter taxes; but still of the same character, and continually increasing, as in Great Britain, with the same causes which first produced them.

I may be asked why I trouble the public with an explanation of the cause, since I can propose no practicable remedy, for present evils. I reply, that the first step towards curing a disease, is to understand its nature. He who shows distinctly wherein an evil consists, has not, indeed, done all, but has done something. He has probed the wound, though he has not prescribed its treatment.

I have become very diffident in dictating specific remedies for the evils I see around me. It is so much easier to expose what is wrong, than to discuss what is right—to detect an abuse, than to remove it. In curing one evil, we sometimes create a greater, and in seeking to avoid one extreme, fall into its opposite.

Still, unless remedies are offered, examined, discussed, how shall improvement ever take place. I suggest, therefore, for consideration, the following.

Is it not practicable to form a community not on the principle of common property, but of labor for equal labor? Might not each member, without giving up his individual property or private rights, furnish to the common stock, in the produce of his particular trade, as much as he drew from it? And would not such a plan give each member the advantage of co-operative union, without depriving him of the competitive incitements to individual industry?

If each member drew from the community storehouse as much only as he placed there, no one could live in idleness on the public stock; and if in proportion to each man's industry were his receipts, his selfish interest would prompt him to industry as at present. While, there being a ready mode of exchanging his particular handiwork for the various articles of necessity, the evils of an overstocked market would be effectually avoided.

Some such modification may succeed; and some such modification is, I am convinced, necessary. Without it, each member is continually wondering whether his neighbor does as much as he; and then there is great temptation for each to act as a spy on the other's conduct. Such a state of things too often produces jealousies and heart burnings, and ever a sort of social slavery. For though there be no legislator so just and mild, and at the same time so powerful, as *enlightened* public opinion, there is none so overbearing and tyrannical as *ignorant* public opinion; nor any to which, a man of spirit and feeling will less willingly submit.

In conclusion, I would suggest to every man who wishes well to his race, the propriety of giving this subject a minute and attentive examination.

4 / Stephen Simpson
Educational Reform

(1831)

Stephen Simpson, a leader and political candidate of the Philadelphia Working Men's party, was widely known for his critical treatise on capitalistic society, *The Working Man's Manual*. Unlike his New York counterparts—the triumvirate of Robert Dale Owen and the "agrarians," George Henry Evans and Thomas Skidmore—Simpson offered no elaborate blueprint for the Good Society. As critical of the prevailing social and economic system as were his colleagues, he focused on the *means* necessary for drastic change and found them in education. Like others in the labor movement, he anticipated from educational reform social benefits not dreamed of by such men as the conservative political economist, Thomas Cooper, or the liberal reformer, Horace Mann.

In relation to the productive faculties of a nation, popular education assumes an importance, not suspected even by its best friends. By implanting the principles of science in the mass of intellect, *invention* is provided with materials for the production of improvements, that may change the whole face of society into one radiant smile of content and enjoyment. The invention of *machinery* is the fruit of an educated age, and the more we diffuse that education, the more we advance the arts and sciences, manufactures and agriculture, to perfection. Not one seed of knowledge dropped into the common mind is lost. On some occasion it will germinate to a profit, and recompense society ten fold for the gift; nor do I mean a mere intellectual reward, but a substantial one of labour, of an increase of the means of sustaining and enjoying life, at the least expenditure of time and toil.

Ignorance and inferiority of mind are the only causes of human degradation; except that of poverty, which is the general concomitant of ignorance—as ignorance is its invariable cause. In the progress of nations, civilized people are generally found to vanquish barbarians, either by the force of superior skill, or the charms of science, literature, and knowledge. Nations, like individuals, hold one another in contempt, or look up with respect and admiration, as they rise or fall in the scale of intelligence and wisdom, refinement and civilization. It is only, however, when we come to scrutinize more closely the elements of a single nation, that we can obtain

Stephen Simpson, *The Working Man's Manual, A New Theory of Political Economy on the Principles of Production the Source of Wealth* ... (Philadelphia, 1831).

an accurate and full perception of the debasing effects of ignorance. This becomes obvious, the moment we penetrate into the manners, and non-intercourse of different classes of society, which we may distinguish into the ignorant, or the enlightened. Between these two classes, one of whom labours, and the other remains in idleness, there exists so great a separation in all the social duties and associations, as almost to constitute them different species. The enlightened and educated look down upon the ignorant as a debased order of beings, and treat them, as matter of course, with contempt; and the ignorant on their part, look up to the refined with a sensation approaching to hatred. It is found, that where vigorous intellect bursts the bonds of its ignorance, in this contemned class, that it is immediately merged into the higher and cultivated class; and, notwithstanding the stigma of labour, comes at length to excite respect. Thus the proof is afforded that it is the *ignorance*, not the *occupation* of the working people, that degrades them on the one hand, and empoverishes them on the other. Owing to this ignorance and degradation, it is, that the educated and enlightened, taking advantage of their contemned condition, have oppressed and bound them in the fetters of servile sub-jection. It is not ignorance that can make laws, organize governments, or administer justice. Education, therefore, is the key to government—it opens the path of power. In vain will you boast of equal rights, and a form of government that secures power to the most humble, when qualified for the task; the blessing will only be nominal whilst the *mass of people* remain ignorant, and incapable of performing those functions that belong to the great civil machine of society. The educated will still occupy the high posts of honour, and devise the system of law and justice; and law and justice thus devised will forever partake of the sentiments peculiar to wisdom and re-finement. Hence the maxim that "those who think must govern those who toil;" a maxim, however, that is predicated on the *ignorance* of those who toil, as a necessary property of their condition. But educate those who toil—teach them *to think*; and they take the place of those who govern. This has been strenuously opposed by the great body of the enlightened, because they were fearful of losing their *exclusive privileges*, by imparting knowledge to the mass of the people.

A system of *general education*, one would hardly imagine, could meet with an opponent in an age so enlightened and so philanthropic—an age so distinguished for the *march of mind*, the diffusion of knowledge, and a severe scrutiny into all the principles that combine in the structure of society. And yet, wonderful to say, *public education for the people* has met with gothic adversaries, and illiberal, narrow-minded traducers. The extension of the lights of knowledge, *by popular education*, to all the people of the republic, has ever been the avowed object of all of our most illustrious statesmen. It teems from the lips of the venerated Washington—it glows in the pen of the immortal Jefferson—it formed the daily toil and the midnight study of the lamented and great Clinton. The text of the friends of liberty was—*to enlighten the people is to promote and cement the public virtue!* The soundness of this text was never questioned *anterior* to the organization of a party, whose object it was to obtain it from the legislature, *as a right*, unjustly withheld. When public instruction was bestowed as the *boon of charity*, it found numerous advocates, and met with no opponents; but now, when we justly demand it as a *right*—and under our constitution it must be a *right* and not a charity—it is not only refused by some, but to our utter amazement, its consequences are painted as baneful to the people, and deprecated as having a fatal tendency upon the good order of government! We seem to have resuscitated from the tomb of time the very spirit of the *feudal ages*, in the breasts of certain bigots, intolerants, aristocrats, and narrowminded *monopolists of knowledge*, who seem as averse to giving the people LIGHT, as they are to paying them for their labour in *hard money*. Actuated by this spirit of an era long past, it is pretended to have been suddenly discovered that *ignorance* is necessary to obedience, and that *public education* is incompatible with public virtue and public order! Sophistry like this is too flimsy to call for confutation; but it reveals a fact that may be useful to us: that although we live under a free constitution, much of the leaven of despotism still remains among us, and that our *theoretical* freedom demands eternal vigilance to preserve it in practice. It is said, that a tax to support common schools would be an *Agrarian Law*, an unjust taking away from the wealth of the rich, for the benefit of the common people. On this principle ALL laws are Agrarian laws; for the rich pay more than the poor individually though not collectively, for the support of government.

Objections to popular education, however, at the present day, come too late to command attention, or require arguments to show their fallacy. The age has happily outrun those who would keep it stationary in ignorance, or arrest its progress towards general knowledge. The cloud of absolute power in governments has passed away from the firmament of the mind; and left it clear and unspecked by one of the fetters of passive submission, non-resistance, and blind credulity. In time long past, the sovereign power was in the king—now it is in the people; positions being thus reversed, it is incumbent on the people to conform their knowledge to their power.

The influence of education on the manners, is not less important than its operation on the mind; between which there exists so close an intimacy— so powerful a sympathy. Civility, politeness, deference, and all the amiable and softer virtues, are generally found to be residents of minds refined and educated; while ignorance assumes manners of corresponding rudeness, and imperious insolence. As it is the tendency of knowledge to inspire diffidence, the more the mind imbibes, the less it presumes to trespass upon the feelings or challenge the opinions of others. Besides that, in educated people there exists a natural assimilation, the general result of which is good breeding; hence one of the most salutary consequences of popular instruction—that those who labour, and have heretofore been rude and insolent, will gradually become polite and civil; and thus remove one of the most serious difficulties that prevents the working people emerging from that debasing condition in which they are now held by the customs of intellect and power. It is to *education*, therefore, that we must mainly look for a redress of that perverted system of society, which dooms the producer to ignorance, to toil, and to penury,[1] to moral degradation, physical want, and social barbarism.

The power of the ballot boxes will do little, without the auxiliary help of our moral and intellectual energies. How can it be a marvel, that wealth practises oppression, when it holds as its allies, all the riches of knowledge, and the exterior semblances of virtue and truth? Moving in the high orbit of science, government and laws; ordaining justice and morality after their own images, how shall we ever counteract the principles of vassalage that now prevail, unless we procure EDUCATION for our offspring, and diffuse SCIENCE among our brethren? It is through this door that we must at last enter into the temple of justice, to consecrate on the altar of reason the true rights of man. Knowledge is *power*, in respect to the procurement of equity to the great mass of the sons of labour. It is the light of intelligence that abashes despotism—it is the fire of intellect that dissolves and melts the chains that enthral seven eighths of mankind to the caprice and luxury of the other few. "*In what way shall this evil be attacked and removed?*" I have answered, by giving our children equal or superior knowledge, virtue and intelligence, to the rich—by EDUCATION to direct and qualify us for government and laws; and by concentrating our SUFFRAGE to enable us to reach that point of influence, at which we shall be able to make the laws conform to the spirit of justice, and the government congenial to the equality of human rights.

---

[1] A great writer observes—"According to ancient practice, *all checks were on the inferior*, to restrain him to the duty of submission; none on the superior, to engage him to the reciprocal duties of gentleness and humanity. In modern times, a bad servant finds not easily a good master, nor a bad master a good servant; and the checks are mutual, *suitably to the inviolable and eternal laws of reason and equity*." The principle admitted in the last sentence, is the pith of this quotation; and this principle it is, that we desire to extend, by the diffusion of education. The ancient practice is still too prevalent; not-withstanding theories of freedom which denounce and supersede it. The checks *ought* to be mutual, but they are not; and where *rights are equal*, the failure becomes an oppression. It is EDUCATION only that can bring this theory of *reciprocal checks* into practice.

5 / Edward Pessen
The Social Blueprint of Secular Perfectionism

(1967)

During the Jacksonian era, leaders of the Working Men's parties and the trade union movement embraced a comprehensive social viewpoint that for all of its inevitable diversity was remarkably homogeneous. The following reading is a discussion of the means and ends favored by these dissenters. They were convinced that the happy appearance of American society only masked a grim reality whose inequity and injustice differed in degree, not kind, from the cruel class society believed to prevail both in England and on the Continent. As the discussion indicates, their ideas were hardly models of internal consistency.

Every leader of the Jacksonian labor movement had a vision of the good society that, were it up to him, would replace or, at the least, drastically modify American society's existing arrangements. Although a few of them were relatively laconic on the matter, perhaps because their glimpse of utopia had been a fleeting one, most of the leaders were quite explicit, and in a few cases downright effusive. If their goals cover a wide spectrum of possibilities, it is also true that for all the seeming divergence of their views, there was much greater agreement in their thinking than even they were aware of. Their consensus tended toward what we today should call a socialist society.

No one of them used the term socialism. Perhaps the radical intellectuals who transformed American social thought early in the twentieth century, with their careful attempt to refrain from using Socialist or Marxist terminology (thus, "personalty" instead of "bourgeoisie"), were not the first to operate on the evident assumption that if the American people might be responsive to radical substantive proposals, it was politic to coin new terms for them. Of course, men so uncompromising as Thomas Skidmore or John Commerford were probably neither intimidated nor trying to be politic in not using a term which, as a matter of fact, was well known and even popular in England and on parts of the Continent.[1] But whether they used the phrase or not, the leaders' expressed hopes were for a society that in most particulars met that era's definition of socialism.

[1] Max Beer, *A History of British Socialism* (2 vols.; London, 1948), I, 102.

The present is by no means unique in ascribing many, sometimes conflicting, meanings to socialism. For since the term achieved popularity early
in the nineteenth century, it has at one time or another been identified with
programs which strive for economic freedom and social solidarity; abolition
of profit; a planned society; common property; realization of natural law;
the total product of society to labor; distribution in accordance with the
quantity and quality of work performed by the individual; individual liberty;
community or democratic management of land and capital; achievement of
religious ideals; the welding together of the worker and society; emancipation
of the proletariat; or combinations of the above.[2] Nor is that all. In view of its
chameleon qualities, there is wisdom in R. H. Tawney's reminder that
"socialism is a word the connotation of which varies not only from generation
to generation, but from decade to decade"; and in Thomas Kirkup's
admonition that "above all things, it is essential to remember that socialism
is not a stereotyped system of dogma. It is . . . living and liable to change."[3]
The common feature of the labor leaders' socialism was its stress on labor.

The solid rock on which their idea of the good society rested was their
belief that labor created all wealth. Those who are familiar with the history
of social thought will know that the idea was not unique with them, even
for the American scene. The fact is, of course, that the idea goes back to
antiquity, was held by the founders of classical economics and our own
Benjamin Franklin, and in their own time had been eloquently expressed
in Shelley's *Song to the Men of England*, which wrote of the workers:

> The seed ye sow, another reaps;
> The wealth ye find, another keeps;
> The robes ye weave, another wears;
> The arms ye forge, another bears.[4]

[2] *Ibid.*; John Strachey, *Theory and Practice of Socialism* (New York, 1936), pp. 115–
117, 119; J. Ramsay MacDonald, *The Socialist Movement* (London, 1911), p. xi;
Harry W. Laidler, *A History of Socialist Thought* (New York, 1927); John H. Noyes,
History of American Socialisms (Philadelphia, 1870); Morris Hillquit, *History of Socialism in the United States* (New York, 1910); Ira Kipnis. *The American Socialist Movement
1897–1912* (New York, 1952), pp. 315, 421; David A. Shannon, *The Socialist Party
of America: A History* (New York, 1955), chap. iii, p. 258; Howard Quint. *The Forging
of American Socialism*, 1953; C. K. Ensor, ed., *Modern Socialism* (London, 1904), p. xvii;
Werner Sombart, *Socialism and the Social Movement* (London, 1909), chap. i; Thomas
Kirkup, *A History of Socialism* (London, 1920), pp. 1, 8; William H. Dawson, *German
Socialism and Ferdinand La Salle* (New York, 1899), p. 3; Reinhold Niebuhr, *Moral Man
and Immoral Society* (New York, 1936); Oscar Jaszi, "Socialism," *Encyclopaedia of Social
Sciences*.

[3] R. H. Tawney, Intro. to Beer, *A History of British Socialism*, p. vii; and Kirkup,
op. cit., p. 2.

[4] Thomas Hutchinson, ed., *The Complete Works of Percy Bysshe Shelley* (London, 1948),
I, 572–573.

As was so often true of any discussion of labor, the leaders were not always precise in defining just what and whom they meant by the term. Most of them, however, meant by labor those who worked with their hands for wages. Skidmore noted that properties willed to an individual were of no value unless they "enable their possessor to live off the labor of others." Evans defined labor as

> those who do the work and fight the battles; who produce the necessaries and comforts of life; who till the earth or dig for its treasures; who build the houses and the ships; who make the clothes, the books, the machinery, the clocks and watches, the musical instruments, and the thousands of things which are necessary to enable men to live and be happy.

Only Simpson, Fisk and, inevitably, English attempted to match this blaze of rhetoric.

Simpson is remindful of Evans when he writes that workers "produce all the wealth of society without sharing a thousandth part of it; . . . they do all the work . . . fight all our battles . . . cause all our enjoyments to flow upon us . . . Without labor there can be no property," and when he concludes that "all capital is . . . produced by the working men of a nation."

Not to be outdone, Fisk asks the workers:

> Who builds their [the rich] marble palaces, who covers their tables with the most costly luxuries . . . ? Who enables them to give their sumptuous entertainments, to roll through the streets in their splendid equipages, to spend hundreds and thousands upon fopperies and gee gaws . . . ? Who does all this? You! Your labor, your toil, your industry, alone produces wealth.

English's passage on the subject, if more brief, was as purple. He asks a labor audience: "Are they [the rich] not provided by our labour with beds of down, with costly furniture . . . ? Do they not live and move; riot and dissipate upon the proceeds of our industry?"

Most of the others were more prosaic, confining themselves to such statements as Commerford's observation that the worker was the "real producer of all the wealth and luxury possessed by the rich and powerful."[5]

[5] Thomas Skidmore, *The Rights of Man to Property* (New York, 1829), pp. 154, 226–227, 239; Skidmore, *Moral Physiology Exposed and Refuted* (New York, 1831), p. 35; *Working Man's Advocate*, Oct. 31, 1829, April 3, and May 1, 15, 1830; *The Man*, Feb. 18, and June 28, 1834; Stephen Simpson, *The Working Man's Manual* (Philadelphia, 1831), pp. 43, 23, 29, 53–55, 64; Theophilus Fisk, *Capital Against Labor* (cited in *Working Man's Advocate*, July 25, 1835); Fisk, *The Banking Bubble Burst* (Charleston, 1837), pp. 3, 25, 30; William English, "Oration Delivered at the Trades' Union Celebration of the 4th of July," *Radical Reformer and Working Man's Advocate*, Sept. 1, 1835, p. 125; John Commerford, "Address Delivered Before the General Trades' Union of New York," in *Working Man's Advocate*, Sept. 19, 1835; the *Union*, April 21, 1836; *Free Enquirer*, Jan. 16, and Feb. 13, 1830; *Daily Sentinel*,

And as their image of American society made clear, they also shared Commerford's view that the working class, "from whose labor spring the articles of exchange, can scarcely obtain sufficient wherewith to make [their] ... families comfortable." Clearly, a better society was needed.

Eloquent or perhaps grandiloquent a number of them were but most of the leaders were not, nor did they claim to be, theorists. For the most part their image of the good society emerges from sparse references, generally made not in the course of developing a model of their final goals, as such, but rather as they dealt with some specific problem. A small number of them, however, were nothing if not theorists. Of these, the man who had the most to say as to the shape society should assume in the future, was—as might be guessed—Thomas Skidmore. And by all odds, the man whose projection of the future was most savagely attacked—by his colleagues within the labor movement as much as by conservative publishers outside it—was the same Thomas Skidmore.

His co-workers fell on his plan, denouncing it for a variety of reasons that included its alleged ineffectiveness, its injustice, its partial tendency, its malicious falseness, and the ease with which it could be used to slander the entire movement.[6] The impression I get is that what really stung them in Skidmore's plan was not so much the blueprint of society it offered—in fact, hardly that at all—but the fact that it actually called for confiscation, to be put into effect immediately. That it was to be put into effect peaceably only if the majority approved did not mollify Skidmore's frightened colleagues. There seems little question, too, that some of them were much more concerned with conservative critics' hostile reaction to Skidmore's program than with any intrinsic deficiencies in it.

Skidmore's program took the form of a plan divided into twenty sections. Its central purpose is clearly indicated in the first section:

> Let a new State Convention be assembled. Let it prepare a new Constitution, and let that Constitution, after having been adopted by the people, decree an abolition of all debts; both at home and abroad, between citizen

---

April 8, 9, 10, 12, 13, 14, 1830; Seth Luther, *An Address on the Origins and Progress of Avarice* (Boston, 1834), pp. 3, 6, 10, 12, 40; Luther, *Address to the Working Men of New England* (3rd ed.; Philadelphia, 1836), p. 25; Charles Douglas, in the *New England Artisan*, May 31, and June 21, 1834; *Radical Reformer*, July 4, 11, 1835; *New Era*, June 9, 1840; "Report of the Resolutions Committee to the First Convention of the National Trades' Union," in *The Man*, Aug. 29, 1834; Ely Moore, *Address Delivered Before the General Trades' Union of the City of New York* (New York, Dec. 2, 1833), p. 20.

[6] See the *Free Enquirer*, Oct. 31, and Nov. 7, 14, 28, 1829; also Oct. 16, 1830. See *Working Man's Advocate*, Jan. 16, 1830; Nov. 14, and Dec. 15, 1829; Aug. 11, 1832; May 8, 1830. See the *Radical*, April, 1841, p. 52; April, 1843, pp. 51–52. Simpson, *The Working Man's Manual*, pp. 27–28, 89, 137–138, 230; Luther, *Origins and Progress of Avarice*, p. 40; English, "Oration Delivered at the Trades' Union Celebration," p. 125; Ely Moore, *Speech in Reply to the Hon. Waddy Thompson*, given in the House of Representatives, May 5, 1836 (Washington, 1836), p. 5.

and foreigner. Let it renounce all property belonging to our citizens, without the State. Let it claim all property within the State, both real and personal, of whatever kind it may be, with the exception of that belonging to resident aliens, and with the further exception of so much personal property, as may be, in the possession of transient owners, not being citizens. Let it order an equal division of all this property among the citizens, of and over the age of maturity in manner yet to be directed. Let it order all transfers or removals of property, except so much as may belong to transient owners, to cease, until the division is accomplished.

The other nineteen sections were essentially concerned with means of implementation.[7]

Disingenuous in the extreme, not the least for its assumptions that a state convention might convene to do the things Skidmore wanted them to do, essentially on his say-so, or that the public, for all its economic and emotional diversity, was some kind of monolith that could not help but respond to his logic, the plan seemed to infuriate its many critics. One suspects they were overwrought.

Many years later, Henry George, who agreed with Skidmore that "to extirpate poverty, to make wages what justice commands they should be, the full earnings of the laborer, we must therefore substitute for the individual ownership of land a common ownership," profited from the lesson taught by the harsh reaction to Skidmore's call for immediate confiscation. While he, too, believed, "we must make land common property," George proposed the method of confiscation of rent rather than of land, since in his words, "great changes can best be brought about under old forms." He hoped to accomplish the same social result as would follow confiscation of wealth but by subtler methods.[8] Skidmore's own contemporaries in the American labor movement were similarly averse to anything resembling confiscation.

---

[7] The plan called for a census of persons and wealth; arrangement for public sale; equitable division of parcels; distribution to all of equal purchasing power; joint bids on large parcels; punishment to those who withheld information respecting their property; guardianship of the property of drunkards and the insane; distribution of the property of those who die during the transaction; annual dividends; the inclusion of residents who were citizens of states organized the same way as New York, for the purpose of sharing in the benefits; public education of all native-born persons; joint disposal of property of deceased husband or wife by the widow(er) and the state; imprisonment of those giving away property (since charity is provided for); the freedom of persons to leave the state; and the guarding of property against foreign competition. Skidmore was so eager to end foreign trade that he cheerfully consented to "let the navy go down forever." Prosperity depended only on the home market. The expropriation was also to be directed against church properties, drawn as they were "from the iniquitous system which has robbed man of his rights forever." (*Rights of Man to Property*, pp. 137–144, 273–283, 342.)

[8] Henry George, *Progress and Poverty*, Modern Library Edition (New York, 1939), p. 328. In view of George's clearcut position, it is hard to understand the statement of his interpreter that George did not favor common ownership in land (George R. Geiger, *The Philosophy of Henry George* [New York, 1933], pp. 130–131).

Without always revealing precisely how it was to be achieved, a number of the leaders looked forward to a society whose material needs would be handled through the mechanism of a common storehouse of goods. Distribution would be based on the principle that was to become a socialist maxim: "From each according to his ability, to each according to his deeds." According to Robert Dale Owen, this ideal state of things would one day replace "individual commercial competition." But first the prevailing marriage and family system, both a consequence and a cause of selfish acquisition, would have to be replaced by a more socially desirable method for uniting the sexes. That there was a transition in Owen's thought is revealed by the two editions of his essay "Wealth and Misery." When first published in 1826, Owen's plan—the "federative system"—called for a common stock into which "each producer puts the articles of wealth he creates, as soon as they are created; and from which he draws articles of necessity and comfort, *as he requires them.*" (Italics mine.) The plan's underlying principle of distribution was to each according to his needs. By the time he had become a leader of the New York Working Men, Owen's scheme—now described as a "common storehouse"—would reward the individual only in proportion to his contribution in labor to its common stock, since without "some such modification . . ., each member is continually wondering whether his neighbor does as much as he; and thus there is a great temptation for each to act as a spy on the other's conduct." The beauty of this change was that it continued to give each member the advantages of "co-operative union," "without depriving him of the competitive incitements to individual industry." Other practical features of Owen's plan were its respect for "individual property or private rights," and its promise to avoid "the evils of an overstocked market."[9] Owen took no steps to put this plan into action, nor did he ever take up the question of how his program based on "competitive incitements" would manage to avoid the pitfalls of the wicked system of "individual commercial competition."

Evans' ideas, always influenced by Owen, also underwent transition. At first he favors producers' co-operatives, as a temporary remedy at the least, in which for only four hours daily labor the workingman would earn far more than he now did in fourteen. By the time he came to publish *The Man*, in 1834, he had been won over to the idea of a common stock, which rewarded labor and others solely according to how much they had contributed to it. "Such," he wrote, "*should* be the state of things, . . . and now . . . is the time to decide whether such shall be." In addition to the cooperative system of production, he also now began to advocate free land as the other solution to mankind's problems.

[9] Robert Dale Owen, "Wealth and Misery," serially in New Harmony *Gazette*, Nov. 8 through Dec. 13, 1826, and also in *Working Man's Advocate*, May 1, 8, 15, 1830; Owen, *Lectures on the Marriages of the Priesthood of the Old Immoral World* (London, 1835), pp. 32, 36, 47, 71–72; *Free Enquirer*, Feb. 13, 1830.

The basic ideas of George Henry Evans, influential land reformer of the 1840s and 1850s, are anticipated in his writing in the 1830s, when he was active in the labor movement. Evans' mounting enthusiasm for free public lands begins to be registered during the latter period. Where in 1833 he is a mild advocate of the safety-valve theory, by the following year he writes that "three-fourths, we verily believe, of all the vice and misery existing in the United States might be eradicated by the just and practicable measure of allowing every necessitous individual to cultivate [without charge] a portion of the uncultivated land." By 1835 Evans is convinced that free public land is the panacea, besides which such a device as trade unionism, for example, pales into insignificance, whether as a temporary or lasting, partial or complete, remedy. Unlike Skidmore, however, Evans seeks no immediate redistribution; private ownership of land, evil though it is, is to be left undisturbed. The free distribution of uncultivated public land will work invincibly to overcome in the future the negative tendencies of the present system. Obviously, the main factor that accounted for the relative popularity and later success of Evans' "new agrarianism," was that, unlike the old, or Skidmore, agrarianism, it did not disturb present title to property.[10]

Other admirers of the common-storehouse plan were Douglas, Ferral, and to an extent, Slamm. Douglas thought that it was "in accordance with the laws of nature and the immutable principles of right and justice" that there be a society "based upon labor, where everyone shall receive for himself the products of his own industry." Ferral asked American workers to support a system based on cooperative production, pooled savings, and a common store of all products, under which "moral justice would exact from every individual, when not incapacitated by natural imbecility or accident, a fair and full equivalent to society for that which he consumes, and also that he should contribute his due portion of labor towards the contingencies of society, for the protection and security he derives therefrom." Slamm expressed a dislike for panaceas, registering his unhappiness at the alleged tendency of Fourier's doctrine to foster free love, while it choked off scientific and artistic progress. He did, however, think that utopian projects were useful in small communities, and that the ideas of Robert Owen and like reformers, far from being offensive, "deserved every consideration."[11] Of course Slamm's expressed approval of socialism may have been motivated by extraneous

---

[10] See the *Working Man's Advocate*, Feb. 20, 1830; April 14, 1832; Jan. 26, and March 2, 1833. Also see *The Man*, Feb. 18, Aug. 29, and June 14, 1834; May 9, 1835.

[11] Douglas in the *New England Artisan*, June 21, 1834; John Ferral, "Report of the Resolutions Committee to the First Convention of the National Trades' Union," in *The Man*, Aug. 29, 1834; Ferral, in the *Radical Reformer*, Sept. 19, 1835, pp. 229–230. On Fourierism in America, see Arthur E. Bestor, "Albert Brisbane, Propagandist for Socialism in the 1840's," *New York History*, XXVIII (April, 1947), No. 2, 128–159. Slamm's *Daily Plebeian* carried for several months as a regular feature a column by Brisbane, explaining Fourierism (*Daily Plebeian*, Jan. 27, 1844; Feb. 6 and March 27, 1845; also *Weekly Plebeian*, March 30, 1844).

considerations rather than felt convictions, since, to hear many tell it, he was a shrewd, artful man. But if this suspicion is well founded, it would only signify the popularity of a doctrine capable of attracting not only zealous admirers but clever dissimulators.

In some cases the rhetoric used by the labor leaders suggests more drastic things than does the actual substance of their thought. For example, Stephen Simpson's discussion of his goals has led Broadus Mitchell to describe Simpson as an important anticipator of Marx.[12] Now it is true that Simpson was critical of the prevalent mode of distribution, as well as of the traditional political economy in which it was justified. He favored a new scheme, according to which the distribution of things is to be almost completely determined by their manner of production. Yet his writings seem more radical than they actually are. Mitchell misinterprets his thought when he describes it as an important anticipation of Marx, because of Simpson's alleged "contention that labor should . . . receive the whole of its production." Simpson never goes that far. What he asks for is not the total product. "As labour is the only basis of wealth," he writes, thus far in accord with the Socialists, "a just proportion of it must be given to the industrious, to enable them to rear their offspring." He thus favors a *larger* share for labor, rather than the whole of the product. This is more a simple call for higher wages than a revolutionary assault on surplus value.

He seeks a higher status as well as better working conditions for labor. "There is, there can be," in his opinion, "but one rule for estimating the value of labour—on principles of equity, benevolence and social harmony—that rule is, human happiness; general competence and as nearly as possible, an equality of the enjoyments of life. The end of labour being happiness—it is self-evident that happiness must regulate the just value of labour." Evidently the precise ratio of this revised formula was to be determined by an arrangement not altogether unlike that governing the establishment of the "just price" in former days, i.e., the intervention of a rational authority guided by its own understanding of the common good.

Simpson himself attempts to forewarn those who might misread his analysis. "It is a fallacy to imagine, that we are aiming to controvert the established doctrines of political economy," he explicitly states. "Our object reaches higher—is more rational—and more laudable. It strikes at a fundamental principle in the distribution of wealth—that Labour shall share with Capital, in the profits of trade, in a more equitable ratio." It turns out that Simpson is urging not confiscation of the property of one class by another, but more equitable sharing by the two.[13]

Commerford would have society based upon "a true system of political economy," in which "those who earn all wealth of the nation [no longer] secure the least; while those who earn the least, monopolize all, by cunning and

[12] Broadus Mitchell, "Stephen Simpson," *Dictionary of American Biography.*
[13] Simpson, *Working Man's Manual*, pp. 82, 87–88, 89, 229.

injustice." A change for the better is needed but it should be a "healthy reformation," rather than a complete alteration. Such language leaves some doubt as to what proportion of society's product labor is to get in the new society. When Moore told New York's unionists that the new system should enable "the producer to enjoy the full benefit of his productions, and thus diffuse the streams of wealth more generally, and consequently, more equally, throughout all the ramifications of society," he manages in one sentence to support the notions that labor should both receive all of the product, and that it should get a larger share. Most of his writings indicate that he meant the latter. The writings of the others justify the conclusion that the Jacksonian labor leaders looked forward to a new society in which labor's reward was at least equal to that of all other groups, both in status and income.[14] Like the utopian Socialists abroad, they would not—with the exception of Skidmore—disturb any man's present private property, for all their inflammatory talk against the institution.

How was the good society to be brought about? It is in their discussion of this issue that in my judgment most of the leaders reveal either their lack of seriousness or their willingness simply to profess certain goals, while showing practically no concern whatever in doing anything likely to accomplish them. Certainly they supported many measures. Not being doctrinaires, they seemed willing to take various paths to heaven. The rub, however, is that although most, if not all, of these paths seemed to lead somewhere good, it was hardly to heaven—or even to their expressed idea of it. This is not to say that they were insincere; for I believe they were sincere, almost to a fault. I am only suggesting that while they evidently wanted a fundamentally different kind of society, they evaded the issue of how to achieve it, settling instead for the advocacy of reforms and solutions that, while useful and benign, had little to do with the ostensible purpose for which they were designed. They no doubt convinced themselves in the process that these measures would have no other effect than to transform American society.

The leaders were ardent champions of educational reform, most of them arguing that this, above all, was the means of correcting the wrongs in American society. Now in working to broaden the educational opportunities of the poor and to destroy the stigma attached to public schools, the labor reformers were fighting a good fight for what in fact was a most worthy reform. This was a reform, nonetheless, that a number of political conservatives also favored. That men of practically every social persuasion could find merit in

[14] See the *Union*, April 21, and May 17, 1836; Moore, *Address Delivered Before the General Trades' Union*, p. 11; *The Man*, November 25, 1834; Luther, *Origin and Progress of Avarice*, p. 18; Luther, *Address to the Working Men of New England*, p. 5; William English, "An Address to the Mechanics and Working Men of the Trades' Union of the City and County of Philadelphia," in the *Pennsylvanian*, Jan. 9, 1834; English, "Oration Delivered at the Trades' Union Celebration"; Fisk, *Capital Against Labor*; Brothers to Lewis, July 18, 1839, in Thomas Brothers, *The United States of North America as They Really Are* (London, 1840), p. 1.

public school reform indicates the universality of the issue, and explains in part this movement's success. But it also raises the question as to whether and how such a reform, no matter how ingeniously its alleged radical consequences are developed in the labor rhetoric, could bring about a completely new society based on the pre-eminence of labor. The distinct impression is given, in fact, that a number of the leaders championed the method of reform through education largely because they wished to avoid a more frontal attack on the institutions they professed to abhor. Such motivation would be perfectly understandable, but it would also reflect on the depth of their feeling for the far-reaching changes they publicly hunger for.

For the most part, the educational opportunity they spoke of, the brave new programs to be set up, were to affect the young, and, thus, by bringing about a revolution in the thinking of the *next* generation, create the intellectual atmosphere likely to bring about the desired changes. It is hard, in view of this, to disagree with the few skeptics, such as Orestes Brownson, the Catholic reformer, who argued that to concentrate on educating the young was in effect to consign the present generation to their dismal fate. Skidmore comes off better with regard to this matter than he usually does, when in response to the proposition that the "right education of the rising generation" is "the most important and consequently has the strongest claim on adults of any question that can be proposed to them," he responds: "But who ever heard . . . so singular a doctrine as this? What! and is it to be said that the welfare of the *adults themselves* is second in importance to the right education of their offspring?"[15] Most of his colleagues seemed to feel precisely that, even if they never said it in so many words. They denounced contemporary society above all for its alleged mistreatment of adult workers, spoke eloquently of the need for something better, and proceeded to stress a reform that would admittedly have little immediate effect on the lives of the working class.

For the leaders were pragmatists. Far from being zealous devotees of a social theory, rigidly construed, they were, in fact, eclectic men, perfectly capable of making no distinction between what seemed to be an ideal society, on the one hand, and slight—if useful—reforms, on the other. They were willing to support various methods of reform, including some that seemed to have little hope of accomplishing their stated objectives. In the manner of sensible men of practical temper, they made a fetish neither of consistency nor of strict logic.

In supporting educational reforms, they showed themselves to be idealists, ready if necessary to sacrifice present well-being for future good. There is no question but that for whatever reasons, emotional or other, a number of the leaders burned with the conviction that education was both a means and an end; that a sound system of educating the young was not only the surest

---

[15] Thomas Skidmore to Amos Gilbert, in *Free Enquirer*, Dec. 17, 1831.

guarantee that society would be changed but, in itself, the central feature of the good society. "The only remedy commensurate with the abuses we purpose to remove," the sovereign measure that struck "at the root of things," according to Owen, was a system of equal national education.

Although almost all of the leaders stressed the importance of education, they had diverse and sometimes conflicting notions as to its values and purposes. Owen and Moore were drawn to it, at least in part, for its conservative implications. Not the least of the reasons the American people should support educational reform is that it "would save their country from the convulsions of a bloody revolution," Owen writes. With a sideward glance in the direction of Skidmore, he notes that "National Education [the particular scheme proposed by Owen] is a measure involving no dangerous revolutions to rouse the passions, and perhaps to blind the judgment of mankind. It presupposes no violent change in the structure of society. It is like the silent flowing of the rising tide, not like the impetuous whirl of the engulfing storm." Moore likewise alluded to equal educational opportunities for poor and rich alike as the means of preventing the rise of factions which "could arise to disturb the public tranquillity, or endanger the public welfare."

This reform likewise appealed to those who believed that man, as he was presently constituted, would not do: he must first purify himself of the unlovely traits fostered by a vicious society. He must first undertake his own regeneration before he could reform institutions, since social "injustice lies deeper than pecuniary inequality; it is beyond the power of money to remedy. It has its roots not in the purse, but in the minds and feelings." The platform for this viewpoint was built by Fanny Wright, when she wrote that "until equality be planted in the mind, in the habits, in the manners, in the feelings, think not it can ever be in the condition." Her thesis was echoed by Owen, when he asked, "What avails it that our present monopolies are destroyed . . . that all pecuniary inequality ceased in a moment, if the ignorance remain that first produced and would soon reproduce it?" His fellow publisher and sometime disciple George Henry Evans agreed.

Education was the nonpareil reform because of its great and varied consequences. It not only made man more knowledgeable and more sociable, it would also remove the deformities inflicted by the piratical society. Evans believed it would make workingmen in the future more virtuous and, in general, lead the way to a new and superior morality. Simpson argued that "knowledge is the great remedy of intemperance; for in proportion as we elevate men in the scale of existence . . . so do we reclaim them from all temptations of degrading vice and ruinous crimes. A reading and intellectual people were never known to be sottish . . . Thus sobriety and political honesty are the twin offspring of education." Luther regarded the sound early education of the child as the best antidote to avarice. In the manual-labor schools he advocated, not only would diseased minds be cured—"suicide would be a thing unknown"—but sickly bodies, as well: "then you will hear but little about dyspepsia." Slamm expected education to destroy the "base feelings" of man. Commerford thought it would "elevate the moral and intellectual character" of future generations of workingmen; while Douglas expected it to "spread sobriety and virtue" among the working class. It is clear that labor's leaders were concerned with the tendency of workers to imbibe heady beverages too freely and that in their estimate the best medicine for this disease was knowledge, rather than the strange rostrums advocated by temperance zealots.

Education would get rid of social, as well as individual, aberrations. Once adopt a sound schooling system and there would be "no need of jails and state prisons, penitentiaries and almshouses, houses of correction and popular executions."

It would also provide workers with a fuller and richer life, befitting the needs of self-respecting men and of a rational and just society. For "without education a portion of the community is cast into the shade." Fairness demanded that "children of the poor, as well as the rich, ought to be instructed both in letters and morals." According to Luther, equal education "would place the rich and the poor on a level in regard to intellectual worth," while also giving the former an interest in work.

Perhaps the most significant result of educational reform, according to a number of the more militant leaders, would be its impact on labor's self-consciousness. They believed that an educated working class would finally appreciate its own true worth. To Ferral, the beauty of the ten hour system was the opportunity it afforded workers to spend their increased leisure in the pursuit of fundamental truths about society. As important a truth as any other, of course, was the one concerning the significance and the destiny of the working class. Evans' succinct comment that a major purpose of education "was to remove the veil of ignorance by which the poor who suffer are prevented from penetrating into the mysteries of that legislation of the rich by which their sufferings are produced," accorded with the prevalent notion that the working people were gulled into subjection by wily oppressors. It goes without saying that the notion of some labor leaders that the role of education was to instill class consciousness into workers was unique with them, not dreamed of by such middle-class champions of educational reform as William Ellery Channing or Horace Mann.

Some of the leaders believed that the great obstacle to the education of the workers was the opposition of the rich and the powerful. With Simpson, they held that "the effort of capital and power, is always on the side of ignorance in the people," because there is always the fear of losing "exclusive privileges by imparting knowledge to the mass of the people." In Fisk's rhetoric, "the great fear of those who grow rich upon [labor's] industry" is that workers will "get time to improve [their] minds," and their eyes will be opened "to the monstrous frauds that have been perpetrated" upon them. "Let their worst fears be realized," he concluded. Of course, the rich did not uniformly display the attitude attributed to them by Simpson and Fisk, but the following excerpt from an editorial in the *National Gazette* in Philadelphia, is a nice example of what the labor critics had in mind:

> The "peasant" must labour during those hours of the day, which his wealthy neighbour can give to the abstract culture of his mind; otherwise, the earth would not yield enough for the subsistence of all: the mechanic cannot abandon the operations of his trade for general studies; if he should, most of the conveniences of life and objects of exchange would be wanting; languor, decay, poverty, discontent would soon be visible among all classes. No government, no statesman, no philanthropist, can furnish what is incompatible with the very organization and being of civil society.

The fact is, of course, that democratization of educational opportunity in America was supported by men of all classes and political persuasions. Horace Mann spoke for humanitarians who sought social justice without social convulsions, when he wrote that "education is . . . the great equalizer of the conditions of men,—the balance-wheel of the social machinery." According to Philip Curoe, in the early nineteenth century men who were little concerned with equality believed that "universal education diminished crime, prevented poverty, and increased production." A developing industrial society required a literate working class, as business leaders increasingly realized. Another valuable feature of popular education was the likelihood that it would counteract the radical, anticommercial doctrines so dangerously prevalent among the working class, and instill in their place respect for the fundamental values required by a stable society. This was the idea suggested by the conservative Thomas Cooper:

> Education universally extended throughout the community, will tend moreover to disabuse the working class of people in respect of a notion that has crept into the minds of our mechanics, and is gradually prevailing, that manual labor is, at present, very inadequately rewarded, owing to combinations of the rich against the poor; that mere mental labor is comparatively worthless; that property or wealth, ought not to be accumulated or transmitted; that to take interest on money lent or profit on capital employed is unjust. These are notions that tend strongly toward an equal division of property, and the right of the poor to plunder the rich. The mistaken and ignorant people who entertain these fallacies as truths, will learn, when they have the opportunity of learning, that the institution of political society originated in the protection of property.

Obviously, class-conscious persons of left and right saw in educational reform the means of propagating necessary social lessons.

Since the accomplishment of a tax-supported, high quality public education system in this country took some doing, there seems little doubt but that the labor contribution to the cause was a significant one, meriting the praise heaped on it by Philip Curoe, Frank Carlton, and Sidney Jackson. Not the least of labor's contributions were the unique educational ideas advocated by some of its leaders. If Owen's plan for state-supported boarding schools, providing "food, clothing and instruction, at the public expense," was not the sole remedy of injustice he claimed it to be, it was nonetheless a provocative idea. If little came of it in practice, the same could not be said of his plans for a broad curriculum that would include agricultural and mechanical, as well as intellectual, subjects. At a time when the common schools were patently inferior, Evans stressed the importance of striving for the highest quality of education in public schools. In curriculum, training of teachers, and pedagogy pains had to be taken to assure that standards in public schools equaled those in private; while with regard to higher education, Evans urged that the poor have equal access with the rich. Simpson was nominated to office by the Philadelphia Working Men primarily because he was known as an enthusiastic supporter of educational reform. He has been praised by Sidney Jackson for the sophistication and prescience of some of his ideas concerning teacher-training and curriculum. Commerford's ideas on the subject were hardly sophisticated, but they were clear enough. He advised the community, and above all its working-class members, constantly to scrutinize the quality of instruction, as well as the "moral character and qualifications of teachers." Underlying this advice was the belief that good schooling, administered by qualified teachers, would move society toward a form of socialism. Questionable as this assumption was, it remains true that in advocating, for whatever reasons, a democratic public-school system of the highest quality, the labor leaders played their part in achieving a reform of the highest importance.[16]

[16] For the discussion of education, see Frank T. Carlton, *Economic Influences upon Educational Progress in the United States, 1820–1850* (Univ. of Wisconsin, *Bulletin*, IV, No. 1, 1908), pp. 39, 50, 53–54; Philip R. V. Curoe, *Educational Attitudes and Policies of Organized Labor in the United States* (New York, 1926), pp. 32–33; Sidney L. Jackson, *America's Struggle for Free Schools* (Washington, D.C., 1941); Robert Dale Owen, *Address on the Hopes and Destinies of the Human Species* (London, 1836), p. 16; Owen, *Republican Government and National Education* (London, n.d.), pp. 11–12, 13–14; *Free Enquirer*, Nov. 7, 1829 and Jan. 16, 1830; Ely Moore, *Address on Civil Government* (New York, 1847), pp. 6–7. See *Working Man's Advocate*, Jan. 16, 1830; May 21, 1831; Feb. 13, March 6, and May 1, 8, 15, 1830. See George Henry Evans, "Report of the New York Association for the Promotion of Education," Sept. 30, 1829, in *Working Man's Advocate*, Nov. 14, 1829; Simpson, *The Working Man's Manual*, pp. 205, 40–41, 42, 212; Luther, *Address to the Working Men of New England*, p. 6; Luther, *Origin and Progress of Avarice*, pp. 34–35, 36; *New Era*, May 1, 1840; *National Trades' Union*, Oct. 10, 1835; Douglas, "Proposals," in *New England Artisan*, March 22 and June 7, 1834; Ferral, in *The Man*, Aug. 29, 1834; Ferral, letter to the editor, *Radical Reformer*, July 4, 1835, p. 62; Fisk, *The Banking Bubble Burst; National Gazette*, July 10, 1830, cited in John R. Commons and Associates, *History of Labour in the United States* (New York, 1918), I, 229; A. Kahler

Most of the leaders believed that, whatever the means used, labor could rely only on itself to right the wrongs it suffered under. Thomas Brothers, himself a hat manufacturer, failed to see inconsistency in his advice that workers "should never admit into their councils one who does not belong to them." They did not hold with Mathew Carey and other benevolent humanitarians that misery would be overcome by appeals to "the humanity of the wealthy employers." Their views were well expressed by Evans when he wrote that how long social abuses "will be suffered to prevail must be decided by the sufferers themselves—the poor laboring classes of the community. The rich could not be expected to take any but the most superficial steps toward remedying social distress."[17] One of the obvious methods that workers had to use to change society was political action.

At times the utterances of the labor leaders convey the belief that political reform is "not enough," especially in the absence of drastic economic changes. Where this idea was expressed, it generally was directed against those who urged reform through the party of Jackson. For as has been shown, labor regarded both parties as humbugs, agreeing with Charles Douglas that "the working class . . . belonged to no party; they were neither disciples of Jacksonism nor Clayism, Van Burenism nor Websterism, nor any other *ism* but *workeyism*." It was not politics as such that they derided but rather what they believed to be the illusion that important reforms could be achieved through co-operation with the major parties. On the other hand, a number of the leaders did advocate labor's independent political action.

The leaders of the Working Men's parties showed by their behavior their belief in the importance of political action. In this case, theory and practice were one, for their words also expressed the same viewpoint. Evans advised that "the leisure hours of working men cannot be more usefully employed than by informing themselves on political subjects—subjects which involve their dearest interests, and on which they have been so designedly kept in ignorance." The trade unionists also emphasized the importance of independent labor politics, even after the disappearance of the labor parties. Douglas never tired of warning workers that on the one hand they must avoid "throwing themselves into the arms of any of the political parties of the day," while on the other, they must take the "political business into their own hands."

---

and E. Hamburger, *Education for an Industrial Age* (New York, 1948); for an analysis of the intellectual history of Thomas Cooper, see Joseph Dorfman, *The Economic Mind in American Civilization* (New York, 1946), II, 527–539; Thomas Cooper, *Elements of Political Economy* (2nd ed.; London, 1831), pp. 333–334; *Daily Sentinel*, April 8, 9, 10, 12, 13, 14, 1830. Evans criticized the plans for a new university on the grounds that "it would only extend the advantages of education to a few who could pay for it, while the large body of working men would be excluded from any participation in the benefit of it for want of means" (*Working Man's Advocate*, March 27, 1830).

[17] *Working Man's Advocate*, April 3, 1830, and May 14, 1831; *The Man*, Feb. 20, 1834; *Radical Reformer*, June 13, and July 18, 1835.

Only by selecting "for their candidates farmers and mechanics, men of virtue and integrity, who are not rich," would they "certainly triumph, and ... destroy the vile system ... which has already reduced them to poverty and degradation." Of course Douglas was an unusually ardent believer in the efficacy of political action. At the first convention of the National Trades' Union, when English, impressed by the early demise of the Philadelphia Working Men, expressed doubts as to both the wisdom and the popularity of political activity by labor, it was Douglas who offered a rebuttal. The question, he said, was not an abstract one, as to whether this or that form of reform was logical or not. If workers suffered because of class legislation, "how were they to get out but by legislating themselves out? They could only advance their interests by choosing such men for legislators as were identified with them." Fisk supported strikes, but he regarded them as halfway measures: "There must be a radical reform—and this can only be accomplished at the ballot boxes," he told workers. Ferral simply reminded labor that at present the servants of the rich controlled law and politics. "The working classes," according to him, "would never effectually remedy the evils under which they were suffering until they carried their grievances to the polls."[18]

The leaders were also fond of invoking the possibility of revolution. Although the memory of Jefferson and the Adamses was still fresh in the minds of Americans during the Jacksonian era, and the term "revolution" therefore still had positive connotations, it was also true that radicals, above all, perhaps because of their sensitivity to conservative criticism, had learned to grow circumspect about using it. Accordingly, only Skidmore explicitly approved of revolution as the suitable means of accomplishing the necessary transformation of society. Revolution was not only a right but a duty in a society that denied to the overwhelming majority of its members the right to property conferred on them by their creator. (Skidmore, unlike the younger Owen, was no atheist.) In his view, revolutions were caused, not by designing men, but by worsening conditions. In 1829 he not only convinced the executive committee of the New York Working Men's party that conditions in their country and state were deteriorating but that, in his words, "the fountain of your distresses is not to be dried up but by a revolution." Believing as he did in the right of revolution, he innocently believed that the people had only to indicate their pleasure, for the necessary change to occur. Of course pains had first to be taken to assure that the revolution was desired by the majority, for otherwise it would be wrong. He feared that some rich men might be inclined to violence to safeguard their wealth; but he was confident that they

[18]*Working Man's Advocate*, Nov. 21, 1829, and March 27, and May 1, 1830; *The Man*, Feb. 18, 1834; Douglas, "Address to the Workingmen of Massachusetts," *New England Artisan*, Oct. 25, 1834, and the *Artisan*, June 21, and Oct. 4, 11, 1834; Fisk, *The Banking Bubble Burst*; Ferral, in *The Man*, Aug. 29, 1834; *Radical Reformer*, July 25, 1835; Ferral, "Remarks to the Convention of the National Trades' Union," in *The Man*, Sept. 6, 1834.

would easily be convinced "that it would be perfectly idle to oppose what so very large a majority should determine to adopt and enforce." But in any case, he was unalterably opposed to violence, for as a contemporary noted, "violence of action ... did not come within the sphere of his designs;—he saw no occasion for [it] ... ; his whole reliance was on the preference which the human mind gives to truth." What need was there for violence, when by Skidmore's naïve estimate, once the workers understood his message, would they not ask with him, concerning the prevailing system, "shall it not be overthrown now?"[19]

As might be expected, the same colleagues who denounced his attacks on private property and his concept of the good society also expressed horror at his advocacy of revolution. For even those men who believed in a co-operative society, would have it develop *alongside* the present one, rather than be imposed in its stead. Thus, although Owen hated private property, his plan for the future scrupulously safeguarded its present possessors. Skidmore, who burned with impatience, would not wait. Other of his colleagues spoke guardedly of the abstract right of revolution—even the careful Moore more than once invoked what after all was a popular Enlightenment doctrine—but especially after the press succeeded in making his ideas anathema, the other leaders took pains to disavow Skidmorism and revolution. And yet a number of them also conveyed the impression that, like it or not, they believed a revolution was imminent, made so by the vicious workings of the system and the greedy men who profited from and controlled it.

A popular oratorical pastime was to indulge in a purple rhetoric that not only predicted imminent revolution—in this case bloody and violent revolution—but, by emphasis and nuance, condoned or at least acquiesced in it. When Brothers asks, in an editorial, "What moral principle will be subverted if the oppressed poor should rise in their *might* and *majesty*, and forcibly take their own, which their oppressors refuse to give up?" he is not approving revolution outright; but he justifies something approximating it: violent social behavior unsanctioned by law but based on a high moral principle. In the same vein, Evans asks: "If the national hive is full, should the bees be expelled or the drones?" Meanwhile, Luther suggests that since a class society incarcerates the weak and the innocent, the task of the decent man is to open prison doors.

No one abhors revolution more than Simpson. He dreads turbulence and disorder. Yet he professes to expect them soon, unless amelioration—about the chances for which he is hopeful but not sanguine—takes place. For he agrees with Skidmore that "all revolutions have been produced by inequality of condition." Either the rich will give in gracefully, or workers will resort to

---

[19]*Rights of Man to Property*, pp. 4, 5–6, 358, 15, 315–316, 17, 271, 335–336, 244; "Report of the Committee of Fifty of the Working Men's Party of New York," in *Working Man's Advocate*, October 31, 1829; Amos Gilbert, "Thomas Skidmore," in *Free Enquirer*, April 6, 1834.

violence. And if they do, who can challenge their right? since "the power to remedy the evil is unquestionable; it resides in the producers of wealth who constitute overwhelmingly a majority of the people." Luther leaves much— but not too much—to the imagination in the following grim passage: "Amid the chilling desolation around them, they [the workers] cast an inquiring glance at their fellow sufferers, and ask the question, 'what shall be done?'" Ferral described the achievement of a shorter working day as labor's "blood-less revolution"; only this concession had interrupted the movement toward a revolution marked by "violence and blood." English reminded rich capital-ists that workers had "the controlling power" in their hands and might be driven to desperation. Fisk warns exploiters of labor that "they would do well to pause. Beneath their feet an earthquake slumbers."

Commerford's views are of interst because they express so well labor's mixed attitudes toward the problem. He makes clear he has no use for the "visionist" "... who would endeavor to disarrange the equilibrium and order of our social arrangements." He wishes "it to be distinctly understood" that he "shall always discountenance anything which may tend to tumult and riot." Yet he sees the same causes which have fomented revolution elsewhere operating here, namely the tendency of the rich to aggrandize the laboring poor. Continued hostility to unions may yet engender a revolutionary spirit here. Already "a moral revolution is silently but steadily progressing," preparing workingmen for "the day of retribution" soon to arrive. In an allusion as vague yet inflammatory as any made by his contemporaries, Commerford writes: "It is not the wages which the laborers of our country at present receive, that stalk before our avaricious task masters like spectres, but it is the more substantial ghosts which are to come, which haunt their grovelling and self-grasping imaginations."[20]

What is one to make of this firebrand talk? Several things, in my opinion. To a large extent it was simply a kind of verbal seasoning, useful in flavoring speeches. These were men, after all, whose activities in so many cases were confined either to talk or to the most sober kind of action. They were not as frank as Skidmore, who at one point conceded that he resorted to "revolution-ary language in order to frighten employers out of lengthening the working

---

[20] *Radical Reformer and Working Man's Advocate*, July 18, and Aug. 29, 1835; *Working Man's Advocate*, Oct. 31, 1829. Evans was later to write: "The very excesses of the priviliged classes will tend to their overthrow. It cannot be, that those who do the work will much longer allow themselves to be defrauded of so large a share of the proceeds of their labor" (*Radical*, Nov., 1841, p. 163). Luther, *Origins and Progress of Avarice*, pp. 30, 6, 18; Simpson, *The Working Man's Manual*, pp. 230, 20, 27, 17; also see the *Pennsylvania Whig*, Aug. 22, 1832; Ferral, in *Radical Reformer*, July 4, 1835; *The Man*, June 29, 1835; English, "Oration Delivered at the Trades' Union Celebration"; Fisk, *The Banking Bubble Burst*; the *Union*, April 21, June 10, May 25, May 28, June 4, and June 9, 1836.

day!"[21] Undoubtedly some of his colleagues hoped, too, that allusions to imminent social convulsions might induce a modest melioration. I think some of them said what they thought their labor audience wanted to hear, while others were simply carried away by their own language, believing every word they uttered. One thing seems clear: no one was frightened—even though some conservatives might profess great fear. Actually, anxiety seemed to be induced much more by trade unionism, with its modest but practical goals, than by revolutionary rhetoric.

It need hardly be said that every one of the labor leaders looked with favor upon trade unions and strikes. Not oddly, the most enthusiastic champions of unionism were the union leaders themselves. According to Moore, unions of journeymen defended labor against capital, neutralized the more vicious tendencies of human selfishness, prevented economic slavery, and preserved the workers' natural rights, added to their dignity, and safeguarded their welfare. Commerford emphasized their importance as defensive alliances which ensured the economically weak, protection against the economically strong. Ferral believed unions not only strengthened labor in its struggle for better hours and wages but could be used to overcome all of "the evils that exist in society." English read great significance into a trades' union movement. His dream was of a union of all the trades; such a body would enable every worker to "provide a comfortable subsistence for his family," education for his young, and a nest egg for his old age, and would gain for him the respect of the community. It would be so strong as to "resist the most formidable oppressions."[22]

Essentially, unionism and strikes were viewed by their American supporters as useful methods for securing and maintaining decent material conditions, rather than methods of changing society. Unlike their fellow English radicals, who already by this time regarded the general strike as a revolutionary political weapon designed to bring about broad and thoroughgoing changes in the social system, the American unionists expected only modest, if useful, tangible benefits from the strike, no matter how many might turn out to support it. This viewpoint of theirs, as well as any other, reveals, in my opinion, their essentially nonrevolutionary cast of mind.

---

[21] See George Henry Evans, "History of the Origin and Progress of the Working Men's Party in New York," in the *Radical*, 1842–1843; *Commercial Advertiser*, April 25, 1829; *Free Enquirer*, April 25, 1829.

[22] Moore, *Address Delivered Before the General Trades' Union*, pp. 8–9, 12, 28; Moore, *Speech* given in the House, May, 5, 1836, p. 11; Commerford, "Address Delivered Before the General Trades' Union," the *Union*, July 1, 1836; John Ferral, Chairman of Committee reporting to the first meeting of the Trades' Union of Pennsylvania, in the *Pennsylvanian*, Dec. 24, 1833, cited in John R. Commons and Associates, *A Documentary History of American Industrial Society* (*Cleveland*, 1910), V, 336; *The Man*, Aug. 29, 1834; English, "Address to the Mechanics and Working Men of the Trades' Union of the City and County of Philadelphia."

Certainly they sincerely hoped for a new society based on social justice and respect for labor. If hoping would have done it, then America would have become a form of socialist community. Since other, tougher means were necessary, they turned instead to a number of practical and exemplary programs, contributing in no small measure to their contemporary reform movement's modest but significant successes. If these measures seemed on close scrutiny to have little chance of bringing about the good society they were ostensibly created to achieve, that fact caused no embarrassment to a group of men who were neither doctrinaires nor strict logicians.

Selected Additional Reading

Bestor, Arthur E., Jr. *Backwoods Utopias: The Sectarian and Owenite Phases of Communitarian Socialism in America* (Philadelphia, 1950).

Blau, Joseph, ed. *Social Theories of Jacksonian Democracy* (Indianapolis, 1950).

Cole, Charles C., Jr. *The Social Ideas of the Northern Evangelists* (New York, 1954).

Curoe, Philip R. V. *Educational Attitudes and Policies of Organized Labor in the United States* (New York, 1926).

Dorfman, Joseph. *The Economic Mind in American Civilization* (New York, 1946), II, ch. 23 and 24.

Miller, Perry. *The Life of the Mind in America from the Revolution to the Civil War* (New York, 1965).

Neufeld, Maurice F. "Realms of Thought and Organized Labor in the Age of Jackson," *Labor History*, X (Winter 1969), pp. 5–43.

Nordhoff, Charles. *The Communistic Societies of the United States* Schocken Books edition, 1965).

Smith, T. L. *Revivalism and Social Reform: American Protestantism on the Eve of the Civil War* (New York, 1957).

Thomas, John L. "Romantic Reform in America, 1815–1865," *American Quarterly*, XVII (Winter 1965), pp. 656–81.

Section Six
Racism and Slavery
Before the Civil War

THOMAS F. GOSSETT

Contents

General Introduction

Racism has been a central element in American thought, as racial conflicts have been central to American experience, from the beginnings of our history. Before the Civil War, though relations between the dominant white culture and the receding Indian cultures were deeply troubled, racism was most powerfully articulated in ideological struggle over the place of black men and women in white America. Both in numbers of people involved and in degree of intensity, the problem of white-black relations exceeded all other racial problems. Institutionally this problem was focused in the question of slavery, and the nearly two-and-a-half centuries of slavery, ending in 1867, have left their mark on both blacks and whites. Though there is today at least some hope that a peaceful solution may eventually be achieved in white-black relations, this task requires an understanding of the historical development of slavery and of racism—an understanding to which racism itself imposes colossal obstacles.

For most of our history, influential white propagandists have argued that blacks were innately different from themselves not merely in appearance but in intelligence and temperament. Over the years, the conclusions of white racism have remained remarkably similar, but the methods of arriving at these conclusions have changed greatly. In the period before the Civil War, most of these arguments depended upon assumptions that no longer command widespread intellectual acceptance. Speak to the most convinced advocate of white superiority today and you are unlikely to hear arguments which derive their ultimate sanction from Noah's curse of his son Ham, as recorded in Genesis. The Biblical argument in defense of slavery, as convincing to its advocates and as troubling to many of its opponents as it once was, now seems archaic to the point of absurdity. Similarly, the "science" of race of the pre-Civil War period is also likely to seem to the modern observer almost equally archaic, depending as it does upon ideas of biology which antedate Darwin and upon theories of human culture which attribute virtually everything strange or different about a people to their racial composition.

Even the archaism of the arguments over the meaning of race in the period before the Civil War has, however, at least one advantage for the reflective modern student. Because he is unlikely to take these arguments seriously, he can see all the more clearly the extent to which the arguments are mere rationalizations. It is what the contestants over the meaning of race want to *do*, or at least the kind of society which they envision, which now attracts the attention of the careful reader. He sees that often their conclusions have been, consciously or not, already determined. It is where they want to go rather than the process by which they reason which ultimately matters more.

The issues of racism would be easier to sort out if we could divide the contestants into two general groups—those who think race is the determinant of character and ability and those who do not. What we discover, however, is that more often than not it is only different varieties of white racism which are competing with one another. It is not merely that there was prejudice against the blacks in the North as well as in the South. The truth is that racism was so powerful that it affected nearly everyone and pervaded the whole range of white opinion. Some of the most distinguished of the opponents of slavery—Thomas Jefferson, Harriet Beecher Stowe, Abraham Lincoln—were convinced that blacks were inherently different from whites inwardly as well as outwardly—and in these supposed differences the idea of black inferiority was never very far away. A kind of "reverse racism" also appears occasionally in black writings of the period, though black spokesmen were much less likely than their white counterparts to be in the grip of theories of innate racial character.

The selections which follow are meant to acquaint you with the major arguments over the meaning of black slavery and of race in American social thought before 1865. In reading them, ask yourself what theories of race are implicit in the arguments? How do these theories become apparent? What do they suggest concerning their authors' conceptions of society? Is there any indication in any of these writings that it is *ideas* of race rather than race itself which have codified and standardized race relationships in American society?

Racism and the Defense of Slavery

"About the last of August [1619] came in a dutch man of warre," wrote John Rolfe of Jamestown, Virginia, as if he were recording an ordinary event, "that sold us twenty Negars."[1] As far as history records, these twenty were the first blacks to set foot on the shores of the English colonies of continental North America. Whether they were sold into slavery or were bound into servitude, like white servants, for a limited period of years, is not now determinable. In any event, black slavery had become deeply rooted in Anglo-America by the close of the first century of colonization, and the status of the black, whether free or slave, had been sharply differentiated from that of the dominant white. How this differentiation came about is not wholly clear and possibly never will be fully clarified.

It should be remembered that the colonists were much less concerned with justifying the institution of slavery than they were in developing a system of labor which suited their needs. It was not easy to attract enough bond servants from Great Britain. Those who came had to be treated well or it would prove difficult to attract others. In any case, the limited term of service meant that they were available only for a limited number of years. As more and more laborers were needed, the plantation owners turned more and more to black slaves. They did so with a minimum of philosophic rationalization. Under these circumstances, black slavery existed in the colonies a good many years before it had a recognizable basis in law. Black slaves very probably had no inkling of the legal ambiguities of their position, and if they had there would have been no way for them to challenge the system.

Gradually the law of the colonies came to distinguish more and more clearly between the white indentured "servant" and the black "slave." For a time, the assumption was apparently implicit that slavery was an interim institution designed to convert the heathen blacks to Christianity, and this

---

[1] Edward Arber, ed., *Travels and Works of Captain John Smith* (Edinburgh, 1910), II, 541.

assumption sometimes led slaveholders to be reluctant to introduce Christianity to their black slaves since it might impair the legality of their ownership of them. Beginning about 1640, there is evidence that whatever the law said, the practice was perpetual servitude for nearly all of the blacks, and in 1660 black slavery began to be codified in law. By the early eighteenth century, slave codes were passed by the colonial legislatures which would not be changed essentially until slavery was ended by the Civil War.

Most of the selections in this section were written by apologists for slavery in the nineteenth century when the institution was under strong attack by abolitionists. An exception is the selection from Thomas Jefferson's *Notes on Virginia* (1785). Although he himself owned slaves, Jefferson saw slavery as an evil institution. His major reason for disliking it, however, was its bad effect on whites since the almost absolute power it conferred on them was morally injurious. Jefferson was convinced that the blacks were inherently inferior and doubted that it would be possible to make them citizens in a free state. For a stimulating and perceptive interpretation of Jefferson's attitudes and ideas on slavery and race the reader may wish to turn to the selection from Winthrop D. Jordan's *White Over Black* that is reprinted in Section One of this volume.

The other readings in this section are chosen as representative defenses of slavery and examples of the ways in which the institution was codified in law and incorporated in the tenets of religion. The importance of religious sanctions for slavery, set forth in these readings by a South Carolina Baptist clergyman, Richard Furman, and inculcated by the slave catechism that follows the selection from Furman, can hardly be exaggerated. Since great numbers of people, including many intellectuals, believed that all parts of the Bible expressed absolutely the intentions of God, Southern apologists for slavery frequently adopted a proof-text method of citing scriptural chapter and verse to show that slavery had God's approval. If slavery was wrong, they argued, why did not the Bible clearly say so? Why had Paul counseled a slave to return to his master (Philemon 1:10–13)? The "curse of Ham" has already been mentioned, but something should be said of the details. Ham, the son of Noah, had laughed at his father because the latter had become drunk and lay sprawled out naked in stupor. When Noah recovered, he cursed Ham and Ham's descendants, saying they would be the servants of Ham's brothers, Shem and Japheth, and of their descendents (Genesis 9:21–27). Though there was no implication in the Bible that Ham was black, the apologists for black slavery argued that no other rational explanation for the existence of the institution was possible.

Defenders of slavery utilized the scientific ideas of race of the time less than we might suppose they would. One reason was the comparatively primitive state of the biology and thus the anthropology of the time. Charles Darwin's *The Origin of Species* was not published until 1859, too late to have any significant part in the debate over slavery. Even if it had appeared earlier, it is unlikely that proponents of slavery would have used it. They were frequently suspicious of what would now be called anthropology because it sometimes seemed to cast doubt on the authenticity of the Biblical record. Nevertheless, scientific ideas of the meaning of race sometimes crop up in the arguments favoring slavery.[2] In general, the scientific opinion of the time bore out the conviction that the blacks were inherently inferior, and some of the scientists went so far as actually to endorse slavery, as did Dr. Samuel Cartwright of New Orleans, a selection from whose essay, "The Prognathous Species of Mankind," is reprinted below.

Besides the Bible and the "science" of anthropology, the white apologists for black slavery developed the third argument that a high civilization must have a stable lower class to perform its menial tasks. In order to free the "superior" upper class for the tasks of civilization, it was argued, someone must be available to do the dirty work, the ordinary tasks of house and field and factory. This theory was common among proponents of slavery and is represented here by the notorious "mudsill" conception of society as developed by Senator James H. Hammond of South Carolina.

Two interpretive readings conclude this group of selections. In the first, the several arguments for slavery are summarized by this country's foremost black historian, John Hope Franklin, professor of history at the University of Chicago, whose book, *From Slavery to Freedom: A History of Negro Americans*, remains the best short study of black history in America. The second reading, by Winthrop D. Jordan, of the University of California at Berkeley, addresses the problem of the origins of American slavery. Did slavery, as some historians have contended, result from antecedent race prejudice, or was racism, as other authorities have held, the consequence of slavery? Jordan reviews the historians' debate over these questions, furnishing a large amount of evidence on the development of race relations and racism in the Anglo-American colonies, and suggests that slavery and racism "may have been equally cause and effect, constantly reacting upon each other, dynamically joining hands to hustle the Negro down the road to complete degradation." It was this mutual reinforcement of idea and institution, of attitudes and social system, that lent great force to the serried arguments of the racist propagandists. There was something of the racist, more or less, in every white American, Northern as well as Southern, to which the defenders of slavery could effectively appeal.

[2] See Thomas F. Gossett, *Race: The History of an Idea in America* (Dallas, Texas, 1963), Chapter IV.

1 / Thomas Jefferson on Black Slavery and Race

(1785)

Thomas Jefferson wrote his *Notes on Virginia*, from which the following selection is taken, in the early 1780's in response to a French request for information on the new state. Though the inquiry came at a time when the misfortunes of war were running against the American forces and Jefferson, then governor of Virginia, was preoccupied in finding a safe place from which to do the governing, he somehow made time to develop an elaborate account, subsequently enlarged before it was printed in 1785, that included observations on such diverse topics as Virginia's rivers, plants, Indians, laws, religions, commerce, currency, and, not least important, slaves. No eighteenth-century treatment of slavery and race more trenchantly reveals the ambiguity of white attitudes on these subjects, or the limitations of the liberalism of the Enlightenment, as viewed, at least, from the more enlightened perspective of the mid-twentieth century. For an extended interpretation of Jefferson's views see the essay by Winthrop D. Jordan that appears in the first section of this volume.

. . . It will probably be asked, Why not retain and incorporate the blacks into the state, and thus save the expence of supplying by importation of white settlers, the vacancies they will leave? Deep rooted prejudices entertained by the whites; ten thousand recollections, by the blacks, of the injuries they have sustained; new provocations; the real distinctions which nature has made; and many other circumstances will divide us into parties, and produce convulsions, which will probably never end but in the extermination of the one or the other race.—To these objections, which are political, may be added others, which are physical and moral. The first difference which strikes us is that of colour. Whether the black of the negro resides in the reticular membrane between the skin and scarfskin, or in the scarfskin itself; whether it proceeds from the colour of the blood, the colour of the bile, or from that

Paul Leicester Ford, ed., *The Works of Thomas Jefferson*, IV (New York & London: G. P. Putnam's Sons, 1904), pp. 49–59.

of some other secretion, the difference is fixed in nature, and is as real as if its seat and cause were better known to us. And is this difference of no importance? Is it not the foundation of a greater or less share of beauty in the two races? Are not the fine mixtures of red and white, the expressions of every passion by greater or less suffusions of colour in the one, preferable to that eternal monotony, which reigns in the countenances, that immovable veil of black which covers all the emotions of the other race? Add to these, flowing hair, a more elegant symmetry of form, their own judgment in favour of the whites, declared by their preference of them as uniformly as is the preference of the Oran ootan for the black woman over those of his own species. The circumstance of superior beauty, is thought worthy attention in the propagation of our horses, dogs, and other domestic animals; why not in that of man? Besides those of colour, figure, and hair, there are other physical distinctions proving a difference of race. They have less hair on the face and body. They secrete less by the kidnies, and more by the glands of the skin, which gives them a very strong and disagreeable odour. This greater degree of transpiration, renders them more tolerant of heat, and less so of cold than the whites. Perhaps too a difference of structure in the pulmonary apparatus, which a late ingenious[1] experimentalist has discovered to be the principal regulator of animal heat, may have disabled them from extricating, in the act of inspiration, so much of that fluid from the outer air, or obliged them in expiration, to part with more of it. They seem to require less sleep. A black after hard labour through the day, will be induced by the slightest amusements to sit up till midnight or later, though knowing he must be out with the first dawn of the morning. They are at least as brave, and more adventuresome. But this may perhaps proceed from a want of forethought, which prevents their seeing a danger till it be present. When present, they do not go through it with more coolness or steadiness than the whites. They are more ardent after their female; but love seems with them to be more an eager desire, than a tender delicate mixture of sentiment and sensation. Their griefs are transient. Those numberless afflictions, which render it doubtful whether heaven has given life to us in mercy or in wrath, are less felt, and sooner forgotten with them. In general, their existence appears to participate more of sensation than reflection. To this must be ascribed their disposition to sleep when abstracted from their diversions, and unemployed in labour. An animal whose body is at rest, and who does not reflect, must be disposed to sleep of course. Comparing them by their faculties of memory, reason, and imagination, it appears to me that in memory they are equal to the whites; in reason much inferior, as I think one could scarcely be found capable of tracing and comprehending the investigations of Euclid: and that in imagination they are dull, tasteless, and anomalous. It would be unfair to follow them to Africa for this investigation. We will consider them here, on the same stage with the whites, and where the

[1] Crawford.—T. J.

facts are not apochryphal on which a judgment is to be formed. It will be right to make great allowances for the difference of condition, of education, of conversation, of the sphere in which they move. Many millions of them have been brought to, and born in America. Most of them, indeed, have been confined to tillage, to their own homes, and their own society: yet many have been so situated, that they might have availed themselves of the conversation of their masters; many have been brought up to the handicraft arts, and from that circumstance have always been associated with the whites. Some have been liberally educated, and all have lived in countries where the arts and sciences are cultivated to a considerable degree, and have had before their eyes samples of the best works from abroad. The Indians, with no advantages of this kind, will often carve figures on their pipes not destitute of design and merit. They will crayon out an animal, a plant, or a country, so as to prove the existence of a germ in their minds which only wants cultivation. They astonish you with strokes of the most sublime oratory; such as prove their reason and sentiment strong, their imagination glowing and elevated. But never yet could I find that a black had uttered a thought above the level of plain narration; never seen even an elementary trait of painting or sculpture. In music they are more generally gifted than the whites, with accurate ears for tune and time, and they have been found capable of imagining a small catch.[1] Whether they will be equal to the composition of a more extensive run of melody, or of complicated harmony, is yet to be proved. Misery is often the parent of the most affecting touches in poetry.—Among the blacks is misery enough, God knows, but no poetry. Love is the peculiar œstrum of the poet. Their love is ardent, but it kindles the senses only, not the imagination. Religion, indeed, has produced a Phyllis Whately;[2] but it could not produce a poet. The compositions published under her name are below the dignity of criticism. The heroes of the Dunciad are to her, as Hercules to the author of that poem. Ignatius Sancoh[3] has approached nearer to merit in composition; yet his letters do more honour to the heart than the head. They breathe the purest effusions of friendship and general philanthropy, and show how great a degree of the latter may be compounded with strong religious zeal. He is often happy in the turn of his compliments, and his style is easy and familiar, except when he affects a Shandean fabrication of words. But his imagination is wild

---

[1] The instrument proper to them is the Banjar, which they brought hither from Africa, and which is the original of the guitar, its chords being precisely the four lower chords of the guitar.—*T. J.*

[2] Phillis Wheatley, author of a number of poems, published at different times, some of which were collected into a volume, published in London in 1773, which has been several times reprinted.

[3] Born in 1729 on a slaveship, and a resident for many years in England. His *Letters, with Memoirs of his Life*, were published in London in two volumes, in 1782. Some account of him, with a reply to Jefferson's criticism of his letters, is given in H. Gregoire's *Enquiry concerning . . . Negroes, Brooklyn*; 1810, p. 227.

and extravagant, escapes incessantly from every restraint of reason and taste, and, in the course of its vagaries, leaves a tract of thought as incoherent and eccentric, as is the course of a meteor through the sky. His subjects should often have led him to a process of sober reasoning; yet we find him always substituting sentiment for demonstration. Upon the whole, though we admit him to the first place among those of his own color who have presented themselves to the public judgment, yet when we compare him with the writers of the race among whom he lived and particularly with the epistolary class in which he has taken his own stand, we are compelled to enrol him at the bottom of the column. This criticism supposes the letters published under his name to be genuine, and to have received amendment from no other hand; points which would not be of easy investigation. The improvement of the blacks in body and mind, in the first instance of their mixture with the whites, has been observed by every one, and proves that their inferiority is not the effect merely of their condition of life. We know that among the Romans, about the Augustan age especially, the condition of their slaves was much more deplorable than that of the blacks on the continent of America. The two sexes were confined in separate apartments, because to raise a child cost the master more than to buy one. Cato, for a very restricted indulgence to his slaves in this particular, took from them a certain price. But in this country the slaves multiply as fast as the free inhabitants. Their situation and manners place the commerce between the two sexes almost without restraint. The same Cato, on a principle of economy, always sold his sick and superannuated slaves. He gives it as a standing precept to a master visiting his farm, to sell his old oxen, old waggons, old tools, old and diseased servants, and everything else become useless, 'Vendat boves vetulos, plaustrum vetus, feramenta vetera, servum senem, servum morbosum, si quid aliud supersit vendat.' Cato de re rusticâ, c. 2. The American slaves cannot enumerate this among the injuries and insults they receive. It was the common practice to expose in the island Æsculapius, in the Tyber, diseased slaves whose cure was like to become tedious.[1] The Emperor Claudius, by an edict, gave freedom to such of them as should recover, and first declared that if any person chose to kill rather than to expose them, it should be deemed homicide. The exposing them is a crime of which no instance has existed with us, and were it to be followed by death, it would be punished capitally. We are told of a certain Vedius Pollio, who, in the presence of Augustus, would have given a slave as food to his fish, for having broken a glass.[2] With the Romans, the regular method of taking the evidence of their slaves was under torture. Here it has been thought better never to resort to their evidence. When a master was murdered, all his slaves, in the same house, or within hearing, were condemned to death. Here punishment

---

[1] Suet. Claud. 25.—*T. J.*
[2] "Seneca de ira. L. 3, 40; de Clementia I, 18; Xiphil. Aug., p. 76." *Note in edition of 1853.*

falls on the guilty only, and as precise proof is required against him as against a freeman. Yet notwithstanding these and other discouraging circumstances among the Romans, their slaves were often their rarest artists. They excelled too in science, insomuch as to be usually employed as tutors to their master's children. Epictetus,[1] Terence, and Phædrus, were slaves. But they were of the race of whites. It is not their condition then, but nature, which has produced the distinction.—Whether further observation will or will not verify the conjecture, that nature has been less bountiful to them in the endowments of the head, I believe that in those of the heart she will be found to have done them justice. That disposition to theft with which they have been branded, must be ascribed to their situation, and not to any depravity of the moral sense. The man in whose favour no laws of property exist, probably feels himself less bound to respect those made in favour of others. When arguing for ourselves, we lay it down as a fundamental, that laws, to be just, must give a reciprocation of right: that, without this, they are mere arbitrary rules of conduct, founded in force, and not in conscience; and it is a problem which I give to the master to solve, whether the religious precepts against the violation of property were not framed for him as well as his slave? And whether the slave may not as justifiably take a little from one who has taken all from him, as he may slay one who would slay him? That a change in the relations in which a man is placed should change his ideas of moral right and wrong, is neither new, nor peculiar to the colour of the blacks. Homer tells us it was so 2600 years ago . . .

> Jove fix'd it certain, that whatever day
> Makes man a slave, takes half his worth away.

But the slaves of which Homer speaks were whites. Notwithstanding these considerations which must weaken their respect for the laws of property, we find among them numerous instances of the most rigid integrity, and as many as among their better instructed masters, of benevolence, gratitude, and unshaken fidelity. The opinion that they are inferior in the faculties of reason and imagination, must be hazarded with great diffidence. To justify a general conclusion, requires many observations, even where the subject may be submitted to the Anatomical knife, to Optical glasses, to analysis by fire or by solvents. How much more then where it is a faculty, not a substance, we are examining; where it eludes the research of all the senses; where the conditions of its existence are various and variously combined; where the effects of those which are present or absent bid defiance to calculation; let me add too, as a circumstance of great tenderness, where our conclusion would degrade a whole race of men from the rank in the scale of beings which their Creator may perhaps have given them. To our reproach it must be said, that though for a century and a half we have had under our eyes the races of black and of red men, they have never yet been viewed by us as sub-

---

[1] In the edition of 1853 the names of Diogenes and Phædon are inserted at this point.

jects of natural history. I advance it, therefore, as a suspicion only, that the blacks, whether originally a distinct race, or made distinct by time and circumstances, are inferior to the whites in the endowments both of body and mind. It is not against experience to suppose that different species of the same genus, or varieties of the same species, may possess different qualifications. Will not a lover of natural history then, one who views the gradations in all the races of animals with the eye of philosophy, excuse an effort to keep those in the department of man as distinct as nature has formed them? This unfortunate difference of colour, and perhaps of faculty, is a powerful obstacle to the emancipation of these people. Many of their advocates, while they wish to vindicate the liberty of human nature, are anxious also to preserve its dignity and beauty. Some of these, embarrassed by the question, "What further is to be done with them?" join themselves in opposition with those who are actuated by sordid avarice only. Among the Romans emancipation required but one effort. The slave, when made free, might mix with, without staining the blood of his master. But with us a second is necessary, unknown to history. When freed, he is to be removed beyond the reach of mixture.

2 / Richard Furman
A Religious Defense of Slavery

(1822)

Richard Furman, a Baptist minister in South Carolina, set forth the main points of the religious argument for slavery in the following "exposition," adopted by the South Carolina Baptist convention in 1822 and addressed to the governor of the state who responded with enthusiastic appreciation.

On the lawfulness of holding slaves, considering it in a moral and religious view, the convention think it their duty to exhibit their sentiments on the present occasion before Your Excellency, because they consider their duty to God, the peace of the state, the satisfaction of scrupulous consciences, and the welfare of the slaves themselves as intimately connected with a right view of the subject. The rather, because certain writers on politics, morals, and religion, and some of them highly respectable, have advanced positions and inculcated sentiments very unfriendly to the principle and practice of holding slaves; and, by some, these sentiments have been advanced among us, tending in their nature *directly* to disturb the domestic peace of the state, to produce insubordination and rebellion among the slaves, and to infringe the rights of our citizens; and *indirectly* to deprive the slaves of religious privileges by awakening in the minds of their masters a fear that acquaintance with the Scriptures and the enjoyment of these privileges would naturally produce the aforementioned effects; because the sentiments in opposition to the holding of slaves have been attributed by their advocates to the Holy Scriptures and to the genius of Christianity.

These sentiments, the convention, on whose behalf I address Your Excellency, cannot think just or well-founded; for the right of holding slaves is clearly established in the Holy Scriptures, both by precept and example. In the Old Testament, the Israelites were directed to purchase their bondmen and bondmaids of the heathen nations; except they were of the

Reprinted from *Rev. Dr. Richard Furman's Exposition of the Views of the Baptists, Relative to the Coloured Population of the United States, in a Communication to the Governor of South-Carolina* (Charleston, S.C., 1823).

Canaanites, for these were to be destroyed. And it is declared that the persons purchased were to be their "bondmen forever," and an "inheritance for them and their children." They were not to go out free in the year of jubilee, as the Hebrews, who had been purchased, were; the line being clearly drawn between them. . .

Had the holding of slaves been a moral evil, it cannot be supposed that the inspired apostles, who feared not the faces of men and were ready to lay down their lives in the cause of their God, would have tolerated it for a moment in the Christian Church. If they had done so on a principle of accommodation, in cases where the masters remained heathen, to avoid offenses and civil commotion, yet, surely, where both master and servant were Christian, as in the case before us, they would have enforced the law of Christ and required that the master should liberate his slave in the first instance. But, instead of this, they let the relationship remain untouched as being lawful and right, and insist on the relative duties.

In proving this subject justifiable by scriptural authority, its morality is also proved; for the Divine Law never sanctions immoral actions.

The Christian Golden Rule of doing to others as we would they should do to us has been urged as an unanswerable argument against holding slaves. But surely this rule is never to be urged against that order of things which the Divine Government has established; nor do our desires become a standard to us, under this rule, unless they have a due regard to justice, propriety, and the general good. . .

If the holding of slaves is lawful, or according to the Scriptures, then this scriptural rule can be considered as requiring no more of the master, in respect of justice (whatever it may do in point of generosity) than what he, if a slave, could consistently wish to be done to himself, while the relationship between master and servant should be still continued.

In this argument, the advocates for emancipation blend the ideas of injustice and cruelty with those which respect the existence of slavery, and consider them as inseparable. But, surely, they may be separated. A bondservant may be treated with justice and humanity as a servant; and a master may, in an important sense, be the guardian and even father of his slaves. . .

That Christian nations have not done all they might, or should have done, on a principle of Christian benevolence for the civilization and conversion of the Africans; that much cruelty has been practised in the slave trade, as the benevolent Wilberforce and others have shown; that much tyranny has been exercised by individuals, as masters over their slaves, and that the religious interests of the latter have been too much neglected by many cannot, will not be denied. But the fullest proof of these facts will not also prove that the holding men in subjection, as slaves, is a moral evil and inconsistent with Christianity. Magistrates, husbands, and fathers have proved tyrants. This does not prove that magistracy, the husband's right to govern, and parental authority are unlawful and wicked. The individual who abuses his authority and acts with cruelty must answer for it at the Divine Tribunal, and civil authority should interpose to prevent or punish it; but neither civil nor ecclesiastical authority can consistently interfere with the possession and legitimate exercise of a right given by the Divine Law...

It appears to be equally clear that those, who by reasoning on abstract principles, are induced to favor the scheme of general emancipation, and who ascribe their sentiments to Christianity, should be particularly careful, however benevolent their intentions may be, that they do not by a perversion of the scriptural doctrine, through their wrong views of it, not only invade the domestic and religious peace and rights of our citizens on this subject but, also by an intemperate zeal, prevent indirectly the religious improvement of the people they design, professedly, to benefit; and, perhaps, become, evidently, the means of producing in our country scenes of anarchy and blood. And all this in a vain attempt to bring about a state of things which, if arrived at, would not probably better the state of that people; which is thought by men of observation to be generally true of the Negroes in the Northern states who have been liberated.

To pious minds it has given pain to hear men, respectable for intelligence and morals, sometimes say that holding slaves is indeed indefensible, but that to us it is necessary and must be supported. On this principle, mere politicians, unmindful of morals, may act. But surely, in a moral and religious view of the subject, this principle is inadmissible. It cannot be said that theft, falsehood, adultery, and murder are become necessary and must be supported. Yet there is reason to believe that some of honest and pious intentions have found their minds embarrassed, if not perverted, on this subject by this plausible but unsound argument. From such embarrassment the view exhibited above affords relief.

The convention, sir, are far from thinking that Christianity fails to inspire the minds of its subjects with benevolent and generous sentiments; or that liberty, rightly understood or enjoyed, is a blessing of little moment. The contrary of these positions they maintain. But they also consider benevolence as consulting the truest and best interests of its objects; and view the happiness of liberty as well as of religion as consisting not in the name or form but in the reality. While men remain in the chains of ignorance and error, and under the dominion of tyrant lusts and passions, they cannot be free. And the more freedom of action they have in this state, they are but the more qualified by it to do injury both to themselves and others. It is, therefore, firmly believed that general emancipation to the Negroes in this country would not, in present circumstances, be for their own happiness, as a body; while it would be extremely injurious to the community at large in various ways; and, if so, then it is not required even by benevolence.

But acts of benevolence and generosity must be free and voluntary; no man has a right to compel another to the performance of them. This is a concern which lies between a man and his God. If a man has obtained slaves by purchase, or inheritance, and the holding of them as such is justifiable by the law of God, why should he be required to liberate them, because it would be a generous action, rather than another, on the same principle, to release his debtors or sell his lands and houses and distribute the proceeds among the poor? These also would be generous actions. Are they, therefore, obligatory? Or, if obligatory, in certain circumstances, as personal, voluntary acts of piety and benevolence, has any man or body of men, civil or ecclesiastic, a right to require them? Surely those who are advocates for compulsory or strenuous measures to bring about emancipation should duly weigh this consideration.

Should, however, a time arrive when the Africans in our country might be found qualified to enjoy freedom, and, when they might obtain it in a manner consistent with the interest and peace of the community at large, the convention would be happy in seeing them free. And so they would, in seeing the state of the poor, the ignorant, and the oppressed of every description and of every country meliorated; so that the reputed free might be free, indeed, and happy. But there seems to be just reason to conclude that a considerable part of the human race, whether they bear openly the character of slaves or are reputed freemen, will continue in such curcumstances, with mere shades of variation, while the world continues. . .

And here I am brought to a part of the general subject which I confess to Your Excellency, the convention, from a sense of their duty as a body of men to whom important concerns of religion are confided, have particularly at heart, and wish it may be seriously considered by all our citizens: This is the religious interests of the Negroes. For though they are slaves, they are also men; and are with ourselves accountable creatures, having immortal souls and being destined to future eternal award. Their religious interests claim a regard from their masters of the most serious nature; and it is indispensable. Nor can the community at large, in a right estimate of their duty and happiness, be indifferent on this subject. To the truly benevolent it must be pleasing to know that a number of masters, as well as ministers and pious individuals of various Christian denominations among us, do conscientiously regard this duty; but there is great reason to believe that it is neglected and disregarded by many.

The convention are particularly unhappy in considering that an idea of the Bible's teaching the doctrine of emancipation as necessary, and, tending to make servants insubordinate to proper authority, has obtained access to any mind; both on account of its direct influence on those who admit it, and the fear it excites in others, producing the effects before noticed. But it is hoped it has been evinced that the idea is an erroneous one, and that it will be seen that the influence of a right acquaintance with that Holy Book tends directly and powerfully, by promoting the fear and love of God, together with just and peaceful sentiments toward men, to produce one of the best securities to the public for the internal and domestic peace of the state.

3 / A Slave Catechism

(1854)

Slaveholders adapted Christianity to their own needs. Slave catechisms can be found which indicate ways in which divine sanction was given to the master-slave relationship. This one was originally printed in an Episcopal magazine published in Charleston, South Carolina. Frederick Douglass (1817–1895), the former slave and leading abolitionist, reprinted it.

Q. Who keeps the snakes and all bad things from hurting you?
A. God does.
Q. Who gave you a master and a mistress?
A. God gave them to me.
Q. Who says that you must obey them?
A. God says that I must.
Q. What book tells you these things?
A. The Bible.
B. How does God do all his work?
A. He always does it right.
Q. Does God love to work?
A. Yes, God is always at work.
Q. Do the angels work?
A. Yes, they do what God tells them.
Q. Do they love to work?
A. Yes, they love to please God.
Q. What does God say about your work?
A. He that will not work shall not eat.
Q. Did Adam and Eve have to work?
A. Yes, they had to keep the garden.
Q. Was it hard to keep that garden?
A. No, it was very easy.
Q. What makes the crops so hard to grow now?
A. Sin makes it.
Q. What makes you lazy?
A. My wicked heart.
Q. How do you know your heart is wicked?
A. I feel it every day.
Q. Who teaches you so many wicked things?
A. The Devil.
Q. Must you let the Devil teach you?
A. No, I must not.

From the *Southern Episcopalian*, Charleston, S.C., reprinted in *Frederick Douglass' Paper*, June 2, 1854.

■ The Biological Argument

4 / Samuel Cartwright
The Prognathous Species of Mankind

(1857)

A New Orleans physician, Samuel Cartwright was a noted exponent of the "scientific" theory of Negro inferiority which stressed the identifying characteristics of the Negro as a "species." These characteristics, in Cartwright's opinion, made the black a natural slave and justified the institution of black slavery.

It is not intended by the use of the term Prognathous to call in question the black man's humanity or the unity of the human races as a *genus*, but to prove that the species of the genus homo are not a unity, but a plurality, each essentially different from the others—one of them being so unlike the other two—the oval-headed Caucasian and the pyramidal-headed Mongolian—as to be actually prognathous, like the brute creation; not that the negro is a brute, or half man and half brute, but a genuine human being, anatomically constructed, about the head and face, more like the monkey tribes and the lower order of animals than any other species of the genus man. Prognathous is a technical term derived from *pro*, before, and *gnathos*, the jaws, indicating that the muzzle or mouth is anterior to the brain. The lower animals, according to Cuvier, are distinguished from the European and Mongol man by the mouth and face projecting further forward in the profile than the brain. He expresses the rule thus: *face anterior*, *cranium posterior*. The typical negroes of adult age, when tried by this rule, are proved to belong to a different species from the man of Europe or Asia, because the head and face are anatomically constructed more after the fashion of the simiadiæ and the brute creation than the Caucasian and Mongolian species of mankind, their mouth and jaws projecting beyond the forehead containing the anterior lobes of the brain. Moreover, their faces are proportionally larger than their crania, instead of smaller, as in the other two species of the genus man. Young monkeys and

Reprinted from Samuel Cartwright, "Natural History of the Prognathous Species of Mankind" (1857), in E. N. Elliott, ed., *Cotton Is King, and Pro-Slavery Arguments* (Augusta, Ga., 1860).

young negroes, however, are not prognathous like their parents, but become so as they grow older. The head of the infant ourang outang is like that of a well formed Caucasian child in the projection and height of the forehead and the convexity of the vertea. The brain appears to be larger than it really is, because the face, at birth, has not attained its proportional size. The face of the Caucasian infant is a little under its proportional size when compared with the cranium. In the infant negro and ourang outang it is greatly so. Although so much smaller in infancy than the cranium, the face of the young monkey ultimately outgrows the cranium; so, also, does the face of the young negro, whereas in the Caucasian, the face always continues to be smaller than the cranium. The superfices of the face at puberty exceeds that of the hairy scalp both in the negro and the monkey, while it is always less in the white man. Young monkeys and young negroes are superior to white children of the same age in memory and other intellectual faculties. The white infant comes into the world with its brain inclosed by fifteen disunited bony plates—the occipital bone being divided into four parts, the sphenoid into three, the frontal into two, each of the two temporals into two, which, with the two parietals, make fifteen plates in all—the vomer and ethmoid not being ossified at birth. The bones of the head are not only disunited, but are more or less overlapped at birth, in consequence of the largeness of the Caucasian child's head and the smallness of its mother's pelvis, giving the head an elongated form, and an irregular, knotty feel to the touch. The negro infant, however, is born with a small, hard, smooth, round head like a gourd. Instead of the frontal and temporal bones being divided into six plates, as in the white child, they form but one bone in the negro infant. The head is not only smaller than that of the white child, but the pelvis of the negress is wider than that of the white woman—its greater obliquity also favors parturition and prevents miscarriage.

Negro children and white children are alike at birth in one remarkable particular—they are both born *white*, and so much alike, as far as color is concerned, as scarcely to be distinguished from each other. In a very short time, however, the skin of the negro infant begins to darken and continues to grow darker until it becomes of a shining black color, provided the child be healthy. The skin will become black whether exposed to the air and light or not. The blackness is not of as deep a shade during the first years of life, as afterward. The black color is not so deep in the female as in the male, nor in the feeble, sickly negro as in the robust and healthy. Blackness is a characteristic of the prognathous species of the genus homo, but all the varieties of all the prognathous species are not equally black. Nor are the individuals of the same family or variety equally so. The lighter shades of color, when not derived from admixture with Mongolian or Caucasian blood, indicate degeneration in the prognathous species. The Hottentots, Bushmen and aborigines of Australia are inferior in mind and body to the typical African of Guinea and the Niger.

The typical negroes themselves are more or less superior or inferior to one another precisely as they approximate to or recede from the typical standard in color and form, due allowance being made for age and sex. The standard is an oily, shining black, and as far as the conformation of the head and face is concerned and the relative proportion of nervous matter outside of the cranium to the quantity of cerebral matter within it, is found between the simiadiae and the Caucasian. Thus, in the typical negro, a perpendicular line, let fall from the forehead, cuts off a large portion of the face, throwing the mouth, the thick lips, and the projecting teeth anterior to the cranium, but not the entire face, as in the lower animals and monkey tribes. When all, or a greater part of the face is thrown anterior to the line, the negro approximates the monkey anatomically more than he does the true Caucasian; and when little or none of the face is anterior to the line, he approximates that mythical being of Dr. Van Evrie, *a black white man*, and almost ceases to be a negro. The black man occasionally seen in Africa, called the *Bature Dutu*, with high nose, thin lips, and long straight hair, is not a negro at all, but a Moor tanned by the climate—because his children, not exposed to the sun, do not become black like himself. The typical negro's nervous system is modeled a little different from the Caucasian and somewhat like the ourang outang. The medullary spinal cord is larger and more developed than in the white man, but less so than in the monkey tribes. The occipital foramen, giving exit to the spinal cord, is a third longer, says Cuvier, in proportion to its breadth, than in the Caucasian, and is so oblique as to form an angle of 30° with the horizon, yet not so oblique as in the simiadiae, but sufficiently so to throw the head somewhat backward and the face upward in the erect position. Hence, from obliquity of the head and the pelvis, the negro walks steadier with a weight on his head, as a pail of water for instance, than without it; whereas, the white man, with a weight on his head, has great difficulty in maintaining his centre of gravity, owing to the occipital foramen forming no angle with the cranium, the pelvis, the spine, or the thighs—all forming a straight line from the crown of the head to the sole of the foot without any of the obliquities seen in the negro's knees, thighs, pelvis and head—and still more evident in the ourang outang . . .

The blackness of the prognathous race, known in the world's history as Canaanites, Cushites, Ethiopians, black men or negroes, is not confined to the skin, but pervades, in a greater or less degree, the whole inward man down to the bones themselves, giving the flesh and the blood, the membranes and every organ and part of the body, except the bones, a darker hue than in the white race. Who knows but what Canaan's mother may have been a genuine Cushite, as black inside as out, and that Cush, which means blackness, was the mark put upon Cain? Whatever may have been the mark set upon Cain, the negro, in all ages of the world, has carried with him a mark equally efficient in preventing him from being slain—the mark of blackness. The wild Arabs and hostile American Indians invariably catch the black wanderer and make a slave of him instead of killing him, as they do the white man.

Nich. Pechlin, in a work written last century entitled "De cute Athiopum," Albinus, in another work, entitled "De sede et causa coloris Athiop," as also the great German anatomists, Meiners, Ebel, and Soemmering, all bear witness to the fact that the muscles, blood, membranes, and all the internal organs of the body, (the bones alone excepted,) are of a darker hue in the negro than in the white man. They estimate the difference in color to be equal to that which exists between the hare and the rabbit. Who ever doubts the fact, or has none of those old and impartial authorities at hand—impartial because they were written before England adopted the policy of pressing religion and science in her service to place white American republican freemen and Guinea negroes upon the same platform—has only to look into the mouth of the first healthy typical negro he meets to be convinced of the truth, that the entire membraneous lining of the inside of the cheeks, lips and gums is of a much darker color than in the white man.

■ The Political Economy of Race

5 / James H. Hammond
The Mud-Sill of Society

(1858)

James H. Hammond, a wealthy planter, lawyer, and editor, who served as governor of South Carolina and in both houses of Congress, held that all civilized societies rested on a "mud-sill" of a laboring class, either free or slave. This mud-sill would be all the more firm as a social foundation if its members were persons of an "inferior" caste or race, capable only of the most menial, muscular tasks. In Hammond's view, the South was blessed with such a race, and the enslaved blacks were both blessed and happy in their slavery. Hammond expressed his gratification on both points in a speech to the United States Senate in 1858, from which the following passage is taken.

In all social systems there must be a class to do the menial duties, to perform the drudgery of life. That is, a class requiring but a low order of intellect and but little skill. Its requisites are vigor, docility, fidelity. Such a class you must have, or you would not have that other class which leads progress, civilization, and refinement. It constitutes the very mud-sill of society and of political government; and you might as well attempt to build a house in the air, as to build either the one or the other, except on this mud-sill. Fortunately for the South, she found a race adapted to that purpose to her hand. A race inferior to her own, but eminently qualified in temper, in vigor, in docility, in capacity to stand the climate, to answer all her purposes. We use them for our purpose, and call them slaves ... I will not characterize that class at the North by that term; but you have it; it is there; it is everywhere; it is eternal.

The Senator from New York said yesterday that the whole world had abolished slavery. Aye, the *name, but not the thing*; all the powers of the earth cannot abolish that. God only can do it when he repeals the *fiat*, "the poor ye always have with you;" for the man who lives by daily labor, and scarcely lives

Reprinted from "Speech on the Admission of Kansas," U.S. Senate, March 4, 1858, in *Selections from the Letters and Speeches of the Hon. James H. Hammond, of South Carolina* (New York, 1866).

at that, and who has to put out his labor in the market, and take the best he can get for it; in short, your whole hireling class of manual laborers and "operatives," as you call them, are essentially slaves. The difference between us is, that our slaves are hired for life and well compensated; there is no starvation, no begging, no want of employment among our people, and not too much employment either. Yours are hired by the day, not cared for, and scantily compensated, which may be proved in the most painful manner, at any hour in any street in any of your large towns. Why, you meet more beggars in one day, in any single street of the city of New York, than you would meet in a lifetime in the whole South. We do not think that whites should be slaves either by law or necessity. Our slaves are black, of another and inferior race. The *status* in which we have placed them is an elevation. They are elevated from the condition in which God first created them, by being made our slaves. None of that race on the whole face of the globe can be compared with the slaves of the South. They are happy, content, unaspiring, and utterly incapable, from intellectual weakness, ever to give us any trouble by their aspirations.

Interpretations

6 / John Hope Franklin
The South Strikes Back

(1947)

Despite the fact that there was considerable Southern sentiment against slavery during the colonial and early national periods, the institution always had its defenders. Almost from the beginning no attack on slavery went unanswered. When Judge Samuel Sewall wrote *The Selling of Joseph*, John Saffin answered his attack on slavery with an enthusiastic rebuttal in 1701. Persons of no less stature than George Whitefield, the great evangelist, and his friend James Habersham sprang to the defense of slavery in the middle of the eighteenth century. When there was some doubt regarding the future of slavery under the new national government, most of the Southern delegates made it clear that they would tolerate no interference with the institution. From the time that Jefferson's *Notes on Virginia* were made public, Southern leaders did not hesitate to use his work to strengthen their contention that Negroes were by nature an inferior race and therefore should be enslaved. Some Southerners conceded that slavery was a political evil, but almost none agreed with anti-slavery antagonists that it was also a great moral evil . . .

Even before the great debate over the admission of Missouri, the anti-slavery movement had assumed something of a sectional character. Emancipation of the slaves in Northern states had proceeded at a time when the institution was becoming more deeply entrenched in the South with the development of the cotton kingdom. The emigration of the majority of anti-slavery men and women from the slave states, moreover, deprived the South of an opportunity to hear the other side of the argument from its neighbors. Professor Dwight L. Dumond insists that this migration deprived the South of men and women "whose combined intelligence, moral courage, and Christian benevolence would have gone far toward modifying the harsher features of slavery, toward preventing so great a unanimity of opinion in that section in support of slavery as a positive good, and toward keeping alive the spirit of

John Hope Franklin, *From Slavery to Freedom*, 3rd ed. Copyright 1947, © 1956, 1967 by Alfred A. Knopf, Inc. Reprinted by permission of the publisher.

free discussion." Later, as anti-slavery men withdrew from the colonization movement and organized militant anti-slavery societies, the South found that it could no longer give any countenance to the enemies of slavery in its midst. The debate over Missouri, the insurrection of Denmark Vesey, and the increased activity of the abolitionists all convinced the men of the South that they must give more attention to the defense of their institution. When the call went out for defenders, they were sufficient both in number and in zeal. They began to strike back at their Northern traducers, blow for blow.

Southerners were now determined not to apologize for slavery. They stopped thinking of it as possessing any undesirable aspects. They evolved the idea, and clung to it with ferocious tenacity, that slavery was a positive good. In 1826 Edward Brown brought out his *Notes on the Origin and Necessity of Slavery*, which drew heavily from a pamphlet published the previous year by Whitemarsh B. Seabrook. Brown declared that "slavery has ever been the stepping ladder by which countries have passed from barbarism to civilization ... It appears ... to be the only state capable of bringing the love of independence and of ease, inherent in man, to the discipline and shelter necessary to his physical wants ..." A few months later Dr. Thomas Cooper of South Carolina published his first pro-slavery pamphlet. One by one, Southern educators and ministers joined in the defense of slavery; and the war of words was on.

The pro-slavery argument was based on a theory of the racial inferiority and biological inequality of the Negro. There were four main postulates of the theory. In the first place, it was contended that slave labor was absolutely essential to the economic development and prosperity of the South. Governor Hammond of South Carolina expressed this point of view clearly: "In all social systems there must be a class to do the menial duties, to perform the drudgery of life ... Its requisites are vigor, docility, fidelity. Such a class you must have or you would not have that other class which leads progress, civilization, and refinement. It constitutes the very mud-sill of society and of political government; and you might as well attempt to build a house in the air, as to build either the one or the other, except on this mud-sill."

In the second place, it was asserted that the Negro race was inferior and destined to occupy a subordinate position. In his *Southern Institutes*, George S. Sawyer stated forcefully this point of view:

> The social, moral, and political, as well as the physical history of the negro race bears strong testimony against them; it furnishes the most undeniable proof of their mental inferiority. In no age or condition has the real negro shown a capacity to throw off the chains of barbarism and brutality that have long bound down the nations of that race; or to rise above the common cloud of darkness that still broods over them.

Dr. John H. Van Evrie, Dr. Joseph Clark Nott, and many others published works in which they subscribed to an ethnological justification of Negro slavery.

Another argument of pro-slavery leaders was that through the ages the church had sanctioned slavery as a means of converting the heathen to Christian civilization. There was, of course, some conflict between the theory that the Negro was incapable of improvement and the notion that he could be civilized and Christianized in slavery; but little attention was paid to this conflict, and each argument was used where it would do the most good. The Rev. James Henley Thornwell, Bishop Stephen Elliott, and Dr. B. M. Palmer were only three among many Southern religious leaders who held fast to this point of view and expressed it in their sermons and writings. With many Northern religious leaders holding to opposite points of view, an intersectional clash of denominations was inevitable. Thus fifteen years before the Civil War the Baptists, Methodists, and Presbyterians had each split into two groups.

Finally, the pro-slavery argument ran, the white race had not degenerated because of slavery but had developed a unique and high degree of culture. George Fitzhugh, Beverly Tucker, and others claimed that a society in which everyone was free was a failure, and that the South had solved its problems by acknowledging the fact that culture and civilization could advance only if slaves were available to do the work.

This war of words became so bitter, and the atmosphere in the South so tense, that free inquiry and free speech disappeared there. People with points of view at variance with the accepted pro-slavery creed were run out of the South. The colleges became a hotbed of secession, and every agency in the community was employed to defend slavery. Even men of letters, like William Gilmore Simms, in keeping with their thinking or with a feeling of necessity, wrote pro-slavery essays, poems, and songs. In words the South struck back with a vengeance.

7 / Winthrop D. Jordan
Modern Tensions and the Origins of American Slavery

(1962)

Thanks to John Smith we know that Negroes first came to the British continental colonies in 1619. What we do not know is exactly when Negroes were first enslaved there. This question has been debated by historians for the past

Winthrop D. Jordan, "Modern Tensions and the Origins of American Slavery," *Journal of Southern History*, XXVIII (February, 1962), 18–30. Copyright 1962 by the Southern Historical Association. Reprinted by permission of the Managing Editor. Footnotes omitted by permission. A modified and much more complete description of the origin of American slavery is in Winthrop D. Jordan, *White Over Black: American Attitudes Toward the Negro, 1550–1812* (Chapel Hill, 1968).

seventy years, the critical point being whether Negroes were enslaved almost from their first importation or whether they were at first simply servants and only later reduced to the status of slaves. The long duration and vigor of the controversy suggest that more than a simple question of dating has been involved. In fact certain current tensions in American society have complicated the historical problem and greatly heightened its significance. Dating the origins of slavery has taken on a striking modern relevance.

During the nineteenth century historians assumed almost universally that the first Negroes came to Virginia as slaves. So close was their acquaintance with the problem of racial slavery that it did not occur to them that Negroes could ever have been anything but slaves. Philip A. Bruce, the first man to probe with some thoroughness into the early years of American slavery, adopted this view in 1896, although he emphasized that the original difference in treatment between white servants and Negroes was merely that Negroes served for life. Just six years later, however, came a challenge from a younger, professionally trained historian, James C. Ballagh. His *A History of Slavery in Virginia* appeared in the *Johns Hopkins University Studies in Historical and Political Science*, an aptly named series which was to usher in the new era of scholarly detachment in the writing of institutional history. Ballagh offered a new and different interpretation; he took the position that the first Negroes served merely as servants and that enslavement did not begin until around 1660, when statutes bearing on slavery were passed for the first time.

There has since been agreement on dating the statutory establishment of slavery, and differences of opinion have centered on when enslavement began in actual practice. Fortunately there has also been general agreement on slavery's distinguishing characteristics: service for life and inheritance of like obligation by any offspring. Writing on the free Negro in Virginia for the Johns Hopkins series, John H. Russell in 1913 tackled the central question and showed that some Negroes were indeed servants but concluded that "between 1640 and 1660 slavery was fast becoming an established fact. In this twenty years the colored population was divided, part being servants and part being slaves, and some who were servants defended themselves with increasing difficulty from the encroachments of slavery." Ulrich B. Phillips, though little interested in the matter, in 1918 accepted Russell's conclusion of early servitude and transition toward slavery after 1640. Helen T. Catterall took much the same position in 1926. On the other hand, in 1921 James M. Wright, discussing the free Negro in Maryland, implied that Negroes were slaves almost from the beginning, and in 1940 Susie M. Ames reviewed several cases in Virginia which seemed to indicate that genuine slavery had existed well before Ballagh's date of 1660.

All this was a very small academic gale, well insulated from the outside world. Yet despite disagreement on dating enslavement, the earlier writers—Bruce, Ballagh, and Russell—shared a common assumption which, though at the time seemingly irrelevant to the main question, has since proved of considerable importance. They assumed that prejudice against the Negro was natural and almost innate in the white man. It would be surprising if they had felt otherwise in this period of segregation statutes, overseas imperialism, immigration restriction, and full-throated Anglo-Saxonism. By the 1920's, however, with the easing of these tensions, the assumption of natural prejudice was dropped unnoticed. Yet only one historian explicitly contradicted that assumption: Ulrich Phillips of Georgia, impressed with the geniality of both slavery and twentieth-century race relations, found no natural prejudice in the white man and expressed his "conviction that Southern racial asperities are mainly superficial, and that the two great elements are fundamentally in accord."

Only when tensions over race relations intensified once more did the older assumption of natural prejudice crop up again. After World War II American Negroes found themselves beneficiaries of New Deal politics and reforms, wartime need for manpower, world-wide repulsion at racist excesses in Nazi Germany, and growingly successful colored anticolonialism. With new militancy Negroes mounted an attack on the citadel of separate but equal, and soon it became clear that America was in for a period of self-conscious reappraisal of its racial arrangements. Writing in this period of heightened tension (1949) a practiced and careful scholar, Wesley F. Craven, raised the old question of the Negro's original status, suggesting that Negroes had been enslaved at an early date. Craven also cautiously resuscitated the idea that white men may have had natural distaste for the Negro, an idea which fitted neatly with the suggestion of early enslavement. Original antipathy would mean rapid debasement.

In the next year (1950) came a sophisticated counterstatement, which contradicted both Craven's dating and implicitly any suggestion of early prejudice. Oscar and Mary F. Handlin in "Origins of the Southern Labor System" offered a case for late enslavement, with servitude as the status of Negroes before about 1660. Originally the status of both Negroes and white servants was far short of freedom, the Handlins maintained, but Negroes failed to benefit from increased freedom for servants in mid-century and became less free rather than more. Embedded in this description of diverging status were broader implications: Late and gradual enslavement undercut the possibility of natural, deep-seated antipathy toward Negroes. On the contrary, if whites and Negroes could share the same status of half freedom for forty years in the seventeenth century, why could they not share full freedom in the twentieth?

The same implications were rendered more explicit by Kenneth M. Stampp in a major reassessment of Southern slavery published two years after the Supreme Court's 1954 school decision. Reading physiology with the eye of faith, Stampp frankly stated his assumption "that innately Negroes *are*, after all, only white men with black skins, nothing more, nothing less."

Closely following the Handlins' article on the origins of slavery itself, he almost directly denied any pattern of early and inherent racial antipathy: "... Negro and white servants of the seventeenth century seemed to be remarkably unconcerned about their visible physical differences." As for "the trend toward special treatment" of the Negro, "physical and cultural differences provided handy excuses to justify it." Distaste for the Negro, then, was in the beginning scarcely more than an appurtenance of slavery.

These views squared nicely with the hopes of those even more directly concerned with the problem of contemporary race relations, sociologists and social psychologists. Liberal on the race question almost to a man, they tended to see slavery as the initial cause of the Negro's current degradation. The modern Negro was the unhappy victim of long association with base status. Sociologists, though uninterested in tired questions of historical evidence, could not easily assume a natural prejudice in the white man as the cause of slavery. Natural or innate prejudice would not only violate their basic assumptions concerning the dominance of culture but would undermine the power of their new Baconian science. For if prejudice was natural there would be little one could do to wipe it out. Prejudice must have followed enslavement, not vice versa, else any liberal program of action would be badly compromised. One prominent social scientist suggested in a UNESCO pamphlet that racial prejudice in the United States commenced with the cotton gin!

Just how closely the question of dating had become tied to the practical matter of action against racial prejudice was made apparent by the suggestions of still another historian. Carl N. Degler grappled with the dating problem in an article frankly entitled "Slavery and the Genesis of American Race Prejudice." The article appeared in 1959, a time when Southern resistance to school desegregation seemed more adamant than ever and the North's hands none too clean, a period of discouragement for those hoping to end racial discrimination. Prejudice against the Negro now appeared firm and deep-seated, less easily eradicated than had been supposed in, say, 1954. It was Degler's view that enslavement began early, as a result of white settlers' prejudice or antipathy toward the first Negroes. Thus not only were the sociologists contradicted but the dating problem was now overtly and consciously tied to the broader question of whether slavery caused prejudice or prejudice caused slavery. A new self-consciousness over the American racial dilemma had snatched an arid historical controversy from the hands of an unsuspecting earlier generation and had tossed it into the arena of current debate.

Ironically there might have been no historical controversy at all if every historian dealing with the subject had exercised greater care with facts and greater restraint in interpretation. Too often the debate entered the realm of inference and assumption. For the crucial early years after 1619 there is simply not enough evidence to indicate with any certainty whether

Negroes were treated like white servants or not. No historian has found anything resembling proof one way or the other. The first Negroes were sold to the English settlers, yet so were other Englishmen. It can be said, however, that Negroes were set apart from white men by the word *Negroes*, and a distinct name is not attached to a group unless it is seen as different. The earliest Virginia census reports plainly distinguished Negroes from white men, sometimes giving Negroes no personal name; and in 1629 every commander of the several plantations was ordered to "take a generall muster of all the inhabitants men woemen and Children as well *Englishe* as Negroes." Difference, however, might or might not involve inferiority.

The first evidence as to the actual status of Negroes does not appear until about 1640. Then it becomes clear that *some* Negroes were serving for life and some children inheriting the same obligations. Here it is necessary to suggest with some candor that the Handlins' statement to the contrary rests on unsatisfactory documentation. That some Negroes were held as slaves after about 1640 is no indication, however, that American slavery popped into the world fully developed at that time. Many historians, most cogently the Handlins, have shown slavery to have been a gradual development, a process not completed until the eighteenth century. The complete deprivation of civil and personal rights, the legal conversion of the Negro into a chattel, in short slavery as Americans came to know it, was not accomplished overnight. Yet these developments practically and logically depended on the practice of hereditary lifetime service, and it is certainly possible to find in the 1640's and 1650's traces of slavery's most essential feature.

The first definite trace appears in 1640 when the Virginia General Court pronounced sentence on three servants who had been retaken after running away to Maryland. Two of them, a Dutchman and a Scot, were ordered to serve their masters for one additional year and then the colony for three more, but "the third being a negro named John Punch shall serve his said master or his assigns for the time of his natural life here or else where." No white servant in America, so far as is known, ever received a like sentence. Later the same month a Negro was again singled out from a group of recaptured runaways; six of the seven were assigned additional time while the Negro was given none, presumably because he was already serving for life. After 1640, too, county court records began to mention Negroes, in part because there were more of them than previously—about two per cent of the Virginia population in 1649. Sales for life, often including any future progeny, were recorded in unmistakable language. In 1646 Francis Pott sold a Negro woman and boy to Stephen Charlton "to the use of him ... forever." Similarly, six years later William Whittington sold to John Pott "one Negro girle named Jowan; aged about Ten yeares and with her Issue and produce duringe her (or either of them) for their Life tyme. And their Successors forever"; and a Maryland man in 1649 deeded two Negro men and a woman "and all their issue both male and Female." The executors of a York County estate in 1647 disposed of eight Negroes—four men, two women, and two children—to Captain John Chisman "to have hold occupy posesse and inioy and every one of the afforementioned Negroes forever[.]" The will of Rowland Burnham of "Rapahanocke," made in 1657, dispensed his considerable number of Negroes and white servants in language which clearly differentiated between the two by specifying that the whites were to serve for their "full terme of tyme" and the Negroes "for ever." Nor did anything in the will indicate that this distinction was exceptional or novel.

In addition to these clear indications that some Negroes were owned for life, there were cases of Negroes held for terms far longer than the normal five or seven years. On the other hand, some Negroes served only the term usual for white servants, and others were completely free. One Negro freeman, Anthony Johnson, himself owned a Negro. Obviously the enslavement of some Negroes did not mean the immediate enslavement of all.

Further evidence of Negroes serving for life lies in the prices paid for them. In many instances the valuations placed on Negroes (in estate inventories and bills of sale) were far higher than for white servants, even those servants with full terms yet to serve. Since there was ordinarily no preference for Negroes as such, higher prices must have meant that Negroes were more highly valued because of their greater length of service. Negro women may have been especially prized, moreover, because their progeny could also be held perpetually. In 1645, for example, two Negro women and a boy were sold for 5,500 pounds of tobacco. Two years earlier William Burdett's inventory listed eight servants (with the time each had still to serve) at valuations ranging from 400 to 1,100 pounds, while a "very anntient" Negro was valued at 3,000 and an eight-year-old Negro girl at 2,000 pounds, with no time-remaining indicated for either. In the late 1650's an inventory of Thomas Ludlow's large estate evaluated a white servant with six years to serve at less than an elderly Negro man and only one half of a Negro woman. The labor owned by James Stone in 1648 was evaluated as follows:

	lb tobo
Thomas Groves, 4 yeares to serve	1300
Francis Bomley for 6 yeares	1500
John Thackstone for 3 yeares	1300
Susan Davis for 3 yeares	1000
Emaniell a Negro man	2000
Roger Stone 3 yeares	1300
Mingo a Negro man	2000

Besides setting a higher value on the two Negroes, Stone's inventory, like Burdett's, failed to indicate the number of years they had still to serve. It would seem safe to assume that the time remaining was omitted in this and similar documents simply because the Negroes were regarded as serving for an unlimited time.

The situation in Maryland was apparently the same. In 1643 Governor Leonard Calvert agreed with John Skinner, "mariner," to exchange certain estates for seventeen sound Negro "slaves," fourteen men and three women between sixteen and twenty-six years old. The total value of these was placed at 24,000 pounds of tobacco, which would work out to 1,000 pounds for the women and 1,500 for the men, prices considerably higher than those paid for white servants at the time.

Wherever Negro women were involved, however, high valuations may have reflected the fact that they could be used for field work while white women generally were not. This discrimination between Negro and white women, of course, fell short of actual enslavement. It meant merely that Negroes were set apart in a way clearly not to their advantage. Yet this is not the only evidence that Negroes were subjected to degrading distinctions not directly related to slavery. In several ways Negroes were singled out for special treatment which suggested a generalized debasing of Negroes as a group. Significantly, the first indications of debasement appeared at about the same time as the first indications of actual enslavement.

The distinction concerning field work is a case in point. It first appeared on the written record in 1643, when Virginia pointedly recognized it in her taxation policy. Previously tithable persons had been defined (1629) as "all those that worke in the ground of what qualitie or condition soever." Now the law stated that all adult men and *Negro* women were to be tithable, and this distinction was made twice again before 1660. Maryland followed a similar course, beginning in 1654. John Hammond, in a 1656 tract defending the tobacco colonies, wrote that servant women were not put to work in the fields but in domestic employments, "yet som wenches that are nasty, and beastly and not fit to be so imployed are put into the ground." Since all Negro women were taxed as working in the fields, it would seem logical to conclude that Virginians found them "nasty" and "beastly." The essentially racial nature of this discrimination was bared by a 1668 law at the time slavery was crystallizing on the statute books:

> Whereas some doubts, have arisen whether negro women set free were still to be accompted tithable according to a former act, *It is declared by this grand assembly* that negro women, though permitted to enjoy their ffreedome yet ought not in all respects to be admitted to a full fruition of the exemptions and impunities of the English, and are still lyable to payment of taxes.

Virginia law set Negroes apart in a second way by denying them the important right and obligation to bear arms. Few restraints could indicate more clearly the denial to Negroes of membership in the white community. This action, in a sense the first foreshadowing of the slave codes, came in 1640, at just the time when other indications first appear that Negroes were subject to special treatment.

Finally, an even more compelling sense of the separateness of Negroes was revealed in early distress concerning sexual union between the races. In 1630 a Virginia court pronounced a now famous sentence: "Hugh Davis to be soundly whipped, before an assembly of Negroes and others for abusing himself to the dishonor of God and shame of Christians, by defiling his body in lying with a negro." While there were other instances of punishment for interracial union in the ensuing years, fornication rather than miscegenation may well have been the primary offense, though in 1651 a Maryland man sued someone who he claimed had said "that he had a black bastard in Virginia." There may have been nothing racial about the 1640 case by which Robert Sweet was compelled "to do penance in church according to laws of England, for getting a negroe woman with child and the woman whipt." About 1650 a white man and a Negro woman were required to stand clad in white sheets before a congregation in Lower Norfolk County for having had relations, but this punishment was sometimes used in ordinary cases of fornication between two whites.

It is certain, however, that in the early 1660's when slavery was gaining statutory recognition, the colonial assemblies legislated with feeling against miscegenation. Nor was this merely a matter of avoiding confusion of status, as was suggested by the Handlins. In 1662 Virginia declared that "if any christian shall commit ffornication with a negro man or woman, hee or shee soe offending" should pay double the usual fine. Two years later Maryland prohibited interracial marriages:

> forasmuch as divers freeborne English women forgettfull of their free Condicon and to the disgrace of our Nation doe intermarry with Negro Slaves by which alsoe divers suites may arise touching the Issue of such woemen and a great damage doth befall the Masters of such Negroes for prevention whereof for deterring such freeborne women from such shame-full Matches . . .

strong language indeed if the problem had only been confusion of status. A Maryland act of 1681 described marriages of white women with Negroes as, among other things, "always to the Satisfaccon of theire Lascivious & Lustfull desires, & to the disgrace not only of the English butt allso of many other Christian Nations." When Virginia finally prohibited all interracial liaisons in 1691, the assembly vigorously denounced miscegenation and its fruits as "that abominable mixture and spurious issue."

One is confronted, then, with the fact that the first evidences of enslavement and of other forms of debasement appeared at about the same time. Such coincidence comports poorly with both views on the causation of prejudice and slavery. If slavery caused prejudice, then invidious distinctions concerning working in the fields, bearing arms, and sexual union should have appeared only after slavery's firm establishment. If prejudice caused slavery, then one would expect to find such lesser discriminations preceding the greater discrimination of outright enslavement.

Perhaps a third explanation of the relationship between slavery and prejudice may be offered, one that might fit the pattern of events as revealed by existing evidence. Both current views share a common starting point: They predicate two factors, prejudice and slavery, and demand a distinct order of causality. No matter how qualified by recognition that the effect may in turn react upon the cause, each approach inevitably tends to deny the validity of its opposite. But what if one were to regard both slavery and prejudice as species of a general debasement of the Negro? Both may have been equally cause and effect, constantly reacting upon each other, dynamically joining hands to hustle the Negro down the road to complete degradation. Mutual causation is, of course, a highly useful concept for describing social situations in the modern world. Indeed it has been widely applied in only slightly altered fashion to the current racial situation: Racial prejudice and the Negro's lowly position are widely accepted as constantly reinforcing each other.

This way of looking at the facts might well fit better with what we know of slavery itself. Slavery was an organized pattern of human relationships. No matter what the law might say, it was of different character than cattle ownership. No matter how degrading, slavery involved human beings. No one seriously pretended otherwise. Slavery was not an isolated economic or institutional phenomenon; it was the practical facet of a general debasement without which slavery could have no rationality. (Prejudice, too, was a form of debasement, a kind of slavery in the mind.) Certainly the urgent need for labor in a virgin country guided the direction which debasement took, molded it, in fact, into an institutional framework. That economic practicalities shaped the external form of debasement should not tempt one to forget, however, that slavery was at bottom a social arrangement, a way of society's ordering its members in its own mind.

Racism and the Attack on Slavery

Introduction

Pro-slavery polemics were characteristically responsive and defensive; slavery's apologists did not initiate the controversy over "the peculiar institution," nor did they establish the terms and categories of the debate. Slavery had to be attacked before anyone in white America comprehended that it needed to be defended—a sign, perhaps, of how deeply racism was engrained in the culture of early America and, indeed, of the whole western world. The attack on slavery originated among the Quakers in the seventeenth century: the earliest known public protest against slavery in America was drawn up by a group of Friends at Germantown, Pennsylvania, in 1688. Throughout the colonial years Quakers took the lead, commonly a lonely lead, in combating slavery. Their most eloquent and vigorous spokesman was John Woolman, whose powerful plea entitled *Some Considerations on the Keeping of Negroes* is excerpted in the readings below. For the most part, however, anti-slavery Quakers were either more concerned with an ethical judgment of the institution than with a political campaign against it or at most were concerned with abolishing it within their own sect alone.

In the early years of American independence, many advocates of freedom from British rule found it difficult to reconcile their advocacy of freedom for themselves with the practice of keeping others in bondage, and a number of them said so quite forcefully, as the passages quoted below under the heading, "The Glorious Cause of Liberty," indicate. Yet though slavery was either abolished or set in the way of extinction in the Northern and Middle states, the Revolution did not significantly affect the social system of the South. One reason was the general and apparently sincere belief that slavery in time would naturally die out. Another was the inability of whites to contemplate with equanimity a genuinely bi-racial society in which blacks would have their equal share of freedom; even the most revolutionary white American tended to take alarm when he began to work out the full implications of the assertion that "all men are created equal." In addition, in 1793 came Eli Whitney's invention of the cotton gin, which effectually confirmed the empire of slavery in the South. Hence it was not till some years later, in the 1820's and 1830's, that the abolition movement can be said to have been taken with real seriousness either in the North, where it rose aggressively, or in the South, where it was earnestly repulsed, and not until the 1850's did slavery become the single most important issue in American politics.

It is almost impossible to overestimate the difficulties which confronted abolitionists in their campaign against slavery. They were few in number and much of the time they encountered either apathy or outright hostility in the North and, of course, almost absolute detestation in the South. Slavery was recognized in the Constitution, and a minority of determined white Southern representatives could prevent any serious attempt legally to abolish the institution. As we have seen, the literal approach to the Bible seemed to lend itself more easily to a defense of slavery than to an attack upon it. In addition, the preponderance of scientific opinion at the time was heavily on the side of the assumption that blacks were innately almost hopelessly inferior to whites. In these circumstances, the abolitionists had to fight the image given them by their opponents North and South of wild men and women or at best sickly humanitarians and do-gooders, unorthodox Christians if Christians at all, and associated with every variety of radicalism—socialism, religious scepticism, women's rights, transcendentalism, vegetarianism, and temperance reform.

It is little wonder that, deprived of any feasible method of changing the law to abolish slavery in the Southern states, the abolitionists should have resorted to highly emotional rhetoric. This characteristic of the movement undoubtedly strikes the modern reader more than it did people at the time. Emotionalism, especially in oratory, was then the dominant method by which issues were presented to the public, and emotion for emotion the abolitionists could easily be matched by the "fire-eater" defenders of slavery. Undoubtedly, a movement like abolitionism, certain to invoke the strongest feelings from the opposition, would be likely to attract people whose earnest conviction was sometimes more apparent than their willingness logically to debate. Thus it happened that some of the advocates of abolitionism frequently boiled over into fanaticism. Wendell Phillips, for example, could on one occasion advise the members of his audience that anyone would be justified in shooting a Federal officer who attempted to enforce the Fugitive Slave Law and on another he called Abraham Lincoln a "slave-hound."[1] At least equally impassioned was William Lloyd Garrison, proprietor of the abolitionist propaganda sheet, *The Liberator*, who came to personify, before John Brown, the cause of anti-slavery in the mind of the slave-holding South, and Harriet Beecher Stowe whose novel, *Uncle Tom's Cabin*, probably did more than any other single piece of writing to win converts to abolitionism and stiffen the resistance of the South. Selections from the writings of Garrison and Mrs.

[1] Quoted from *The Liberator*, April 11, 1851, in Irving H. Bartlett, *Wendell Phillips—Brahmin Radical* (Boston, 1961), p. 222.

Stowe are included among the materials in this section that illustrate the character of white abolitionism.

Some of the abolitionists used the Bible as the Southern proponents of slavery did, citing chapter and verse. The tendency was, however, to emphasize the great ethical truths of Christianity rather than specific citations which could be directly applied to the institution of slavery. The abolitionists argued, for example, that Adam and Eve were the parents of all humanity and therefore that it was wrong for the white branch of the human race to enslave the black branch. They argued that slavery was inconsistent with the Golden Rule, the injunction that one should do unto others as he would have others do to himself (Matthew 7:12). Deprived of firm support from the anthropologists of the time, they appealed to those scientific men who were anti-slavery or attempted to show, when they dealt with the subject at all, that such a variety of opinions existed on the meaning of the concept of race that "ethnology," as it was then called, was not yet an authoritative discipline. Their strongest arguments, however, were derived from an examination of the system of slavery itself—the whippings, brandings, and maimings, the separation of families, the denial of the right to permanent marriage, the pitiful plight of runaways. The inherent cruelties of slavery provided the abolitionists with an almost inexhaustible supply of arguments against it.

Blacks, too, took a vigorous part in the struggle against slavery. Slave uprisings in the South, such as the Nat Turner Rebellion of 1831, made it evident that conditions of life on the plantations were far from universally tolerable and that the desire for freedom ran deep among the slaves. The free blacks of the North, concerned about the plight of their brothers held in bondage, eagerly assisted white abolitionists in the frontal assault on slavery. Led by such outstanding men as Frederick Douglass, the foremost black abolitionist of the nineteenth century, northern blacks acted as conductors on the "Underground Railroad," raised money for the antislavery cause within their own community, conducted public meetings to protest slavery and racism, propagandized abolition by means of black newspapers and tracts, and cooperated enthusiastically, if not always in perfect harmony, with white abolitionists. At the same time, the beginnings of black nationalism appeared among blacks who sought escape from racism by the establishment of black colonies or nations abroad to which American blacks were urged to emigrate.

8 / John Woolman and the Quaker Opposition to Slavery

(1754)

"Suppose then, that our Ancestors and we had been exposed to constant servitude ..."

Among the early protests against slavery were those of the Quakers. The nature of the Quaker faith was such as to emphasize the role of the community of members and to attempt to deepen and expand it. Thus, the Quaker movement early came to recognize the evils of slavery as an impediment to the wider community. John Woolman (1720–1772) was the most persuasive of the Quakers in his arguments against slavery, and he had real insight into the evils which slavery involved. He himself was suddenly struck by the evils of slavery when, at the age of twenty-three, he was asked to write a bill of sale for a black slave. Later, on a trip from his native New Jersey, Woolman encountered slave plantations in Maryland and Virginia. He shrewdly observed how slavery helped to cause the very characteristics in blacks which white men argued were inherently a part of the blacks' nature:

> Suppose then, that our Ancestors and we had been exposed to constant servitude, in the more servile and inferior Employments of Life; that we had been destitute of the Help of Reading and good Company; that amongst ourselves we had had few wise and pious Instructors; that the Religious amongst our Superiors seldom took Notice of us; that while others, in Ease, have plentifully heaped up the Fruit of our Labour, we had receiv'd barely enough to relieve Nature, and being wholly at the Command of others, had generally been treated as a contemptible, ignorant Part of Mankind: Should we, in that Case, be less abject than they now are? Again, if Oppression be so hard to bear, that a wise Man is made mad by it, Eccl. vii. 7, then a Series of those Things, altering the Behaviour and Manners of a People, is what may reasonably be expected.... These and other Circumstances, rightly considered, will lessen that too great Disparity which some make between us and them.

John Woolman, *Some Considerations on the Keeping of Negroes* (Philadelphia, 1754).

Woolman also recognized that the damage was not merely to the character of the black slaves but to that of the white masters as well. He further recognized that this damage took place in the whites even while they were still children:

> And if Children are not only educated in the Way of so great Temptation, but have also the Opportunity of lording it over their Fellow Creatures, and being Masters of Men in their Childhood, how can we hope otherwise than that their tender Minds will be possessed with Thoughts too high for them?

Woolman correctly forecast that slavery was an evil which would some day demand an accounting:

> I saw in these Southern provinces so many vices and corruptions, increased by this [slave] trade and this way of life, that it appeared to me as a dark gloominess hanging over the land; and though now many willingly run into it, yet in future the consequences will be grievous to posterity.

In a later edition of *Some Considerations on the Keeping of Negroes*, published in 1762, Woolman again perceptively analyzed the evils of slavery:

> Placing on Men the ignominious Title SLAVE, dressing them in uncomely Garments, keeping them to servile Labour, in which they are often dirty, tends gradually to fix a Notion in the Mind, that they are a Sort of People below us in Nature, and leads us to consider them as such in all our Conclusions about them. And, moreover, a Person, which in our Esteem is mean and contemptible, if their Language or Behaviour toward us is unseemly or disrespectful, it excites Wrath more powerfully than the like Conduct in one we accounted our Equal or Superior; and where this happens to be the Case, it disqualifies for candid Judgment; for it is unfit for a Person to sit as Judge in a Case where his own Personal Resentments are stirred up; and, as Members of Society in a well framed Government, we are mutually dependant. Present Interest incites to Duty, and makes each Man attentive to the Convenience of others; but he whose Will is a Law to Others, and can enforce Obedience by Punishment; he whose Wants are supplied without feeling any Obligation to make equal Returns to his Benefactor, his irregular Appetites find an open Field for Motion, and he is in Danger of growing hard, and inattentive to their Convenience who labour for his Support; and so loses that Disposition, in which alone Men are fit to govern.
>
> The *English* Government hath been commended by candid Foreigners for the Disuse of Racks and Tortures, so much practised in some States; but this multiplying Slaves now leads to it; for where People exact hard Labour of others, without a suitable Reward, and are resolved to continue in that Way, Severity to such who oppose them becomes the Consequence; and several *Negroe* Criminals, among the *English* in *America*, have been executed in a lingering, painful Way, very terrifying to others.

It is a happy Case to set out right, and persevere in the same Way: A wrong Beginning leads into many Difficulties; for to support one Evil, another becomes customary; two produces more; and the further Men proceed in this Way, the greater their Dangers, their Doubts and Fears; and the more painful and perplexing are their Circumstances; so that such who are true Friends to the real and lasting Interest of our Country, and candidly consider the Tendency of Things, cannot but feel some Concern on this Account.

9 / "The Glorious Cause of Liberty": Anti-Slavery in the Period of the American Revolution

Thomas Paine, 1775:

How just, how suitable to our crime is the punishment with which providence threatens us! We have enslaved multitudes . . . and now are threatened with the same . . . no other vice . . . has brought so much guilt on the land . . .

The Reverend Francis Alison, 1768:

I am assured the Common father of all men will severely plead a Controversy against these Colonies for Enslaving Negroes, . . . and possibly for this wickedness God threatens us with slavery.

Abigail Adams, 1774:

It always appeared a most iniquitous scheme to me to fight ourselves for what we are daily robbing and plundering from those who have as good a right to freedom as we have.

Correspondent to a Trenton, New Jersey, newspaper, 1780:

. . . if after we have made such a declaration to the world, we continue to hold our fellow creatures in slavery, our words must rise up in judgement against us, and by the breath of our own mouths we shall stand condemned.

Benjamin Rush, 1769:

It would be useless for us to denounce the servitude to which the Parliament of Great Britain wishes to reduce us, while we continue to keep our fellow creatures in slavery just because their color is different from ours.

James Otis, 1764:

> ... the Colonists are by the law of nature free born, as indeed all men are, white and black.

David Cooper, 1783:

> If these solemn *truths*, uttered at such an awful crisis, are *self-evident*: unless we can shew the African race are not *men*, words can hardly express the amazement which naturally arises on reflecting, that the very people who make these pompous declarations are slave-holders, and, by their legislative conduct, tell us, that these blessings were only meant to be the *rights* of *white-men* not of all *men* ...

Correspondent to a Philadelphia paper, 1768:

> How suits it with the glorious cause of Liberty to keep your fellow men in bondage, men equally the work of your great Creator, men formed for freedom as yourselves?

10 / The Anti-Slavery of William Lloyd Garrison

(1837)

Why is it unconstitutional to pity and defend them?
Because they are black.

In his passionate rhetoric, William Lloyd Garrison (1805–1879), the spearhead of New England abolitionism, came near matching the hottest of the Southern firebrands. In addition, he outdid them—at least for a time—in advocating secession, though he meant secession of the North. He argued that a Constitution which permitted slavery was a "Covenant with Death and an Agreement with Hell." Garrison frequently quarreled with his friends and split the Anti-Slavery Society asunder because many of them would not agree with his advocacy of immediate emancipation. As editor of *The Liberator*, an abolition journal published in Boston from 1831 to 1865, Garrison brought to anti-slavery a dedicated will and a burning passion. "I will be as harsh as truth and as uncompromising as justice," he declared. "I will not equivocate— I will not excuse—I will not retreat a single inch—and I will be *heard*!"

In one of the selections which follow from *The Liberator*, it is interesting to see Garrison's observations on racial intermixture. Nearly all the anthropologists of the period, if one can call them that, assumed almost as a matter of course that blacks were inferior and therefore that intermixture was a bad thing. Garrison makes the matter one of individual choice, not of the law, though there are indications that he was uncomfortable on this subject. He quickly turned the argument against the apologists for slavery by arguing that they were the true race mixers.

A Short Catechism

Adapted to All Parts of the United States

1. Why is American slaveholding in all cases not sinful?
   Because its victims are *black*.
2. Why is gradual emancipation right?
   Because the slaves are *black*.
3. Why is immediate emancipation wrong and dangerous?
   Because the slaves are *black*.
4. Why ought one-sixth portion of the American population to be exiled from their native soil?
   Because they are *black*.
5. Why would the slaves if emancipated, cut the throats of their masters.
   Because they are *black*.
6. Why are our slaves not fit for freedom?
   Because they are *black*.
7. Why are American slaveholders not thieves, tyrants and men-stealers?
   Because their victims are *black*.
8. Why does the Bible justify American slavery?
   Because its victims are *black*.
9. Why ought not the Priest and the Levite, "passing by on the other side," to be sternly rebuked?
   Because the man who has fallen among thieves, and lies weltering in his blood, is *black*.
10. Why are abolitionists fanatics, madmen and incendiaries?
    Because those for whom they plead are *black*.
11. Why are they wrong in their principles and measures?
    Because the slaves are *black*.
12. Why is all the prudence, moderation, judiciousness, philanthropy and piety on the side of their opponents?
    Because the slaves are *black*.
13. Why ought not the free discussion of slavery to be tolerated?
    Because its victims are *black*.
14. Why is Lynch law, as applied to abolitionists, better than common law?
    Because the slaves, whom they seek to emancipate, are *black*.

From *The Liberator*, November 17, 1837.

15. Why are the slaves contented and happy?
    Because they are *black!*
16. Why don't they want to be free?
    Because they are *black!*
17. Why are they not created in the image of God?
    Because their skin is *black.*
18. Why are they not cruelly treated, but enjoy unusual comforts and privileges?
    Because they are *black!*
19. Why are they not our brethren and countrymen?
    Because they are *black.*
20. Why is it unconstitutional to pity and defend them?
    Because they are *black.*
21. Why is it a violation of the national compact to rebuke their masters?
    Because they are *black.*
22. Why will they be lazy, improvident, and worthless, if set free?
    Because their skin is *black.*
23. Why will the whites wish to amalgamate with them in a state of freedom?
    Because they are *black!!*
24. Why must the Union be dissolved, should Congress abolish slavery in the District of Columbia?
    Because the slaves in that District are *black.*
25. Why are abolitionists justly treated as outlaws in one half of the Union?
    Because those whose cause they espouse are *black.*
26. Why is slavery "the corner-stone of our republican edifice?"
    Because its victims are *black.*

We have thus given twenty-six replies to those who assail our principles and measures—that is, one reply, unanswerable and all-comprehensive, to all the cavils, complaints, criticisms, objections, and difficulties which swarm in each State in the Union, against our holy enterprize. The victims are BLACK! "That alters the case!" There is not an individual in all this country, who is not conscious before God, that if the slaves at the South should be today miraculously transformed into men of white complexions, tomorrow the abolitionists would be recognized and cheered as the best friends of their race; their principles would be eulogized as sound and incontrovertible, and their measures as rational and indispensable! Then, indeed, immediate emancipation would be the right of the slaves, and the duty of the masters! . . .

Letter to *The Liberator*, published March 31, 1832.
To Wm. Lloyd Garrison:
There has been accidentally thrown in my way a paper headed "*The Liberator.*" The beautiful cuts with which it is decorated attracted my attention, and induced me to peruse its contents. Your paper, Sir, is a lame and

impotent production, designed obviously for the most base and infamous purpose; and can have no other ultimate effect than to render the negroes dissatisfied with their condition, and thereby make it necessary to hold them in stricter subjection ...

There is another small matter between us, Master Garrison. You don't seem to like the law of your State, which prohibits the unholy alliance between white and black. Suppose you were to take a fancy to a brute; would you not make the same objections to the law against Sodomy? Answer me *that*, Master Garrison. The white man or woman who would consent to marry a negro, deserves to be hung with a knotty grape vine, without benefit of Clergy. "*Fleas* are not *Lobsters*—d—m their souls." Negroes and white men are essentially distinct in their nature. It is a most *odious* and *odorous* comparison. The dark complexion, peculiar features, woolly hair and small skulls of the negroes, are not their only characteristics. Their blood is not of the temperature of ours by two degrees; and their mental capacities are an hundred degrees below that of some of their white "brethren," as you pleased to call us. It is idle to take the intelligence of a few individuals, as a criterion by which to judge of their intellect as a people. Such instances only serve to unite these two links in the chain of creation, which extends from the honorable, free-born, high-born, high-bred Virginian, down to the meanest reptile in existence, such as your ignoble self. The progeny of a Yankee and Negro would indeed be a nondescript in natural history; uniting the selfishness, duplicity, canting hypocrisy and vicious propensities of the one, to the recklessness, obstinacy and folly of the other: in short, just such a monster as yourself. Publish this without mutilation or alteration. I dare you. Answer me without equivocation or evasion. I defy you. And if your infamous and villanous paper should ever again pollute my sight, *I'll* publish you from Dan to Beersheba, until you cry "hold, enough."

Hotspur

Garrison's reply:

... The logic of this writer dishonors his understanding: but a man-stealer may as well attempt to fly, as to reason coherently on the subject of slavery ...

I have never expressed any opinion of the propriety or impropriety of inter-marriage with persons of color. I neither advocate nor oppose an honorable amalgamation. It is not my province, nor that of any body of men, to regulate human affection or prescribe objects of attachment. I call for the repeal of the marriage law of this State, because it not only discredits the good sense of the Commonwealth, but is a direct invasion of an inalienable right, and one of the links of that chain which binds millions of our race in servitude. But the impudence of the Virginia "hotspur" is exceeded only by his indecency. *He* scouts a *lawful* connexion between whites and blacks, who is doubtless holding an illicit and constant commerce with his female slaves! Ay, even the "honor-able, free-born, high-bred Virginian" is nightly mingling his *pure* blood with other blood, between the temperature of which are "two degrees"! and he often contrives to live by selling off a certain number of his own children annually!! I might tell some tales, with regard to this intercourse, even of the first men in Virginia; but their recital would be too disgusting for the public eye.

11 / Harriet Beecher Stowe: *Uncle Tom's Cabin*

(1852)

"A black woman . . . threw her arms round that unfortunate piece of merchandise before enumerated—'John, aged thirty.'"

Harriet Beecher Stowe was certainly the most powerful of the abolitionist writers. *Uncle Tom's Cabin* (1852) was the greatest fictional success of nineteenth century America. It still makes impressive reading. Mrs. Stowe was the daughter, the sister, and the wife of clergymen. She was familiar from childhood with all the subtleties of theological argument, with the detection of logical fallacies, and with the knowledge of how to transform argument into transcendently moral terms. When it was published, *Uncle Tom's Cabin* was furiously resented in the white South as presenting an unfair portrait of the South and of slavery. Nowadays, it is the advocates of black equality who often are embarrassed by the book. The sentimentality is heavily laid on, particularly in the death scene of Little Eva. More important, modern readers recognize that in her defense of the black, Mrs. Stowe has her own stereotype. She sees blacks as inherently religious, meek, loyal, inclined to gaudiness in dress. These conceptions are serious faults, certainly, since it is possible to read the book and think of blacks not as beings like other people but as inferior beings to whom whites should show kindliness and sympathy. On its strong points, however, the book is a mercilessly logical indictment of slavery. Every conceivable argument in favor of the system Mrs. Stowe anticipates and destroys. Better than any other writer of her time, she shows that slavery was a ghastly commentary on the ideals of Christianity.

In the passages below, Uncle Tom has been sold by Mr. Shelby, his kindly Kentucky owner, because of financial difficulties. Haley is a slave trader who is transporting Uncle Tom down the Ohio and the Mississippi rivers to Louisiana where he ultimately will end up as the slave of cruel master, Simon Legree. The scene which follows takes place on the steamboat on the way to New Orleans.

Harriet Beecher Stowe, *Uncle Tom's Cabin* (Boston, 1852).

The La Belle Rivière, as brave and beautiful a boat as ever walked the waters of her namesake river, was floating gayly down the stream, under a brilliant sky, the stripes and stars of free America waving and fluttering over head; the guards crowded with well-dressed ladies and gentlemen walking and enjoying the delightful day. All was full of life, buoyant and rejoicing;—all but Haley's gang [his slaves], who were stored, with other freight, on the lower deck, and who, somehow, did not seem to appreciate their various privileges, as they sat in a knot, talking to each other in low tones.

"Boys," said Haley, coming up, briskly, "I hope you keep up good heart, and are cheerful. Now, no sulks, ye see; keep stiff upper lip, boys; do well by me, and I'll do well by you."

The boys addressed responded the invariable "Yes, Mas'r," for ages the watchword of poor Africa; but it's to be owned they did not look particularly cheerful; they had their various little prejudices in favor of wives, mothers, sisters, and children, seen for the last time,—and though "they that wasted them required of them mirth," it was not instantly forthcoming.

"I've got a wife," spoke out the article enumerated as "John, aged thirty," and he laid his chained hand on Tom's knee,—"and she don't know a word about this, poor girl!"

"Where does she live?" said Tom.

"In a tavern a piece down here," said John; "I wish, now, I *could* see her once more in this world," he added.

Poor John! It *was* rather natural; and the tears that fell, as he spoke, came as naturally as if he had been a white man. Tom drew a long breath from a sore heart, and tried, in his poor way, to comfort him.

And over head, in the cabin, sat fathers and mothers, husbands and wives; and merry, dancing children moved round among them, like so many little butterflies, and everything was going on quite easy and comfortable.

"O, mamma," said a boy, who had just come up from below, "there's a negro trader on board, and he's brought four or five slaves down there."

"Poor creatures!" said the mother, in a tone between grief and indignation.

"What's that?" said another lady.

"Some poor slaves below," said the mother.

"And they've got chains on," said the boy.

"What a shame to our country that such sights are to be seen!" said another lady.

"O, there's a great deal to be said on both sides of the subject," said a genteel woman, who sat at her state-room door sewing, while her little girl and boy were playing round her. "I've been south, and I must say I think the negroes are better off than they would be to be free."

"In some respects, some of them are well off, I grant," said the lady to whose remark she had answered. "The most dreadful part of slavery, to my mind, is its outrages on the feelings and affections,—the separating of families, for example."

That *is* a bad thing, certainly," said the other lady, holding up a baby's dress she had just completed, and looking intently on its trimmings; "but then, I fancy, it don't occur often."

"O, it does," said the first lady, eagerly; "I've lived many years in Kentucky and Virginia both, and I've seen enough to make any one's heart sick. Suppose, ma'am, your two children, there, should be taken from you, and sold?"

"We can't reason from our feelings to those of this class of persons," said the other lady, sorting out some worsteds on her lap.

"Indeed, ma'am you can know nothing of them, if you say so," answered the first lady, warmly. "I was born and brought up among them. I know they *do* feel, just as keenly,—even more so, perhaps,—as we do."

The lady said "Indeed!" yawned, and looked out the cabin window, and finally repeated, for a finale, the remark with which she had begun,—"After all, I think they are better off than they would be to be free."

"It's undoubtedly the intention of Providence that the African race should be servants,—kept in a low condition," said a grave-looking gentleman in black, a clergyman, seated by the cabin door. "'Cursed be Canaan; a servant of servants shall he be,' the scripture says."

"I say, stranger, is that ar what that text means?" said a tall man, standing by.

"Undoubtedly. It pleased Providence, for some inscrutable reason, to doom the race to bondage, ages ago; and we must not set up our opinion against that."

"Well, then, we'll all go ahead and buy up niggers," said the man, "if that's the way of Providence,—won't we, Squire?" said he, turning to Haley, who had been standing, with his hands in his pockets, by the stove, and intently listening to the conversation.

"Yes," continued the tall man, "we must all be resigned to the decrees of Providence. Niggers must be sold, and trucked round, and kept under; it's what they's made for. 'Pears like this yer view's quite refreshing, an't it, stranger?" said he to Haley.

"I never thought on't," said Haley. "I could n't have said as much, myself; I ha'nt no larning. I took up the trade just to make a living; if 't an't right, I calculated to 'pent on 't in time, *ye* know."

"And now you'll save yerself the trouble, won't ye?" said the tall man. "See what 't is, now, to know scripture. If ye'd only studied yer Bible, like this yer good man, ye might have know'd it before, and saved ye a heap o' trouble. Ye could jist have said, 'Cussed be'—what's his name?—'and 't would all have come right.'" And the stranger, who was no other than the honest drover whom we introduced to our readers in the Kentucky tavern, sat down, and began smoking, with a curious smile on his long, dry face.

A tall, slender young man, with a face expressive of great feeling and intelligence, here broke in, and repeated the words, "'All things whatsoever ye would that men should do unto you, do ye even so unto them.' I suppose," he added, "*that* is scripture, as much as 'Cursed be Canaan.'"

"Wal, it seems quite *as* plain a text, stranger," said John the drover, "to poor fellows like us, now;" and John smoked on like a volcano.

The young man paused, looked as if he was going to say more, when suddenly the boat stopped, and the company made the usual steamboat rush, to see where they were landing.

"Both them ar chaps parsons?" said John to one of the men, as they were going out.

The man nodded.

As the boat stopped, a black woman came running wildly up the plank, darted into the crowd, flew up to where the slave gang sat, and threw her arms round that unfortunate piece of merchandise before enumerated—"John, aged thirty," and with sobs and tears bemoaned him as her husband.

But what needs tell the story, told too oft,—every day told,—of heartstrings rent and broken,—the weak broken and torn for the profit and convenience of the strong! It needs not to be told;—every day is telling it,—telling it, too, in the ear of One who is not deaf, though he be long silent.

The young man who had spoken for the cause of humanity and God before stood with folded arms, looking on this scene. He turned, and Haley was standing at his side. "My friend," he said, speaking with thick utterance, "how can you, how dare you, carry on a trade like this? Look at those poor creatures! Here I am, rejoicing in my heart that I am going home to my wife and child; and the same bell which is a signal to carry me onward towards them will part this poor man and his wife forever. Depend upon it, God will bring you into judgment for this."

The trader turned away in silence.

"I say, now," said the drover, touching his elbow, "there's differences in parsons, an't there? 'Cussed be Canaan' don't seem to go down with this 'un, does it?"

Haley gave an uneasy growl.

"And that ar an't the worst on't," said John; "mabbe it won't go down with the Lord, neither, when ye come to settle with Him, one o' these days, as all on us must, I reckon."

Haley walked reflectively to the other end of the boat.

"If I make pretty handsomely on one or two next gangs," he thought, "I reckon I'll stop off this yer; it's really getting dangerous." And he took out his pocket-book, and began adding over his accounts,—a process which many gentlemen besides Mr. Haley have found a specific for an uneasy conscience.

The boat swept proudly away from the shore, and all went on merrily, as before. Men talked, and loafed, and read, and smoked. Women sewed, and children played, and the boat passed on her way.

Blacks Attack Slavery and Racism

■ **Black Revolutionaries**

12 / Nat Turner's Rebellion

(1831)

"I saw white spirits and black spirits engaged in battle, and the sun was darkened . . . and blood flowed in streams . . ."

Nat Turner (1800–1831) led the most remarkable of the slave revolts in the United States. He was a slave preacher. He could read and write, and the statements attributed to him suggest a man of considerable complexity, a prophet who spoke in the cadences of the Bible, and one who recognized the inconsistency of the facts of slavery as he knew them with the ideal of Christianity. In 1831, Turner received what he thought to be a sign from God that he should lead a revolt. About sixty slaves took part in the uprising, and they killed fifty-four white people. The following is an account by Thomas R. Gray, a reporter; in it is found nearly all the evidence we have concerning the character of Nat Turner. The rebellion made a deep impression on the white South and encouraged extremists in their conviction that even a discussion of slavery was on its face subversive.

Agreeable to his own appointment, on the evening he was committed to prison, with permission of the jailer, I visited NAT on Tuesday the 1st November, when, without being questioned at all, he commenced his narrative in the following words:—

Sir,—You have asked me to give a history of the motives which induced me to undertake the late insurrection, as you call it—To do so I must go back to the days of my infancy, and even before I was born. I was thirty-one years of age the 2d of October last, and born the property of Benj. Turner, of this county. In my childhood a circumstance occurred which made an indelible impression on my mind, and laid the ground work of that enthusiasm which has terminated so fatally to many, both white and black, and for which I am about to atone at the gallows. It is here necessary to relate this

Reprinted from *The Confessions of Nat Turner ... As Fully and Voluntarily Made to Thomas R. Gray* (Baltimore, 1831).

circumstance—trifling as it may seem, it was the commencement of that belief which has grown with time, and even now, sir, in this dungeon, helpless and forsaken as I am, I cannot divest myself of. Being at play with other children, when three or four years old, I was telling them something, which my mother overhearing, said it had happened before I was born—I stuck to my story, however, and related somethings which went, in her opinion, to confirm it—others being called on were greatly astonished, knowing that these had happened, and caused them to say in my hearing, I surely would be a prophet, as the Lord had shewn me things that had happened before my birth . . .

And about this time I had a vision—and I saw white spirits and black spirits engaged in battle, and the sun was darkened—the thunder rolled in the Heavens, and blood flowed in streams—and I heard a voice saying, "Such is your luck, such you are called to see, and let it come rough or smooth, you must surely bear it." I now withdrew myself as much as my situation would permit, from the intercourse of my fellow servants, for the avowed purpose of serving the Spirit more fully—and it appeared to me, and reminded me of the things it had already shown me, and that it would then reveal to me the knowledge of the elements, the revolution of the planets, the operation of tides, and changes of the seasons. After this revelation in the year 1825, and the knowledge of the elements being made known to me, I sought more than ever to obtain true holiness before the great day of judgment should appear, and then I began to receive the true knowledge of faith. And from the first steps of righteousness until the last, was I made perfect; and the Holy Ghost was with me, and said, "Behold me as I stand in the Heavens"—and I looked and saw the forms of men in different attitudes—and there were lights in the sky to which the children of darkness gave other names than what they really were—for they were the lights of the Saviour's hands, stretched forth from east to west, even as they were extended on the cross on Calvary for the redemption of sinners. And I wondered greatly at these miracles, and prayed to be informed of a certainty of the meaning thereof—and shortly afterwards, while laboring in the field, I discovered drops of blood on the corn as though it were dew from heaven—and I communicated it to many, both white and black, in the neighborhood—and I then found on the leaves in the woods hieroglyphic characters, and numbers, with the forms of men in different attitudes, portrayed in blood, and representing the figures I had seen before in the heavens. And now the Holy Ghost had revealed itself to me, and made plain the miracles it had shown me—For as the blood of Christ had been shed on this earth, and had ascended to heaven for the salvation of sinners, and was now returning to earth again in the form of dew—and as the leaves on the trees bore the impression of the figures I had seen in the heavens, it was plain to me that the Saviour was about to lay down the yoke he had borne for the sins of men, and the great day of judgment was at hand . . .

Since the commencement of 1830, I had been living with Mr. Joseph Travis, who was to me a kind master, and placed the greatest confidence in me; in fact, I had no cause to complain of his treatment of me. On Saturday evening, the 20th of August, it was agreed between Henry, Hark and myself, to prepare a dinner the next day for the men we expected, and then to concert a plan, as we had not yet determined on any. Hark, on the following morning, brought a pig, and Henry brandy, and being joined by Sam, Nelson, Will and Jack, they prepared in the woods a dinner, where, about three o'clock, I joined them.

Q. Why were you so backward in joining them.

A. The same reason that had caused me not to mix with them for years before.

I saluted them on coming up, and asked Will how came he there, he answered, his life was worth no more than others, and his liberty as dear to him. I asked him if he thought to obtain it? He said he would, or lose his life. This was enough to put him in full confidence. Jack, I knew, was only a tool in the hands of Hark. It was quickly agreed we should commence at home (Mr. J. Travis') on that night, and until we had armed and equipped ourselves, and gathered sufficient force, neither age nor sex was to be spared, (which was invariably adhered to.) We remained at the feast, until about two hours in the night, when we went to the house and found Austin; they all went to the cider press and drank, except myself. On returning to the house, Hark went to the door with an axe, for the purpose of breaking it open, as we knew we were strong enough to murder the family, if they were awaked by the noise; but reflecting that it might create an alarm in the neighborhood, we determined to enter the house secretly, and murder them whilst sleeping. Hark got a ladder and set it against the chimney, on which I ascended, and hoisting a window, entered and came down stairs, unbarred the door, and removed the guns from their places. It was then observed that I must spill the first blood. On which, armed with a hatchet, and accompanied by Will, I entered my master's chamber, it being dark, I could not give a death blow, the hatchet glanced from his head, he sprang from the bed, and called his wife, it was his last word, Will laid him dead, with a blow of his axe, and Mrs. Travis shared the same fate, as she lay in bed. The murder of this family, five in number, was the work of a moment, not one of them awoke; there was a little infant sleeping in a cradle, that was forgotten, until we had left the house and gone some distance, when Henry and Will returned and killed it; we got here, four guns that would shoot, and several old muskets, with a pound or two of powder. We remained some time at the barn, where we paraded; I formed them in a line as soldiers, and after carrying them off to Mr. Salathur Francis', about six hundred yards distant, Sam and Will went to the door and knocked. Mr. Francis asked who was there, Sam replied it was him, and he had a letter for him, on which he got up and came to the door; they immediately seized him, and dragging him out a little from the door, he was dispatched by repeated blows on the head; there was no other white person in the family. We started from there for Mrs. Reese's, maintaining the most perfect silence on our march, where finding the door unlocked, we entered, and murdered Mrs. Reese in her bed, while sleeping; her son awoke, but it was only to sleep the sleep of death; he had only time to say who is that, and he was no more. From Mrs. Reese's we went to Mrs. Turner's, a mile distant, which we reached about sunrise, on Monday morning. Henry, Austin, and Sam, went to the still, where, finding Mr. Peebles, Austin shot him, and the rest of us went to the house; as we approached, the family discovered us, and shut the door. Vain hope! Will, with one stroke of his axe, opened it, and we entered and found Mrs. Turner and Mrs. Newsome in the middle of a room, almost frightened to death. Will immediately killed Mrs. Turner, with one blow of his axe. I took Mrs. Newsome by the hand, and with the sword I had when I was apprehended, I struck her several blows over the head, but not being able to kill her, as the sword was dull. Will turning around and discovering it, despatched her also. A general destruction of property and search for money and ammunition, always succeeded the murders. By this time my company amounted to fifteen, and nine men mounted, who started for Mrs. Whitehead's, (the other six were to go through a by way to Mr. Bryant's, and rejoin us at Mrs. Whitehead's,) as we approached the house we discovered Mr. Richard Whitehead standing in the cotton patch, near the lane fence; we called him over into the lane, and Will, the executioner, was near at hand, with his fatal axe, to send him to an untimely grave . . .

I here proceeded to make some inquiries of him, after assuring him of the certain death that awaited him, and that concealment would only bring destruction on the innocent as well as guilty, of his own color, if he knew of any extensive or concerted plan. His answer was, I do not. When I questioned him as to the insurrection in North Carolina happening about the same time, he denied any knowledge of it; and when I looked him in the face as though I would search his inmost thoughts, he replied, "I see sir, you doubt my word; but can you not think the same ideas, and strange appearances about this time in the heaven's might prompt others, as well as myself, to this undertaking." I now had much conversation with and asked him many questions, having forborne to do so previously, except in the cases noted in parenthesis; but during his statement, I had, unnoticed by him, taken notes as to some particular circumstances, and having the advantage of his statement before me in writing, on the evening of the third day that I had been with him, I began a cross examination, and found his statement corroborated by every circumstance coming within my own knowledge or the confessions of others whom had been either killed or executed, and whom he had not seen nor had any knowledge since 22d of August last, he expressed himself fully satisfied as to the impracticability of his attempt. It has been said he was ignorant and cowardly, and that his object was to murder and rob for the purpose of obtaining money to make his escape. It is notorious, that he was never known to have a dollar in his life; to swear an oath, or drink a drop of spirits. As to his ignorance, he certainly never had the advantages of education, but he can read and write, (it was taught him by his parents,) and for natural intelligence and quickness of apprehension, is surpassed by few men I have ever seen. As to his being a coward, his reason as given for not resisting Mr. Phipps, shews the decision of his character. When he saw Mr. Phipps present his gun, he said he knew it was impossible for him to escape as the woods were full of men; he therefore thought it was better to surrender, and trust to fortune for his escape. He is a complete fanatic, or plays his part most admirably. On other subjects he possesses an uncommon share of intelligence, with a mind capable of attaining any thing; but warped and perverted by the influence of early impressions. He is below the ordinary in stature, though strong and active, having the true negro face, every feature of which is strongly marked. I shall not attempt to describe the effect of his narrative, as told and commented on by himself, in the condemned hole of the prison. The calm, deliberate composure with which he spoke of his late deeds and intentions, the expression of his fiend-like face when excited by enthusiasm, still bearing the stains of the blood of helpless innocence about him; clothed with rags and covered with chains; yet daring to raise his manacled hands to heaven, with a spirit soaring above the attributes of man; I looked on him and my blood curdled in my veins . . .

**13 / Frederick Douglass
My Bondage and My Freedom**

(1855)

"I have seen him in a tempest of passion . . ."

Frederick Douglass (1817?–1895) was the leading black in the anti-slavery movement. Born in Talbot County, Maryland, he was for a time a house slave in Baltimore, where his mistress taught him to read. On the death of his owner, he was sold as a field hand in rural Maryland. He escaped in 1838 and worked in the North for a time as a laborer. He attended a meeting of the Massachusetts Anti-Slavery Society and was asked to speak himself. He proved so extraordinarily effective that he was employed as an agent and a speaker for the society. He later established an anti-slavery newspaper, *The North Star*, which was published for seventeen years. During the Civil War he helped recruit black soldiers for the 54th and 55th Massachusetts Regiments, and after the war he spoke widely on civil rights for blacks. In later years he served the government as Secretary of the Santo Domingo Commission, Marshal and Recorder of the Deeds of the District of Columbia, and Minister of the United States to Haiti.

Although my old master—Capt. Anthony—gave me at first ... very little attention, and although that little was of a remarkably mild and gentle description, a few months only were sufficient to convince me that mildness and gentleness were not the prevailing or governing traits of his character. These excellent qualities were displayed only occasionally. He could, when it suited him, appear to be literally insensible to the claims of humanity, when appealed to by the helpless against an aggressor, and he could himself commit outrages, deep, dark and nameless. Yet he was not by nature worse than other men. Had he been brought up in a free state, surrounded by the just restraints of free society—restraints which are necessary to the

---

Douglass first published his autobiography in 1845 and wrote three subsequent revisions in 1855, 1881, and 1892. This selection is from *My Bondage and My Freedom* (New York, 1855). Chapter 5.

freedom of all its members, alike and equally—Capt. Anthony might have been as humane a man, and every way as respectable, as many who now oppose the slave system; certainly as humane and respectable as are members of society generally. The slaveholder, as well as the slave, is the victim of the slave system. A man's character greatly takes its hue and shape from the form and color of things about him. Under the whole heavens there is no relation more unfavorable to the development of honorable character, than that sustained by the slaveholder to the slave. Reason is imprisoned here, and passions run wild. Like the fires of the prairie, once lighted, they are at the mercy of every wind, and must burn, till they have consumed all that is combustible within their remorseless grasp. Capt. Anthony could be kind, and, at times, he even showed an affectionate disposition. Could the reader have seen him gently leading me by the hand—as he sometimes did—patting me on the head, speaking to me in soft, caressing tones and calling me his "little Indian boy," he would have deemed him a kind old man, and, really, almost fatherly. But the pleasant moods of a slaveholder are remarkably brittle; they are easily snapped; they neither come often, nor remain long. His temper is subjected to perpetual trials; but, since these trials are never borne patiently, they add nothing to his natural stock of patience.

Old master very early impressed me with the idea that he was an unhappy man. Even to my child's eye, he wore a troubled, and at times, a haggard aspect. His strange movements excited my curiosity, and awakened my compassion. He seldom walked alone without muttering to himself; and he occasionally stormed about, as if defying an army of invisible foes. "He would do this, that, and the other; he'd be d—d if he did not,"—was the usual form of his threats. Most of his leisure was spent in walking, cursing and gesticulating like one possessed by a demon. Most evidently, he was a wretched man, at war with his own soul, and with all the world around him. To be overheard by the children, disturbed him very little. He made no more of *our* presence, than of that of the ducks and geese which he met on the green. He little thought that the little black urchins around him, could see, through those vocal crevices, the very secrets of his heart. Slaveholders ever underrate the intelligence with which they have to grapple. I really understood the old man's mutterings, attitudes and gestures, about as well as he did himself. But slaveholders never encourage that kind of communication, with the slaves, by which they might learn to measure the depths of his knowledge. Ignorance is a high virtue in a human chattel; and as the master studies to keep the slave ignorant, the slave is cunning enough to make the master think he succeeds. The slave fully appreciates the saying, "where ignorance is bliss, 'tis folly to be wise." When old master's gestures were violent, ending with a threatening shake of the head, and a sharp snap of his middle finger and thumb, I deemed it wise to keep at a respectable distance from him; for, at such times, trifling faults stood, in his eyes, as momentous offenses; and, having both the power and the disposition, the victim had only to be near him to catch the punishment, deserved or undeserved.

One of the first circumstances that opened my eyes to the cruelty and wickedness of slavery, and the heartlessness of my old master, was the refusal of the latter to interpose his authority, to protect and shield a young woman, who had been most cruelly abused and beaten by his overseer in Tuckahoe. This overseer—a Mr. Plummer—was a man like most of his class, little better than a human brute; and, in addition to his general profligacy and repulsive coarseness, the creature was a miserable drunkard. He was, probably, employed by my old master, less on account of the excellence of his services, than for the cheap rate at which they could be obtained. He was not fit to have the management of a drove of mules. In a fit of drunken madness, he committed the outrage which brought the young woman in question down to my old master's for protection. This young woman was the daughter of Milly, an own aunt of mine. The poor girl, on arriving at our house, presented a pitiable appearance. She had left in haste, and without preparation; and, probably, without the knowledge of Mr. Plummer. She had traveled twelve miles, bare-footed, bare-necked and bare-headed. Her neck and shoulders were covered with scars, newly made; and, not content with marring her neck and shoulders, with the cowhide, the cowardly brute had dealt her a blow on the head with a hickory club, which cut a horrible gash, and left her face literally covered with blood. In this condition, the poor young woman came down, to implore protection at the hands of my old master. I expected to see him boil over with rage at the revolting deed, and to hear him fill the air with curses upon the brutal Plummer; but I was disappointed. He sternly told her, in an angry tone, he "believed she deserved every bit of it," and, if she did not go home instantly, he would himself take the remaining skin from her neck and back. Thus was the poor girl compelled to return, without redress, and perhaps to receive an additional flogging for daring to appeal to old master against the overseer.

14 / National Emigration Convention of Colored People "A People, To Be Free, Must Necessarily be Their Own Rulers"

(1854)

Though many black men and women actively participated in the abolitionist movement, some blacks reacted to slavery in the South and racial discrimination in the North by abandoning all faith that the United States could resolve its racial crisis. From the late 1840's through the cheerless decade of the 1850's these blacks advocated various forms of black nationalism, prominent among them the idea of emigration and colonization overseas. The declaration of the National Emigration Convention of Colored People (1854), reprinted in part below, was written by Martin R. Delany, often called "The Father of Black Nationalism." Delany, a pre-Civil War abolitionist, editor, and physician, advocated colonization in Central America. Later he shifted his preference to the Niger Delta in West Africa and in 1859 ventured to that place, securing an agreement from the Yoruba rulers to permit American blacks to settle there. Delany's declaration forcefully documents the struggle by blacks to assert their pride of race in mid-nineteenth-century America. While the efforts of the emigrationists of the 1850's produced no concrete results, they did reflect the frustrations experienced by "free" blacks in the North who daily encountered racial prejudice, and they publicized a pattern of response to the inferior condition of the black man in America that has played a significant role in the history of American blacks down to the present time.

To the colored inhabitants of the United States

Fellow-Countrymen!—The duty assigned us is an important one, comprehending all that pertains to our destiny and that of our posterity—present and prospectively. And while it must be admitted, that the subject is one of the greatest magnitude, requiring all that talents, prudence and wisdom might

---

Reprinted from "Political Destiny of the Colored Race, on the American Continent," *Proceedings of the National Emigration Convention of Colored People...1854* (Pittsburgh, 1854).

adduce, and while it would be folly to pretend to give you the combined result of these three agencies, we shall satisfy ourselves with doing our duty to the best of our ability, and that in the plainest, most simple and comprehensive manner.

Our object, then, shall be to place before you our true position in this country—the United States,—the improbability of realizing our desires, and the sure, practicable and infallible remedy for the evils we now endure.

We have not addressed you as *citizens*—a term desired and ever cherished by us—because such you have never been. We have not addressed you as *freemen*,—because such privileges have never been enjoyed by any colored man in the United States. Why then should we flatter your credulity, by inducing you to believe that which neither has now, nor never before had an existence. Our oppressors are ever gratified at our manifest satisfaction, especially when that satisfaction is founded upon false premises; an assumption on our part, of the enjoyment of rights and privileges which never have been conceded, and which, according to the present system of the United States policy, we never can enjoy ...

Let it then be understood, as a great principle of political economy, that no people can be free who themselves do not constitute an essential part of the *ruling element* of the country in which they live. Whether this element be founded upon a true or false, a just or an unjust basis; this position in community is necessary to personal safety. The liberty of no man is secure, who controls not his own political destiny. What is true of an individual, is true of a family; and that which is true of a family, is also true concerning a whole people. To suppose otherwise, is that delusion which at once induces its victim, through a period of long suffering, patiently to submit to every species of wrong; trusting against probability, and hoping against all reasonable grounds of expectation, for the granting of privileges and enjoyment of rights, which never will be attained. This delusion reveals the true secret of the power which holds in peaceable subjection, all the oppressed in every part of the world.

A people, to be free, must necessarily be *their own rulers*: that is, *each individual* must, in himself, embody the *essential ingredient*—so to speak—of the *sovereign principle* which composes the *true basis* of his liberty. This principle, when not exercised by himself, may, at his pleasure, be delegated to another—his true representative ...

In the United States, our degradation being once—as it has in a hundred instances been done—legally determined, our color is sufficient, independently of costume, education, or other distinguishing marks, to keep up that distinction.

In Europe, when an inferior is elevated to the rank of equality with the superior class, the law first comes to his aid, which, in its decrees, entirely destroys his identity as an inferior, leaving no trace of his former condition visible.

In the United States, among the whites, their color is made, by law and custom, the mark of distinction and superiority; while the color of the blacks is a badge of degradation, acknowledged by statute, organic law, and the common consent of the people.

With this view of the case—which we hold to be correct—to elevate to equality the degraded subject of law and custom, it can only be done, as in Europe, by an entire destruction of the identity of the former condition of the applicant. Even were this desirable—which we by no means admit— with the deep seated prejudices engendered by oppression, with which we have to contend, ages incalculable might reasonably be expected to roll around, before this could honorably be accomplished; otherwise, we should encourage and at once commence an indiscriminate concubinage and immoral commerce, of our mothers, sisters, wives and daughters, revolting to think of, and a physical curse to humanity.

If this state of things be to succeed, then, as in Egypt, under the dread of the inscrutible approach of the destroying angel, to appease the hatred of our oppressors, as a license to the passions of every white, let the lintel of each door of every black man, be stained with the blood of virgin purity and unsullied matron fidelity. Let it be written along the cornice in capitals, "The *will* of the white man is the rule of my household." Remove the protection to our chambers and nurseries, that the places once sacred, may henceforth become the unrestrained resort of the vagrant and rabble, always provided that the licensed commissioner of lust shall wear the indisputable impress of a *white* skin.

But we have fully discovered and comprehended the great political disease with which we are affected, the cause of its origin and continuance; and what is now left for us to do, is to discover and apply a sovereign remedy—a healing balm to a sorely diseased body—a wrecked but not entirely shattered system. We propose for this disease a remedy. That remedy is Emigration. This Emigration should be well advised, and like remedies applied to remove the disease from the physical system of man, skillfully and carefully applied, within the proper time, directed to operate on that part of the system, whose greatest tendency shall be, to benefit the whole . . .

Our friends in this and other countries, anxious for our elevation, have for years been erroneously urging us to lose our identity as a distinct race, declaring that we were the same as other people . . . The truth is, we are not identical with the Anglo-Saxon or any other race of the Caucasian or pure white type of the human family, and the sooner we know and acknowledge this truth, the better for ourselves and posterity.

The English, French, Irish, German, Italian, Turk, Persion, Greek, Jew, and all other races, have their native or inherent peculiarities, and why not our race? We are not willing, therefore, at all times and under all circumstances to be moulded into various shapes of eccentricity, to suit the caprices and conveniences of every kind of people. We are not more suitable to everybody than everybody is suitable to us; therefore, no more like other people than others are like us.

We have then inherent traits, attributes—so to speak—and native characteristics, peculiar to our race—whether pure or mixed blood—and all that is required of us is to cultivate these and develope them in their purity, to make them desirable and emulated by the rest of the world.

That the colored races have the highest traits of civilization, will not be disputed. They are civil, peaceable and religious to a fault. In mathematics, sculpture and architecture, as arts and sciences, commerce and internal improvements as enterprises, the white race may probably excel; but in languages, oratory, poetry, music and painting as arts and sciences, and in ethics, metaphysics, theology and legal jurisprudence; in plain language— in the true principles of morals, correctness of thought, religion, and law or civil government, there is no doubt but the black race will yet instruct the world.

It would be duplicity longer to disguise the fact, that the great issue, sooner or later, upon which much be disputed the world's destiny, will be a question of black and white; and every individual will be called upon for his identity with one or the other. The blacks and colored races are four-sixths of all the population of the world; and these people are fast tending to a common cause with each other. The white races are but one-third of the population of the globe—or one of them to two of us—and it cannot much longer continue, that two-thirds will passively submit to the universal domination of this one-third. And it is notorious that the only progress made in territorial domain, in the last three centuries, by the whites, has been a usurpation and encroachment on the rights and native soil of some of the colored races . . .

Interpretations

15 / Russell B. Nye
The Ideology of Abolitionism

(1969)

In the following selection, Russel B. Nye, professor of English at Michigan State University, sets the anti-slavery movement in the context of the thrust for humanitarian reform in many areas of American society during the early nineteenth century. He also identifies the intellectual sources—religious and secular, native and foreign—from which the abolitionists drew inspiration. As Nye points out, though united by a fervent desire to destroy slavery, the abolitionists were deeply divided over the question of how to accomplish their goal, a division that perhaps reflected abolitionist indebtedness to a wide variety of ideological stimuli.

Nineteenth-century reform touched on almost every aspect of American life—education, labor, politics, debt, war, dress, health, family life, church, prisons, the poor, the crippled, and the unfortunate. Horace Mann worked tirelessly for better public education, while Bronson Alcott, George Bancroft, and others experimented with innovations in pedagogy, some European-inspired, some native. Dorothea Dix made her way through the states inspecting prisons and poorhouses, writing precise and damning reports that rocked legislatures. Samuel Gridley Howe of Boston and T. H. Gallaudet of Philadelphia dedicated themselves to improving the lot of the blind and deaf; David Low Dodge of New York and William Ladd of Maine hoped to outlaw war. Fanny Wright, Margaret Fuller, Lucy Stone, the Blackwell sisters, and other strong-minded women campaigned for the rights of women; Amelia Bloomer, agitating for reforms in dress, left her name immortalized in an unlovely article of feminine apparel. Temperance converts, proudly wearing the white badge, paraded by thousands to listen to the impassioned lectures of reformed drunkards like John Hawkins and John B. Gough. Readers of the Scotsman Owen and the Frenchman Fourier planned utopian

Russel B. Nye, *William Lloyd Garrison and the Humanitarian Reformers*. Copyright © 1969 by Little, Brown and Company Inc. Reprinted by permission of the publisher.

communities in the rolling farmlands of New England and Ohio, and others, touched by the prevailing religious excitement, founded Christian communist societies based on New Testament injunctions. The American Bible Society, the Society for Foreign Missions, and the American Tract Society sent out agents and lecturers to spread the Gospel around the world. And on the fringes of the reform movement there existed societies to abolish flogging in the Navy, to promote the eating of whole wheat, to abolish corsets, to distribute Bibles to criminals, and to communicate with spirits. There were so many thing to do, so little time, and such a long way to go before men lived together in harmony and peace! Nineteenth-century America was in a hurry to have its Kingdom of Heaven in the here and now.

The reform movement had deep roots at home and abroad. Nineteenth-century Americans were direct heirs of the eighteenth-century Enlightenment, with its traditions of natural rights, human equality, and human perfectibility. The Declaration of Independence guaranteed every man a right to life, liberty, and the pursuit of happiness—unjust laws, imperfect institutions, and social disjointures subverted that right. Christianity guaranteed men the right to live as brothers, children of God; a brutally competitive society violated the spirit of Christian ethics. War, drunkenness, poverty, crime, and ignorance nullified those divinely-inspired concepts on which the Republic had been founded. At the same time, Europe provided example and theory for American reformers, for there was in the Western world at large a powerful trend toward recognition of human rights, of the reality of human duties, of the plight of the poor, the oppressed, and the enslaved. Philanthropic groups in England and on the Continent sought out a variety of social and economic ills and strove to cure them by humanitarian efforts. The Reform Bill, the Chartist movement, the Factory Act, the repeal of the Corn Laws, and the West Indies Emancipation Act were successful British attempts at reform, while in Europe and in Latin America the period was dotted with revolutions.

The Romantic Movement reinforced the bequest of "natural rights." The keynote of romanticism was its tremendous and unshakable faith in man, in his capacity to perceive his problems and in his ability to solve them— a faith reflected in the two most representative Americans of the age, Emerson and Jackson. In the individual, the Romantic Era believed, divinity dwelt; to him was revealed truth and right; every man was his own oracle. The American Unitarians and transcendentalists created their deity in man's image—"the idea of God," Channing said, ". . . is the idea of our own spiritual nature, purified and enlarged to infinity."

On another level, the Perfectionists who followed the great evangelist Charles Grandison Finney added their reinforcement to reform. Sin, said Finney, was selfishness; virtue was "disinterested benevolence." Any human being could be saved by the simple process of exchanging selfishness for selflessness. Any human being could attain a state of Christian perfection in this world by his own efforts. But salvation alone, continued Finney, was not enough. The "perfected" one must make his religion active; he must "have the determination to aim at being useful in the highest degree possible." Salvation was not the end but the beginning of a useful life. Finney's theology was, in effect, another affirmation of the belief in progress that permeated the times, and the "doctrine of usefulness" had a direct relationship with contemporary reforms. If Finney's converts searched for ways to make themselves useful, there were a multitude of opportunities ready at hand—particularly in the movement to abolish the sinful, unchristian institution of slavery. They flocked to the abolitionist societies by scores. It was no accident that Finney's two theological seminaries at Oneida and Oberlin eventually produced the majority of abolitionist agents, nor that in its early phases the antislavery crusade had strong overtones of Perfectionist evangelism.

Emerson caught the spirit of his times best. The age moved, he wrote, from the belief "that there is an infinite worthiness in man, which will appear at the call of worth, and that all particular reforms are the removing of impediments." So too Andrew Jackson and his muddy-booted hordes deified the common man as politically sufficient unto himself. "I believe," wrote one politician, echoing Jackson and Emerson (and Finney too), "man becomes more and more endowed with divinity; and as he does he becomes more Godlike in his character and capable of governing himself. Let us go on elevating our people, perfecting our institutions, until democracy shall reach such a point of perfection that we can acclaim with truth that the voice of the people is the voice of God."

Nineteenth-century American reform drew much of its vitality from the militant democracy of the period, from that fervent and complex faith in themselves that de Tocqueville noted in the Americans of 1836. The young nation had survived two wars against the world's greatest military and economic power, created a philosophy of revolution, and built a republic upon it. Democracy was won; the task now remained to consolidate it. Free from entanglements with the decadent societies of the Old World, Emerson's Young Americans eagerly looked forward to creating new ideas and new institutions, or to cleansing old ones of prejudice and evil. In the American concept of democracy, the individual was both a means and a goal. The goal was the complete development of the individual's capacities; the means by which this was to be attained was the reform of every institution or tradition that prevented realization of the individual's powers. In this manner the age of Emerson and Jackson identified nationalism and democracy with progress and perfectibility, providing both a natural and a supernatural basis for reform.

The movement to abolish Negro chattel slavery was part of this pattern, motivated by the same factors that produced the women's rights, evangelical, pacifistic, utopian, humanitarian, and Perfectionist movements. Slavery existed near enough to touch the orbit of every American's life, yet geographically far enough removed from the lives of some to allow it to be judged more or less objectively. It was confined to a portion of the nation whose political and economic interests differed sharply from those of the nonslaveholding sections. The system was politically accessible, subject to state and Federal law. It had obvious religious, social, and moral implications for Americans of every class. At first only one of many reforms, abolition bulked larger and larger in the total, until, at the end, it overshadowed or absorbed nearly all of them.

Abolitionists, and those who sympathized with them, believed slavery to be a direct denial of elementary human rights. When their opponents seemed willing to dispense with the safeguards of the Constitution and to deny the self-evident truths of the Declaration of Independence, the abolitionists gathered more and more support until theirs became the dominant issue of the era. Eventually the issue involved the question of whether the nation would continue to exist, and if so, whether it would remain democratic. It could not, as Lincoln pointed out, endure permanently half-slave and half-free, but would become all one or the other. Before the Civil War came, the abolitionists found themselves allied with a much wider movement to protect the basic rights of democracy—freedom of speech, assembly, and press; academic freedom; the rights of petition and jury trial; freedom of transit and the mails; the entire natural-rights tradition—and to preserve the Union that guaranteed them. "The anti-slavery struggle," Garrison could write quite truthfully in 1852, "was commenced primarily and exclusively with reference to the emancipation of the enslaved inhabitants of the Africa race in our land; in it now are seen to be included the rights and liberties of all classes of people, without regard to complexion."

The arguments over slavery that developed after 1830 were extremely complex. Antislavery groups were not always able to agree among themselves. Earlier antislavery societies intended to appeal to the national conscience, to change public opinion, and thus to build a great body of Northern and Southern antislavery sentiment that would eventually force the abolition of slavery by legislative action. Their attack on the institution rested on several principles, any one of which might be stressed to the exclusion of others.

First, said some, slavery was immoral and barbaric. The practice of slavebreeding for the market, the refusal of slaveholders to sanction slave marriages or to recognize the slave family as a unit, struck at the very foundations of morality. Relations between master and slave encouraged immoral behavior in Negro and white alike. The system was cruel and inhumane; Theodore Weld's *Slavery As It Is,* Mrs. Stowe's *Uncle Tom's Cabin*, and scores of other studies and novels attempted to document the accusation with stories of whippings, cruel confinements, slave marts, broken families, bloodhounds, and tortures.

Further, slavery was unchristian. Chattel slavery, abolitionists argued, arrogated to one man power over another which rightfully belonged only to God. It was impossible, in the abolitionist view, for a man to be both a slaveholder and a Christian, as it was impossible for an American church to remain Christian while condoning slavery. Such opinions aroused bitter argument within the Protestant churches. The Wesleyan Methodists withdrew from the Methodist Convention of 1843 in protest against its failure to take a stand against slavery, and two years later the Southern Methodists seceded to form the Methodist Episcopal Church, South. The Southern Baptist Convention split on the same issue, while the Presbyterians managed to postpone a division until 1857, when their Southern congregations severed relations.

Next, slavery was undemocratic. It produced a small, powerful class of aristocratic landowners who (abolitionists claimed) had entered into a secret "slave power conspiracy" to extend slavery throughout the nation. The abolitionists carefully charted the progress of this "conspiracy" and issued regular warnings; after the Dred Scott decision of 1857, they pointed out, it needed but one more favorable court decision to achieve its goal. If the Southern "slaveocracy" joined forces with Northern industrial capitalists, abolitionists believed, the two oligarchies together could and would rule the nation—only the abolition of slavery could prevent the combined tyranny of those whom Wendell Phillips strikingly called "The Lords of the Lash and the Lords of the Loom."

Slavery, abolitionists agreed, was economically unsound and wasteful. The poor white man in the South could not compete with unpaid slave labor; so long as slavery existed he would remain poor. And last of all, some antislavery men claimed that slavery was simply illegal, since the Declaration of Independence banned slavery by its affirmation of every man's natural right' to life, liberty, and equality. If the Declaration were considered simply a statement of intent, rather than law, abolitionists pointed to the Constitution, which implicitly, at least, banned slavery by outlawing the slave trade. Even if the Constitution did not explicitly abolish slavery, it was because the framers of the document considered it unnecessary to label as illegal an institution already banished by the terms of the Declaration. If the Constitution did actually sanction slavery (as certain commentators believed it might under the guaranteed property clause) the true Christian must perforce obey a "higher law" of morality and reject not only the Constitution but any law based upon it.

Whatever their reasons for believing slavery wrong, all abolitionists believed wholeheartedly that it must be abolished, and soon. They found great difficulty, however, in agreeing on exactly how. One group believed that a national campaign for moral regeneration—an evangelical religious crusade—would cause the abolition of slavery by unanimous consent, North and South. Appeals to the national conscience, thought Theodore Weld, could convince slaveholder and nonslaveholder alike that the system was against God and Christianity. Another school of thought believed that slavery could best be eliminated by working within the existing political framework—either through the two major parties, which could legislate slavery out of existence, or through a third party, which might gain control of the Federal government to accomplish the same end. A third group, believing that the Constitution legalized slavery and that there were no legal means of abolishing it, advocated either abandoning the Constitution for a new one or seceding from any government founded on it. If the Constitution sanctioned an institution which violated "higher laws" of morality and justice, a man must follow his conscience and refuse to remain within the Union founded on that Constitution.

16 / Leon F. Litwack
The Emancipation of the Negro Abolitionist

(1965)

The conflict between blacks and their white supporters is older than many people suppose. In the following essay, Leon F. Litwack, professor of history at the University of California, Berkeley, discusses the complex matter of the relationship between whites and blacks in the anti-slavery movement. Black abolitionists discovered, first of all, that some of the white abolitionists put little emphasis on the goal of racial equality. Such a goal would have involved them in heated controversies in the North. Therefore, the white abolitionists tended to concentrate on the evils of slavery in the South. Even on this subject, they sometimes seemed more interested in absolving the North of responsibility for slavery than in freeing the black slaves.

When William Lloyd Garrison launched his antislavery offensive, Negro abolitionists responded with warm enthusiasm. It "has roused up a Spirit in our Young People," one Negro leader wrote, "that had been slumbering for years." Encouraged by this emergence of antislavery militancy among whites, Negroes helped to sustain *The Liberator*, joined the newly formed abolition societies, and cheered the announced intention of white abolitionists to establish a Negro industrial college. It appeared to be an auspicious beginning of effective interracial cooperation for mutual goals. But the attempted coalition, though not unproductive, was to reveal to the abolitionists—white

Leon Litwack, "The Emancipation of the Negro Abolitionist," in Martin Duberman, ed., *The Antislavery Vanguard: New Essays on the Abolitionists* (Princeton: Princeton University Press, 1965). Reprinted without footnotes by permission of Princeton University Press.

and black—fundamental differences in assumptions, goals, and emphasis. "Thus, was the cause espoused," Negro leader Martin R. Delany wrote in 1852, "and thus did we expect much. But in all this, we were doomed to disappointment, sad, sad disappointment. Instead of realizing what we had hoped for, we find ourselves occupying the very same position in relation to our Anti-Slavery friends, as we do in relation to the proslavery part of the community—a mere secondary, underling position." The time had come, he insisted, for Negroes to break the chains of this bondage.

The Negro's initial enthusiasm was readily understandable. Several years of independent Negro agitation had produced few results. And now, in the wake of the Nat Turner insurrection, new racial tensions gripped large sections of the country, for not only the South but the North, too, was forced to consider the possible consequences of a disgruntled racial minority in its midst. Both sections embraced the prevailing image of the Negro as an inferior race, incapable of assuming any of the responsibilities of citizenship, but in the North the Negro could at least challenge this assumption and strive to improve his position. Thus Garrison's antislavery debut had come at an opportune moment. Subjected to incessant harassment and racist propaganda, the Negro found encouragement in the advent of a movement which forcefully challenged the colonizationists, the doctrine of racial inferiority, and any antislavery which did not include as an objective the elevation of the free Negro—politically, socially, and economically. The publication of *The Liberator*, Garrison declared, had "operated like a trumpet-call" on the Northern Negro community. "They have risen in their hopes and feelings to the perfect stature of men: in this city, every one of them is as tall as a giant."

Notwithstanding some opposition or misgivings, most of the white abolition societies admitted Negroes, and some elevated them to positions on the executive committee. The Negro's most important function, however, was that of an antislavery lecturer, for "eloquent" Negro speakers were able to draw "in most places far larger" audiences than their white counterparts. "The public have itching ears to hear a colored man speak," one abolitionist wrote to Garrison, "and particularly *a slave*. Multitudes will flock to hear one of this class speak." Such was the response to Frederick Douglass, for example, that he soon became a leading abolitionist orator. The Negro who committed himself to the abolitionist cause incurred obvious risks. If the average white man expected anything of the Negro, it was that he acquiesce in the racial status quo and act the clownish, childish, carefree, irresponsible Uncle Tom that whites had long presumed him to be. But the Negro abolitionist betrayed the white man's trust and confidence; more than that, he confounded by his very example the white man's rationale for a benevolent guardianship over an inferior and helpless race. Rare, indeed, was the Negro abolitionist who did not have to face a hostile mob at some point in his antislavery career; it was the price he paid for having committed the most unpardonable sin of all—impudence.

In a society racked by racial tensions, misunderstanding and suspicion were almost bound to precipitate divisions between white and black abolitionists. Such questions as Negro membership in abolition societies and race mixing at antislavery functions, for example, provoked considerable debate among white abolitionists. Many feared that a bold defiance of prevailing customs might endanger the eventual success of the antislavery cause. Outside of official gatherings, such intercourse also posed challenges to well-meaning white abolitionists. Sarah Forten, a Philadelphia Negro, recalled a white friend who told her that when walking with a Negro "the darker the night, the better Abolitionist was I." Nevertheless, she was willing to forgive such conduct on the ground that abolitionists were often forced to make "great sacrifices to public sentiment." Still, it was disconcerting. "Many, very many anxious to take up the cross," she lamented, "but how few are strong enough to bear it." Less forgiving was the Rev. Theodore S. Wright, who entreated white abolitionists to "annihilate in their own bosoms the cord of caste. We must be consistent—recognize the colored man in every respect as a man and brother." And this must be applied, he said, to "the church, the stage, the steamboat, the public house, in all places." . . .

Of what use, asked Negroes, was the right to vote, attend school, and enter the homes of abolitionists if it was still impossible to gain access to any but the most menial employment. The economic condition of the Negro was at best deplorable, and the new waves of immigrants, competing for many positions which Negroes had long monopolized, only made matters worse. Although some white abolitionists had agitated vigorously in the areas of civil rights and educational opportunities, little had been done in the way of economic assistance, except to call upon Negroes to improve themselves. Perhaps this simply reflected the dominant middle-class ideology of self-help which affected abolitionists, like other whites, but Negroes found little encouragement in such a doctrine and appealed to the antislavery movement to meet this true test of its stated determination to elevate the free Negro.

That the Negro should have placed considerable emphasis on the economic question is understandable. To many Negroes, in fact, this was a key point if they were ever to achieve the respect of white society. The abolitionist, then, was called upon to render practical assistance. But when the *Colored American* reviewed the economic plight of the Negro in the wake of the Panic of 1837, it noted that not one local abolitionist had placed a Negro in any conspicuous position in his business establishment; in fact, it could not even find a Negro in the offices of the New York Anti-Slavery Society. The newspaper beseeched abolitionists to correct this grievous situation, and preferably not by passing a resolution at their next convention. In the absence of any measurable progress along these lines, Negro delegates to an abolition convention in 1852 charged that the antislavery movement had failed in its responsibility. Proposals had been made to leading abolitionists to employ

Negroes in their commercial establishments but the appeal had been largely in vain. True, one delegate conceded, Negroes had found employment in Arthur Tappan's department store, but, he added, only in a menial capacity. "Wherever the colored man is connected with the houses of these gentlemen, it is as the lowest drudges."

In demanding economic assistance, the Negro denied any desire for preferential treatment; he simply wanted an equal opportunity to compete for respectable employment. And since many white abolitionists were in a position to make this possible, they were asked to give practical implementation to their antislavery professions. After all, one Negro leader argued, the struggle for equal rights cannot be won on "the bare ground of abstract principles"; abolitionists must strive not only to abolish chattel slavery but "that other kind of slavery" which doomed the free Negro to economic dependence and pauperism; indeed, he deplored the preoccupation of abolitionists with such reforms as capital punishment, temperance, and women's rights, while they refused in their own establishments to afford equal economic opportunities to depressed Negroes. But such strictures yielded few concrete results, thus prompting a Negro convention delegate to charge that some of those who professed to be "the strongest abolitionists" have refused to grant Negroes anything but sympathy; they have persistently evaded a more practical application of their principles. True, some "might employ a colored boy as a porter or packer," but most abolitionists "would as soon put a hod-carrier to the clerk's desk as a colored boy, ever so well educated though he be." It was left to Frederick Douglass to issue a more direct challenge to the abolitionists: "What boss anti-slavery mechanic will take a black boy into his wheelwright's shop, his blacksmith's shop, his joiner's shop, his cabinet shop? Here is something *practical*; where are the whites and where are the blacks that will respond to it?" The response was difficult to discern. This "is not the song that anti-slavery sung," wrote the disillusioned Delany, "in the first love of the new faith, proclaimed by its disciples."

Perhaps the Negro had been unrealistic in his expectations. By the late 1830's, at any rate, Negro leaders began to reassess their role in the anti-slavery movement; increasing factional quarrels among the whites made such a reappraisal all the more necessary. Although some Negro abolitionists, such as Robert Purvis and Charles Remond, remained loyal Garrisonians, a growing restlessness within the Negro abolitionist camp manifested itself in more frequent demands for ideological and political independence; moreover, as Negroes became more articulate themselves, they tended increasingly to voice their own aspirations and to question the white abolitionist's prerogative to speak for them. "As long as we let them think and act for us," the *Colored American* warned in 1839, "as long as we will bow to their opinions, and acknowledge that their word is counsel, and their will is law; so long they will outwardly treat us as men, while in their hearts they still hold us as slaves."

Under the editorial supervision of Charles B. Ray and Philip A. Bell, the

Colored American was the most prominent voice of this quest for independent expression. Published in New York, the newspaper first took to task the recently formed American Moral Reform Society, dominated largely by pro-Garrison Philadelphia Negroes, for its criticism of separate Negro conventions and the term "colored people," both of which allegedly implied degradation. To the *Colored America*, such positions not only were preposterous but they ignored the primary problems facing the Negro in a hostile society. "[W]hile these sages are frightened half to death, at the idea of being called colored, their FRIENDS and their FOES, in the convention, in the Assembly and in the Senate; through the pulpit and the press, call them nothing else but NEGROES, NEGROES, THE NEGROES OF PENNSYLVANIA."

When the Garrisonian press claimed that separate Negro conventions perpetuated the idea of segregation, the *Colored American* and its supporters reaffirmed their defense of independent action. The multiplicity of wrongs inflicted on the Negro, Samuel Ward argued, made frequent meetings and independent organization indispensable; his white friends, he thought, would appreciate this need if they had "worn a colored skin from October '17 to June '40, as I have, in this pseudo-republic." Although conceding some valuable service by the white antislavery men, Ward was still dissatisfied, especially with those "abolitionists in *profession*" who had yet to conquer prejudice within themselves. "Too many," he regretted, ". . . best love the colored man at a distance."

If there remained any doubts as to the determination of Negroes to voice their opinions, regardless of prevailing antislavery creeds, Henry Highland Garnet quickly dispelled them in 1843 when he told a national Negro convention that slaves would be justified in using violent means to win their freedom. The convention refused by a single vote to endorse the address; nevertheless, the issue had been permanently raised and the narrow vote suggested a growing impatience among Negroes with the traditional reliance on moral force to conquer slavery. But the aftermath of this debate was in many ways even more revealing. Condemned by *The Liberator* for his militant appeal to the slaves and for his endorsement of the Liberty Party, Garnet accepted the challenge. "If it has come to this," he replied, "that I must think and act as you do, because you are an abolitionist, or be exterminated by your thunder, then I do not hesitate to say that your abolitionism is abject slavery." Six years later, an Ohio Negro convention ordered the "gratuitous" circulation of Garnet's convention address; and by this time Frederick Douglass, who had opposed Garnet at the convention, was on the verge of breaking with the Garrisonians and adding his considerable force and prestige to the cause of independent Negro expression and agitation.

The Douglass heresy, made public at the American Anti-Slavery Society convention of 1851, struck particular dismay into the Garrisonian camp, for he had been their principal Negro spokesman. The estrangement stemmed from Douglass' revised position on the dissolution of the Union, political action, nonresistance, and the nature of the Constitution In each case, he broke with prevailing Garrisonian ideology. To seek the dissolution of the Union, he now argued, was to violate his duty as an abolitionist, for it left the slave helpless; to abstain from voting was to ignore "a legitimate and powerful means for abolishing slavery"; and to hold that the Constitution was a proslavery document was to distort both its letter and spirit. The Garrisonians, Douglass charged, had abandoned the original purposes of the antislavery movement. "It started to free the slave," he contended. "It ends by leaving the slave to free himself. It started with the purpose to imbue the heart of the nation with sentiments favorable to the abolition of slavery, and ends by seeking to free the North from all responsibility of slavery." To Douglass, this was not practical antislavery; his alleged apostasy, he insisted, was not from "the Anti-Slavery Cause, for all know that I am as faithful to that cause as I ever was," but from "Garrisonism."

Even before these ideological differences, there had been indications that Douglass was growing restive in the Garrisonian camp. When he first began to lecture, his white friends told him to confine his remarks to his experiences as a slave, for that was what the audiences wanted to hear. "Give us the facts," an abolitionist remarked to Douglass, "we will take care of the philosophy." But Douglass soon found it impossible to confine himself in this way; indeed, his rapid intellectual development had already created some concern among his friends. "People won't believe you ever were a slave, Frederick, if you keep on this way," one abolitionist exclaimed, and another added, "Be yourself and tell your story. Better have a little of the plantation speech than not; it is not best that you seem too learned." . . .

When the still restive Douglass decided to establish a newspaper in Rochester, despite the contrary advice of his Garrisonian friends, the subsequent break was almost assured, for he now had an independent means of expression. The newspaper project, Douglass contended, was no reflection on the quality of existing antislavery journals; the time had come, however, for Negroes to demonstrate their own capabilities, to produce their own authors, editors, and journals, and to be their "own representatives and advocates, not exclusively, but peculiarly—not distinct from, but in connection with our white friends." But since independence also involved divergence in antislavery creed, it was insufferable to the Garrisonians. Before long, Garrison and Douglass were engaged in a vituperative editorial war, while other abolitionists looked on in dismay. To Douglass, it was ironic that the proved champions of human freedom—the Garrisonians—should presume to suppress dissent within their own movement. Apparently the only true faith was that proclaimed in Boston. "They talk down there," he wrote to Gerrit Smith, "just as if the Anti-Slavery Cause belonged to them—and as if all Anti-Slavery ideas originated with them and that no man has a right to 'peep or mutter' on the subject, who does not hold letters patent from them." Such subordination was more than an ex-slave could accept.

Whatever the merits of the conflicting abolition doctrines, Douglass' actions, when combined with those of various state and national Negro conventions, dramatized the increasing demand of Negro abolitionists for a greater voice in the tactics, strategy, and creed of the movement. And this reflected not only conflict over doctrine but considerable dissatisfaction with the pace of the equal rights struggle in the North. Some Negroes questioned whether or not racial equality had been relegated to a position of secondary importance in the abolition crusade. "I have seen constitutions of abolition societies," one Negro leader charged, "where nothing was said about the improvement of the man of color! They have overlooked the great sin of prejudice. They have passed by this foul monster, which is at once the parent and offspring of slavery." Pursuing this subject, the *Colored American* charged that the American Anti-Slavery Society had made "secondary and collateral what ought to have been the primary object of all their efforts. In their strong zeal and fiery indignation against slavery in the South, they half over-looked slavery in the North." Indeed, more is known of slavery in the Carolinas "than of the deep and damning thralldom which grinds to the dust, the colored inhabitants of New York." On the eve of the election of 1860, Douglass noted with regret that the equal suffrage movement in New York was almost exclusively in the hands of Negroes, for neither abolitionists nor Republicans "seem to care much for it." But these differences in emphasis were perhaps inevitable and never effectively reconciled; the black abolitionist was generally moved by compelling personal need, his white cohort acted more from the abstractions of conscience; for one, the primary problem was the Negro; for the other, the slave. Each sought, in his own way, to enlarge the area of freedom.

During the crucial decade of the 1850's, the Negro abolitionist grew ever more restive and impatient. The Fugitive Slave Act, the resurgence of the American Colonization Society, the unsuccessful attempts to win equal suffrage, and, finally, the Dred Scott decision, impressed many Negroes with the increasing helplessness of their position in the face of the white man's apparent determination to maintain racial supremacy. Despite two decades of militant antislavery, the Negro's position seemed little improved. More-over, the emergence of the Republican party made the very term "anti-slavery" difficult to define with any precision. If the Republican party was "antislavery," why did it refuse to move against racial oppression in the free states? and why in some areas did it proclaim principles of white supremacy? If the Kansas free staters were, indeed, "antislavery," how does one account for their determined efforts to keep all Negroes out of the territory? The answer was obvious: it was possible to be both "antislavery" and anti-Negro, to proclaim both free soil and white supremacy. "Opposing slavery and hating its victims," Douglass observed, "has come to be a very common form of abolitionism." Disillusioned with Republican pronouncements, an Illinois Negro leader was moved to declare that he cared "nothing about that antislavery which wants to make the Territories free, while it is unwilling to extend to me, as a man, in the free States, all the rights of a man." Of course, many white abolitionists had come to an identical conclusion about the "cowardly and contemptible" antislavery of the Republican party. When Stephen S. Foster accordingly called for a convention to reorganize the abolitionist movement, Douglass enthusiastically endorsed the proposal. Reviewing the history of the antislavery struggle, the Negro leader contrasted the heroic beginnings of militant abolitionism with the "Sentimental Abolitionism" of the Republican party, the "fratricidal conduct" of the American Anti-Slavery Society, and the political impotency of the Liberty party. If the "noble objects" of Foster's convention were put into effect, abolitionists—white and black—might once again unite into "one solid abolition organization" which would agitate for the exercise of Federal and State power to abolish the institution of slavery. Thus might the confusion between Republican antislavery and true abolitionism be ended.

But in the absence of any such unified movement, the Negro abolitionist continued to advance an increasingly independent position. Tired of exhortations to be patient and await that "impartial and just God" who would inevitably rid the nation of slavery, Negroes began to talk of organized insubordination, slave insurrections, the use of physical force to resist the newly passed Fugitive Slave Act, the organization of state leagues to combat repressive legislation, and, in view of the Dred Scott decision, some even argued that Negroes no longer had any obligation to the United States and should welcome the overthrow of the government if necessary to exterminate slavery. The vindication of the Negro's rights now seemed to demand a position more advanced than that of moral suasion. "Every slavehunter who meets a bloody death in his infernal business," Douglass wrote, "is an argument in favor of the manhood of our race." Had not John Brown demonstrated, a Boston Negro leader asserted, that physical force might prove more effective than the "gradual diffusion of anti-slavery gospel." Although he hoped that slavery might be abolished peaceably, "if, as appears to be the case, there is no use in crying peace, then let us not shrink from the responsibility. My motto has always been, 'Better die freemen than live to be slaves.'"

The espousal of increasingly radical measures mirrored the Negro's deepening sense of alienation from American society. The antislavery crusade had not altered the image of the Negro in the eyes of white America, nor measurably improved his position. "We are slaves in the midst of freedom," Delany wrote, "waiting patiently, and unconcernedly—indifferently, and stupidly, for masters to come and lay claim to us, trusting to their generosity, whether or not they will own us and carry us into endless bondage ... I must admit, that I have no hopes in this country—no confidence in the American people." The movement which Delany advocated in the 1850's, that of emigration, began to attract more Negroes; it enunciated a vigorous race nationalism, rejected the democratic pretensions of white Americans, questioned the motives and effectiveness of white abolitionsts, and urged the establishment of an independent Negro state. To remain any longer in the United States was to remain "the dupes of, and deluded by the whites, even our most professed anti-slavery friends." The Negro must find his own identity, apart from that of the whites. "The truth is," an emigration convention declared, "we are not identical with the Anglo-Saxon or any other race of the Caucasian or pure white type of the human family, and the sooner we know and acknowledge this truth, the better for ourselves and posterity." Although most Negroes rejected emigration, they did so uneasily, for the logic of the argument seemed difficult to refute ...

On the eve of the Civil War, most Negroes aspired no higher than the goal of incorporation into white American society. Nevertheless, a strong undercurrent of race pride and consciousness, made explicit in the emigration movement, was clearly present, and white reformers would henceforth have to contend with its implications. Although the "wealth, the intellect, the Legislation (State and Federal), the pulpit, and the science of America" still tended to dismiss the Negro "as something less than a man," one Negro journal prophesied in 1859 that such arguments would become increasingly insupportable and that "this great black sluggard" may yet "shake the pillars of the commonweal." In the meantime, the Negro had begun to produce his own spokesmen and media of expression; he had achieved increased recognition within the antislavery movement, and though he continued to express his appreciation of the efforts and sacrifices of white abolitionists, he made it clear that they were no longer to dominate the cause or confine its limits. The entire question of racial equality was at issue, not merely the elimination of chattel slavery. "The time is come," a Negro conference announced in 1854, "when our people must assume the rank of a first-rate power in the battle against caste and Slavery; it is emphatically our battle; no one else can fight it for us, and with God's help we must fight it ourselves.—Our relations to the Anti-Slavery movement must be and are changed. Instead of depending upon it we must lead it."

Abraham Lincoln and the Problem of Race

Introduction

Lincoln has been so enshrined among Americans as the Great Emancipator that it has been a temptation for his admirers to forget how ambiguous his attitudes on race and slavery were. Yet it is also important to remember that if he had argued from the beginning that black slaves should become free citizens he might have developed a reputation as a social philosopher but it is most unlikely that he ever would have become President of the United States. For much of his life, Lincoln was torn between two conflicting convictions—a detestation of slavery and a doubt that black people were inherently capable of exercising citizenship in a free society. Just as much, he doubted that white opinion could ever be changed so much as to admit the black as a free citizen in this country.

As we can see from the following selections, Lincoln expressed a variety of opinions about black people. He could sympathize with their cruel treatment under slavery, he could act to prevent extension of slavery into the territories but—until nearly the end of his career—he could not really envision the black as an American citizen. Thus we have him arguing in his debate with Stephen A. Douglas that he never had been and was not then, in 1858, in favor of "making voters or jurors of negroes, nor of qualifying them to hold office, not to intermarry with white people . . ."

When the Civil War came, Lincoln resisted all appeals to identify the cause of the North with that of anti-slavery. To have done so would have jeopardized support for the government in the border states where slavery was still legal, but even if the situation had been otherwise, it is not at all certain that Lincoln would then have favored black citizenship. For the first year or so of the Civil War he insisted on linking the idea of emancipation of the

The selections in this section from Lincoln's writings are from Roy P. Basler, ed., *The Collected Works of Abraham Lincoln* (New Brunswick, N.J.: Rutgers University Press, 1953), as follows: "Fragments on Slavery," II, pp. 222–223; Speech at Peoria, II, pp. 255–256; Letter to Speed, II, pp. 320–323; Debate at Charleston, III, pp. 145–146; Address on Colonization, V, pp. 370–374; Letter to Greeley, V, pp. 388–389.

blacks with the idea of colonization abroad. He was opposed to sending the freedmen to Liberia in Africa because he thought the climate was unhealthy, and therefore he explored the possibilities for a black settlement somewhere in Central America. This idea was vigorously protested by several Central American governments.

As the difficulties of colonization of blacks multiplied, Lincoln's attitude toward the War was changing. It was not the purpose of the War, he came to believe, simply to restore the Union as it was, but to bring about "a new birth of freedom." Thus, toward the end of the War, he seemed to be moving toward the policy of accepting the black not merely as a nonslave but as a citizen and a voter. In 1864, he wrote a letter privately to the governor of the newly reconstructed State of Louisiana in which he broached the subject of allowing some of the blacks to vote. He asked "whether some of the colored people may not be let in, as, for instance, the very intelligent, and especially those who have fought gallantly in our ranks. They would probably help in some trying time in the future to keep the jewel of Liberty in the family of freedom." At the same time, ambivalent and "political" to the last, Lincoln was unwilling to force the new governor to accept black voters if he did not wish to have them.[1] The selections which follow show both the range and the ambivalence of Lincoln's thoughts on slavery and on the status of slave and free blacks.

In the interpretive essay that concludes this section Lincoln's views are placed in social and political perspectives by Professor Eric Foner. Foner shows that the ideology of Lincoln's Republican party was deeply streaked with racism, yet he also shows that these same Republican politicians took stands in favor of black rights that set them at odds with the prevailing attitudes of the time and place. If their "free labor ideology" was racist, it was at least less so than general public opinion in the Republican heartland of the Midwest where the fear of free black competition was quite common. In Foner's perspective, Lincoln's racism must be qualified by Lincoln's liberalism, and his liberalism by his racism. Yet Foner also makes it clear that the liberal principles of democracy, individualism, and equality were intended, with only a very few exceptions, for whites only, and that "the very social mobility for which the West has been celebrated may have tended to exaggerate racial prejudice." The readings thus end on the same note with which they began: from Jefferson to Lincoln, American social thought was afflicted—is still afflicted—by profound ambiguities on the subject of race. To overcome those ambiguities by understanding them may take Americans, black and white alike, an appreciable distance toward the "one nation, indivisible" that has yet to be created out of the races who inhabit this land.

---

[1] Letter to Michael Hahn, March 13, 1864, in Roy P. Basler, ed., *The Collected Works of Abraham Lincoln* (New Brunswick, N.J., 1953), VII, 243. See also Benjamin Quarles, *Lincoln and the Negro* (New York, 1962), pp. 108–12.

17 / Abraham Lincoln
Fragments on Slavery

(July 1, 1854?)

The ant, who has toiled and dragged a crumb to his nest, will furiously defend the fruit of his labor, against whatever robber assails him. So plain, that the most dumb and stupid slave that ever toiled for a master, does constantly *know* that he is wronged. So plain that no one, high or low, ever does mistake it, except in a plainly *selfish* way; for although volume upon volume is written to prove slavery a very good thing, we never hear of the man who wishes to take the good of it, *by being a slave himself.*

Most governments have been based, practically, on the denial of equal rights of men, as I have, in part, stated them; *ours* began, by *affirming* those rights. They said, some men are too *ignorant*, and *vicious*, to share in government. Possibly so, said we; and, by your system, you would always keep them ignorant, and vicious. We proposed to give *all* a chance; and we expected the weak to grow stronger, the ignorant, wiser; and all better, and happier together . . .

If A. can prove, however conclusively, that he may, of right, enslave B.— why may not B. snatch the same argument, and prove equally, that he may enslave A.?—

You say A. is white, and B. is black. It is *color*, then; the lighter, having the right to enslave the darker? Take care. By this rule, you are to be slave to the first man you meet, with fairer skin than your own.

You do not mean *color* exactly?—You mean the whites are intellectually the superiors of the blacks, and, therefore have the right to enslave them? Take care again. By this rule, you are to be slave to the first man you meet, with an intellect superior to your own.

But, say you, it is a question of *interest;* and, if you can make it your *interest*, you have the right to enslave another. Very well. And if he can make it his interest, he has the right to enslave you.

18 / Abraham Lincoln
Speech at Peoria, Illinois

(October 16, 1854)

When southern people tell us they are no more responsible for the origin of slavery, then we; I acknowledge the fact. When it is said that the institution exists; and that it is very difficult to get rid of it, in any satisfactory way, I can understand and appreciate the saying. I surely will not blame them for not doing what I should not know how to do myself. If all earthly power were given me, I should not know what to do, as to the existing institution. My first impulse would be to free all the slaves, and send them to Liberia,—to their own native land. But a moment's reflection would convince me, that whatever of high hope, (as I think there is) there may be in this, in the long run, its sudden execution is impossible. If they were all landed there in a day, they would all perish in the next ten days; and there are not surplus shipping and surplus money enough in the world to carry them there in many times ten days. What then? Free them all, and keep them among us as underlings? Is it quite certain that this betters their condition? I think I would not hold one in slavery, at any rate, yet the point is not clear enough for me to denounce people upon. What next? Free them, and make them politically and socially, our equals? My own feelings will not admit of this; and if mine would, we well know that those of the great mass of white people will not. Whether this feeling accords with justice and sound judgment, is not the sole question, if indeed, it is any part of it. A universal feeling, whether well or ill-founded, can not be safely disregarded. We can not, then, make them equals. It does seem to me that systems of gradual emancipation might be adopted; but for their tardiness in this, I will not undertake to judge our brethren of the south.

19 / Abraham Lincoln
Letter to Joshua F. Speed

(Aug. 24, 1855)

Dear Speed:
    You know what a poor correspondent I am. Ever since I received your very agreeable letter of the 22nd of May I have been intending to write you in answer to it. You suggest that in political action now, you and I would differ. I suppose we would; not quite as much, however, as you may think. You know I dislike slavery; and you fully admit the abstract wrong of it. So

far there is no cause of difference. But you say that sooner than yield your legal right to the slave—especially at the bidding of those who are not themselves interested, you would see the Union dissolved. I am not aware that *any one* is bidding you to yield that right; very certainly *I* am not. I leave that matter entirely to yourself. I also acknowledge *your* rights and *my* obligations, under the constitution, in regard to your slaves. I confess I hate to see the poor creatures hunted down, and caught, and carried back to their stripes, and unrewarded toils; but I bite my lip and keep quiet. In 1841 you and I had together a tedious low-water trip, on a Steam Boat from Louisville to St. Louis. You may remember, as I well do, that from Louisville to the mouth of the Ohio there were, on board, ten or a dozen slaves, shackled together with irons. That sight was a continual torment to me; and I see something like it every time I touch the Ohio, or any other slave-border. It is hardly fair for you to assume, that I have no interest in a thing which has, and continually exercises, the power of making me miserable. You ought rather to appreciate how much the great body of the Northern people do crucify their feelings, in order to maintain their loyalty to the constitution and the Union . . .

You enquire where I now stand. That is a disputed point. I think I am a whig; but others say there are no whigs, and that I am an abolitionist. When I was at Washington I voted for the Wilmot Proviso as good as forty times, and I never heard of anyone attempting to unwhig me for that. I now do no more than oppose the *extension* of slavery.

I am not a Know-Nothing. That is certain. How could I be? How can any one who abhors the oppression of negroes, be in favor of degrading classes of white people? Our progress in degeneracy appears to me to be pretty rapid. As a nation, we began by declaring that *"all men are created equal."* We now practically read it "all men are created equal, *except negroes.*" When the Know-Nothings get control, it will read "all men are created equal, except negroes, *and foreigners*, *and catholics.*" When it comes to this I should prefer emigrating to some country where they make no pretence of loving liberty— to Russia, for instance, where despotism can be taken pure, and without the base alloy of hypocracy . . .

20 / Abraham Lincoln
Fourth Debate with Stephen A. Douglas
at Charleston, Illinois

(September 18, 1858)

While I was at the hotel today an elderly gentleman called upon me to know whether I was really in favor of producing a perfect equality between the negroes and white people. [Great laughter.] While I had not proposed to myself on this occasion to say much on that subject, yet as the question was asked me I thought I would occupy perhaps five minutes in saying something in regard to it. I will say then that I am not, nor ever have been in favor of bringing about in any way the social and political equality of the white and black races, [applause]—that I am not nor ever have been in favor of making voters or jurors of negroes, nor of qualifying them to hold office, nor to intermarry with white people; and I will say in addition to this that there is a physical difference between the white and black races which I believe will for ever forbid the two races living together on terms of social and political equality. And inasmuch as they cannot so live, while they do remain together there must be the position of superior and inferior, and I as much as any other man am in favor of having the superior position assigned to the white race. I say upon this occasion I do not perceive that because the white man is to have the superior position the negro should be denied everything. I do not understand that because I do not want a negro woman for a slave I must necessarily want her for a wife. [Cheers and laughter.] My understanding is that I can just let her alone. I am now in my fiftieth year, and I certainly never have had a black woman for either a slave or a wife. So it seems to me quite possible for us to get along without making either slaves or wives of negroes. I will add to this that I have never seen to my knowledge a man, woman or child who was in favor of producing a perfect equality, social and political, between negroes and white men . . . I will also add to the remarks I have made, (for I am not going to enter at large upon this subject,) that I have never had the least apprehension that I or my friends would marry negroes if there was no law to keep them from it, [laughter] but as Judge Douglas and his friends seem to be in great apprehension that they might, if there were no law to keep them from it, [roars of laughter] I give him the most solemn pledge that I will to the very last stand by the law of this State, which forbids the marrying of white people with negroes. [Continued laughter and applause.] . . .

21 / Abraham Lincoln
Address on Colonization
to a Deputation of Negroes

(August 14, 1862)

This afternoon the President of the United States gave audience to a Committee of colored men at the White House. They were introduced by the Rev. J. Mitchell, Commissioner of Emigration. E. M. Thomas, the Chairman, remarked that they were there by invitation to hear what the Executive had to say to them. Having all been seated, the President, after a few preliminary observations, informed them that a sum of money had been appropriated by Congress, and placed at his disposition for the purpose of aiding the colonization in some country of the people, or a portion of them, of African descent, thereby making it his duty, as it had for a long time been his inclination, to favor that cause; and why, he asked, should the people of your race be colonized, and where? Why should they leave this country? This is, perhaps, the first question for proper consideration. You and we are different races. We have between us a broader difference than exists between almost any other two races. Whether it is right or wrong I need not discuss, but this physical difference is a great disadvantage to us both, as I think your race suffer very greatly, many of them by living among us, while ours suffer from your presence. In a word we suffer on each side. If this is admitted, it affords a reason at least why we should be separated. You here are freemen I suppose.

A Voice: Yes, sir.

The President—Perhaps you have long been free, or all your lives. Your race are suffering, in my judgment, the greatest wrong inflicted on any people. But even when you cease to be slaves, you are yet far removed from being placed on an equality with the white race. You are cut off from many of the advantages which the other race enjoy. The aspiration of men is to enjoy equality with the best when free, but on this broad continent, not a single man of your race is made the equal of a single man of ours. Go where you are treated the best, and the ban is still upon you.

I do not propose to discuss this, but to present it as a fact with which we have to deal. I cannot alter it if I would. It is a fact, about which we all think and feel alike, I and you. We look to our condition, owing to the existence of the two races on this continent. I need not recount to you the effects upon white men, growing out of the institution of Slavery. I believe in its general evil effects on the white race. See our present condition—the country engaged in war!—our white men cutting one another's throats, none knowing how far it will extend; and then consider what we know to be the truth. But for your race among us there could not be war, although many men engaged on either side do not care for you one way or the other. Nevertheless, I repeat, without the institution of Slavery and the colored race as a basis, the war could not have an existence.

It is better for us both, therefore, to be separated. I know that there are free men among you, who even if they could better their condition are not as much inclined to go out of the country as those, who being slaves could obtain their freedom on this condition. I suppose one of the principal difficulties in the way of colonization is that the free colored man cannot see that his comfort would be advanced by it. You may believe you can live in Washington or elsewhere in the United States the remainder of your life [as easily], perhaps more so than you can in any foreign country, and hence you may come to the conclusion that you have nothing to do with the idea of going to a foreign country. This is (I speak in no unkind sense) an extremely selfish view of the case.

But you ought to do something to help those who are not so fortunate as yourselves. There is an unwillingness on the part of our people, harsh as it may be, for you free colored people to remain with us. Now, if you could give a start to white people, you would open a wide door for many to be made free. If we deal with those who are not free at the beginning, and whose intellects are clouded by Slavery, we have very poor materials to start with. If intelligent colored men, such as are before me, would move in this matter, much might be accomplished. It is exceedingly important that we have men at the beginning capable of thinking as white men, and not those who have been systematically oppressed.

There is much to encourage you. For the sake of your race you should sacrifice something of your present comfort for the purpose of being as grand in that respect as the white people. It is a cheering thought throughout life that something can be done to ameliorate the condition of those who have been subject to the hard usage of the world. It is difficult to make a man miserable while he feels he is worthy of himself, and claims kindred to the great God who made him. In the American Revolutionary war sacrifices were made by men engaged in it; but they were cheered by the future. Gen. Washington himself endured greater physical hardships than if he had remained a British subject. Yet he was a happy man, because he was engaged in benefiting his race—something for the children of his neighbors, having none of his own.

The colony of Liberia has been in existence a long time. In a certain sense it is a success. The old President of Liberia, Roberts, has just been with me—the first time I ever saw him. He says they have within the bounds of that colony between 300,000 and 400,000 people, or more than in some of our old States, such as Rhode Island or Delaware, or in some of our newer States, and less than in some of our larger ones. They are not all American colonists, or their descendants. Something less than 12,000 have been sent thither from this country. Many of the original settlers have died, yet, like people elsewhere, their offspring outnumber those deceased.

The question is if the colored people are persuaded to go anywhere, why not there? One reason for an unwillingness to do so is that some of you would rather remain within reach of the country of your nativity. I do not know how much attachment you may have toward our race. It does not strike me that you have the greatest reason to love them. But still you are attached to them at all events.

The place I am thinking about having for a colony is in Central America. It is nearer to us than Liberia—not much more than one-fourth as far as Liberia, and within seven days' run by steamers. Unlike Liberia it is on a great line of travel—it is a highway. The country is a very excellent one for any people, and with great natural resources and advantages, and especially because of the similarity of climate with your native land—thus being suited to your physical condition.

The particular place I have in view is to be a great highway from the Atlantic or Caribbean Sea to the Pacific Ocean, and this particular place has all the advantages for a colony. On both sides there are harbors among the finest in the world. Again, there is evidence of very rich coal mines. A certain amount of coal is valuable in any country, and there may be more than enough for the wants of the country. Why I attach so much importance to coal is, it will afford an opportunity to the inhabitants for immediate employment till they get ready to settle permanently in their homes.

If you take colonists where there is no good landing, there is a bad show; and so where there is nothing to cultivate, and of which to make a farm. But if something is started so that you can get your daily bread as soon as you reach there, it is a great advantage. Coal land is the best thing I know of with which to commence an enterprise.

To return, you have been talked to upon this subject, and told that a speculation is intended by gentlemen, who have an interest in the country, including the coal mines. We have been mistaken all our lives if we do not know whites as well as blacks look to their self-interest. Unless among those deficient of intellect everybody you trade with makes something. You meet with these things here as elsewhere.

If such persons have what will be an advantage to them, the question is whether it cannot be made of advantage to you. You are intelligent, and know that success does not as much depend on external help as on self-reliance. Much, therefore, depends upon yourselves. As to the coal mines, I think I see the means available for your self-reliance.

I shall, if I get a sufficient number of you engaged, have provisions made that you shall not be wronged. If you will engage in the enterprise I will spend some of the money intrusted to me. I am not sure you will succeed. The Government may lose the money, but we cannot succeed unless we try; but we think with care, we can succeed.

22 / Abraham Lincoln
Letter to Horace Greeley

(August 22, 1862)

Dear Sir:

I have just read yours of the 19th. addressed to myself through the New-York Tribune. If there be in it any statements, or assumptions of fact, which I may know to be erroneous, I do not, now and here, controvert them. If there be in it any inferences which I may believe to be falsely drawn, I do not now and here, argue against them. If there be perceptible in it an impatient and dictatorial tone, I waive it in deference to an old friend, whose heart I have always supposed to be right.

As to the policy I "seem to be pursuing" as you say, I have not meant to leave any one in doubt.

I would save the Union. I would save it the shortest way under the Constitution. The sooner the national authority can be restored; the nearer the Union will be "the Union as it was." If there be those who would not save the Union, unless they could at the same time *save* slavery, I do not agree with them. If there be those who would not save the Union unless they could at the same time *destroy* slavery, I do not agree with them. My paramount object in this struggle *is* to save the Union, and is *not* either to save or to destroy slavery. If I could save the Union without freeing *any* slave I would do it; and if I could save it by freeing some and leaving others alone I would also do that. What I do about slavery, and the colored race, I do because I believe it helps to save the Union; and what I forbear, I forbear because I do *not* believe it would help to save the Union. I shall do *less* whenever I shall believe what I am doing hurts the cause, and I shall do *more* whenever I shall believe doing more will help the cause. I shall try to correct errors when shown to be errors; and I shall adopt new views so fast as they shall appear to be true views.

I have here stated my purpose according to my view of *official* duty; and I intend no modification of my oft-expressed *personal* wish that all men every where could be free.

Yours,

A. Lincoln

Interpretation

23 / Eric Foner
The Republicans and Race

(1970)

On his visit to the United States in the 1830's, Alexis de Tocqueville made his justly famous observation that racial prejudice seemed to be stronger in the North than in the South, and was most intense in the western states which had never known slavery. Several recent historical studies have shown that racial prejudice was all but universal in antebellum northern society. Only five states, all in New England, allowed the black man equal suffrage, and even there he was confined to menial occupations and subjected to constant discrimination. In the West, Negroes were often excluded from the public schools, and four states—Indiana, Illinois, Iowa, and Oregon—even barred them from entering their territory. This pervasive prejudice made the question of the proper place of the black man in American society the most troublesome and perplexing one the Republicans faced before the Civil War. Like the Democrats, Republicans often made use of electoral appeals which smacked of racism, and some historians have interpreted this as proof that there existed no fundamental differences between the two parties' racial attitudes. Yet the Republicans did develop a policy which recognized the essential humanity of the Negro, and demanded protection for certain basic rights which the Democrats denied him. Although deeply flawed by an acceptance of many racial stereotypes, and limited by the free labor ideology's assumption that the major responsibility for a person's success or failure rested with himself, not society, the Republican stand on race relations went against the prevailing opinion of the 1850's, and proved a distinct political liability in a racist society.

Nowhere did race present more political difficulties than in the Northwest. Why was this area, which some historians have seen as the very breeding ground of democracy and egalitarian individualism, marked by such intense racial prejudice? Clearly one important reason was the large population of

Abridged from *Free Soil, Free Labor, Free Men: The Ideology of the Republican Party before the Civil War* by Eric Foner. Copyright © 1970 by Eric Foner. Reprinted without footnotes by permission of Oxford University Press, Inc.

southern origin—men and women who had migrated to escape the influences of slavery, but had brought with them the anti-Negro outlook of slave society. As one Republican of southern background put it, "It is not probable, sir, with the prejudices of my early education, that I would be likely to have too great sympathy for negroes." However, states like Michigan and Wisconsin, whose population came largely from the East, also revealed racial prejudice, although to a lesser degree than Indiana, Illinois, and Ohio. It may be that the greater social mobility of western society helped make fear of the Negro—and therefore prejudice—more severe. In the East, no one questioned that the free black should occupy a subordinate position in society, even where he had substantial legal equality. In the more fluid social structure of the West, however, free Negroes might be able to rise socially and economically. This fear had an especially potent appeal in the lower West, which foresaw an influx of freedmen, ready to challenge the status and prerogatives of white men, should emancipation take place. Where the social order was least stratified—as in the frontier states of Kansas, California, and Oregon—legal discrimination was most severe. Thus, paradoxically, the very social mobility for which the West has been celebrated may have tended to exaggerate racial prejudice.

Although many Republicans agreed with the black abolitionist Frederick Douglass that racism was "the greatest of all obstacles in the way of the anti-slavery cause," they also knew that advocacy of the free Negro's rights might prove politically disastrous. Horace Greeley, for example, explained in 1846 that though he favored equal suffrage for New York Negroes, a proposal to establish it would certainly be defeated in a popular referendum. Prejudiced voters were to blame, Greeley wrote: "You know how numerous and potent this class is.". . .

At times during the 1850's it seemed that the only weapon in the Democrats' political arsenal was the charge that the Republicans were pro-Negro. "Whenever we resist the expansion of slavery into the territories," Wilson complained, "we have a lecture about the equality of the races. When we propose the homestead policy . . . we have lectures about the equality of the races." Such attacks had always been a problem for anti-slavery men, but in the 1850's they were greatly increased. In the Lincoln-Douglas campaign of 1858, the organ of the Democratic party urged readers to "Keep it before the people of Illinois that the Abolition-Republican party headed by Abraham Lincoln are in favor of negro equality . . ." Francis P. Blair later described this charge as the "incessant theme" of Douglas's campaign. The Wisconsin Democracy labeled the Republicans the "Nigger party," and in Indiana, a Democratic parade featured a group of young ladies carrying the banner, "Fathers, save us from nigger husbands." . . . It is not surprising that Chase complained that Democrats had little interest in any issue but race. All they wanted, he said, was "simply to talk about the universal nigger question, as they call it. All that they seem to say is 'nigger, nigger, nigger.'". . .

The use of the race issue as a potent political weapon by the Democrats led many Republicans to reply in kind. Especially in the West, Republican spokesmen insisted that they, not the Democrats, were the real "white man's party," and they often vehemently denied any intention of giving legal or social equality to free Negroes. The astute politician David Davis, Lincoln's friend and adviser, insisted during the 1858 campaign that Republican orators "distinctly and emphatically disavow *negro suffrage*, negroes holding office, serving on juries and the like." When Democrats charged that anti-slavery spokesmen subordinated the rights of whites to those of Negroes, Republicans responded that they hoped to keep the territories open to free white settlers by barring slavery. It required no effort to show, an Iowa Congressman wrote, that the Democratic, not the Republican party, "exalts and spreads Africans at the expense of the white race." Because they opposed Democratic plans to "flood Kansas and the other Territories with negro slaves," Republicans claimed "that we are the only white man's party in the country." And when Democrats accused them of favoring the intermixing of the races, Republicans responded that keeping the races separate by barring slavery from the territories would prevent this very intermixing. Said a leading Iowa Republican, "It is the institution of slavery which is the great parent of amalgamation. Gentlemen need not fear it from those opposed to that institution."

To a large extent, these expressions of racism were political replies to Democratic accusations rather than gratuitous insults to the black race. Few Republicans were as blatantly prejudiced as the New York *Tribune's* associate editor James S. Pike, who so despised the Negro race that he hoped the South would secede, taking its black population with it. Some Republicans who insisted they were advocating the rights of the white race made sure to add that they did not wish "to disclaim any sympathy" for Negroes. Yet inherent in the anti-slavery outlook of many Republicans was a strong overtone of racism. For the whole free labor argument against the extension of slavery contained a crucial ambiguity. Was it the institution of slavery, or the presence of the Negro, which degraded the white laborer? Sometimes Republicans clearly stated that the institution itself, not the race of the slave, was to blame. An Ohio Congressman declared that while he agreed that a black population represented a nuisance, "a free white man could live where there are negroes, and maintain his freedom; but no white non-slaveholder can live where slave laws, customs, and habits pertain, and retain [his] rights . . ." The radical *National Era* informed the South, "We are not opposed to the extension of either class of your population, provided it be *free*, but to the existencê of slavery and migration of *slaves*." More often, however, Republicans indicated that they made little distinction between free Negroes and slaves, and felt that association with any black degraded the white race. "I want to have nothing to do, either with the free negro or the slave negro . . . ," said Lyman Trumbull. "We wish to settle the Territories with free white men." And Simon Cameron of Pennsylvania stated that he wished to keep Negroes out of the territories, because the white laborer "must be depressed wherever the Negro is his competitor in the field or the workshop.". . .

Another index of the scope of racism within the Republican party was the wide acceptance of plans for colonizing blacks outside the United States. Colonization as a solution to the race problem and as an adjunct of gradual emancipation had been advocated for many years. Many of the founding fathers, including Jefferson, Madison, and Henry, had been opposed to slavery but had believed in coupling emancipation with deportation of the freedmen. Later, the American Colonization Society attempted to establish colonies in Africa, but the fact that both free Negroes and abolitionists viewed the plan as an attempt to strengthen the slave system, by removing free blacks from the country, prevented its ever being put in full operation . . .

At the root of all colonization plans, including the Republican one, was the assumption that the United States was, or should be, a nation of white men. "It is certainly the wish of every patriot," Francis P. Blair wrote in 1858, "that all within the limits of our Union should be homogeneous in race and of our own blood." Another colonizationist, Senator James R. Doolittle of Wisconsin, said the plan would "keep our Anglo-Saxon institutions as well as our Anglo-Saxon blood pure and uncontaminated." Some supporters frankly expressed their conviction that free Negroes were "a grievous nuisance to every State of the Union," and that colonization "would relieve us from the curse of free blacks." They were convinced that these were the views of a majority of Americans. "The great mass of white men," said Preston King, desired the separation of the two races, and even a lukewarm supporter of colonization like Salmon P. Chase admitted that his state desired "a homogeneous population." The strong element of racism in the colonization idea was candidly acknowledged by an Iowa Republican. Speaking of free Negroes and slaves, he declared, "I have my prejudices against them. My prejudice is such as to lead me to desire that they shall not be left in this country . . . I am, therefore, a colonizationist."

But there was much more than simple racism to the Republican colonization plan. It is significant that its leading advocates, the Blairs, were deeply involved in the politics of Missouri and Maryland. In these border states the slave system seemed weak, and emancipation sentiment was rising. The Blairs were anti-slavery slaveholders who shared the assumptions of their class regarding race, and who attacked slavery primarily because of its effect upon southern white labor. The Blairs hoped to build up a Republican party in the South, based on the poor whites, which would gradually abolish slavery. The one great obstacle, as they saw it, was the antipathy of the non-slaveholding whites toward the Negro, and their fear that emancipation would lead to equality and intermixing of the races. "It is this compounding of the races," Blair explained to a northern anti-slavery leader, "which is supposed to be the aim of abolitionism, that enables slaveholders to excite such abhorrence against abolitionists throughout the South." Blair's son Frank, the first Republican Congressman from a slave state, agreed. "The idea of liberating the slaves and allowing them to remain in the country," he told a New England audience, "is one that never will be tolerated." Only when the non-slaveholders of the South were convinced that the removal of the black population would go hand in hand with emancipation, would their latent anti-slavery inclinations find political expression.

To the Blairs, therefore, colonization was an essential part of a larger plan to destroy slavery from within the southern states. Endorsement of colonization by the Republican party would be "an enabling act to the emancipationists of the South," for it would effectively rebut the slaveholders' charges that abolition meant Negro equality . . .

The Republican colonizationists also recognized that lying deeper than the issue of slavery was the dark question of race. Even with its racism, colonization included a genuine humanitarian element, for many Republicans sincerely believed racial prejudice in the United States was so powerful that the Negro could never attain any kind of legal or social equality. "In this country," said the New York *Evening Post*, "the colored man has no future to which he can look forward, with hope of pleasure." Ben Wade agreed that free Negroes were "despised by all, repudiated by all; outcasts upon the face of the earth, without any fault of theirs that I know of." He deplored the prejudice, but believed it "perfectly impossible that these two races can inhabit the same place and be prosperous and happy.". . .

During the 1850's, a good number of abolitionists and black leaders remained aloof from the Republican party because of its racist elements. An influential Negro newspaper charged in 1860 that anti-slavery meant little more to the Republicans than "opposition to the black man," and the black orator H. Ford Douglass told a Massachusetts abolitionist audience that no party deserved their votes "unless that party is willing to extend to the black man all the rights of a citizen." On the other hand, prominent blacks like Frederick Douglass and Dr. John Rock actively supported Frémont and Lincoln, and colored conventions throughout the North endorsed Republican candidates. These men recognized that the basic fault of the Republicans' racial attitude was not simple racism but ambivalence. Even Republicans who attacked racial prejudice and defended Negro rights were not free from prejudice, for almost all accepted in some degree the racial stereotypes of their time. Even Seward and Chase, with their long records of advocacy of Negro rights, had this problem. Seward could lecture a Michigan audience during the campaign of 1856 on the necessity for giving blacks the rights to vote—a position which could hardly be of political advantage—but at the same time, he viewed the Negro as a "foreign and feeble" element of the population which, unlike European immigrants, could never be assimilated and would eventually "altogether disappear." And Chase could insist during the gubernatorial campaign of 1857, at great political hazard, that one of his aims was to have it acknowledged "that colored people have rights and privileges which they have not now." But he also believed that an eventual separation of the races was both inevitable and necessary . . .

Many of the Republican criticisms of free Negroes were shared by black leaders. "The colored people," Frederick Douglass told Harriet Beecher Stowe, "are wanting in self-reliance," and he deplored their tendency to remain in menial occupations. Some colored conventions advised Negroes to leave the cities and take jobs on farms as a means of self-improvement, and other spokesmen insisted that frugality, self-reliance, and a "better regulation of our domestic habits," were essential preconditions to social advancement. The black leaders insisted, however, that the Negro's deficiencies in character and achievement were wholly the result of prejudice and discrimination, and they objected to the "tone of assumed superiority and arrogant complacency," with which Republicans like Greeley criticized black citizens. But black spokesmen accepted the free labor idea that independence was the key to respectability, and that "to be dependent is to be degraded." And they insisted that they desired not any special privileges or aid, but merely equality of opportunity. "Remove all obstacles, and give the black man an equal chance," the black spokesmen said, ". . . and then should he not succeed, he will not ask you or anyone else to mourn over his failure."

During the 1850's, Republicans accepted the idea that the Negro should be given an "equal chance" to prove himself capable of economic advancement, and their actions in state legislatures and in Congress had the effect of breaking down some of the legal inequalities which surrounded the black citizen. "I want every man to have the chance—and I believe a black man is entitled to it—in which he *can* better his condition . . . ," Lincoln insisted in 1860. The limitations of the Republican outlook did not become fully manifest until the tragic failure of Reconstruction. Given the long history of slavery and the continuing fact of discrimination, the mere granting of civil equality was not enough to guarantee real equality of opportunity for northern Negroes, much less for newly freed southern slaves. Many Republicans, of course, never expected the Negro to attain complete equality. Greeley had written before the war that, free or slave, Negroes would always occupy an inferior social position, and during Reconstruction, Seward observed philosophically, "They are God's poor; they always have been and always will be everywhere." But even the more radical Republicans, who sincerely hoped that the Negro could rise to economic and social equality, shrank from a long period of federal protection of Negro rights and a redistribution of southern property. The free labor ideology, based on the premise that all Americans, whatever their origins, could achieve social advancement if given equal protection of the law, was only an incomplete version of the full commitment which would have been necessary to make these hopes fully realized.

Suggested Reading

Botkin, Benjamin F., ed. *Lay My Burden Down: A Folk History of Slavery* (Chicago, 1945).

Davis, David Brion. *The Problem of Slavery in Western Culture* (Ithaca, N.Y., 1966).

Degler, Carl N. "Slavery and the Genesis of American Race Prejudice," *Comparative Studies in Society and History*, II (October, 1959).

Elkins, Stanley M. *Slavery: A Problem in American Institutional and Intellectual Life* (Chicago, 1959, 1968).

Franklin, John Hope. *From Slavery to Freedom: A History of American Negroes*, 2nd ed., rev. (New York, 1963).

Frazier, E. Franklin. *The Negro in the United States*, 2nd ed. (New York, 1957).

Furnas, J. C. *Goodbye to Uncle Tom* (New York, 1956).

Genovese, Eugene D. *The Political Economy of Slavery: Studies in the Economy and Society of the Slave South* (New York, 1965).

Gossett, Thomas F. *Race, the History of an Idea in America* (Dallas, Texas, 1963).

Handlin, Oscar. *Race and Nationality in American Life* (Boston, 1957).

Herskovits, Melville J. *The Myth of the Negro Past* (New York, London, 1941).

Johnson, Guion G. *Ante-Bellum North Carolina: A Social History* (Chapel Hill, N.C., 1937).

Jordan, Winthrop D. *White Over Black: The Development of American Attitudes toward the Negro, 1550–1812* (Chapel Hill, N.C., 1968).

Lane, Ann J., ed. *The Debate Over Slavery: Stanley Elkins and His Critics* (Urbana, Ill., 1971).

Litwack, Leon. *North of Slavery: The Negro in the Free States, 1790–1860* Chicago, 1961).

Myrdal, Gunnar, *et al. An American Dilemma; The Negro Problem and Modern Democracy*, 2 vols. (New York, London, 1944).

Quarles, Benjamin. *Lincoln and the Negro* (New York, 1962).

Stampp, Kenneth M. *The Peculiar Institution: Slavery in the Antebellum South* (New York, 1956).

Stanton, William R. *The Leopard's Spots: Scientific Attitudes Toward Race in America, 1815–1859* (Chicago, 1960).

Weinstein, Allen, and Frank Otto Gatell, eds. *American Negro Slavery: A Modern Reader* (New York, London, 1968).

Woodson, Carter G., and Charles H. Wesley. *The Negro in Our History*, 10th ed. (Washington, 1962).

ABCDE798765432